CHILDREN'S DAILY PRAYER

for the School Year 2013–2014

Teresa Marshall

LTP

LITURGY
TRAINING
PUBLICATIONS

Nihil Obstat
Very Reverend Daniel A. Smilanic, JCD
Vicar for Canonical Services
Archdiocese of Chicago
December 12, 2012

Imprimatur
Reverend John F. Canary, STL, DMin
Vicar General
Archdiocese of Chicago
December 12, 2012

The *Nihil Obstat* and *Imprimatur* are official declarations that the material is free form doctrinal or moral error, and thus is granted permission to publish in accordance with c. 827. No legal responsibility is assumed by the grant of this permission. No implication is contained herein that those who have granted the *Nihil Obstat* and *Imprimatur* agree with the content, opinions, or statements expressed.

Many of the concepts and guidelines, as well as various prayer services offered in this book were originally conceived and developed by Dr. Sofia Cavalletti, Ms. Gianna Gobbi, and their collaborators. Theological underpinnings and many elements of these prayer services were first documented in Cavalletti's foundational books including, *The Religious Potential of the Child* and *The Religious Potential of the Child Age 6–12*.

Liturgy Training Publications acknowledges the significant contribution made by Elizabeth McMahon Jeep to the development of *Children's Daily Prayer*. Ms. Jeep worked tirelessly for more than 15 years to help this resource become the essential annual prayer resource for children and their parents, teachers, and catechists. We are indebted to her for her authorship and guidance.

As a publisher, LTP works toward responsible stewardship of the environment. We printed the text of *Children's Daily Prayer* with soy-based ink on paper certified to the SFI (Sustainable Forestry Initiative[R]) Certified Fiber Sourcing Standard CERT–0048284, confirming that the paper manufacturer takes a responsible approach to obtaining fiber. The wood pulp that was required in the making of this paper was sourced from sawmill residuals or pulp logs unsuitable for other uses. A thermo mechanical pulp process in manufacturing provides 100% more efficient use of wood fiber than the conventional process.

Additionally, this paper was produced using completely chlorine-free technology. Biomass fuels were used in manufacturing for lower greenhouse gas emissions, and therefore a reduced carbon footprint.

CHILDREN'S DAILY PRAYER 2013–2014 © 2013 Archdiocese of Chicago: Liturgy Training Publications, 3949 South Racine Avenue, Chicago IL 60609; 1-800-933-1800; orders@ltp.org; fax 1-800-933-7094. All rights reserved. See our website at www.LTP.org.

CHILDREN'S DAILY PRAYER was illustrated by Paula Wiggins.

Printed in the United States of America.

ISBN 978-1-61671-076-7

CDP14

INSTRUCTIONS FOR PRAYER FOR THE DAY AND WEEK

FOR THE WHOLE GROUP

Amen means: "Yes! I believe it is true!" Let your "Amen" be heard by all.

The Gospel reader always begins with, "A reading from the holy Gospel according to . . . ." The group responds, "Glory to you, O Lord." When the reading ends, the reader says, "The Gospel of the Lord." Everyone responds, "Praise to you, Lord Jesus Christ."

FOR THE LEADER

1. Find the correct page and read it silently. Parts in bold black type are for everyone. All others are for you alone.

2. Practice reading your part aloud, and pronounce every syllable clearly. The parts marked with ◆ and ✚ are instructions for what to do. Follow the instructions but do not read them or the headings aloud. If you stumble over a word, repeat it until you can say it smoothly.

3. Pause after "A reading from the holy Gospel according to . . . " so the class can respond. Pause again after "The Gospel of the Lord." Remember to allow for silence when the instructions call for it, especially after the Gospel and after reading the questions "For Silent Reflection."

4. Pause after "Let us bring our hopes and needs to God . . . " so that individuals may offer their prayers aloud or in silence. After each petition, the group responds, "Lord, hear our prayer."

5. When you make the Sign of the Cross, use your right hand and do it slowly and reverently, first touching your forehead ("In the name of the Father"), next just below your chest ("and of the Son"), then your left shoulder ("and of the Holy Spirit"), and finally your right shoulder ("Amen").

6. At prayer time, stand in the front of the class straight and tall. Ask the students to use their reproducible sheet of Psalms for reading their part. Read slowly and clearly.

IF THERE ARE TWO LEADERS

One leader reads the Reading or Gospel while the other reads all of the other parts. Practice reading your part(s). Both leaders should stand in front of the class during the entire prayer.

Remember to read very slowly, with a loud, clear voice.

CONTENTS

CONTENTS

SUPPLEMENTAL RESOURCES ON OUR WEBSITE: WWW.LTP.ORG

(Click on "Resources," then "Product Supplements," then look for cover icon of Children's Daily Prayer)

Reference Bibliography

Also on This Day
(Fuller explanations of Buddhist, Hindu, Jewish, and Muslim Observances)

The editors appreciate your feedback.
E-mail: cdp@ltp.org.

INTRODUCTION

CHOOSE OR ADAPT PRAYER ELEMENTS TO FIT YOUR SITUATION

For schools and home-schooling families, this book provides an order of prayer for each day of the school year (Prayer for the Day). For religious education settings, it provides an order of prayer for once a week (Prayer for the Week). Not every prayer element in these orders of prayer will be useful in every situation. From the elements listed below, you can choose the ones that will be most effective for your group, setting, and time available:

OPENING

Introduces any saint to be remembered that day; may give context for the scripture reading; and explains difficult words in the reading.

SIGN OF THE CROSS

A must! The ritual action Catholics use to begin and end prayer.

PSALM

Use the short version on the prayer page or the longer version on the Reproducible Psalms pages.

READING OR GOSPEL

The Scripture selection on the prayer page is an excerpt from one of the readings of the Mass for the day (except for the Prayer for the Week, which always uses the Sunday Gospel). In this plan, children are praying with Scripture from the day's Mass along with the rest of the Church. If you have a different plan for using Scripture in daily prayer (perhaps for very young children), substitute a different Scripture reading.

FOR SILENT REFLECTION

This is designed to be a time of silence so that the children can ponder the scripture they have heard and experience the value of silence in prayer. But if you prefer to use this time for a discussion about the reading, substitute your own instruction and questions.

CLOSING PRAYER

This prayer element begins with intercessions and ends with a brief prayer related either to the Scripture or the memorial, feast, or solemnity of the day. You could ask children to prepare intercessions or encourage them to offer their own intentions spontaneously.

PRAYER SERVICES

Additional prayer services are offered for specific times, memorials, feasts, or solemnities. (Check the table of contents.) You may prefer to use one of these instead of the Prayer for the Day.

GRACE BEFORE MEALS AND PRAYER AT DAY'S END

In order to instill in children the habit of prayer, use these prayers before lunch or at the end of the day.

PSALMS AND CANTICLES

A few extras are provided at the end of the book, but you will find many more in your Bible. Substitute these for any of the Psalm excerpts in the orders of prayer or pray these with the children at any time.

HOME PRAYER

To give families resources for prayer at home, photocopy these pages to send home or access PDF files of these from the LTP website. These files may be printed or sent to families as e-mail attachments. (See More Children's Daily Prayer Resources on our website.)

TIPS FOR GIVING CHILDREN A GREATER ROLE IN PRAYER

1. If customarily an adult reads the prayers in this book over the school public address system, consider inviting children from the upper grades to do the reading instead. Two or three children could each take a part and lead prayer together. Be sure the children rotate, so that every child gets an opportunity to grow in this way.

2. If you have already given the older children the task of reading the prayer over the public address system, consider inviting a larger group of children to prepare the readings and then send them to lead prayer in person within the various classrooms.

3. If your older students are already going out to the classrooms to lead prayer in person for the younger classes, ask the older ones to help orient the younger ones to the order of prayer. The older ones can help the younger ones to practice the readings so that the younger ones can lead prayer within their own classrooms.

4. If each class now has its own personal communal prayer time, consider allowing the children to write their own prayers to add just before the Closing Prayer. Some creative children may even write an alternate Closing Prayer.

CREATING A SACRED SPACE AND TIME FOR PRAYER

We are always praying in a particular time of the Church year, so think first about the time.

1. Read the introduction to each liturgical time before it begins.
2. Use the language in the introduction to help the children understand the character of the time.
3. Find practical suggestions for how to celebrate that time in a classroom setting:
   - how to arrange a special prayer area and prayer table within the classroom
   - which colors and objects to use on the prayer table
   - which songs to sing in each liturgical time
   - suggestions for special prayers for that liturgical time and how best to introduce them to children
   - help with adapting ideas from this book to these special circumstances (for catechists who meet with students once a week)

HOW CHILDREN PRAY

THE YOUNGEST CHILDREN

Young children (up until age 6) will pray simple but profound acclamations when they are given a real opportunity to hear the Word of God or to experience the language of signs found in our liturgy. Their spontaneous prayers most often reflect their joy in the Word of God, their thanksgiving for God's goodness, and the pleasure they receive in relationship with Christ. Here are some examples of prayers collected by catechists: "Thank you, Lord, for the light!" (a 3-year-old); "Thank you for everything!" (a 4-year-old); "I love you!" (a 3-year-old); and "I want to take a bath in your light." (a 4-year-old).

These prayers point to the young child's ability to appreciate the greatest of realities: life in relationship with God.

When praying with these "little ones," it is best to proclaim the Scripture (explaining difficult words in advance to help their understanding) and then to ask one or two open-ended questions to help them to reflect on what the passage is saying to them. If you then invite them to say something to Jesus about what they've heard, you may be surprised at what comes out of the mouths of those budding little theologians!

PRAYING WITH OLDER CHILDREN

Older children (ages 6–12) begin to appreciate the gift of prayer language. We should go slowly and use a light touch, though. When they're younger, give them one beautiful phrase ("Our Father, who art in heaven.") that they can begin to appreciate and love. As they grow you can add a second phrase, then a third. But make sure that they understand the words they are using, and encourage them to pray slowly.

Older children also enjoy leading prayer and composing their own prayers. If you give them each a small prayer journal and give them time to write in it, they will produce exquisite prayers and little theological drawings (particularly if you give them time to write and draw right after reading Scripture together).

PSALMS

The psalms offer a treasure trove of prayer language. Consider praying with one or two verses at a time. You could write one or two verses onto an unlined index card and prop it up on your prayer table. You can invite older children to copy them into their prayer journals. But remember to go over each word with the class, asking them to reflect on what the prayer wants to say to God. Children need time to explore the rich implications in their prayer. Also, psalms may be sung or chanted (after all, they were written as songs). There are many beautiful musical settings for the psalms. Experiment until you find the tunes that most move your students.

MUSIC IN PRAYER

It is a fact that the songs we sing in church are all prayers, so include singing in your classroom prayer life. What a wonderful difference it makes! Don't be shy, and don't worry about how well you sing. Even if you don't think you have a good voice, children will happily sing with you. So go ahead and make a joyful noise! Children enjoy the chance to lift their voices to God. You may even have a few gifted singers in the class who can help you lead the singing.

The best music to use in the classroom is what your parish sings during the Sunday liturgy. Especially good to sing with the children are the Penitential Act ("Lord Have Mercy, Christ Have Mercy, Lord Have Mercy"), the Gloria, the Gospel Acclamation (Alleluia), the Holy, Holy, Holy (Sanctus), the Memorial Acclamations (for example, "Save us, Savior of the world"), the Great Amen, the Our Father, and the Lamb of God (Agnus Dei). But any songs, hymns, or chants that your parish sings would be a good choice. Your parish music director or diocesan director of music can be good resources.

Also, in the introductions to each liturgical time, you will find a wealth of music suggestions.

ART AS PRAYER

Try to suggest that the children draw a picture after having heard the Scripture reading. Their drawings often reveal their joy and love in ways that language can't always express. Some children are more visual than verbal. Drawing allows them a way to lengthen and deepen their enjoyment of prayer time.

For these "prayer" drawings, don't give the children assignments or themes, and don't offer a lot of fancy art supplies or media. The best, most reverent drawings come from children who are simply invited to draw something that has to do with what they have just heard in the Scripture reading, something to do with the Mass, or anything to do with God. These open-ended suggestions allow the Holy Spirit room to enter into the children's work.

PRAYER CANNOT BE EVALUATED

This book is most often used in school or religious education programs. In these settings, teachers are often required to give children a grade in religion. Teachers and catechists who have any choice in the matter should make certain *not to give the children a grade for prayer!* Prayer expresses an inner, mysterious reality, and teachers can provide an environment in which prayer can flourish. Prayer is a person's conversation with God. Consider Jesus's teaching on prayer (Matthew 6:5–13) or take a close look at his parable of the Pharisee and the tax collector (Luke 18:9–14). We don't want the children to pray for the benefit of a grade or praise from the teacher; but rather, we want them to pray to the Father "in secret."

JOY

In all you do with the children, feel free to communicate your joy to them. Joy is a great sign of the presence of Christ. If you take pleasure in your students' company, they will understand that they are precious children of God. If you take pleasure in your work, they will understand that work is a beautiful gift. If you listen to them and take their words seriously, you will be incarnating Christ, who so valued children. While you must keep order and an atmosphere of dignity in your classrooms, don't be afraid of a little silliness at times. Both laughter and tears are signs of the presence of the Holy Spirit.

ABOUT THE AUTHOR

Teresa Marshall facilitates the Rite of Christian Initiation of Adults and liturgical ministries at St. Vincent de Paul Catholic Church in Andover, Kansas, a suburb of Wichita. She embarked on her journey into pastoral ministries 13 years ago after a career in corporate communications and journalism. She has an MA in pastoral ministries from St. Mary's University, Winona, Minnesota, and an MA in communications from Wichita State University, Kansas.

ABOUT THE ARTIST AND THE ART

Paula Wiggins, who lives and works in Cincinnati, is the artist for *Children's Daily Prayer 2013–2014.* With a combination of line drawing and scratchboard technique, she has given us a cover that evokes three great movements in salvation history. On the left panel is the Incarnation, when God became flesh in order to be with us. On the center panel is the Eucharist, when Jesus gave us his Body and Blood and, by washing the feet of his disciples, taught us that we must care for others. On the right panel we reflect on the Resurrection, the coming of the Holy Spirit at Pentecost, and Christ's Ascension to the right hand of the Father, and we remember Christ's promise to return at the end of time. On the back cover, Paula's pictures show us prayer and Scripture reading, and they illustrate several beloved parables: the lost coin, the sower, the good shepherd, and the vine and the branches.

Inside the book, on the top of the page for each day's prayer, you will find a special little picture that reflects on the liturgical time. During Ordinary Time in the Autumn, a sturdy mustard tree with tiny seeds blowing from it reminds us of the parable of the mustard seed. For Advent we find the familiar Advent wreath. During the short season of Christmas Time, there is a manger scene with sheep and a dove. As we begin counting Ordinary Time, we find an oyster shell with pearls—an image for the parable of the pearl of great price. During Lent, bare branches remind us of this time of living simply, without decoration and distraction, so that we can feel God's presence. During Easter Time, we find the empty tomb in the early dawn of the first Easter. And as we return to Ordinary Time after Pentecost, a beautiful grape vine reminds us of Jesus's parable of the vine and the branches.

At the beginning of each new liturgical time, special art accompanies the Grace Before Meals and Prayer at Day's End, and you will find appropriate scenes for the various prayer services throughout the year. Finally, notice the harps accompanying the psalms, reminding us that these prayers were originally sung. The incense on the pages of canticles pictures the way we want our prayers to rise to God. Thank you, Paula, for giving us images to accompany our prayer!

MORE CHILDREN'S DAILY PRAYER RESOURCES ON OUR WEBSITE

For an updated list of additional resources (printed in previous editions of *Children's Daily Prayer* as "Reference Bibliography"), please go to http://www.ltp.org/t-productsupplements.aspx.

For more information about the holidays and observances listed under Also on This Day, please go to http://www.ltp.org/t-productsupplements.aspx.

A NOTE ABOUT COPIES

As a purchaser of this book, you have permission to duplicate only the Reproducible Psalms pages, the Grace Before Meals and Prayer at Day's End pages, the Prayer Services, and the Home Prayer pages; these copies may be used only with your class or group; and the Home Prayer pages may be used only in the students' households. You may not duplicate the psalms or prayers unless you are using them with this book. Other parts of this book may not be duplicated without the permission of Liturgy Training Publications or the copyright holders listed on the acknowledgments page.

ORDINARY TIME, AUTUMN

Psalm for Sunday, August 4—Friday, September 13

Psalm 66:1–3a, 5, 8, 16–17

LEADER: Make a joyful noise to God, all the earth.

ALL: **Make a joyful noise to God, all the earth.**

LEADER: Make a joyful noise to God, all the earth;
sing the glory of his name;
Give to him glorious praise.
Say to God, "How awesome are your
    deeds!"

ALL: **Make a joyful noise to God, all the earth.**

Short version: use above only; Long version: use above and below.

SIDE A: Come and see what God has done;
he is awesome in his deeds
    among mortals.
Bless our God, you peoples;
    let the sound of his praise be heard.

SIDE B: Come and hear, all you who fear God,
    And I will tell you what
he has done for me.
I cried aloud to him,
    And he was extolled with my tongue.

ALL: **Make a joyful noise to God, all the earth**

ORDINARY TIME, AUTUMN

Psalm for Sunday, September 15—Friday, October 18

Psalm 145:2–3, 4–5, 10–11

LEADER: I will praise your name for ever, LORD.

ALL: **I will praise your name for ever, LORD.**

LEADER: Every day will I bless you,

    and I will praise your name for ever
    and ever.
Great is the LORD and greatly to be
    praised;
    his greatness is unsearchable.

ALL: **I will praise your name for ever, LORD.**

Short version: use above only; Long version: use above and below.

SIDE A: One generation shall laud your works
    to another, and shall declare your
    mighty acts.
On the glorious splendor of your majesty,
    and on your wondrous works,
    I will meditate.

SIDE B: All your works shall give thanks to you,
    O LORD, and all your faithful shall
    bless you.
They shall speak of the glory of your
    kingdom, and tell of your power.

ALL: **I will praise your name for ever, LORD.**

CHILDREN'S DAILY PRAYER 2013–2014 © 2013 Archdiocese of Chicago: Liturgy Training Publications, 3949 South Racine Avenue, Chicago IL 60609. All rights reserved. Orders: 1-800-933-1800 or www.LTP.org. Scripture excerpts are taken from *The New Revised Standard Version Bible: Catholic Edition*, © 1989, Division of Christian Education of the National Council of the Churches of Christ in the United States of America. Used with permission. All rights reserved.

REPRODUCIBLE PSALMS
ORDINARY TIME, AUTUMN, ADVENT

ORDINARY TIME, AUTUMN

Psalm for Sunday, October 20—Friday, November 29

Psalm 98:1, 2–3, 3–4

LEADER: The LORD has made known his victory.

ALL: **The LORD has made known his victory.**

LEADER: O sing to the LORD a new song,
for he has done marvelous things.
His right hand and his holy arm have
gained him victory.

ALL: **The LORD has made known his victory.**

Short version: use above only; Long version: use above and below.

SIDE A: The LORD has made known his victory;
he has revealed his vindication in the
sight of the nations.
He has remembered his steadfast love
and faithfulness to the house of Israel.

SIDE B: All the ends of the earth have seen the
victory of our God.
Make a joyful noise to the LORD,
all the earth; break forth into joyous
song and sing praises.

ALL: **The LORD has made known his victory.**

ADVENT

Psalm for Sunday, December 1—Sunday, December 22

Psalm 85:4a, 8, 10–11, 12–13

LEADER: Restore us again, O God of our
salvation!

ALL: **Restore us again, O God of our
salvation!**

LEADER: Let me hear what God the LORD will
speak,
for he will speak peace to his people,
to his faithful, to those who turn to
him in their hearts.

ALL: **Restore us again, O God of our
salvation!**

Short version: use above only; Long version: use above and below.

SIDE A: Steadfast love and faithfulness will meet;
righteousness and peace will kiss
each other.
Faithfulness will spring up from the
ground,
and righteousness will look down
from the sky.

SIDE B: The LORD will give what is good,
and our land will yield its increase.
Righteousness will go before him,
and will make a path for his steps.

ALL: **Restore us again, O God of our
salvation!**

CHILDREN'S DAILY PRAYER 2013–2014 © 2013 Archdiocese of Chicago: Liturgy Training Publications, 3949 South Racine Avenue, Chicago IL 60609. All rights reserved. Orders: 1-800-933-1800 or www.LTP.org. Scripture excerpts are taken from *The New Revised Standard Version Bible: Catholic Edition*, © 1989, Division of Christian Education of the National Council of the Churches of Christ in the United States of America. Used with permission. All rights reserved.

CHRISTMAS

Psalm for Monday, January 6—Sunday, January 12

Psalm 96:1–2a, 2b–3, 5b–6, 11a

LEADER: Let the heavens be glad and the earth
rejoice!

ALL: **Let the heavens be glad and the earth
rejoice!**

LEADER: Sing to the LORD a new song;
sing to the LORD, all the earth.
Sing to the LORD; bless his name.

ALL: **Let the heavens be glad and the earth
rejoice!**

Short version: use above only; Long version: use above and below.

SIDE A: Tell of his salvation from day to day.

Declare his glory among the nations,
his marvelous works among all the
peoples.

SIDE B: The LORD made the heavens.
Honor and majesty are before him;
strength and beauty are in his sanctuary.

ALL: **Let the heavens be glad and the earth
rejoice!**

ORDINARY TIME, WINTER

Psalm for Monday, January 13—Tuesday, March 4

Psalm 23:1–3a, 3b–4, 5, 6

LEADER: I shall dwell in the house of the LORD my
whole life long.

ALL: **I shall dwell in the house of the LORD my
whole life long.**

LEADER: The LORD is my shepherd, I shall not
want.
He makes me lie down in green
pastures;
he leads me beside still waters;
he restores my soul.

ALL: **I shall dwell in the house of the LORD my
whole life long.**

Short version: use above only; Long version: use above and below.

SIDE A: He leads me in right paths
for his name's sake.
Even though I walk through the darkest
valley,
I fear no evil; for you are with me;
your rod and your staff—
they comfort me.

SIDE B: You prepare a table before me
in the presence of my enemies;
you anoint my head with oil;
my cup overflows.

ALL: **I shall dwell in the house of the LORD my
whole life long.**

CHILDREN'S DAILY PRAYER 2013–2014 © 2013 Archdiocese of Chicago: Liturgy Training Publications, 3949 South Racine Avenue, Chicago IL 60609. All rights reserved. Orders: 1-800-933-1800 or www.LTP.org. Scripture excerpts are taken from The New Revised Standard Version Bible: Catholic Edition, © 1989, Division of Christian Education of the National Council of the Churches of Christ in the United States of America. Used with permission. All rights reserved.

REPRODUCIBLE PSALMS
LENT

LENT

Psalm for Wednesday, March 5—Thursday, April 17

Psalm 34:4–5, 6–7, 16–17, 18–19

LEADER: The LORD saves the crushed in spirit.

ALL: **The LORD saves the crushed in spirit.**

LEADER: I sought the LORD, and he answered me,
and delivered me from all my fears.
Look to him, and be radiant;
so your faces shall never be ashamed.

ALL: **The LORD saves the crushed in spirit.**

Short version: use above only; Long version: use above and below.

SIDE A: This poor soul cried, and was heard by
the LORD,
and was saved from every trouble.
The angel of the LORD encamps
around those who fear him, and
delivers them.

SIDE B: The face of the LORD is against evildoers,
to cut off the remembrance of them
from the earth.
When the righteous cry for help,
the LORD hears,
and rescues them from all their
troubles.

ALL: **The LORD saves the crushed in spirit.**

LEADER: The LORD is near to the brokenhearted,
and saves the crushed in spirit.
Many are the afflictions of the righteous,
but the LORD rescues them from them
all.

ALL: **The LORD saves the crushed in spirit.**

CHILDREN'S DAILY PRAYER 2013–2014 © 2013 Archdiocese of Chicago: Liturgy Training Publications, 3949 South Racine Avenue, Chicago IL 60609. All rights reserved. Orders: 1-800-933-1800 or www.LTP.org. Scripture excerpts are taken from *The New Revised Standard Version Bible: Catholic Edition,* © 1989, Division of Christian Education of the National Council of the Churches of Christ in the United States of America. Used with permission. All rights reserved.

REPRODUCIBLE PSALMS
EASTER

EASTER

Psalm for Sunday, April 20—Friday, May 16, 2014

Psalm 105:1–2, 3–4, 6–7

LEADER: Let the hearts of those who seek the Lord
rejoice.

ALL: **Let the hearts of those who seek the Lord
rejoice.**

LEADER: O give thanks to the Lord, call on
his name,
make known his deeds among
the peoples.
Sing to him, sing praises to him;
tell of all his wonderful works.

ALL: **Let the hearts of those who seek
the Lord rejoice.**

Short version: use above only; Long version: use above and below.

SIDE A: Glory in his holy name;
let the hearts of those who seek the
Lord rejoice.
Seek the Lord and his strength;
seek his presence continually.

SIDE B: O offspring of his servant Abraham,
children of Jacob, his chosen ones.
He is the Lord our God;
his judgments are in all the earth.

ALL: **Let the hearts of those who seek
the Lord rejoice.**

EASTER

Psalm for Sunday, May 18—Sunday, June 8

Psalm 118:1–2 and 4, 22–24, 25–27a

LEADER: The stone that the builders rejected
has become the chief cornerstone.

ALL: **The stone that the builders rejected
has become the chief cornerstone.**

LEADER: O give thanks to the Lord, for he is good;
his steadfast love endures forever!
Let Israel say,
"His steadfast love endures forever."
Let those who fear the Lord say,
"His steadfast love endures forever."

ALL: **The stone that the builders rejected
has become the chief cornerstone.**

Short version: use above only; Long version: use above and below.

SIDE A: The stone that the builders rejected
has become the chief cornerstone.
This is the Lord's doing;
it is marvelous in our eyes.
This is the day that the Lord has made;
let us rejoice and be glad in it.

SIDE B: Save us, we beseech you, O Lord!
O Lord, we beseech you, give us
success!
Blessed is the one who comes in the name
of the Lord.
We bless you from the house
of the Lord.
The Lord is God,
and he has given us light.

ALL: **The stone that the builders rejected
has become the chief cornerstone.**

CHILDREN'S DAILY PRAYER 2013–2014 © 2013 Archdiocese of Chicago: Liturgy Training Publications, 3949 South Racine Avenue, Chicago IL 60609. All rights reserved. Orders: 1-800-933-1800 or www.LTP.org. Scripture excerpts are taken from *The New Revised Standard Version Bible: Catholic Edition*, © 1989, Division of Christian Education of the National Council of the Churches of Christ in the United States of America. Used with permission. All rights reserved.

REPRODUCIBLE PSALMS
ORDINARY TIME

ORDINARY TIME, SUMMER

Psalm for Monday, June 9—Friday, June 27

Psalm 85:8–9, 10–11, 12–13

LEADER: The LORD speaks of peace to his people.

ALL: **The LORD speaks of peace to his people.**

LEADER: Let me hear what God the LORD will
    speak,
    for he will speak peace to his people,
    to his faithful, to those who turn to
      him in their hearts.
  Surely his salvation is at hand for those
    who fear him,
    that his glory may dwell in our land.

ALL: **The LORD speaks of peace to his people.**

Short version: use above only; Long version: use above and below.

SIDE A: Steadfast love and faithfulness will meet;
    righteousness and peace will kiss
    each other.
  Faithfulness will spring up from the
    ground,
    and righteousness will look down
    from the sky.

SIDE B: The LORD will give what is good,
    and our land will yield its increase.
  Righteousness will go before him,
    and will make a path for his steps.

ALL: **The LORD speaks of peace to his people.**

CHILDREN'S DAILY PRAYER 2013–2014 © 2013 Archdiocese of Chicago: Liturgy Training Publications, 3949 South Racine Avenue, Chicago IL 60609. All rights reserved. Orders: 1-800-933-1800 or www.LTP.org. Scripture excerpts are taken from The New Revised Standard Version Bible: Catholic Edition, © 1989, Division of Christian Education of the National Council of the Churches of Christ in the United States of America. Used with permission. All rights reserved.

ORDINARY TIME AUTUMN

SUNDAY, AUGUST 4, 2013, TO WEDNESDAY, NOVEMBER 27, 2013

ORDINARY TIME

AUTUMN

THE MEANING OF ORDINARY TIME

"Jesus also said, 'With what can we compare the kingdom of God, or what parable will we use for it? It is like a mustard seed, which, when sown upon the ground, is the smallest of all the seeds on earth; yet when it is sown it grows up and becomes the greatest of all shrubs, and puts forth large branches, so that the birds of the air can make nests in its shade' " (Mark 4:30–32).

Jesus told us that the kingdom of God has already arrived. We are living the mysterious reality of the kingdom of God *right now!* We need a new way of looking to see this kingdom in our world today.

Mustard seeds from the Holy Land are much smaller than the mustard seeds you buy in the grocery store. They are so small you can barely see them. The kingdom can be found in the tiny, overlooked, and forgotten. We must search for it.

What happens to the mustard seed? When it is planted in the ground, it grows into a tree, with large spreading branches. The kingdom is not only here with us; it is alive and growing. We can see the kingdom at work in our bodies, hearts, and minds. We can't tell our arms or legs to grow even one inch, but God has filled us with his life, so that we do grow, according to his amazing plan. Our hearts and minds are also full of life and made to grow in wonderful ways.

Times and seasons in the kingdom of God, in contrast to those in the secular calendar, are valued in a different, altogether new way. The Christian calendar even has a different shape! Instead of a rectangle, we draw all the days of a year in a circle. Instead of marking off times according to the weather, the people of the kingdom celebrate those great moments when God has revealed his love for us in marvelous and mysterious ways. There are two celebrations on the calendar that are more precious to us than any of the others: Christmas and Easter. In both, we can see the miracle of the mustard seed at work. At Christmas, we celebrate that the Son of God became flesh as a tiny, vulnerable baby. At Easter, we rejoice in the miracle that

his lifeless, broken human body was buried, like a seed planted in the earth, and that he came out of the tomb alive in a risen body. Now peoples of every country and city in the world can find shelter and rest in the Church, his mystical body.

These are the times of the Church year: *Advent,* the time of preparation before *Christmas Time*; and *Lent,* another period of preparation before *Easter Time.* The fifth time of the Church year is called *Ordinary Time.*

Ordinary Time begins after Christmas (after the Baptism of the Lord), continues until Ash Wednesday when it stops for Lent and Easter, then picks up again after Pentecost Sunday and runs through the summer and autumn until the beginning of Advent. It is a time of growth and change. Sometimes that growth is hidden like that of the mustard seed when it is planted in the ground. Sometimes we are well aware of the growth taking place all around us and inside us. But to remind us that we are growing in grace and in the love of God, each Sunday in Ordinary Time has a number and the numbers increase each week.

PREPARING TO CELEBRATE ORDINARY TIME IN THE CLASSROOM

For Ordinary Time in autumn, *Children's Daily Prayer* provides several special prayer services to use in the classroom or with larger groups: to celebrate the beginning of the school year, to pray for peace (on September 11), to honor Our Lady of the Rosary (October 7), and to celebrate All Saints (November 1) and Thanksgiving. The Home Prayer pages can be duplicated for the students to take home and share with their families: Morning Prayer for Families Departing for the Day; Home Prayer for All Saints and All Souls, called Celebrating the Saints; Remembering the Dead; and a Meal Prayer for Thanksgiving. At the end of this time you will find a Home Prayer page for praying with an Advent Wreath. It's placed at the end of Ordinary Time so you won't forget to send it home with the students *before* the First Sunday of Advent.

SACRED SPACE

With the start of the school year, you have the opportunity to make adjustments to your prayer area. Take a long look around your classroom and decide whether you would like to keep the prayer table where it is or move it to a new spot. You want it to be in a place where the children will see it often and remember to go to it in their free moments. Also, the prayer table should not be too high. A coffee table is the perfect height. You may wish to buy one or two inexpensive cushions to place before your prayer table so that children will feel invited to sit or kneel there. The most essential things for your prayer table are a cross or crucifix, a Bible, and a candle. Cover the prayer table with a plain green cloth and remind the children that green, the color of hope and life, is the color of Ordinary Time. If you can, set the Bible on a bookstand or use a beautiful cushion as a "throne" to prop it up. When you orient the children to the prayer table, point out the small candle beside the Bible, and remind them that Jesus said, "I am the Light of the world" (John 8:12). You might even light the candle, open the Bible, and read that verse to the class. Other objects you might want to include on your prayer table include a simple statue of Christ or Mary, an image of a saint, or a small vase with a fresh flower. Try to avoid clutter! Choose objects that are beautiful, avoiding anything that looks like a toy.

SACRED MUSIC

One of the best ways to help the children enter into the special qualities of this or any liturgical time is by teaching them the music of the Church. The best music for this purpose is what your parish community sings during Sunday Mass. Teach the children how your church sings "Glory to God in the highest," the "Holy, Holy, Holy," the Great Amen, or the Memorial Acclamation, such as, "Save us, Savior of the world . . ." You may even wish to invite the music director for your parish to come one day to teach this music. Some songs

and hymns that children love to sing in Ordinary Time are "For the Beauty of the Earth," "Make Me a Channel of Your Peace," and "I Want to Walk As a Child of the Light."

PRAYERS FOR ORDINARY TIME

During this season, take some time to discuss the meaning of the Our Father with the children in your class. In particular, discuss the kingdom of God (you may wish to review the material in "The Meaning of Ordinary Time" beforehand) and what it means to ask God for his kingdom to come. Go through the prayer a few words at a time. You might even try taking a few deep breaths between each phrase. This helps children relax and listen. Pause, listen, and invite the children to tell you what they hear. Explore with them what Jesus is teaching us about how we should pray: We ask for God's name to be treated as blessed and holy, for the coming of the kingdom of God, for God's will to be accomplished on earth, for our "daily bread," for forgiveness, and for strength in the face of temptation.

A NOTE TO CATECHISTS

Because you meet with your students once a week, you may wish to use the Prayer for the Week pages. These weekly prayer pages contain an excerpt from the Sunday Gospel and will help to prepare the children for Mass. Sometimes, though, you may wish to substitute the Prayer for the Day if it falls on an important solemnity, feast, or memorial of the Church (All Saints, for example).

In this introduction, you will see the suggestion to consider the best placement for your prayer table. You may have to set up a prayer table each time you meet with your group. Think in advance about where to place the prayer table and then always set it up in the same place.

3

GRACE BEFORE MEALS

FOR ORDINARY TIME • Autumn 2013

LEADER:

Lord, you gift us with your love in so many ways.

ALL: We praise you and thank you!

✚ All make the Sign of the Cross.

In the name of the Father, and of the Son, and of the Holy Spirit. Amen.

LEADER:

Father, Son, and Spirit,
you bring us joy
through your abundant grace.
As we gather to share this meal,
may we be grateful for the
loving people who prepared it
every step of the way.
We thank all those in lands far from us
and those nearby who
helped grow, nurture, package,
transport, store, and cook our food.
We bless these brothers and sisters
as we bless each other here,
for you created all of us in
your image of goodness and love.
May this meal nourish our bodies
to give you glory and to build your kingdom.
We ask this through Jesus Christ, our Lord.

✚ All make the Sign of the Cross.

In the name of the Father, and of the Son, and of the Holy Spirit. Amen.

4

PRAYER AT DAY'S END

FOR ORDINARY TIME • Autumn 2013

LEADER:
God of all wisdom,
we offer back to you
all that we have done today
through the gift of your gentle Spirit.

ALL: For your love is in our hearts!

✜ All make the Sign of the Cross.

In the name of the Father, and of the Son, and of the Holy Spirit. Amen.

LEADER:
We are grateful for
the signs and wonders of this day,
for the ordinary events and its surprises,
big and small.
We thank you for the
loving people who surround us.
May we continue to reflect your goodness
to others in your name.
We ask this through your beloved Son, Jesus.

✜ All make the Sign of the Cross.

In the name of the Father, and of the Son, and of the Holy Spirit. Amen.

5

PRAYER SERVICE
BEGINNING OF THE YEAR FOR SCHOOL STAFF

Seek volunteers to lead this prayer service. You may involve up to seven leaders (as marked below). The fourth leader will need a Bible for the Scripture passage. Choose hymns for the beginning and ending if you wish.

FIRST LEADER:
We gather in Christ's name
to celebrate all of God's children.
Let us ask the Holy Spirit for guidance
as we begin our journey again with them.

◆ Gesture for all to stand.

Together we enter this time of prayer as we make the Sign of the Cross.

✚ All make the Sign of the Cross.

In the name of the Father, and of the Son, and of the Holy Spirit. Amen.

SECOND LEADER:
Spirit of God,
enlighten our minds
as we begin another school year, for
these children are gifts of new life.
Draw us closer to all
that is good and true
so that through us
all that they see
is you.
We ask this through Christ our Lord.

Amen.

THIRD LEADER:
Spirit of your Son Jesus,
grant us your wisdom and
integrity each and every day,
for you are the breath of all
that is holy.

CHILDREN'S DAILY PRAYER 2013–2014, © 2013 Archdiocese of Chicago: Liturgy Training Publications. All rights reserved. Orders: 1-800-933-1800 or www.LTP.org.

BEGINNING OF THE YEAR FOR SCHOOL STAFF

Refresh us with ideas that
inspire our youth with your energy
and enthusiasm.
We ask this in Christ's name.

Amen.

◆ Gesture for all to sit.

FOURTH LEADER: Romans 8:31b–35, 37–39
A reading from St. Paul to the Romans

◆ Read the Scripture passage from the Bible.

The Word of the Lord.

◆ All observe silence.

FIFTH LEADER:

◆ Gesture for all to stand.

Let us bring our hopes and needs to God as we
pray from the Opening Prayer of our Church
leadership as they embarked on the Second
Vatican Council, 50 years ago. Our response
will be: **Guide us with your love.**

For light and strength to know your will,
to make it our own,
and to live it in our lives,
we pray to the Lord.

ALL: Guide us with your love.

For justice for all;
enable us to uphold the rights of others;
do not allow us to be misled by ignorance
or corrupted by fear or favor,
we pray to the Lord.

ALL: Guide us with your love.

Unite us to yourself in the bond of love
and keep us faithful to all that is true,
we pray to the Lord.

ALL: Guide us with your love.

May we temper justice with love,
so that all our discussions and reflections
may be pleasing to you, and earn the reward
promised to good and faithful servants,
we pray to the Lord.

ALL: Guide us with your love.

SIXTH LEADER:
Let us pray as Jesus taught us:
Our Father . . . Amen.

◆ Pause and then say:

Let us offer one another the sign
of Christ's peace.

◆ All offer one another a sign of peace.

SEVENTH LEADER:
Let us pray:
God, our Creator,
your presence through the
Holy Spirit strengthens us
for the days ahead.
Guide us with your patience
and compassion as we
mentor our future leaders in Christ.
Amen.

✦ All make the Sign of the Cross.

**In the name of the Father, and of the
Son, and of the Holy Spirit. Amen.**

PRAYER SERVICE
BEGINNING OF THE YEAR FOR STUDENTS

This prayer service may be led by the eighth grade students or by older students. The third and fifth leaders will need a Bible for the passages from Matthew and Luke. Take time to help the third and fifth leaders practice the readings. You may wish to sing "This Little Light of Mine" as the opening and closing songs. If the group will sing, prepare someone to lead the songs.

FIRST LEADER:

We are embarking on a journey together
in this brand new school year.
As we look ahead at all that this year might reveal,
let us remember Jesus,
who will walk beside us every step of the way.

SONG LEADER:

Let us begin by singing the first few verses of our song.

◆ Gesture for all to stand, and lead the first few verses of the song.

SECOND LEADER:

✚ All make the Sign of the Cross.

In the name of the Father, and of the Son, and of the Holy Spirit. Amen.

Let us pray:
God our Creator,
we were made in
your image and likeness.
Help us to be gentle with
ourselves and each other
as we mature this year with your grace.

CHILDREN'S DAILY PRAYER 2013–2014, © 2013 Archdiocese of Chicago: Liturgy Training Publications. All rights reserved. Orders: 1-800-933-1800 or www.LTP.org.

BEGINNING OF THE YEAR FOR STUDENTS

Guide us in our studies and help us develop
with knowledge and maturity.
We ask this through Christ our Lord.
Amen.

◆ Remain standing and sing Alleluia.

THIRD LEADER: Matthew 5:14–16
A reading from the holy Gospel according to
Matthew

◆ Read the Gospel passage from the Bible.

The Gospel of the Lord.

◆ All sit and observe silence.

FOURTH LEADER:

◆ Gesture for all to stand.

Let us bring our hopes and needs to God as we
pray, Let your light shine through us.

ALL: Let your light shine through us.

Help us to show honor and respect
to all those who teach and coach us,
we pray to the Lord.

ALL: Let your light shine through us.

Guide us with your counsel, Lord,
when we are frustrated with our studies,
we pray to the Lord.

ALL: Let your light shine through us.

Help us to take care of our
minds and bodies
so that we give you glory in
everything we do,
we pray to the Lord.

ALL: Let your light shine through us.

Help us to remember all that we learn
so that we can apply it to our lives
in the months and years ahead,
we pray to the Lord.

ALL: Let your light shine through us.

FIFTH LEADER:
Let us listen to what Jesus teaches
to his disciples:

Luke 6:31–36

A reading from the holy Gospel according to
Luke

◆ Read the Gospel passage from the Bible.

The Gospel of the Lord.

SIXTH LEADER:
Let us pray,
O God,
we know you are with us on this journey.
Help us to love one another
as you love us.
Guide us with your light of mercy and justice.
May we be considerate with our friends
and respectful of all who lead us.
Help us to learn and grow in your
wisdom throughout this year.
We ask this through Christ our Lord.
Amen.

✝ All make the Sign of the Cross.

**In the name of the Father, and of the
Son, and of the Holy Spirit. Amen.**

SONG LEADER:
Please join in singing the final verses of our
closing song.

HOME PRAYER
MORNING PRAYER FOR FAMILIES DEPARTING FOR THE DAY

Gather the household in one room. (Breakfast is an ideal opportunity or at the door, just as everyone is ready to depart.) This prayer may be led by a parent or other adult.

LEADER:

Jesus was fully human and fully divine.
We hear of story after story where he used all of his senses
and touched people to heal and connect,
often sending them forth in a whole new way.
Today we bless our senses as we leave for the day,
as we are sent forth from our domestic "church" to be
Jesus for others.

So let's remember to bless your ears, eyes, and nose before you go
and know all the good that Christ will do through you
during this day.

As I hold your head in my hands,
I will gently kiss your ears and say,
"May your ears listen for God's voice."

And your eyes, saying,
"May your eyes see the face of Jesus in others."
And your nose, saying,
"May you follow the Holy Spirit's way."

LEADER:

Almighty God,
maker of all that lives:
you gave us the senses of
touch, hearing, sight, smell, and taste
to enjoy all of your creation abundantly.
May you give us the courage
to listen with ears of compassion,
see with eyes focused on the world's beauty,
smell the fragrance of the Spirit's movement, and
touch your path of truth.
Guide us in all our actions and decisions today.
May we love you fully as we love others.
We ask this through Christ our Lord.

ALL: Amen.

> ✚ As each person departs for the day, exchange a kiss of peace and trace a small cross on each forehead.

10 CHILDREN'S DAILY PRAYER 2013–2014, © 2013 Archdiocese of Chicago: Liturgy Training Publications, 3949 South Racine Avenue, Chicago IL 60609. All rights reserved. Orders: 1-800-933-1800 or www.LTP.org. Scripture excerpts are taken from *The New Revised Standard Version Bible: Catholic Edition*, copyright © 1989, Division of Christian Education of the National Council of the Churches of Christ in the United States of America. Used with permission. All rights reserved.

OPENING

In today's Gospel, Jesus warns his followers about greediness. He tells the story about a successful landowner who decides to store his abundant crops and live a life of leisure. Notice what God tells the man if he continues on this path.

✛ All make the Sign of the Cross.

In the name of the Father, and of the Son, and of the Holy Spirit. Amen.

PSALM   (For a longer psalm, see page xi.) Psalm 66:1–3a, 5 and 8, 16–17

Make a joyful noise to God, all the earth.

Make a joyful noise to God, all the earth.

Make a joyful noise to God, all the earth;
sing the glory of his name;
Give to him glorious praise.
Say to God, "How awesome are your
   deeds!"

Make a joyful noise to God, all the earth.

◆ All stand and sing **Alleluia.**

GOSPEL   Luke 12:16–21

A reading from the holy Gospel according to Luke

Jesus told them a parable: "The land of a rich man produced abundantly. And he thought to himself, 'What should I do, for I have no place to store my crops?' Then he said, 'I will do this: I will pull down my barns and build larger ones, and there I will store all my grain and my goods. And I will say to my soul, 'Soul, you have ample goods laid up for many years; relax, eat, drink, be merry.' But God said to him, 'You fool! This very night your life is being demanded of you. And the things you have prepared, whose will they be?' So it is with those who store up treasures for themselves but are not rich toward God."

The Gospel of the Lord.

◆ All sit and observe silence.

FOR SILENT REFLECTION

How is this rich man greedy? What do you think Jesus is saying about how we should use our gifts and possessions?

CLOSING PRAYER

Let us stand and bring our hopes and needs to God as we pray, "Lord, hear our prayer."

◆ All may add their own prayers here.

Let us pray: **Our Father . . . Amen.**

Almighty God,
we are blessed with so much.
You ask us to live fully in the
present moment
and to keep our focus on you and
all that is good.
Help us to remember
that our time on this earth is
just a brief moment
in all of eternity.
May we live fully today,
aware that our lives are a gift from you.
Amen.

✛ All make the Sign of the Cross.

PRAYER FOR **MONDAY**
AUGUST 5, 2013

OPENING

In today's Gospel, Jesus multiplies a small number of bread loaves and fish to feed thousands of people. This miracle is one we've heard proclaimed many times, but can be experienced in a new way as we remember the hungry of this world.

✝ All make the Sign of the Cross.

In the name of the Father, and of the Son, and of the Holy Spirit. Amen.

PSALM   (For a longer psalm, see page xi.) Psalm 66:1–3a, 5 and 8, 16–17

Make a joyful noise to God, all the earth.

Make a joyful noise to God, all the earth.

Make a joyful noise to God, all the earth;
  sing the glory of his name;
  Give to him glorious praise.
Say to God, "How awesome are your deeds!"

Make a joyful noise to God, all the earth.

◆ All stand and sing **Alleluia.**

GOSPEL   Matthew 14:15–21

A reading from the holy Gospel according to Matthew

When it was evening, the disciples came to him and said, "This is a deserted place, and the hour is now late; send the crowds away so that they may go into the villages and buy food for themselves." Jesus said to them, "They need not go away; you give them something to eat." They replied, "We have nothing here but five loaves and two fish." And he said, "Bring them here to me." Then he ordered the crowds to sit down on the grass. Taking the five loaves and the two fish, he looked up to heaven, and blessed and broke the loaves, and gave them to the disciples, and the disciples gave them to the crowds. And all ate and were filled; and they took up what was left over of the broken pieces, twelve baskets full. And those who ate were about five thousand men, besides women and children.

The Gospel of the Lord.

◆ All sit and observe silence.

FOR SILENT REFLECTION

What are some of the ways in which I share my talents, skills, and resources with others now?

CLOSING PRAYER

Let us stand and bring our hopes and needs to God as we pray, "Lord, hear our prayer."

◆ All may add their own prayers here.

Let us pray: **Our Father . . . Amen.**

Lord Jesus,
you feed us when we are hungry and thirsty.
Help us to be generous and compassionate
when those we meet are in need of comfort.
Give us courage to follow your words.
We ask this in your name.
Amen.

✝ All make the Sign of the Cross.

OPENING

In today's Gospel, Jesus goes up the mountain to pray with his close friends, and they witness some amazing things.

✝ All make the Sign of the Cross.

In the name of the Father, and of the Son, and of the Holy Spirit. Amen.

PSALM

(For a longer psalm, see page xi.) Psalm 66:1–3a, 5 and 8, 16–17

Make a joyful noise to God, all the earth.

Make a joyful noise to God, all the earth.

Make a joyful noise to God, all the earth;
   sing the glory of his name;
   Give to him glorious praise.
Say to God, "How awesome are your deeds!"

Make a joyful noise to God, all the earth.

◆ All stand and sing **Alleluia**.

GOSPEL

Luke 9:28–35

A reading from the holy Gospel according to Luke

Now about eight days after these sayings Jesus took with him Peter and John and James, and went up on the mountain to pray. And while he was praying, the appearance of his face changed, and his clothes became dazzling white. Suddenly they saw two men, Moses and Elijah, talking to him. They appeared in glory and were speaking of his departure, which he was about to accomplish at Jerusalem. Now Peter and his companions were weighed down with sleep; but since they had stayed awake, they saw his glory and the two men who stood with him. Just as they were leaving him, Peter said to Jesus, "Master, it is good for us to be here; let us make three dwellings, one for you, one for Moses, and one for Elijah"—not knowing what he said. While he was saying this, a cloud came and overshadowed them; and they were terrified as they entered the cloud. Then from the cloud came a voice that said, "This is my Son, my Chosen; listen to him!"

The Gospel of the Lord.

◆ All sit and observe silence.

FOR SILENT REFLECTION

How do I allow Christ to be the light in my life through my daily actions of goodness and truth?

CLOSING PRAYER

Let us stand and bring our hopes and needs to God as we pray, "Lord, hear our prayer."

◆ All may add their own prayers here.

Let us pray: **Our Father . . . Amen.**

Lord, our God,
your awesome presence is everywhere.
May we radiate the light of Christ through our daily acts of goodness.
May we give you glory through your life-giving Spirit.
Amen.

✝ All make the Sign of the Cross.

PRAYER FOR **WEDNESDAY** AUGUST 7, 2013

OPENING

Today we remember St. Sixtus II and his deacons who died for their faith in the year 258. We also remember St. Cajetan, who was ordained in 1516 and dedicated himself to caring for the poor and sick.

✚ All make the Sign of the Cross.

In the name of the Father, and of the Son, and of the Holy Spirit. Amen.

PSALM

(For a longer psalm, see page xi.) Psalm 66:1–3a, 5 and 8, 16–17

Make a joyful noise to God, all the earth.

Make a joyful noise to God, all the earth.

Make a joyful noise to God, all the earth;
   sing the glory of his name;
   Give to him glorious praise.
Say to God, "How awesome are your deeds!"

Make a joyful noise to God, all the earth.

◆ All stand and sing **Alleluia.**

GOSPEL

Matthew 15:21–28

A reading from the holy Gospel according to Matthew

Jesus left that place and went away to the district of Tyre [TAI-er] and Sidon [SAI-duhn]. Just then a Canaanite woman from that region came out and started shouting, "Have mercy on me, Lord, Son of David; my daughter is tormented by a demon." But he did not answer her at all. And his disciples came and urged him, saying, "Send her away, for she keeps shouting after us." He answered, "I was sent only to the lost sheep of the house of Israel." But she came and knelt before him, saying, "Lord, help me." He answered, "It is not fair to take the children's food and throw it to the dogs." She said, "Yes, Lord, yet even the dogs eat the crumbs that fall from their masters' table." Then Jesus answered her, "Woman, great is your faith! Let it be done for you as you wish." And her daughter was healed instantly.

The Gospel of the Lord.

◆ All sit and observe silence.

FOR SILENT REFLECTION

Have you ever felt ignored in your prayers to God? Why do you think Jesus waited to respond to the woman?

CLOSING PRAYER

Let us stand and bring our hopes and needs to God as we pray, "Lord, hear our prayer."

◆ All may add their own prayers here.

Let us pray: **Our Father . . . Amen.**

Lord Jesus,
we come to you with needs for our family
and friends and you listen to us.
Encourage us to continue our conversation
with you,
for it is the path to your healing and strength.
We ask this in your name.
Amen.

✚ All make the Sign of the Cross.

OPENING

Today we remember St. Dominic, born in Spain in 1170, who inspired many people to study Scripture, and to live simply and prayerfully.

✝ All make the Sign of the Cross.

In the name of the Father, and of the Son, and of the Holy Spirit. Amen.

PSALM   (For a longer psalm, see page xi.) Psalm 66:1–3a, 5 and 8, 16–17

Make a joyful noise to God, all the earth.

Make a joyful noise to God, all the earth.

Make a joyful noise to God, all the earth;
   sing the glory of his name;
   Give to him glorious praise.
Say to God, "How awesome are your deeds!"

Make a joyful noise to God, all the earth.

◆ All stand and sing **Alleluia.**

GOSPEL   Matthew 16:13–20

A reading from the holy Gospel according to Matthew

Now when Jesus came into the district of Caesarea [sez-suh-REE-uh] Philippi [fih-LIP-I], he asked his disciples, "Who do people say that the Son of Man is?" And they said, "Some say John the Baptist, but others Elijah, and still others Jeremiah or one of the prophets." He said to them, "But who do you say that I am?" Simon Peter answered, "You are the Messiah [meh-SĪ-uh], the Son of the living God." And Jesus answered him, "Blessed are you, Simon son of Jonah! For flesh and blood has not revealed this to you, but my Father in heaven. And I tell you, you are Peter, and on this rock I will build my church, and the gates of Hades will not prevail against it. I will give you the keys of the kingdom of heaven, and whatever you bind on earth will be bound in heaven, and whatever you loose on earth will be loosed in heaven."

The Gospel of the Lord.

◆ All sit and observe silence.

FOR SILENT REFLECTION

In what way is the Church a rock for you in your faith?

CLOSING PRAYER

Let us stand and bring our hopes and needs to God as we pray, "Lord, hear our prayer."

◆ All may add their own prayers here.

Let us pray: **Our Father . . . Amen.**

Lord Jesus,
Help us to lean on you and on
the beliefs of the Church
for they are the building blocks of our faith.
We ask this in your name.

Amen.

✝ All make the Sign of the Cross.

ALSO ON THIS DAY: Eid al-Fitr (Islamic celebration marking the end of Ramadan, the month of fasting)

OPENING

Today we remember St. Teresa Benedicta of the Cross, known as Edith Stein, who was born into a Jewish family in Poland. She was a professor who had stopped believing in God, but reversed her beliefs after reading about the life of St. Teresa of Avila. She became a Carmelite nun and a respected author, who died in Auschwitz.

✛ All make the Sign of the Cross.

In the name of the Father, and of the Son, and of the Holy Spirit. Amen.

PSALM   (For a longer psalm, see page xi.) Psalm 66:1–3a, 5 and 8, 16–17

Make a joyful noise to God, all the earth.

Make a joyful noise to God, all the earth.

Make a joyful noise to God, all the earth;
   sing the glory of his name;
   Give to him glorious praise.
Say to God, "How awesome are your deeds!"

Make a joyful noise to God, all the earth.

◆ All stand and sing **Alleluia.**

GOSPEL   Matthew 16:24–28

A reading from the holy Gospel according to Matthew

Then Jesus told his disciples, "If any want to become my followers, let them deny themselves and take up their cross and follow me. For those who want to save their life will lose it, and those who lose their life for my sake will find it. For what will it profit them if they gain the whole world but forfeit their life? Or what will they give in return for their life? "For the Son of Man is to come with his angels in the glory of his Father, and then he will repay everyone for what has been done. Truly I tell you, there are some standing here who will not taste death before they see the Son of Man coming in his kingdom."

The Gospel of the Lord.

◆ All sit and observe silence.

FOR SILENT REFLECTION

What does it mean "to take up our cross"? How can I remain a true disciple of Christ?

CLOSING PRAYER

Let us stand and bring our hopes and needs to God as we pray, "Lord, hear our prayer."

◆ All may add their own prayers here.

Let us pray: **Our Father . . . Amen.**

Lord Jesus,
you remind us
of what we truly need: belief in you.
Sometimes we don't understand
what our "cross" really is, but we know
you will be with us on the journey.
We believe in your promise of life everlasting.
We pray this in your name.

Amen.

✛ All make the Sign of the Cross.

PRAYER FOR THE WEEK

OPENING

In today's Gospel, Jesus tells a story about a master who returns home after attending a wedding feast. Notice how the homeowner rewards his helpers when he discovers they're still alert and willing to help.

✚ *All make the Sign of the Cross.*

In the name of the Father, and of the Son, and of the Holy Spirit. Amen.

PSALM   (For a longer psalm, see page xi.) Psalm 66:1–3a, 5 and 8, 16–17

Make a joyful noise to God, all the earth.

Make a joyful noise to God, all the earth.

Make a joyful noise to God, all the earth;
   sing the glory of his name;
   Give to him glorious praise.
Say to God, "How awesome are your deeds!"

Make a joyful noise to God, all the earth.

◆ *All stand and sing* **Alleluia.**

GOSPEL   Luke 12:35–40

A reading from the holy Gospel according to Luke

Jesus said to his disciples: "Be dressed for action and have your lamps lit; be like those who are waiting for their master to return from the wedding banquet, so that they may open the door for him as soon as he comes and knocks. Blessed are those slaves whom the master finds alert when he comes; truly I tell you, he will fasten his belt and have them sit down to eat, and he will come and serve them. If he comes during the middle of the night, or near dawn, and finds them so, blessed are those slaves. But know this: if the owner of the house had known at what hour the thief was coming, he would not have let his house be broken into. You also must be ready, for the Son of Man is coming at an unexpected hour."

The Gospel of the Lord.

◆ *All sit and observe silence.*

FOR SILENT REFLECTION

Why does Jesus want us to be watchful and ready? What could be considered a "thief" in today's world?

CLOSING PRAYER

Let us stand and bring our hopes and needs to God as we pray, "Lord, hear our prayer."

◆ *All may add their own prayers here.*

Let us pray: **Our Father . . . Amen.**

Lord Jesus,
you influence our thoughts and actions
as we talk with you throughout the day.
You teach us with your examples of love
and servant leadership.
Help us to be aware of how we can always be
loving to others in word and deed.
We ask this in your name

Amen.

✚ *All make the Sign of the Cross.*

17

PRAYER FOR **MONDAY**
AUGUST 12, 2013

OPENING

Today we remember St. Jane Frances de Chantal, born in 1572 in Dijon, France. She was a wife and mother in French high society. After her husband died, she became a nun and founder of a religious community. In today's Gospel, see what Jesus's friends discover in a fish's mouth.

✛ All make the Sign of the Cross.

In the name of the Father, and of the Son, and of the Holy Spirit. Amen.

PSALM (For a longer psalm, see page xi.) Psalm 66:1–3a, 5 and 8, 16–17

Make a joyful noise to God, all the earth.

Make a joyful noise to God, all the earth.

Make a joyful noise to God, all the earth;
   sing the glory of his name;
   Give to him glorious praise.
Say to God, "How awesome are your deeds!"

Make a joyful noise to God, all the earth.

◆ All stand and sing **Alleluia.**

GOSPEL   Matthew 17:22–27

A reading from the holy Gospel according to Matthew

As they were gathering in Galilee [GAL-ih-lee], Jesus said to them, "The Son of Man is going to be betrayed into human hands, and they will kill him, and on the third day he will be raised." And they were greatly distressed. When they reached Capernaum [kuh-PERR-nay-uhm], the collectors of the temple tax came to Peter and said, "Does your teacher not pay the temple tax?" He said, "Yes, he does." And when he came home, Jesus spoke of it first, asking, "What do you think, Simon? From whom do kings of the earth take toll or tribute? From their children or from others?" When Peter said, "From others," Jesus said to him, "Then the children are free. However, so that we do not give offense to them, go to the sea and cast a hook; take the first fish that comes up; and when you open its mouth, you will find a coin; take that and give it to them for you and me."

The Gospel of the Lord.

◆ All sit and observe silence.

FOR SILENT REFLECTION

Jesus reveals to Peter who is Lord of all creation. How do I see God working in the world today, despite negative news that I often hear?

CLOSING PRAYER

Let us stand and bring our hopes and needs to God as we pray, "Lord, hear our prayer."

◆ All may add their own prayers here.

Let us pray: **Our Father . . . Amen.**

Almighty God,
you created our universe and everything that lives and breathes on earth.
May we glorify you with our lives as we study and move through our day.
We ask this through Christ our Lord.

Amen.

✛ All make the Sign of the Cross.

OPENING

Today we remember St. Pontian [PON-tee-un] and St. Hippolytus [hi-PAW-lih-tuhs], who had been bitter enemies, but reconciled while in prison together. The writings of Hippolytus have been a source for those studying Roman liturgy and the structure of the early church.

✛ All make the Sign of the Cross.

In the name of the Father, and of the Son, and of the Holy Spirit. Amen.

PSALM (For a longer psalm, see page xi.) Psalm 66:1–3a, 5 and 8, 16–17

Make a joyful noise to God, all the earth.

Make a joyful noise to God, all the earth.

Make a joyful noise to God, all the earth;
   sing the glory of his name;
   Give to him glorious praise.
Say to God, "How awesome are your deeds!"

Make a joyful noise to God, all the earth.

◆ All stand and sing **Alleluia.**

GOSPEL Matthew 18:1–5, 10, 12–13

A reading from the holy Gospel according to Matthew

At that time the disciples came to Jesus and asked, "Who is the greatest in the kingdom of heaven?" He called a child, whom he put among them, and said, "Truly I tell you, unless you change and become like children, you will never enter the kingdom of heaven. Whoever becomes humble like this child is the greatest in the kingdom of heaven. Whoever welcomes one such child in my name welcomes me. "Take care that you do not despise one of these little ones; for, I tell you, in heaven their angels continually see the face of my Father in heaven. What do you think? If a shepherd has a hundred sheep, and one of them has gone astray, does he not leave the ninety-nine on the mountains and go in search of the one that went astray? And if he finds it, truly I tell you, he rejoices over it more than over the ninety-nine that never went astray."

The Gospel of the Lord.

◆ All sit and observe silence.

FOR SILENT REFLECTION

Why does Jesus ask adults to become like children? How do I follow Jesus, the shepherd?

CLOSING PRAYER

Let us stand and bring our hopes and needs to God as we pray, "Lord, hear our prayer."

◆ All may add their own prayers here.

Let us pray: **Our Father . . . Amen.**

Lord Jesus,
you are our most loving shepherd,
and we are secure in your arms.
You care for us in so many ways,
leading us to safe meadows and mountain springs.
Help us to trust you more and more.
We ask this in your name.

Amen.

✛ All make the Sign of the Cross.

PRAYER FOR **WEDNESDAY** AUGUST 14, 2013

OPENING

Today we remember St. Maximilian Mary Kolbe. He was captured by Nazi soldiers, and suffered in a concentration camp. His last act of heroism was standing up for someone selected to die through starvation. He volunteered to take that prisoner's place because he had a family.

✠ All make the Sign of the Cross.

In the name of the Father, and of the Son, and of the Holy Spirit. Amen.

PSALM

(For a longer psalm, see page xi.) Psalm 66:1–3a, 5 and 8, 16–17

Make a joyful noise to God, all the earth.

Make a joyful noise to God, all the earth.

Make a joyful noise to God, all the earth;
   sing the glory of his name;
   Give to him glorious praise.
Say to God, "How awesome are your deeds!"

Make a joyful noise to God, all the earth.

◆ All stand and sing **Alleluia.**

GOSPEL

Matthew 18:15–20

A reading from the holy Gospel according to Matthew

Jesus said to his disciples: "If another member of the church sins against you, go and point out the fault when the two of you are alone. If the member listens to you, you have regained that one. But if you are not listened to, take one or two others along with you, so that every word may be confirmed by the evidence of two or three witnesses. If the member refuses to listen to them, tell it to the church; and if the offender refuses to listen even to the church, let such a one be to you as a Gentile and a tax collector. Truly I tell you, whatever you bind on earth will be bound in heaven, and whatever you loose on earth will be loosed in heaven. Again, truly I tell you, if two of you agree on earth about anything you ask, it will be done for you by my Father in heaven. For where two or three are gathered in my name, I am there among them."

The Gospel of the Lord.

◆ All sit and observe silence.

FOR SILENT REFLECTION

Are there times you could follow Jesus's guidelines when someone hurts you?

CLOSING PRAYER

Let us stand and bring our hopes and needs to God as we pray, "Lord, hear our prayer."

◆ All may add their own prayers here.

Let us pray: **Our Father . . . Amen.**

Lord Jesus,
you are the source of all wisdom.
You provide a guide for resolving conflict
in our everyday matters.
Help us to find solutions with one another.
Give us courage to call upon you
in times of stress.
We ask this in your name.

Amen.

✠ All make the Sign of the Cross.

OPENING

Today, on the Solemnity of the Assumption of the Blessed Virgin Mary, we remember the Mother of Jesus, who was taken, body and soul, into heaven. In today's Gospel, we see how Mary's elderly cousin (and her unborn child) react as Mary greets Elizabeth.

✚ All make the Sign of the Cross.

In the name of the Father, and of the Son, and of the Holy Spirit. Amen.

PSALM (For a longer psalm, see page xi.) Psalm 66:1–3a, 5 and 8, 16–17

Make a joyful noise to God, all the earth.

Make a joyful noise to God, all the earth.

Make a joyful noise to God, all the earth;
   sing the glory of his name;
   Give to him glorious praise.
Say to God, "How awesome are your deeds!"

Make a joyful noise to God, all the earth.

◆ All stand and sing **Alleluia.**

GOSPEL   Luke 1:39–45

A reading from the holy Gospel according to Luke

In those days Mary set out and went with haste to a Judean town in the hill country, where she entered the house of Zechariah [zeh-uh-RI-uh] and greeted Elizabeth. When Elizabeth heard Mary's greeting, the child leaped in her womb. And Elizabeth was filled with the Holy Spirit and exclaimed with a loud cry, "Blessed are you among women, and blessed is the fruit of your womb. And why has this happened to me, that the mother of my Lord comes to me? For as soon as I heard the sound of your greeting, the child in my womb leaped for joy. And blessed is she who believed that there would be a fulfillment of what was spoken to her by the Lord."

The Gospel of the Lord.

◆ All sit and observe silence.

FOR SILENT REFLECTION

Why do you think Elizabeth called Mary "blessed among women"? How do you think Mary felt at this time?

CLOSING PRAYER

Let us stand and bring our hopes and needs to God as we pray, "Lord, hear our prayer."

◆ All may add their own prayers here.

Let us pray: **Our Father . . . Amen.**

Almighty God,
you gave us your Son Jesus
through the gift of Mary.
We honor her because of her courage to
say, "yes" to your Spirit.
Help us to be brave like the blessed Mary,
who prays with us to you.
We ask this through Christ our Lord.

Amen.

✚ All make the Sign of the Cross.

PRAYER FOR **FRIDAY** AUGUST 16, 2013

OPENING

Today we remember St. Stephen of Hungary, who became king of his country in 1001. He was known for his zeal in building churches and support for priests. In today's Gospel, we hear Jesus talk about the holiness of marriage and the troubling issue of divorce.

✛ All make the Sign of the Cross.

In the name of the Father, and of the Son, and of the Holy Spirit. Amen.

PSALM   (For a longer psalm, see page xi.) Psalm 66:1–3a, 5 and 8, 16–17

Make a joyful noise to God, all the earth.

Make a joyful noise to God, all the earth.

Make a joyful noise to God, all the earth;
  sing the glory of his name;
  Give to him glorious praise.
Say to God, "How awesome are your deeds!"

Make a joyful noise to God, all the earth.

◆ All stand and sing **Alleluia.**

GOSPEL   Matthew 19:3–6

A reading from the holy Gospel according to Matthew

Some Pharisees came to him, and to test him they asked, "Is it lawful for a man to divorce his wife for any cause?" He answered, "Have you not read that the one who made them at the beginning 'made them male and female,' and said, 'For this reason a man shall leave his father and mother and be joined to his wife,

and the two shall become one flesh'? So they are no longer two, but one flesh. Therefore what God has joined together, let no one separate."

The Gospel of the Lord.

◆ All sit and observe silence.

FOR SILENT REFLECTION

How can I be a support to a friend whose parents are separated or going through a divorce?

CLOSING PRAYER

Let us stand and bring our hopes and needs to God as we pray, "Lord, hear our prayer."

◆ All may add their own prayers here.

Let us pray: **Our Father . . . Amen.**

Lord God,
you show us the way in good times as well as those hard to bear.
Help married couples
in their vocation of love.
Help us to trust in you as we
nurture family life.
We ask this through Christ our Lord.

Amen.

✛ All make the Sign of the Cross.

OPENING

Today's Gospel describes struggle for those who follow Jesus's way. While it is true that faith in Christ can foster unity and peace, it can also cause division among family members, especially those who have different beliefs.

✦ All make the Sign of the Cross.

In the name of the Father, and of the Son, and of the Holy Spirit. Amen.

PSALM

(For a longer psalm, see page xi.) Psalm 66:1–3a, 5 and 8, 16–17

Make a joyful noise to God, all the earth.

Make a joyful noise to God, all the earth.

Make a joyful noise to God, all the earth;
sing the glory of his name;
Give to him glorious praise.
Say to God, "How awesome are your deeds!"

Make a joyful noise to God, all the earth.

◆ All stand and sing **Alleluia.**

GOSPEL

Luke 12:49–53

A reading from the holy Gospel according to Luke

Jesus said to his disciples: "I came to bring fire to the earth, and how I wish it were already kindled! I have a baptism with which to be baptized, and what stress I am under until it is completed! Do you think that I have come to bring peace to the earth? No, I tell you, but rather division! From now on five in one household will be divided, three against two and two against three; they will be divided: father against son and son against father, mother against daughter and daughter against mother, mother-in-law against her daughter-in-law and daughter-in-law against mother-in-law."

The Gospel of the Lord.

◆ All sit and observe silence.

FOR SILENT REFLECTION

Who are your brothers and sisters in Christ? Why do you think Jesus describes strife when someone follows him?

CLOSING PRAYER

Let us stand and bring our hopes and needs to God as we pray, "Lord, hear our prayer."

◆ All may add their own prayers here.

Let us pray: **Our Father . . . Amen.**

Almighty God,
it is not easy to be your Son's disciple.
We are asked to do what is right,
which can be a struggle at times.
Help us to be true to your Word
as we love others as your beloved sons and
daughters.
We ask this through Christ our Lord.

Amen.

✦ All make the Sign of the Cross.

PRAYER FOR **MONDAY** AUGUST 19, 2013

OPENING

Today we remember St. John Eudes [yood], who lived from 1601–1680 in France. Ordained at the age of 24, he became known for his compassion and gift of preaching. He personally cared for those sick from the plague. To prevent his fellow religious from getting ill, he lived in a large barrel or cask in an isolated field.

✚ All make the Sign of the Cross.

In the name of the Father, and of the Son, and of the Holy Spirit. Amen.

PSALM
(For a longer psalm, see page xi.) Psalm 66:1–3a, 5 and 8, 16–17

Make a joyful noise to God, all the earth.

Make a joyful noise to God, all the earth.

Make a joyful noise to God, all the earth;
   sing the glory of his name;
   Give to him glorious praise.
Say to God, "How awesome are your deeds!"

Make a joyful noise to God, all the earth.

◆ All stand and sing **Alleluia.**

GOSPEL
Matthew 19:16–22

A reading from the holy Gospel according to Matthew

Someone came to Jesus and said, "Teacher, what good deed must I do to have eternal life?" And he said to him, "Why do you ask me about what is good? There is only one who is good. If you wish to enter into life, keep the commandments." He said to him, "Which ones?"

And Jesus said, "You shall not murder; You shall not commit adultery; You shall not steal; You shall not bear false witness; Honor your father and mother; also, You shall love your neighbor as yourself." The young man said to him, "I have kept all these; what do I still lack?" Jesus said to him, "If you wish to be perfect, go, sell your possessions, and give the money to the poor, and you will have treasure in heaven; then come, follow me." When the young man heard this word, he went away grieving, for he had many possessions.

The Gospel of the Lord.

◆ All sit and observe silence.

FOR SILENT REFLECTION

How do I show respect for my mother and father, or those who care for me?

CLOSING PRAYER

Let us stand and bring our hopes and needs to God as we pray, "Lord, hear our prayer."

◆ All may add their own prayers here.

Let us pray: **Our Father . . . Amen.**

Gracious God,
you give us direction in this life.
We honor your laws for treating others
and ourselves
with dignity and respect.
Continue to guide us on our journey of faith.
We ask this through Christ our Lord.

Amen.

✚ All make the Sign of the Cross.

OPENING

We remember St. Bernard of Clairvaux [clare-VOH]. He served as a counselor during a time of social upheaval throughout Europe in the early 12th century and was later named Doctor of the Church.

✝ All make the Sign of the Cross.

In the name of the Father, and of the Son, and of the Holy Spirit. Amen.

PSALM   (For a longer psalm, see page xi.) Psalm 66:1–3a, 5 and 8, 16–17

Make a joyful noise to God, all the earth.

Make a joyful noise to God, all the earth.

Make a joyful noise to God, all the earth;
    sing the glory of his name;
    Give to him glorious praise.
Say to God, "How awesome are your deeds!"

Make a joyful noise to God, all the earth.

◆ All stand and sing **Alleluia.**

GOSPEL   Matthew 19:23–26

A reading from the holy Gospel according to Matthew

Jesus said to his disciples, "Truly I tell you, it will be hard for a rich person to enter the kingdom of heaven. Again I tell you, it is easier for a camel to go through the eye of a needle than for someone who is rich to enter the kingdom of God." When the disciples heard this, they were greatly astounded and said, "Then who can be saved?" But Jesus looked at them and said, "For mortals it is impossible, but for God all things are possible."

The Gospel of the Lord.

◆ All sit and observe silence.

FOR SILENT REFLECTION

Why does Jesus tell us that with God all things are possible?

CLOSING PRAYER

Let us stand and bring our hopes and needs to God as we pray, "Lord, hear our prayer."

◆ All may add their own prayers here.

Let us pray: **Our Father . . . Amen.**

Lord God,
we are your disciples in a
world that has many distractions.
You ask us to focus on all that is good.
Help us to take time to
clear all the sights and sounds
from our busy days
so that we can follow you,
wherever it may take us:
in this day, in this lifetime.
We ask this through Christ our Lord.
Amen.

✝ All make the Sign of the Cross.

PRAYER FOR **WEDNESDAY** AUGUST 21, 2013

OPENING

Pope Pius X, whose feast we celebrate today, encouraged Italian Catholics to become more politically active and helped in several world relief efforts.

✝ All make the Sign of the Cross.

In the name of the Father, and of the Son, and of the Holy Spirit. Amen.

PSALM

(For a longer psalm, see page xi.) Psalm 66:1–3a, 5 and 8, 16–17

Make a joyful noise to God, all the earth.

Make a joyful noise to God, all the earth.

Make a joyful noise to God, all the earth;
sing the glory of his name;
Give to him glorious praise.
Say to God, "How awesome are your deeds!"

Make a joyful noise to God, all the earth.

◆ All stand and sing **Alleluia.**

GOSPEL

Matthew 20:1–15

A reading from the holy Gospel according to Matthew

"For the kingdom of heaven is like a landowner who went out early in the morning to hire laborers for his vineyard. After agreeing with the laborers for the usual daily wage, he sent them into his vineyard. When he went out about nine o'clock, he saw others standing idle in the marketplace; and he said to them, 'You also go into the vineyard. When he went out again about noon and about three o'clock, he did the same. And about five o'clock he found others standing around; and he said to them,

'Why are you standing here idle all day?' They said to him, 'Because no one has hired us.' He said, 'You also go into the vineyard.' When evening came, the owner of the vineyard said to his manager, 'Call the laborers and give them their pay.' When those hired about five o'clock came, each of them received the usual daily wage. Now when the first came, they thought they would receive more; but each of them also received the usual daily wage. They grumbled against the landowner, saying, 'These last worked only one hour, and you have made them equal to us.' But he replied, 'Friend, I am doing you no wrong; did you not agree with me for the usual daily wage? I choose to give to this last the same as I give to you.'"

The Gospel of the Lord.

◆ All sit and observe silence.

FOR SILENT REFLECTION

When have I grumbled at what seemed to be unfair?

CLOSING PRAYER

Let us stand and bring our hopes and needs to God as we pray, "Lord, hear our prayer."

◆ All may add their own prayers here.

Let us pray: **Our Father . . . Amen.**

Creator God,
give us courage to work hard and with joy.
We ask this through Jesus, your Son.

Amen.

✝ All make the Sign of the Cross.

OPENING

Today is the feast of the Queenship of Mary, in which we honor the Mother of our Lord Jesus Christ, and reflect on her active role in God's plan for our salvation.

✦ All make the Sign of the Cross.

In the name of the Father, and of the Son, and of the Holy Spirit. Amen.

PSALM

(For a longer psalm, see page xi.) Psalm 66:1–3a, 5 and 8, 16–17

Make a joyful noise to God, all the earth.

Make a joyful noise to God, all the earth.

Make a joyful noise to God, all the earth;
   sing the glory of his name;
   Give to him glorious praise.
Say to God, "How awesome are your deeds!"

Make a joyful noise to God, all the earth.

◆ All stand and sing **Alleluia.**

GOSPEL

Matthew 22:1–10

A reading from the holy Gospel according to Matthew

Once more Jesus spoke to them in parables, saying: "The kingdom of heaven may be compared to a king who gave a wedding banquet for his son. He sent his slaves to call those who had been invited to the wedding banquet, but they would not come. Again he sent other slaves, saying, 'Tell those who have been invited: Look, I have prepared my dinner, my oxen and my fat calves have been slaughtered, and everything is ready; come to the wedding banquet.' But they made light of it and went away, one to his farm, another to his business. Then he said to his slaves, 'The wedding is ready, but those invited were not worthy. Go therefore into the main streets, and invite everyone you find to the wedding banquet.' Those slaves went out into the streets and gathered all whom they found, both good and bad; so the wedding hall was filled with guests."

The Gospel of the Lord.

◆ All sit and observe silence.

FOR SILENT REFLECTION

Can I imagine God's eternal banquet ready for me to enjoy? Do I sometimes say "no" to Jesus's invitation to love?

CLOSING PRAYER

Let us stand and bring our hopes and needs to God as we pray, "Lord, hear our prayer."

◆ All may add their own prayers here.

Let us pray: **Our Father . . . Amen.**

Loving Father,
as your sons and daughters, we are
grateful to feast among family and friends.
Your Spirit calls to us here on earth,
serving as a reminder of
your great celebration with the saints
of heaven.
We ask this through Christ our Lord.

Amen.

✦ All make the Sign of the Cross.

PRAYER FOR **FRIDAY** AUGUST 23, 2013

OPENING

Today we remember St. Rose of Lima, who suffered humiliation from her family as she devoted herself to Christ. She cared for homeless children, the elderly, and the sick, and inspired others to develop more social services for the impoverished in Peru. In the Gospel today, Jesus summarizes all laws into two simple, yet profound statements.

✚ All make the Sign of the Cross.

In the name of the Father, and of the Son, and of the Holy Spirit. Amen.

PSALM (For a longer psalm, see page xi.) Psalm 66:1–3a, 5 and 8, 16–17

Make a joyful noise to God, all the earth.

Make a joyful noise to God, all the earth.

Make a joyful noise to God, all the earth;
 sing the glory of his name;
 Give to him glorious praise.
Say to God, "How awesome are your deeds!"

Make a joyful noise to God, all the earth.

◆ All stand and sing **Alleluia.**

GOSPEL Matthew 22:34–40

A reading from the holy Gospel according to Matthew

When the Pharisees [FAYR-uh-seez] heard that Jesus had silenced the Sadducees [SAD-yoo-seez], they gathered together, and one of them, a lawyer, asked him a question to test him. "Teacher, which commandment in the law is the greatest?" He said to him, "'You shall love the Lord your God with all your heart, and with all your soul, and with all your mind.' This is the greatest and first commandment. And a second is like it: 'You shall love your neighbor as yourself.' On these two commandments hang all the law and the prophets."

The Gospel of the Lord.

◆ All sit and observe silence.

FOR SILENT REFLECTION

What does it look like to love with our "whole heart" and our "whole soul" and "all our mind"?

CLOSING PRAYER

Let us stand and bring our hopes and needs to God as we pray, "Lord, hear our prayer."

◆ All may add their own prayers here.

Let us pray: **Our Father . . . Amen.**

Almighty God,
you are pure love.
You created everything to be good,
and we are made in your image.
Through your Son,
you teach us to love God entirely
and to love each other as
we love ourselves.
Help us to recognize holiness
in each other.
Guide us as we care for our own
spiritual, physical, and emotional beings too.
We ask this through Christ our Lord.

Amen.

✚ All make the Sign of the Cross.

OPENING

In today's Gospel, Jesus uses the image of a narrow doorway to the kingdom of heaven.

✝ All make the Sign of the Cross.

In the name of the Father, and of the Son, and of the Holy Spirit. Amen.

PSALM
(For a longer psalm, see page xi.) Psalm 66:1–3a, 5 and 8, 16–17

Make a joyful noise to God, all the earth.

Make a joyful noise to God, all the earth.

Make a joyful noise to God, all the earth;
   sing the glory of his name;
   Give to him glorious praise.
Say to God, "How awesome are your deeds!"

Make a joyful noise to God, all the earth.

◆ All stand and sing **Alleluia**.

GOSPEL
Luke 13:23–30

A reading from the holy Gospel according to Luke

Someone asked him, "Lord, will only a few be saved?" He said to them, "Strive to enter through the narrow door; for many, I tell you, will try to enter and will not be able. When once the owner of the house has got up and shut the door, and you begin to stand outside and to knock at the door, saying, 'Lord, open to us,' then in reply he will say to you, 'I do not know where you come from.' Then you will begin to say, 'We ate and drank with you, and you taught in our streets.' But he will say, 'I do not know where you come from; go away from me, all you evildoers!' There will be weeping and gnashing of teeth when you see Abraham and Isaac and Jacob and all the prophets in the kingdom of God, and you yourselves thrown out. Then people will come from east and west, from north and south, and will eat in the kingdom of God. Indeed, some are last who will be first, and some are first who will be last."

The Gospel of the Lord.

◆ All sit and observe silence.

FOR SILENT REFLECTION

What do you imagine it will be like to "eat in the kingdom of God"?

CLOSING PRAYER

Let us stand and bring our hopes and needs to God as we pray, "Lord, hear our prayer."

◆ All may add their own prayers here.

Let us pray: **Our Father . . . Amen.**

Lord God,
you are the source of all wisdom and justice.
You alone know our hearts and can guide us
through the narrow door.
We are mindful of the challenges ahead,
but we know your Word is our guide.
Keep us connected with you
if we should wander from your path.
We ask this through Christ our Lord.

Amen.

✝ All make the Sign of the Cross.

PRAYER FOR **MONDAY**
AUGUST 26, 2013

OPENING

In today's reading, St. Paul gives encouraging news to the people of Thessalonia [theh-suh-LO-nih-uh]. See if you can identify why Paul also is pleased with their spiritual growth.

✝ All make the Sign of the Cross.

In the name of the Father, and of the Son, and of the Holy Spirit. Amen.

PSALM (For a longer psalm, see page xi.) Psalm 66:1–3a, 5 and 8, 16–17

Make a joyful noise to God, all the earth.

Make a joyful noise to God, all the earth.

Make a joyful noise to God, all the earth;
   sing the glory of his name;
   Give to him glorious praise.
Say to God, "How awesome are your deeds!"

Make a joyful noise to God, all the earth.

READING 1 Thessalonians 1:2–5, 8b–10

A reading from the first Letter of St. Paul to the Thessalonians

We always give thanks to God for all of you and mention you in our prayers, constantly remembering before our God and Father your work of faith and labor of love and steadfastness of hope in our Lord Jesus Christ. For we know, brothers and sisters beloved by God, that he has chosen you, because our message of the gospel came to you not in word only, but also in power and in the Holy Spirit and with full conviction; just as you know what kind of persons we proved to be among you for your sake. For The word of the Lord has sounded forth from you not only in Macedonia and Achaia, but in every place your faith in God has become known, so that we have no need to speak about it. For the people of those regions report about us what kind of welcome we had among you, and how you turned to God from idols, to serve a living and true God, and to wait for his Son from heaven, whom he raised from the dead—Jesus, who rescues us from the wrath that is coming.

The Word of the Lord.

◆ All observe silence.

FOR SILENT REFLECTION

I am a chosen one, a beloved child of God. What helps me to remember how precious I am in God's eyes?

CLOSING PRAYER

Let us stand and bring our hopes and needs to God as we pray, "Lord, hear our prayer."

◆ All may add their own prayers here.

Let us pray: **Our Father . . . Amen.**

Jesus our Savior,
you bring us messages of hope
through your kind words in Scripture.
Help us to be true to our calling
as sons and daughters of our Creator.
Help us to have the same courage
to tell your story of hope.
We ask this in your name.

Amen.

✝ All make the Sign of the Cross.

OPENING

Today we remember St. Monica, the mother of one of our faith tradition's great heroes, St. Augustine. Monica was patient and persistent in helping Augustine to change his immoral ways. As a young student, Augustine tried to elude his mother, moving from one location to another, but she always followed him in the hope that he would change his lifestyle. Augustine converted before Monica's death in 387.

✛ All make the Sign of the Cross.

In the name of the Father, and of the Son, and of the Holy Spirit. Amen.

PSALM   (For a longer psalm, see page xi.) Psalm 66:1–3a, 5 and 8, 16–17

Make a joyful noise to God, all the earth.

Make a joyful noise to God, all the earth.

Make a joyful noise to God, all the earth;
    sing the glory of his name;
    Give to him glorious praise.
Say to God, "How awesome are your deeds!"

Make a joyful noise to God, all the earth.

READING   1 Thessalonians 2:1–2, 5–8

A reading from the first Letter of St. Paul to the Thessalonians [theh-suh-LO-nih-uhnz]

You yourselves know, brothers and sisters, that our coming to you was not in vain, but though we had already suffered and been shamefully mistreated at Philippi, as you know, we had courage in our God to declare to you the gospel of God in spite of great opposition. As you know and as God is our witness, we never came with words of flattery or with a pretext for greed; nor did we seek praise from mortals, whether from you or from others, though we might have made demands as apostles of Christ. But we were gentle among you, like a nurse tenderly caring for her own children. So deeply do we care for you that we are determined to share with you not only the gospel of God but also our own selves, because you have become very dear to us.

The Word of the Lord.

◆ All observe silence.

FOR SILENT REFLECTION

What are some of the tender ways that God and others care for us?

CLOSING PRAYER

Let us stand and bring our hopes and needs to God as we pray, "Lord, hear our prayer."

◆ All may add their own prayers here.

Let us pray: **Our Father . . . Amen.**

Lord God of all,
your Spirit fills the hearts of all who
carry Jesus's message of hope.
You instill in us bravery and fortitude
when we are facing tough times.
May we remember those
who help us nurture our relationship
with God.
We ask this through Jesus, your Son.

Amen.

✛ All make the Sign of the Cross.

PRAYER FOR **WEDNESDAY** AUGUST 28, 2013

OPENING

Today we remember St. Augustine of Hippo, one of the great Catholic writers and Doctors of the Church, who influenced many thinkers. Known for his conversion, (with the help of his mother St. Monica), Augustine studied under St. Ambrose in Italy, and later produced many works that helped shape Catholic theology.

◆ All make the Sign of the Cross.

In the name of the Father, and of the Son, and of the Holy Spirit. Amen.

PSALM (For a longer psalm, see page xi.) Psalm 66:1–3a, 5 and 8, 16–17

Make a joyful noise to God, all the earth.

Make a joyful noise to God, all the earth.

Make a joyful noise to God, all the earth;
    sing the glory of his name;
    Give to him glorious praise.
Say to God, "How awesome are your deeds!"

Make a joyful noise to God, all the earth.

◆ All stand and sing **Alleluia.**

GOSPEL Matthew 23:27–28

A reading from the holy Gospel according to Matthew

Jesus said, "Woe to you, scribes and Pharisees [FAHR-uh-seez], hypocrites [HIP-o-crits]! For you are like whitewashed tombs, which on the outside look beautiful, but inside they are full of the bones of the dead and of all kinds of filth. So you also on the outside look righteous to others, but inside you are full of hypocrisy and lawlessness."

The Gospel of the Lord.

◆ All sit and observe silence.

FOR SILENT REFLECTION

Are there aspects of me that I cover up or "whitewash"? What do I do for appearances' sake?

CLOSING PRAYER

Let us stand and bring our hopes and needs to God as we pray, "Lord, hear our prayer."

◆ All may add their own prayers here.

Let us pray: **Our Father . . . Amen.**

Almighty God,
you see clearly all things in all ways.
You know what is real or fake,
and what is covered up or cleaned
just for appearances.
Help us to be authentic with
our intentions and actions
so that honesty is a part of
everything we do.
We ask this through Christ our Lord.
Amen.

✚ All make the Sign of the Cross.

OPENING

Today we remember St. John the Baptist and how he was martyred for his faith. We recall how this greatest of prophets suffered in prison and was beheaded at the request of a drunken king. He will always be known as the humble disciple who pointed the way to our Savior and declared, "Behold, the Lamb of God."

✚ All make the Sign of the Cross.

In the name of the Father, and of the Son, and of the Holy Spirit. Amen.

PSALM
(For a longer psalm, see page xi.) Psalm 66:1–3a, 5 and 8, 16–17

Make a joyful noise to God, all the earth.

Make a joyful noise to God, all the earth.

Make a joyful noise to God, all the earth;
   sing the glory of his name;
   Give to him glorious praise.
Say to God, "How awesome are your deeds!"

Make a joyful noise to God, all the earth.

READING
1 Thessalonians 3:7–13

A reading from the first Letter of St. Paul to the Thessalonians [theh-suh-LO-nih-uhnz]

For this reason, brothers and sisters, during all our distress and persecution we have been encouraged about you through your faith. For we now live, if you continue to stand firm in the Lord. How can we thank God enough for you in return for all the joy that we feel before our God because of you? Night and day we pray most earnestly that we may see you face to face and restore whatever is lacking in your faith.

Now may our God and Father himself and our Lord Jesus direct our way to you. And may the Lord make you increase and abound in love for one another and for all, just as we abound in love for you. And may he so strengthen your hearts in holiness that you may be blameless before our God and Father at the coming of our Lord Jesus with all his saints.

The Word of the Lord.

◆ All observe silence.

FOR SILENT REFLECTION

How do we encourage one another in faith?

CLOSING PRAYER

Let us stand and bring our hopes and needs to God as we pray, "Lord, hear our prayer."

◆ All may add their own prayers here.

Let us pray: **Our Father . . . Amen.**

Lord Jesus,
you sent your servant Paul
to bring good news to people in distant lands.
Help us to be courageous
with our missionaries of hope:
our parents, teachers, coaches, helpers,
and friends.
We ask this in your name.

Amen.

✚ All make the Sign of the Cross.

PRAYER FOR **FRIDAY**
AUGUST 30, 2013

OPENING

In today's Gospel, we learn about some wise people and some people who are not so smart. How could the foolish ones have been better prepared?

✠ All make the Sign of the Cross.

In the name of the Father, and of the Son, and of the Holy Spirit. Amen.

PSALM

(For a longer psalm, see page xi.) Psalm 66:1–3a, 5 and 8, 16–17

Make a joyful noise to God, all the earth.

Make a joyful noise to God, all the earth.

Make a joyful noise to God, all the earth;
   sing the glory of his name;
   Give to him glorious praise.
Say to God, "How awesome are your deeds!"

Make a joyful noise to God, all the earth.

◆ All stand and sing **Alleluia.**

GOSPEL

Matthew 25:1–12

A reading from the holy Gospel according to Matthew

Jesus told his disciples this parable: "The kingdom of heaven will be like this. Ten bridesmaids took their lamps and went to meet the bridegroom. Five of them were foolish, and five were wise. When the foolish took their lamps, they took no oil with them; but the wise took flasks of oil with their lamps. As the bridegroom was delayed, all of them became drowsy and slept. But at midnight there was a shout, 'Look! Here is the bridegroom! Come out to meet him.' Then all those bridesmaids got up and trimmed their lamps. The foolish said to the wise, 'Give us some of your oil, for our lamps are going out.' But the wise replied, 'No! there will not be enough for you and for us; you had better go to the dealers and buy some for yourselves.' And while they went to buy it, the bridegroom came, and those who were ready went with him into the wedding banquet; and the door was shut.

The Gospel of the Lord.

◆ All sit and observe silence.

FOR SILENT REFLECTION

How can we help others in need without rescuing them all the time? How can I be a witness to Jesus and encourage others to be responsible?

CLOSING PRAYER

Let us stand and bring our hopes and needs to God as we pray, "Lord, hear our prayer."

◆ All may add their own prayers here.

Let us pray: **Our Father . . . Amen.**

Lord Jesus,
you advise us to be ready,
for we know not the hour
when the "bridegroom" returns.
Give us the courage to use
our resources wisely and for your glory.
We ask this in your name.

Amen.

✠ All make the Sign of the Cross.

OPENING

In his parable about a wedding banquet, Jesus strongly suggests how a person who chooses to act humbly can open a more glorious place in God's kingdom.

✚ All make the Sign of the Cross.

In the name of the Father, and of the Son, and of the Holy Spirit. Amen.

PSALM   (For a longer psalm, see page xi.) Psalm 66:1–3a, 5 and 8, 16–17

Make a joyful noise to God, all the earth.

Make a joyful noise to God, all the earth.

Make a joyful noise to God, all the earth;
    sing the glory of his name;
    Give to him glorious praise.
Say to God, "How awesome are your deeds!"

Make a joyful noise to God, all the earth.

◆ All stand and sing **Alleluia.**

GOSPEL   Luke 14:1, 7–11

A reading from the holy Gospel according to Luke

On one occasion when Jesus was going to the house of a leader of the Pharisees to eat a meal on the sabbath, they were watching him closely.

When he noticed how the guests chose the places of honor, he told them a parable. "When you are invited by someone to a wedding banquet, do not sit down at the place of honor, in case someone more distinguished than you has been invited by your host; and the host who invited both of you may come and say to you, 'Give this person your place,' and then in disgrace you would start to take the lowest place. But when you are invited, go and sit down at the lowest place, so that when your host comes, he may say to you, 'Friend, move up higher'; then you will be honored in the presence of all who sit at the table with you. For all who exalt themselves will be humbled, and those who humble themselves will be exalted."

The Gospel of the Lord.

◆ All sit and observe silence.

FOR SILENT REFLECTION

Have your assumptions ever led you to feel disappointed? Why did this happen?

CLOSING PRAYER

Let us stand and bring our hopes and needs to God as we pray, "Lord, hear our prayer."

◆ All may add their own prayers here.

Let us pray: **Our Father . . . Amen.**

Lord of all,
your presence at our earthly banquet
helps us to remember who
should be given the highest priority.
Help us to make room at the table for those
less fortunate than us.
Keep us willing to welcome others whom
you embrace with your bounty of love.
We ask this through Christ our Lord.

Amen.

✚ All make the Sign of the Cross.

PRAYER FOR **MONDAY**
SEPTEMBER 2, 2013

OPENING

On this Labor Day, many of us take time to relax and enjoy an extended summer weekend. This federal holiday helps us remember all workers who contribute to the financial and social well-being of society.

✝ All make the Sign of the Cross.

In the name of the Father, and of the Son, and of the Holy Spirit. Amen.

PSALM   (For a longer psalm, see page xi.) Psalm 66:1–3a, 5 and 8, 16–17

Make a joyful noise to God, all the earth.

Make a joyful noise to God, all the earth.

Make a joyful noise to God, all the earth;
sing the glory of his name;
Give to him glorious praise.
Say to God, "How awesome are your deeds!"

Make a joyful noise to God, all the earth.

◆ All stand and sing **Alleluia.**

GOSPEL   Luke 4:16–21

A reading from the holy Gospel according to Luke

When Jesus came to Nazareth, where he had been brought up, he went to the synagogue [SIN-a-gog] on the sabbath day, as was his custom. He stood up to read, and the scroll of the prophet Isaiah [I-ZAY-uh] was given to him. He unrolled the scroll and found the place where it was written: "The Spirit of the Lord is upon me, because he has anointed me to bring good news to the poor. He has sent me to proclaim release to the captives and recovery of sight to the blind, to let the oppressed go free, to proclaim the year of the Lord's favor." And he rolled up the scroll, gave it back to the attendant, and sat down. The eyes of all in the synagogue were fixed on him. Then he began to say to them, "Today this scripture has been fulfilled in your hearing."

The Gospel of the Lord.

◆ All sit and observe silence.

FOR SILENT REFLECTION

Are there times when I don't recognize Christ's presence among my neighbors?

CLOSING PRAYER

Let us stand and bring our hopes and needs to God as we pray, "Lord, hear our prayer."

◆ All may add their own prayers here.

Let us pray: **Our Father . . . Amen.**

Lord Jesus,
you revealed your truth
and they rejected you.
Help us to recognize you among
our friends, neighbors, and family members,
for your presence is everywhere.
In your name we pray.

Amen.

✝ All make the Sign of the Cross.

OPENING

Today we remember Pope Gregory the Great, who served during a difficult time in Church history. Pope Gregory was known for his directness in managing papal affairs. He also helped shape Catholic worship and teaching. He died in 604 and was honored with the title of Doctor of the Church.

✚ All make the Sign of the Cross.

In the name of the Father, and of the Son, and of the Holy Spirit. Amen.

PSALM   (For a longer psalm, see page xi.) Psalm 66:1–3a, 5 and 8, 16–17

Make a joyful noise to God, all the earth.

Make a joyful noise to God, all the earth.

Make a joyful noise to God, all the earth;
   sing the glory of his name;
   Give to him glorious praise.
Say to God, "How awesome are your deeds!"

Make a joyful noise to God, all the earth.

READING   1 Thessalonians 5:1–6, 9–10

A reading from the first Letter of St. Paul to the Thessalonians [theh-suh-LO-nih-uhnz]

Now concerning the times and the seasons, brothers and sisters, you do not need to have anything written to you. For you yourselves know very well that the day of the Lord will come like a thief in the night. When they say, "There is peace and security," then sudden destruction will come upon them, as labor pains come upon a pregnant woman, and there will be no escape! But you, beloved, are not in darkness, for that day to surprise you like a thief; for you are all children of light and children of the day; we are not of the night or of darkness. So then let us not fall asleep as others do, but let us keep awake and be sober; For God has destined us not for wrath but for obtaining salvation through our Lord Jesus Christ, who died for us, so that whether we are awake or asleep we may live with him.

The Word of the Lord.

◆ All observe silence.

FOR SILENT REFLECTION

In what ways do I reveal how I am a child of light and of the day?

CLOSING PRAYER

Let us stand and bring our hopes and needs to God as we pray, "Lord, hear our prayer."

◆ All may add their own prayers here.

Let us pray: **Our Father . . . Amen.**

Holy God,
we thank you for the tremendous gift
of your Son.
We await his return,
for he gives us hope in this life.
Your servant Paul reassures us
that we have been saved by Christ.
Help us to live as "children of light"
to guide others to Jesus.
We ask this through Christ, your Son.

Amen.

✚ All make the Sign of the Cross.

PRAYER FOR **WEDNESDAY** **SEPTEMBER 4, 2013**

OPENING

In today's Gospel, we learn how Jesus heals Simon's mother-in-law, who promptly begins serving them.

✛ All make the Sign of the Cross.

In the name of the Father, and of the Son, and of the Holy Spirit. Amen.

PSALM (For a longer psalm, see page xi.) Psalm 66:1–3a, 5 and 8, 16–17

Make a joyful noise to God, all the earth.

Make a joyful noise to God, all the earth.

Make a joyful noise to God, all the earth;
   sing the glory of his name;
   Give to him glorious praise.
Say to God, "How awesome are your deeds!"

Make a joyful noise to God, all the earth.

◆ All stand and sing **Alleluia.**

GOSPEL Luke 4:38–43

A reading from the holy Gospel according to Luke

After leaving the synagogue, Jesus entered Simon's house. Now Simon's mother-in-law was suffering from a high fever, and they asked him about her. Then he stood over her and rebuked the fever, and it left her. Immediately she got up and began to serve them. As the sun was setting, all those who had any who were sick with various kinds of diseases brought them to him; and he laid his hands on each of them and cured them. Demons also came out of many, shouting, "You are the Son of God!"

But he rebuked them and would not allow them to speak, because they knew that he was the Messiah. At daybreak he departed and went into a deserted place. And the crowds were looking for him; and when they reached him, they wanted to prevent him from leaving them. But he said to them, "I must proclaim the good news of the kingdom of God to the other cities also; for I was sent for this purpose."

The Gospel of the Lord.

◆ All sit and observe silence.

FOR SILENT REFLECTION

Do I know of people who have been healed, who then inspired others with their story?

CLOSING PRAYER

Let us stand and bring our hopes and needs to God as we pray, "Lord, hear our prayer."

◆ All may add their own prayers here.

Let us pray: **Our Father . . . Amen.**

God Almighty,
you created each of us with
gifts and talents to share with others.
Help us to recognize our holy qualities
just as your Son felt called to
share his healing gifts.
We ask this through Christ our Lord.

Amen.

✛ All make the Sign of the Cross.

ALSO ON THIS DAY: Rosh Hashanah (Jewish New Year begins at sunset).

38

OPENING

Some future apostles are surprised to catch boatfuls of fish in the Gospel today. Jesus compares their bounty with people, who will fill their "nets" as they leave everything to follow him.

✛ All make the Sign of the Cross.

In the name of the Father, and of the Son, and of the Holy Spirit. Amen.

PSALM   (For a longer psalm, see page xi.) Psalm 66:1–3a, 5 and 8, 16–17

Make a joyful noise to God, all the earth.

Make a joyful noise to God, all the earth.

Make a joyful noise to God, all the earth;
   sing the glory of his name;
   Give to him glorious praise.
Say to God, "How awesome are your deeds!"

Make a joyful noise to God, all the earth.

◆ All stand and sing **Alleluia.**

GOSPEL   Luke 5:1–7a

A reading from the holy Gospel according to Luke

Once while Jesus was standing beside the lake of Gennesaret [gehn-NEHS-uh-ret], and the crowd was pressing in on him to hear the word of God, he saw two boats there at the shore of the lake; the fishermen had gone out of them and were washing their nets. He got into one of the boats, the one belonging to Simon, and asked him to put out a little way from the shore. Then he sat down and taught the crowds from the boat. When he had finished speaking, he said to Simon, "Put out into the deep water and let down your nets for a catch." Simon answered, "Master, we have worked all night long but have caught nothing. Yet if you say so, I will let down the nets." When they had done this, they caught so many fish that their nets were beginning to break. So they signaled their partners in the other boat to come and help them. And they came and filled both boats.

The Gospel of the Lord.

◆ All sit and observe silence.

FOR SILENT REFLECTION

Have you ever been amazed by what seemed to be God's miracles? Are there small miracles that happen every day?

CLOSING PRAYER

Let us stand and bring our hopes and needs to God as we pray, "Lord, hear our prayer."

◆ All may add their own prayers here.

Let us pray: **Our Father . . . Amen.**

Lord Jesus,
you fill our nets with
so many extravagant gifts.
Help us to remain grateful
for your grace.
Inspire us with your persistence in love,
and in giving us more chances
to follow you.
In your name we pray.

Amen.

✛ All make the Sign of the Cross.

PRAYER FOR **FRIDAY** **SEPTEMBER 6, 2013**

OPENING

In today's Gospel, Jesus challenges the stubborn, outdated thinking of scribes and Pharisees [FAIR-uh-seez]. He reveals his true identity.

✦ All make the Sign of the Cross.

In the name of the Father, and of the Son, and of the Holy Spirit. Amen.

PSALM
(For a longer psalm, see page xi.) Psalm 66:1–3a, 5 and 8, 16–17

Make a joyful noise to God, all the earth.

Make a joyful noise to God, all the earth.

Make a joyful noise to God, all the earth;
   sing the glory of his name;
   Give to him glorious praise.
Say to God, "How awesome are your deeds!"

Make a joyful noise to God, all the earth.

◆ All stand and sing **Alleluia.**

GOSPEL
Luke 5:33–39

A reading from the holy Gospel according to Luke

The scribes and Pharisees [FAIR-uh-seez] said to Jesus, "John's disciples, like the disciples of the Pharisees, frequently fast and pray, but your disciples eat and drink. Jesus said to them, "You cannot make wedding guests fast while the bridegroom is with them, can you? The days will come when the bridegroom will be taken away from them, and then they will fast in those days." He also told them a parable: "No one tears a piece from a new garment and sews it on an old garment; otherwise the new will be torn, and the piece from the new will not match the old. And no one puts new wine into old wineskins; otherwise the new wine will burst the skins and will be spilled, and the skins will be destroyed. But new wine must be put into fresh wineskins. And no one after drinking old wine desires new wine, but says, 'The old is good.'"

The Gospel of the Lord.

◆ All sit and observe silence.

FOR SILENT REFLECTION

What new thing does Jesus bring to us? How does his message change us?

CLOSING PRAYER

Let us stand and bring our hopes and needs to God as we pray, "Lord, hear our prayer."

◆ All may add their own prayers here.

Let us pray: **Our Father . . . Amen.**

Lord Jesus,
you reveal your identity as the "bridegroom,"
the One to whom we should target our
thoughts and actions.
Your arrival was declared by the
prophets and John the Baptist.
Help us to recognize you in
one another.
Keep us focused on you as we
live fully and gracefully in this day.

Amen.

✦ All make the Sign of the Cross.

OPENING

In today's Gospel, Jesus challenges his disciples. He redefines our priorities as Christians living in a world often filled with greed.

✝ All make the Sign of the Cross.

In the name of the Father, and of the Son, and of the Holy Spirit. Amen.

PSALM
(For a longer psalm, see page xi.) Psalm 66:1–3a, 5 and 8, 16–17

Make a joyful noise to God, all the earth.

Make a joyful noise to God, all the earth.

Make a joyful noise to God, all the earth;
    sing the glory of his name;
    Give to him glorious praise.
Say to God, "How awesome are your deeds!"

Make a joyful noise to God, all the earth.

◆ All stand and sing **Alleluia.**

GOSPEL
Luke 14:25–33

A reading from the holy Gospel according to Luke

Now large crowds were traveling with him; and he turned and said to them, "Whoever comes to me and does not hate father and mother, wife and children, brothers and sisters, yes, and even life itself, cannot be my disciple. Whoever does not carry the cross and follow me cannot be my disciple. For which of you, intending to build a tower, does not first sit down and estimate the cost, to see whether he has enough to complete it? Otherwise, when he has laid a foundation and is not able to finish, all who see it will begin to ridicule him, saying, 'This fellow began to build and was not able to finish.' Or what king, going out to wage war against another king, will not sit down first and consider whether he is able with ten thousand to oppose the one who comes against him with twenty thousand? If he cannot, then, while the other is still far away, he sends a delegation and asks for the terms of peace. So therefore, none of you can become my disciple if you do not give up all your possessions."

The Gospel of the Lord.

◆ All sit and observe silence.

FOR SILENT REFLECTION

What must I do to be a disciple of Christ?

CLOSING PRAYER

Let us stand and bring our hopes and needs to God as we pray, "Lord, hear our prayer."

◆ All may add their own prayers here.

Let us pray: **Our Father . . . Amen.**

Lord Jesus,
you describe a difficult path
for your followers.
We are anxious about this journey,
but know that you travel with us.
Keep us close to you as we release
earthly burdens that cause us to stray.
We ask this in your name.

Amen.

✝ All make the Sign of the Cross.

ALSO ON THIS DAY: Grandparents' Day (U.S.A.)

PRAYER FOR **MONDAY** SEPTEMBER 9, 2013

OPENING

Today we remember St. Peter Claver, a missionary who left his home in Spain in 1610 to work in Cartagena (in Colombia). There he ministered to thousands of African slaves who were deathly sick after being transported by ship to the Americas. In today's Gospel, we see Jesus defying the Sabbath law for more noble reasons.

✛ All make the Sign of the Cross.

PSALM (For a longer psalm, see page xi.) Psalm 66:1–3a, 5 and 8, 16–17

Make a joyful noise to God, all the earth.

Make a joyful noise to God, all the earth.

Make a joyful noise to God, all the earth;
  sing the glory of his name;
  Give to him glorious praise.
Say to God, "How awesome are your deeds!"

Make a joyful noise to God, all the earth.

◆ All stand and sing **Alleluia.**

GOSPEL Luke 6:6–11

A reading from the holy Gospel according to Luke

On another sabbath he entered the synagogue [SIN-uh-gog] and taught, and there was a man there whose right hand was withered. The scribes and the Pharisees [FAIR-uh-seez] watched him to see whether he would cure on the sabbath, so that they might find an accusation against him. Even though he knew what they were thinking, he said to the man who had the withered hand, "Come and stand here." He got up and stood there. Then Jesus said to them, "I ask you, is it lawful to do good or to do harm on the sabbath, to save life or to destroy it?" After looking around at all of them, he said to him, "Stretch out your hand." He did so, and his hand was restored. But they were filled with fury and discussed with one another what they might do to Jesus.

The Gospel of the Lord.

◆ All sit and observe silence.

FOR SILENT REFLECTION

Are there laws that do more harm than good? What happens when the intent of a rule is ignored?

CLOSING PRAYER

Let us stand and bring our hopes and needs to God as we pray, "Lord, hear our prayer."

◆ All may add their own prayers here.

Let us pray: **Our Father . . . Amen.**

Jesus, our Savior,
you angered leaders when you revealed
how laws cause more harm
when they are abused.
Your commandments of love are
most important.
Lead us to to do good and to cherish the
dignity of all life.
We ask this in your name.

Amen.

✛ All make the Sign of the Cross.

42

PRAYER SERVICE
FOR PEACE ON SEPTEMBER 11

Prepare six leaders for this service. The second leader will need a Bible for the Scripture and may need help practicing for the reading. You may begin by singing "Healer of Our Every Ill," "Song of the Body of Christ," or "This Is My Song," or perhaps begin in silence with a simple tolling of a hand bell.

FIRST LEADER:
May the grace and peace of our Lord Jesus Christ be with us, now and for ever.

Amen.

Let us pray:
Lord Jesus Christ,
we remember all those who died
on that September day in 2001,
people from different faiths and
backgrounds and ways of life.
We turn to you now, Lord of all,
to give us the courage of forgiveness.
May you envelop our hearts
with your Spirit of peace.

Amen.

◆ All stand and sing **Alleluia**.

SECOND LEADER: Luke 6:36–37
A reading from the holy Gospel according to Luke

◆ Read the Gospel passage from the Bible.

The Gospel of the Lord.

THIRD LEADER:
Let us pause and pray in silence for all those who have died in wars and other conflicts around the world.

◆ Allow a minute of silence.

FOURTH LEADER:
We recall the beautiful prayer of peace of St. Francis of Assisi:

Lord, make me an instrument of your peace;
where there is hatred, let me sow love;
where there is injury, pardon;
where there is doubt, faith;
where there is despair, hope;
where there is darkness, light;
and where there is sadness, joy.
Grant that I may not so much seek
to be consoled as to console;
to be understood as to understand,
to be loved as to love;
for it is in giving that we receive,
it is in pardoning that we are pardoned,
and it is in dying that we are born to
eternal life.

Amen.

FIFTH LEADER:
Now let us offer to one another a sign of Christ's peace:

◆ All offer one another a sign of peace.

SIXTH LEADER:
And may the Lord bless us,

✛ All make the Sign of the Cross.

protect us from all evil,
and bring us to everlasting life.

Amen.

PRAYER FOR **TUESDAY** SEPTEMBER 10, 2013

OPENING

In today's Gospel, Jesus names his Twelve Apostles from among many disciples. Notice how many people gathered to listen to Jesus.

✠ All make the Sign of the Cross.

In the name of the Father, and of the Son, and of the Holy Spirit. Amen.

PSALM

(For a longer psalm, see page xi.) Psalm 66:1–3a, 5 and 8, 16–17

Make a joyful noise to God, all the earth.

Make a joyful noise to God, all the earth.

Make a joyful noise to God, all the earth;
  sing the glory of his name;
  Give to him glorious praise.
Say to God, "How awesome are your deeds!"

Make a joyful noise to God, all the earth.

◆ All stand and sing **Alleluia.**

GOSPEL

Luke 6:12–19

A reading from the holy Gospel according to Luke

Now during those days he went out to the mountain to pray; and he spent the night in prayer to God. And when day came, he called his disciples and chose twelve of them, whom he also named apostles: Simon, whom he named Peter, and his brother Andrew, and James, and John, and Philip, and Bartholomew, and Matthew, and Thomas, and James son of Alphaeus [AL-fee-uhs], and Simon, who was called the Zealot, and Judas son of James, and Judas Iscariot, who became a traitor. He came down with them and stood on a level place, with a great crowd of his disciples and a great multitude of people from all Judea, Jerusalem, and the coast of Tyre [TAI-er] and Sidon. They had come to hear him and to be healed of their diseases; and those who were troubled with unclean spirits were cured. And all in the crowd were trying to touch him, for power came out from him and healed all of them.

The Gospel of the Lord.

◆ All sit and observe silence.

FOR SILENT REFLECTION

Is there a way to accomplish great things without a team? Who are your supporters?

CLOSING PRAYER

Let us stand and bring our hopes and needs to God as we pray, "Lord, hear our prayer."

◆ All may add their own prayers here.

Let us pray: **Our Father . . . Amen.**

Lord Jesus,
you pray to our Creator to
stay connected to the Almighty One,
the source of all wisdom.
Help us to remember how
God can be a guide for all our decisions.
We ask this in your name.

Amen.

✠ All make the Sign of the Cross.

OPENING

Today is a National Day of Mourning and Remembrance. Nearly 3,000 people lost their lives in the terrorist attack on this day in 2001. Today's Gospel reassures those who still mourn that more joyful times await them.

✦ All make the Sign of the Cross.

In the name of the Father, and of the Son, and of the Holy Spirit. Amen.

PSALM
(For a longer psalm, see page xi.) Psalm 66:1–3a, 5 and 8, 16–17

Make a joyful noise to God, all the earth.

Make a joyful noise to God, all the earth.

Make a joyful noise to God, all the earth;
    sing the glory of his name;
    Give to him glorious praise.
Say to God, "How awesome are your deeds!"

Make a joyful noise to God, all the earth.

◆ All stand and sing **Alleluia.**

GOSPEL
Luke 6:20–26

A reading from the holy Gospel according to Luke

Jesus looked up at his disciples and said: "Blessed are you who are poor, for yours is the kingdom of God. Blessed are you who are hungry now, for you will be filled. Blessed are you who weep now, for you will laugh. Blessed are you when people hate you, and when they exclude you, revile you, and defame you on account of the Son of Man. Rejoice in that day and leap for joy, for surely your reward is great in heaven; for that is what their ancestors did to the prophets. But woe to you who are rich, for you have received your consolation. Woe to you who are full now, for you will be hungry. Woe to you who are laughing now, for you will mourn and weep. Woe to you when all speak well of you, for that is what their ancestors did to the false prophets."

The Gospel of the Lord.

◆ All sit and observe silence.

FOR SILENT REFLECTION

Do you know people who are dealing with difficult issues right now? How can you encourage them?

CLOSING PRAYER

Let us stand and bring our hopes and needs to God as we pray, "Lord, hear our prayer."

◆ All may add their own prayers here.

Let us pray: **Our Father . . . Amen.**

Lord Jesus Christ,
we look to you for comfort when it seems
like life brings us sadness or despair.
You give us so much hope.
Help us to always look to you
for strength.

Amen.

✦ All make the Sign of the Cross.

PRAYER FOR **THURSDAY SEPTEMBER 12, 2013**

OPENING

Today is the feast of the Holy Name of Mary, declared in the 17th century by Pope Innocent XI. As a counterpart to the feast of the Holy Name of Jesus (January 3), this feast reinforces how many people call upon Mary's intercessory help in times of distress.

✝ All make the Sign of the Cross.

In the name of the Father, and of the Son, and of the Holy Spirit. Amen.

PSALM

(For a longer psalm, see page xi.) Psalm 66:1–3a, 5 and 8, 16–17

Make a joyful noise to God, all the earth.

Make a joyful noise to God, all the earth.

Make a joyful noise to God, all the earth;
    sing the glory of his name;
    Give to him glorious praise.
Say to God, "How awesome are your deeds!"

Make a joyful noise to God, all the earth.

◆ All stand and sing **Alleluia.**

GOSPEL

Luke 6:27–35a

A reading from the holy Gospel according to Luke

Jesus said to his disciples: "But I say to you that listen, love your enemies, do good to those who hate you, bless those who curse you, pray for those who abuse you. If anyone strikes you on the cheek, offer the other also; and from anyone who takes away your coat do not withhold even your shirt. Give to everyone who begs from you; and if anyone takes away your goods, do not ask for them again. Do to others as you would have them do to you. If you love those who love you, what credit is that to you? For even sinners love those who love them. If you do good to those who do good to you, what credit is that to you? For even sinners do the same. If you lend to those from whom you hope to receive, what credit is that to you? Even sinners lend to sinners, to receive as much again. But love your enemies, do good, and lend, expecting nothing in return."

The Gospel of the Lord.

◆ All sit and observe silence.

FOR SILENT REFLECTION

How do you treat people who are unkind to you? What can you do to follow more closely Jesus's commandments to love?

CLOSING PRAYER

Let us stand and bring our hopes and needs to God as we pray, "Lord, hear our prayer."

◆ All may add their own prayers here.

Let us pray: **Our Father . . . Amen.**

Jesus our Redeemer,
you give us lessons that are
so hard to follow sometimes.
Give us patience and
renewed hope in your power.
We ask this in your name.

Amen.

✝ All make the Sign of the Cross.

46

OPENING

Today we remember St. John Chrysostom, bishop of Constantinople [con-STAN-tin-O-pul], who was known as an energetic preacher. As he became critical of corrupt bishops and the rich, he became the target of scandals. He was eventually exiled and died in 407. In today's Gospel, Jesus calls upon all of us to look at ourselves before criticizing others.

✝ All make the Sign of the Cross.

In the name of the Father, and of the Son, and of the Holy Spirit. Amen.

PSALM (For a longer psalm, see page xi.) Psalm 66:1–3a, 5 and 8, 16–17

Make a joyful noise to God, all the earth.

Make a joyful noise to God, all the earth.

Make a joyful noise to God, all the earth;
    sing the glory of his name;
    Give to him glorious praise.
Say to God, "How awesome are your deeds!"

Make a joyful noise to God, all the earth.

◆ All stand and sing **Alleluia.**

GOSPEL   Luke 6:39–42

A reading from the holy Gospel according to Luke

Jesus told his disciples a parable: "Can a blind person guide a blind person? Will not both fall into a pit? A disciple is not above the teacher, but everyone who is fully qualified will be like the teacher. Why do you see the speck in your neighbor's eye, but do not notice the log in your own eye? Or how can you say to your neighbor, 'Friend, let me take out the speck in your eye,' when you yourself do not see the log in your own eye? You hypocrite, first take the log out of your own eye, and then you will see clearly to take the speck out of your neighbor's eye."

The Gospel of the Lord.

◆ All sit and observe silence.

FOR SILENT REFLECTION

Have I been critical of someone lately? What is the "log" in my own eye?

CLOSING PRAYER

Let us stand and bring our hopes and needs to God as we pray, "Lord, hear our prayer."

◆ All may add their own prayers here.

Let us pray: **Our Father . . . Amen.**

Jesus our Savior,
you remind us how hurtful we can be
when we criticize others.
Help us to focus on improving ourselves
before pointing out faults.
Keep us attentive to
what you ask of us
instead of pointing out
our neighbors' mistakes.
In your name we pray.

Amen.

✝ All make the Sign of the Cross.

PRAYER FOR THE WEEK

OPENING

In today's Gospel, Jesus reassures those who have strayed from the faith but chosen to return.

✚ All make the Sign of the Cross.

In the name of the Father, and of the Son, and of the Holy Spirit. Amen.

PSALM (For a longer psalm, see page xi.) Psalm 145:2–3, 4–5, 10–11

I will praise your name for ever.

I will praise your name for ever.

Every day I will bless you,
    and praise your name for ever and ever.
Great is the LORD, and greatly to be praised;
    his greatness is unsearchable.

I will praise your name for ever.

◆ All stand and sing **Alleluia.**

GOSPEL   Luke 15:3–10

A reading from the holy Gospel according to Luke

So he told them this parable: "Which one of you, having a hundred sheep and losing one of them, does not leave the ninety-nine in the wilderness and go after the one that is lost until he finds it? When he has found it, he lays it on his shoulders and rejoices. And when he comes home, he calls together his friends and neighbors, saying to them, 'Rejoice with me, for I have found my sheep that was lost.' Just so, I tell you, there will be more joy in heaven over one sinner who repents than over ninety-nine righteous persons who need no repentance. Or what woman having ten silver coins, if she loses one of them, does not light a lamp, sweep the house, and search carefully until she finds it? When she has found it, she calls together her friends and neighbors, saying, 'Rejoice with me, for I have found the coin that I had lost.' Just so, I tell you, there is joy in the presence of the angels of God over one sinner who repents."

The Gospel of the Lord.

◆ All sit and observe silence.

FOR SILENT REFLECTION

Why is there is great joy when what was lost is found?

CLOSING PRAYER

Let us stand and bring our hopes and needs to God as we pray, "Lord, hear our prayer."

◆ All may add their own prayers here.

Let us pray: **Our Father . . . Amen.**

Jesus our Shepherd,
how grateful we are to recall these
comforting messages of hope!
You search for us when we are lost.
Help us to stay connected to you.
We ask this in your name.

Amen.

✚ All make the Sign of the Cross.

ALSO ON THIS DAY: Catechetical Sunday

OPENING

Today we remember Sts. Cornelius [kohr-NEEL-ee-uhs] and Cyprian [SIP-ree-uhn]. After Cornelius was elected pope, he helped shape our understanding of the Sacrament of Penance.

✝ All make the Sign of the Cross.

In the name of the Father, and of the Son, and of the Holy Spirit. Amen.

PSALM   (For a longer psalm, see page xi.) Psalm 145:2–3, 4–5, 10–11

I will praise your name for ever.

I will praise your name for ever.

Every day I will bless you,
  and praise your name for ever and ever.
Great is the LORD, and greatly to be praised;
  his greatness is unsearchable.

I will praise your name for ever.

◆ All stand and sing **Alleluia.**

GOSPEL   Luke 7:1–10

A reading from the holy Gospel according to Luke

A centurion there had a slave whom he valued highly, and who was ill and close to death. When he heard about Jesus, he sent some Jewish elders to him, asking him to come and heal his slave. When they came to Jesus, they appealed to him earnestly, saying, "He is worthy of having you do this for him, for he loves our people, and it is he who built our synagogue for us." And Jesus went with them, but when he was not far from the house, the centurion sent friends to say to him, "Lord, do not trouble yourself, for I am not worthy to have you come under my roof; therefore I did not presume to come to you. But only speak the word, and let my servant be healed. For I also am a man set under authority, with soldiers under me; and I say to one, 'Go,' and he goes, and to another, 'Come,' and he comes, and to my slave, 'Do this,' and the slave does it." When Jesus heard this he was amazed at him, and turning to the crowd that followed him, he said, "I tell you, not even in Israel have I found such faith." When those who had been sent returned to the house, they found the slave in good health.

The Gospel of the Lord.

◆ All sit and observe silence.

FOR SILENT REFLECTION

When do we hear or say the centurion's words?

CLOSING PRAYER

Let us stand and bring our hopes and needs to God as we pray, "Lord, hear our prayer."

◆ All may add their own prayers here.

Let us pray: **Our Father . . . Amen.**

Son of the Most High,
you have power to heal.
May our trust in you be as great
as the centurion's.
We ask this in your name.

Amen.

✝ All make the Sign of the Cross.

PRAYER FOR **TUESDAY** **SEPTEMBER 17, 2013**

OPENING

Today we remember St. Robert Bellarmine [BELL-er-mun]. Ordained in 1570, he was a professor who was named a cardinal because of his influence in guiding Church leaders. In today's Gospel, we see Jesus filled with compassion for a widow who was about to lose her only son.

✠ All make the Sign of the Cross.

In the name of the Father, and of the Son, and of the Holy Spirit. Amen.

PSALM (For a longer psalm, see page xi.) Psalm 145:2–3, 4–5, 10–11

I will praise your name for ever.

I will praise your name for ever.

Every day I will bless you,
  and praise your name for ever and ever.
Great is the LORD, and greatly to be praised;
  his greatness is unsearchable.

I will praise your name for ever.

◆ All stand and sing **Alleluia.**

GOSPEL   Luke 7:11–17

Jesus went to a town called Nain, and his disciples and a large crowd went with him. As he approached the gate of the town, a man who had died was being carried out. He was his mother's only son, and she was a widow; and with her was a large crowd from the town. When the Lord saw her, he had compassion for her and said to her, "Do not weep." Then he came forward and touched the bier, and the bearers stood still. And he said, "Young man, I say to you, rise!" The dead man sat up and began to speak, and Jesus gave him to his mother. Fear seized all of them; and they glorified God, saying, "A great prophet has risen among us!" and "God has looked favorably on his people!" This word about him spread throughout Judea and all the surrounding country.

The Gospel of the Lord.

◆ All sit and observe silence.

FOR SILENT REFLECTION

As I see positive change and goodness in my life and in others' lives, do I thank Jesus the healer?

CLOSING PRAYER

Let us stand and bring our hopes and needs to God as we pray, "Lord, hear our prayer."

◆ All may add their own prayers here.

Let us pray: **Our Father . . . Amen.**

Lord Jesus,
you are tender with those
who are experiencing loss.
You showed compassion with the widow
just as you do for us.
Help us to remember that
we, too, will rise with you in
the next life as we declare your name
throughout the world.
We ask this in your name.

Amen.

✠ All make the Sign of the Cross.

OPENING

Today's Gospel shows Jesus reminding the crowds that God has acted through the prophets in different ways over the centuries, and that the truth of Christ will be revealed in time.

✝ All make the Sign of the Cross.

In the name of the Father, and of the Son, and of the Holy Spirit. Amen.

PSALM (For a longer psalm, see page xi.) Psalm 145:2–3, 4–5, 10–11

I will praise your name for ever.

I will praise your name for ever.

Every day I will bless you,
  and praise your name for ever and ever.
Great is the LORD, and greatly to be praised;
  his greatness is unsearchable.

I will praise your name for ever.

◆ All stand and sing **Alleluia.**

GOSPEL   Luke 7:31–35

A reading from the holy Gospel according to Luke

Jesus said to the crowds: "To what then will I compare the people of this generation, and what are they like? They are like children sitting in the marketplace and calling to one another, 'We played the flute for you, and you did not dance; we wailed, and you did not weep.' For John the Baptist has come eating no bread and drinking no wine, and you say, 'He has a demon'; the Son of Man has come eating and drinking, and you say, 'Look, a glutton and a drunkard, a friend of tax collectors and sinners!' Nevertheless, wisdom is vindicated by all her children."

The Gospel of the Lord.

◆ All sit and observe silence.

FOR SILENT REFLECTION

How can I become more aware of God's holy activity today?

CLOSING PRAYER

Let us stand and bring our hopes and needs to God as we pray, "Lord, hear our prayer."

◆ All may add their own prayers here.

Let us pray: **Our Father . . . Amen.**

Jesus our Savior,
we, as your people, can be fickle and
stubborn at times.
We often ignore miracles that happen
right before our eyes.
We have huge expectations that
separate us from your goodness.
Help us to be grateful for
your presence with us now and always.
We ask this in your name.

Amen.

✝ All make the Sign of the Cross.

51

PRAYER FOR **THURSDAY** SEPTEMBER 19, 2013

OPENING

In today's Gospel, we hear about the woman who washed Jesus's feet. She wept as she wiped them, using perfumed oil. After Jesus forgives her sins, the Pharisees begin to question Jesus's claim to such great power.

✦ All make the Sign of the Cross.

In the name of the Father, and of the Son, and of the Holy Spirit. Amen.

PSALM (For a longer psalm, see page xi.) Psalm 145:2–3, 4–5, 10–11

I will praise your name for ever.

I will praise your name for ever.

Every day I will bless you,
   and praise your name for ever and ever.
Great is the LORD, and greatly to be praised;
   his greatness is unsearchable.

I will praise your name for ever.

◆ All stand and sing **Alleluia.**

GOSPEL   Luke 7:36–39, 44–48

A reading from the holy Gospel according to Luke

One of the Pharisees asked Jesus to eat with him, and he went into the Pharisee's house and took his place at the table. And a woman in the city, who was a sinner, having learned that he was eating in the Pharisee's house, brought an alabaster jar of ointment. She stood behind him at his feet, weeping, and began to bathe his feet with her tears and to dry them with her hair. Then she continued kissing his feet and anointing them with the ointment. Now when the Pharisee who had invited him saw it, he said to himself, "If this man were a prophet, he would have known who and what kind of woman this is who is touching him—that she is a sinner." Then turning toward the woman, Jesus said to Simon, "Do you see this woman? I entered your house; you gave me no water for my feet, but she has bathed my feet with her tears and dried them with her hair. Therefore, I tell you, her sins, which were many, have been forgiven; hence she has shown great love. But the one to whom little is forgiven, loves little."

The Gospel of the Lord.

◆ All sit and observe silence.

FOR SILENT REFLECTION

Who have I forgiven? How can I better appreciate God's gift of forgiveness?

CLOSING PRAYER

Let us stand and bring our hopes and needs to God as we pray, "Lord, hear our prayer."

◆ All may add their own prayers here.

Let us pray: **Our Father . . . Amen.**

Jesus our Savior,
through another's tears, you
help us understand the
depth of your forgiveness.
Help us to receive your gift of
reconciliation.
We ask this in you name.

Amen.

✦ All make the Sign of the Cross.

OPENING

Today we remember Sts. Andrew Kim Tae-gŏn, Paul Chŏng Ha-sang, and companions, who were missionaries throughout Korea in the 19th century, under severe government oppression. In today's reading from St. Paul to Timothy, he gives his friend a pep talk and guides him when he is opposed by disbelievers and the authorities.

✛ All make the Sign of the Cross.

In the name of the Father, and of the Son, and of the Holy Spirit. Amen.

PSALM (For a longer psalm, see page xi.) Psalm 145:2–3, 4–5, 10–11

I will praise your name for ever.

I will praise your name for ever.

Every day I will bless you,
 and praise your name for ever and ever.
Great is the LORD, and greatly to be praised;
 his greatness is unsearchable.

I will praise your name for ever.

READING   1 Timothy 6:6c–12

A reading from the first Letter of St. Paul to Timothy

Of course, there is great gain in godliness combined with contentment; for we brought nothing into the world, so that we can take nothing out of it; but if we have food and clothing, we will be content with these. But those who want to be rich fall into temptation and are trapped by many senseless and harmful desires that plunge people into ruin and destruction. For the love of money is a root of all kinds of evil, and in their eagerness to be rich some have wandered away from the faith and pierced themselves with many pains. But as for you, man of God, shun all this; pursue righteousness, godliness, faith, love, endurance, gentleness. Fight the good fight of the faith; take hold of the eternal life, to which you were called and for which you made the good confession in the presence of many witnesses.

The Word of the Lord.

◆ All observe silence.

FOR SILENT REFLECTION

Who are the people in my life who show me how to be good?

CLOSING PRAYER

Let us stand and bring our hopes and needs to God as we pray, "Lord, hear our prayer."

◆ All may add their own prayers here.

Let us pray: **Our Father . . . Amen.**

Loving God,
keep us mindful of how
a humble lifestyle can
help us on our journey to you.
We ask this through Christ our Lord.

Amen.

✛ All make the Sign of the Cross.

PRAYER FOR THE WEEK

OPENING

In today's Gospel, Jesus speaks of the importance of being honest and being faithful in small matters as well as important ones.

✛ All make the Sign of the Cross.

In the name of the Father, and of the Son, and of the Holy Spirit. Amen.

PSALM (For a longer psalm, see page xi.) Psalm 145:2–3, 4–5, 10–11

I will praise your name for ever.

I will praise your name for ever.

Every day I will bless you,
   and praise your name for ever and ever.
Great is the LORD, and greatly to be praised;
   his greatness is unsearchable.

I will praise your name for ever.

◆ All stand and sing **Alleluia.**

GOSPEL   Luke 16:10–13

A reading from the holy Gospel according to Luke

"Whoever is faithful in a very little is faithful also in much; and whoever is dishonest in a very little is dishonest also in much. If then you have not been faithful with the dishonest wealth, who will entrust to you the true riches? And if you have not been faithful with what belongs to another, who will give you what is your own? No slave can serve two masters; for a slave will either hate the one and love the other, or be devoted to the one and despise the other. You cannot serve God and wealth."

The Gospel of the Lord.

◆ All sit and observe silence.

FOR SILENT REFLECTION

Why is it important to be honest in little ways? Why is it important to be honest with our friends and family?

CLOSING PRAYER

Let us stand and bring our hopes and needs to God as we pray, "Lord, hear our prayer."

◆ All may add their own prayers here.

Let us pray: **Our Father . . . Amen.**

Jesus, our teacher,
you revealed for us how important it is
to act creatively and practically to
achieve goals that point to you,
source of all goodness.
Help us to put your words into action
with sound judgment and grace.
In your name we pray.

Amen.

✛ All make the Sign of the Cross.

OPENING

Today we remember St. Pius of Pietrelcina, a Capuchin priest from Italy, who died in 1968. Known as a spiritual director, he counseled others to recognize God in all things and to "pray, hope and don't worry." In today's Gospel, Jesus reminds us of the gift of God's truth.

✜ All make the Sign of the Cross.

In the name of the Father, and of the Son, and of the Holy Spirit. Amen.

PSALM   (For a longer psalm, see page xi.) Psalm 145:2–3, 4–5, 10–11

I will praise your name for ever.

I will praise your name for ever.

Every day I will bless you,
    and praise your name for ever and ever.
Great is the LORD, and greatly to be praised;
    his greatness is unsearchable.

I will praise your name for ever.

◆ All stand and sing **Alleluia.**

GOSPEL   Luke 8:16–18

A reading from the holy Gospel according to Luke

Jesus said to the crowd: "No one after lighting a lamp hides it under a jar, or puts it under a bed, but puts it on a lampstand, so that those who enter may see the light. For nothing is hidden that will not be disclosed, nor is anything secret that will not become known and come to light. Then pay attention to how you listen; for to those who have, more will be given; and from those who do not have, even what they seem to have will be taken away."

The Gospel of the Lord.

◆ All sit and observe silence.

FOR SILENT REFLECTION

What are my personal gifts and talents that I should let shine? How can I best share them?

CLOSING PRAYER

Let us stand and bring our hopes and needs to God as we pray, "Lord, hear our prayer."

◆ All may add their own prayers here.

Let us pray: **Our Father . . . Amen.**

God almighty,
you are our proud, heavenly parent.
We are your children who can
allow your light to shine
through our talents and skills.
Guide us as we learn more about
our gifts in school and at play.
We ask this through Christ our Lord.

Amen.

✜ All make the Sign of the Cross.

PRAYER FOR **TUESDAY** **SEPTEMBER 24, 2013**

OPENING

In today's Gospel, we learn more about our true brothers and sisters in Christ.

✚ All make the Sign of the Cross.

In the name of the Father, and of the Son, and of the Holy Spirit. Amen.

PSALM (For a longer psalm, see page xi.) Psalm 145:2–3, 4–5, 10–11

I will praise your name for ever.

I will praise your name for ever.

Every day I will bless you,
and praise your name for ever and ever.
Great is the LORD, and greatly to be praised;
his greatness is unsearchable.

I will praise your name for ever.

◆ All stand and sing **Alleluia.**

GOSPEL   Luke 8:19–21

A reading from the holy Gospel according to Luke

The mother of Jesus and his brothers came to him, but they could not reach him because of the crowd. And he was told, "Your mother and your brothers are standing outside, wanting to see you." But he said to them, "My mother and my brothers are those who hear the word of God and do it."

The Gospel of the Lord.

◆ All sit and observe silence.

FOR SILENT REFLECTION

How can I show my love to all my kin in Christ?

CLOSING PRAYER

Let us stand and bring our hopes and needs to God as we pray, "Lord, hear our prayer."

◆ All may add their own prayers here.

Let us pray: **Our Father . . . Amen.**

Lord Jesus,
you regard all your believers
as your brothers and sisters,
and for this we are especially blessed.
Help us to appreciate
being among your kin,
as members of your glorious
extended family.
We ask this in your name.

Amen.

✚ All make the Sign of the Cross.

OPENING

Jesus tells us what to pack as we welcome others to learn about his promise of new life. We, too, are called to be his disciples and to witness to the Good News.

✝ All make the Sign of the Cross.

In the name of the Father, and of the Son, and of the Holy Spirit. Amen.

PSALM (For a longer psalm, see page xi.) Psalm 145:2–3, 4–5, 10–11

I will praise your name for ever.

I will praise your name for ever.

Every day I will bless you,
   and praise your name for ever and ever.
Great is the LORD, and greatly to be praised;
   his greatness is unsearchable.

I will praise your name for ever.

◆ All stand and sing **Alleluia.**

GOSPEL   Luke 9:1–6

A reading from the holy Gospel according to Luke

Jesus called the twelve together and gave them power and authority over all demons and to cure diseases, and he sent them out to proclaim the kingdom of God and to heal. He said to them, "Take nothing for your journey, no staff, nor bag, nor bread, nor money—not even an extra tunic. Whatever house you enter, stay there, and leave from there. Wherever they do not welcome you, as you are leaving that town shake the dust off your feet as a testimony against them." They departed and went through the villages, bringing the good news and curing diseases everywhere.

The Gospel of the Lord.

◆ All sit and observe silence.

FOR SILENT REFLECTION

How can I spread the Good News of Jesus to others in my daily actions?

CLOSING PRAYER

Let us stand and bring our hopes and needs to God as we pray, "Lord, hear our prayer."

◆ All may add their own prayers here.

Let us pray: **Our Father . . . Amen.**

Lord Jesus,
you ask us to travel lightly here on earth,
and to use your gifts to
spread your healing Word to all.
Guide us today as we
bring your Good News to others
by word and deed.

Amen.

✝ All make the Sign of the Cross.

PRAYER FOR **THURSDAY SEPTEMBER 26, 2013**

OPENING

Today we remember Sts. Cosmas and Damian, who were twin brothers and physicians. They practiced in Syria and often did so free of charge. Their practice led many people to become Christian, which angered the authorities. They were persecuted for their faith, dying in 287. They are the patron saints for surgeons, physicians, and dentists. In today's Gospel, we learn more about Herod, who hears about Jesus from others' reports, and wants to find him.

✝ All make the Sign of the Cross.

In the name of the Father, and of the Son, and of the Holy Spirit. Amen.

PSALM   (For a longer psalm, see page xi.) Psalm 145:2–3, 4–5, 10–11

I will praise your name for ever.

I will praise your name for ever.

Every day I will bless you,
   and praise your name for ever and ever.
Great is the LORD, and greatly to be praised;
   his greatness is unsearchable.

I will praise your name for ever.

◆ All stand and sing **Alleluia.**

GOSPEL   Luke 9:7–9

A reading from the holy Gospel according to Luke

Herod the ruler heard about all that had taken place, and he was perplexed, because it was said by some that John had been raised from the dead, by some that Elijah had appeared, and by others that one of the ancient prophets had arisen. Herod said, "John I beheaded; but who is this about whom I hear such things?" And he tried to see him.

The Gospel of the Lord.

◆ All sit and observe silence.

FOR SILENT REFLECTION

How do I learn about what is going on with my friends? Do I believe rumors? What's the best way to handle rumors?

CLOSING PRAYER

Let us stand and bring our hopes and needs to God as we pray, "Lord, hear our prayer."

◆ All may add their own prayers here.

Let us pray: **Our Father . . . Amen.**

Dear Lord,
sometimes life can pose some
dangers that we must avoid.
Please keep us safe from harm,
and protect all who are in danger.
We ask this in your name.

Amen.

✝ All make the Sign of the Cross.

OPENING

Today we remember St. Vincent de Paul, a French priest in 1600, who was once kidnapped by Turkish pirates. He was sold into slavery but began ministering to other slaves, even convincing his "owner" to become a Christian. Later in life, he established charity groups and hospitals that offered physical relief for the poor and sick. He was also known as a retreat director for the clergy and founded the first seminaries. In today's Gospel, Jesus asks his close friends what people are saying about him.

✦ All make the Sign of the Cross.

In the name of the Father, and of the Son, and of the Holy Spirit. Amen.

PSALM (For a longer psalm, see page xi.) Psalm 145:2–3, 4–5, 10–11

I will praise your name for ever.

I will praise your name for ever.

Every day I will bless you,
  and praise your name for ever and ever.
Great is the LORD, and greatly to be praised;
  his greatness is unsearchable.

I will praise your name for ever.

◆ All stand and sing **Alleluia.**

GOSPEL   Luke 9:18–22

A reading from the holy Gospel according to Luke

Once when Jesus was praying alone, with only the disciples near him, he asked them, "Who do the crowds say that I am?" They answered, "John the Baptist; but others, Elijah; and still others, that one of the ancient prophets has arisen." He said to them, "But who do you say that I am?" Peter answered, "The Messiah of God." He sternly ordered and commanded them not to tell anyone, saying, "The Son of Man must undergo great suffering, and be rejected by the elders, chief priests, and scribes, and be killed, and on the third day be raised."

The Gospel of the Lord.

◆ All sit and observe silence.

FOR SILENT REFLECTION

What do others say about me? How could I solve misunderstandings about what I do and say?

CLOSING PRAYER

Let us stand and bring our hopes and needs to God as we pray, "Lord, hear our prayer."

◆ All may add their own prayers here.

Let us pray: **Our Father . . . Amen.**

Jesus, Son of God,
you are our Lord,
our leader in this life and the next.
Guide us as we learn more
about your role as our Savior.
Although your path became more painful,
God led you to new life
as you will lead us.
In your name we pray.

Amen.

✦ All make the Sign of the Cross.

ALSO ON THIS DAY: Native American Day (U.S.A.)

PRAYER FOR THE WEEK

OPENING

In today's Gospel, Jesus warns us against avoiding the poor and sick among us, for we are all God's children.

✠ All make the Sign of the Cross.

In the name of the Father, and of the Son, and of the Holy Spirit. Amen.

PSALM (For a longer psalm, see page xi.) Psalm 145:2–3, 4–5, 10–11

I will praise your name for ever.

I will praise your name for ever.

Every day I will bless you,
  and praise your name for ever and ever.
Great is the LORD, and greatly to be praised;
  his greatness is unsearchable.

I will praise your name for ever.

◆ All stand and sing **Alleluia.**

GOSPEL   Luke 16:19–25

A reading from the holy Gospel according to Luke

"There was a rich man who was dressed in purple and fine linen and who feasted sumptuously every day. And at his gate lay a poor man named Lazarus [LAZ-uh-ruhs], covered with sores, who longed to satisfy his hunger with what fell from the rich man's table; even the dogs would come and lick his sores. The poor man died and was carried away by the angels to be with Abraham. The rich man also died and was buried. In Hades, where he was being tormented, he looked up and saw Abraham far away with Lazarus by his side. He called out,

'Father Abraham, have mercy on me, and send Lazarus to dip the tip of his finger in water and cool my tongue; for I am in agony in these flames.' But Abraham said, 'Child, remember that during your lifetime you received your good things, and Lazarus in like manner evil things; but now he is comforted here, and you are in agony.'"

The Gospel of the Lord.

◆ All sit and observe silence.

FOR SILENT REFLECTION

Why do you think that God is concerned about the poor and the helpless?

CLOSING PRAYER

Let us stand and bring our hopes and needs to God as we pray, "Lord, hear our prayer."

◆ All may add their own prayers here.

Let us pray: **Our Father . . . Amen.**

Jesus our helper and Savior,
your stories trouble our hearts
for many of us live with abundance.
Guide us as we help the helpless.
Give us courage to find solutions
as we see in the news so many who
are sick, hungry, and have no homes.
Help us to connect with people who are
working to solve these local and global
problems.
In your name we pray.

Amen.

✠ All make the Sign of the Cross.

OPENING

Today we remember St. Jerome, a highly respected Scripture scholar, known for his translation of the Bible which came to be called the Vulgate. He was a master of the Latin, Greek, and Hebrew languages, and went to Rome and later Germany to continue his studies. He later traveled throughout Palestine and lived as a mystic, finally settling in Bethlehem, in the cave believed to be the birthplace of Christ. He died there in 420. In today's Gospel, Jesus surprises followers with his description of the "greatest."

✚ All make the Sign of the Cross.

In the name of the Father, and of the Son, and of the Holy Spirit. Amen.

PSALM (For a longer psalm, see page xi.) Psalm 145:2–3, 4–5, 10–11

I will praise your name for ever.

I will praise your name for ever.

Every day I will bless you,
    and praise your name for ever and ever.
Great is the LORD, and greatly to be praised;
    his greatness is unsearchable.

I will praise your name for ever.

◆ All stand and sing **Alleluia.**

GOSPEL   Luke 9:46–50

A reading from the holy Gospel according to Luke

An argument arose among them as to which one of them was the greatest. But Jesus, aware of their inner thoughts, took a little child and put it by his side, and said to them, "Whoever welcomes this child in my name welcomes me, and whoever welcomes me welcomes the one who sent me; for the least among all of you is the greatest." John answered, "Master, we saw someone casting out demons in your name, and we tried to stop him, because he does not follow with us." But Jesus said to him, "Do not stop him; for whoever is not against you is for you."

The Gospel of the Lord.

◆ All sit and observe silence.

FOR SILENT REFLECTION

What are the qualities of a child to which Jesus is referring? What adults do you know who have the faith of a child?

CLOSING PRAYER

Let us stand and bring our hopes and needs to God as we pray, "Lord, hear our prayer."

◆ All may add their own prayers here.

Let us pray: **Our Father . . . Amen.**

Lord Jesus,
you embrace the child in all of us.
You reach for the humble of heart,
as well as the fun-loving spirits who enjoy simplicity.
Help us to trust in your
guidance and leadership.
In your name we pray.

Amen.

✚ All make the Sign of the Cross.

PRAYER FOR **TUESDAY** **OCTOBER 1, 2013**

OPENING

Today we remember St. Thérèse of Lisieux [Li-SOO], known as the "Little Flower of Jesus," who entered the Carmelite convent at the age of 15. Her life of humility and prayer, as well as her writings, particularly her autobiography *Story of a Soul*, established her as a model of virtue and goodness. She suffered from illness most of her life, dying in 1897 from tuberculosis at the age of 24. In today's Gospel, Jesus strongly tells James and John what he thinks about retaliation after a community's rejection.

✚ All make the Sign of the Cross.

In the name of the Father, and of the Son, and of the Holy Spirit. Amen.

PSALM (For a longer psalm, see page xi.) Psalm 145:2–3, 4–5, 10–11

I will praise your name for ever.

I will praise your name for ever.

Every day I will bless you,
    and praise your name for ever and ever.
Great is the LORD, and greatly to be praised;
    his greatness is unsearchable.

I will praise your name for ever.

◆ All stand and sing **Alleluia.**

GOSPEL   Luke 9:51–56

A reading from the holy Gospel according to Luke

When the days drew near for Jesus to be taken up, he set his face to go to Jerusalem. And he sent messengers ahead of him. On their way they entered a village of the Samaritans to make ready for him; but they did not receive him, because his face was set toward Jerusalem. When his disciples James and John saw it, they said, "Lord, do you want us to command fire to come down from heaven and consume them?" But he turned and rebuked them. Then they went on to another village.

The Gospel of the Lord.

◆ All sit and observe silence.

FOR SILENT REFLECTION

When have I felt rejected? How did I deal with it? When have I rejected others?

CLOSING PRAYER

Let us stand and bring our hopes and needs to God as we pray, "Lord, hear our prayer."

◆ All may add their own prayers here.

Let us pray: **Our Father . . . Amen.**

Lord Jesus,
you felt rejection from
people who should have welcomed
and celebrated your God-filled presence.
Give us the insight to
recognize you in the midst of
our busy lives.
Help us to see your face in
everyone whom we meet,
today and every day.
In your name we pray.

Amen.

✚ All make the Sign of the Cross.

OPENING

Today is the feast of the Guardian Angels. We remember how God also loves and nurtures us through angels who guide us throughout our lives.

✚ All make the Sign of the Cross.

In the name of the Father, and of the Son, and of the Holy Spirit. Amen.

PSALM (For a longer psalm, see page xi.) Psalm 145:2–3, 4–5, 10–11

I will praise your name for ever.

I will praise your name for ever.

Every day I will bless you,
    and praise your name for ever and ever.
Great is the LORD, and greatly to be praised;
    his greatness is unsearchable.

I will praise your name for ever.

READING   Nehemiah 2:1–5, 8

A reading from the Book of Nehemiah

In the month of Nisan, in the twentieth year of King Artaxerxes [ahr-tuh-ZUHRK-seez], when wine was served him, I carried the wine and gave it to the king. Now, I had never been sad in his presence before. So the king said to me, "Why is your face sad, since you are not sick? This can only be sadness of the heart." Then I was very much afraid. I said to the king, "May the king live forever! Why should my face not be sad, when the city, the place of my ancestors' graves, lies waste, and its gates have been destroyed by fire?" Then the king said to me, "What do you request?" So I prayed to the

God of heaven. Then I said to the king, "If it pleases the king, and if your servant has found favor with you, I ask that you send me to Judah, to the city of my ancestors' graves, so that I may rebuild it." And the king granted me what I asked, for the gracious hand of my God was upon me.

The Word of the Lord.

◆ All observe silence.

FOR SILENT REFLECTION

When do I listen to my Creator? What are some of my best times for prayer?

CLOSING PRAYER

Let us stand and bring our hopes and needs to God as we pray, "Lord, hear our prayer."

◆ All may add their own prayers here.

Let us pray: **Our Father . . . Amen.**

Lord God Almighty,
you speak to each of us in
different ways;
all we have to do is listen.
Help us to be like Nehemiah,
who had the courage to ask the king to
release him to do God's will.
Give us the boldness to
act on your behalf, even when it feels
uncomfortable.
We ask this through Christ our Lord.

Amen.

✚ All make the Sign of the Cross.

PRAYER FOR **THURSDAY** OCTOBER 3, 2013

OPENING

In today's Gospel, Jesus gives us direction on how to accept hospitality as we become missionaries in his name.

✝ All make the Sign of the Cross.

In the name of the Father, and of the Son, and of the Holy Spirit. Amen.

PSALM   (For a longer psalm, see page xi.) Psalm 145:2–3, 4–5, 10–11

I will praise your name for ever.

I will praise your name for ever.

Every day I will bless you,
   and praise your name for ever and ever.
Great is the LORD, and greatly to be praised;
   his greatness is unsearchable.

I will praise your name for ever.

◆ All stand and sing **Alleluia.**

GOSPEL   Luke 10:1–9

A reading from the holy Gospel according to Luke

Jesus appointed seventy others and sent them on ahead of him in pairs to every town and place where he himself intended to go. He said to them, "The harvest is plentiful, but the laborers are few; therefore ask the Lord of the harvest to send out laborers into his harvest. Go on your way. See, I am sending you out like lambs into the midst of wolves. Carry no purse, no bag, no sandals; and greet no one on the road. Whatever house you enter, first say, 'Peace to this house!' And if anyone is there who shares in peace, your peace will rest on that person; but if not, it will return to you. Remain in the same house, eating and drinking whatever they provide, for the laborer deserves to be paid. Do not move about from house to house. Whenever you enter a town and its people welcome you, eat what is set before you; cure the sick who are there, and say to them, 'The kingdom of God has come near to you.'"

The Gospel of the Lord.

◆ All sit and observe silence.

FOR SILENT REFLECTION

Have you experienced someone's hospitality when traveling with friends or family?

CLOSING PRAYER

Let us stand and bring our hopes and needs to God as we pray, "Lord, hear our prayer."

◆ All may add their own prayers here.

Let us pray: **Our Father . . . Amen.**

Lord Jesus,
you instruct us on the simplicity of
spreading your Gospel of love.
We are your laborers for the harvest.
Give us courage to travel without
"baggage" as we help each other
on the road to God's kingdom.
We ask this in your name.
Amen.

✝ All make the Sign of the Cross.

OPENING

Today we remember St. Francis of Assisi, a lover of animals, nature, and champion of the poor. He gave up all his possessions so that he could preach on the streets of Italy, and before long several prominent citizens joined his group. The pope eventually recognized the order and called it the Franciscans. Francis called all creatures his "brothers and sisters." He believed that humans are to be the stewards of all of nature. He died in 1226. In today's Gospel, Jesus warns us about those who reject his words of truth.

✚ All make the Sign of the Cross.

In the name of the Father, and of the Son, and of the Holy Spirit. Amen.

PSALM (For a longer psalm, see page xi.) Psalm 145:2–3, 4–5, 10–11

I will praise your name for ever.

I will praise your name for ever.

Every day I will bless you,
 and praise your name for ever and ever.
Great is the LORD, and greatly to be praised;
 his greatness is unsearchable.

I will praise your name for ever.

◆ All stand and sing **Alleluia.**

GOSPEL   Luke 10:13–16

A reading from the holy Gospel according to Luke

Jesus said to them, "Woe to you, Chorazin [koh-RAY-zihn]! Woe to you, Bethsaida [beth-SAY-uh-duh]! For if the deeds of power done in you had been done in Tyre [TI-er] and Sidon [SI-duhn], they would have repented long ago, sitting in sackcloth and ashes. But at the judgment it will be more tolerable for Tyre and Sidon than for you. And you, Capernaum, will you be exalted to heaven? No, you will be brought down to Hades. Whoever listens to you listens to me, and whoever rejects you rejects me, and whoever rejects me rejects the one who sent me."

The Gospel of the Lord.

◆ All sit and observe silence.

FOR SILENT REFLECTION

How do we listen to Jesus? Who helps us to understand his words?

CLOSING PRAYER

Let us stand and bring our hopes and needs to God as we pray, "Lord, hear our prayer."

◆ All may add their own prayers here.

Let us pray: **Our Father . . . Amen.**

Lord Jesus,
you warn residents about
not repenting and following your ways.
We listen as you lead us with
your wisdom and truth.
Guide us as we spread the word
about you in our communities.
We ask this in your name.

Amen.

✚ All make the Sign of the Cross.

PRAYER SERVICE
MEMORIAL OF OUR LADY OF THE ROSARY

Prepare eight leaders for this service. The third and fourth leaders will need Bibles for the Scripture passages and may need help practicing the readings. You may wish to begin by singing "The Servant Song" and end with "We Have Been Told." If the group will sing, prepare a song leader.

FIRST LEADER:
May the grace and peace of our Lord Jesus Christ be with us, now and forever.

Amen.

SECOND LEADER:
Today we celebrate Mary,
the Mother of our Lord Jesus,
whose life of holiness always pointed
toward Christ our Savior.
And today we honor her with this feast
in thanksgiving for the Rosary
that highlights the mysteries of
the life and Death of our Messiah.
May we say, "yes" to God
as she did throughout her life.
We ask this through Christ our Lord.

Amen.

◆ All stand and sing **Alleluia.**

THIRD LEADER: Luke 1:39–45
A reading from the holy Gospel according to Luke

◆ Read the passage from a Bible.

The Gospel of the Lord.

Response: **Praise to you, Lord Jesus Christ.**

CHILDREN'S DAILY PRAYER 2013–2014, © 2013 Archdiocese of Chicago: Liturgy Training Publications. All rights reserved. Orders: 1-800-933-1800 or www.LTP.org.

MEMORIAL OF OUR LADY OF THE ROSARY

FOURTH LEADER: Luke 1:46–56

A reading from the holy Gospel according to Luke

◆ Read the passage from a Bible.

The Gospel of the Lord.

Response: **Praise to you, Lord Jesus Christ.**

◆ All sit and observe silence.

FIFTH LEADER:

Lord Jesus,
your Mother's life
was centered around you.
Through the gift of the Rosary,
we can reflect on the key events
in your life filled with
joy, sorrow, and glory.
Guide us toward living as fully
as Mary did as we meditate on
your mysteries.
In your name we pray.

Amen.

SIXTH LEADER:

Together let's pray one decade of
the Rosary in honor of this
feast of our Mother Mary:
Hail Mary, full of grace
the Lord is with you,
blessed are you among women
and blessed is the fruit of your womb, Jesus,
Holy Mary, Mother of God,
pray for us sinners,
now and at the hour of our death.

Amen.

Glory be to the Father,
and to the Son,
and to the Holy Spirit.

Amen.

SEVENTH LEADER:

Loving Jesus,
fill our hearts with the same
loving response as Mary had
when the angel Gabriel asked her
to be the Mother of our Lord.
May we be mindful of how you
also remained faithful to God's will
through the tragedies and joys
of your life.
Help us to be vessels of your grace.
We ask this through Christ our Lord.

Amen.

EIGHTH LEADER:

May the love of God,

✢ All make the Sign of the Cross.

Father, Son, and Holy Spirit,
keep us connected with the help of
our Mother Mary,
now and forever.

Amen.

CHILDREN'S DAILY PRAYER 2013–2014 © 2013 Archdiocese of Chicago: Liturgy Training Publications, 3949 South Racine Avenue, Chicago IL 60609. All rights reserved. Orders: 1-800-933-1800 or www.LTP.org. Scripture excerpts are taken from *The New Revised Standard Version Bible: Catholic Edition*, © 1989, Division of Christian Education of the National Council of the Churches of Christ in the United States of America. Used with permission. All rights reserved.

OPENING

Today's Gospel is a challenge as we consider the strength of our faith.

✛ All make the Sign of the Cross.

In the name of the Father, and of the Son, and of the Holy Spirit. Amen.

PSALM   (For a longer psalm, see page xi.) Psalm 145:2–3, 4–5, 10–11

I will praise your name for ever.

I will praise your name for ever.

Every day I will bless you,
  and praise your name for ever and ever.
Great is the LORD, and greatly to be praised;
  his greatness is unsearchable.

I will praise your name for ever.

◆ All stand and sing **Alleluia.**

GOSPEL   Luke 17:5–10

A reading from the holy Gospel according to Luke

The apostles said to the Lord, "Increase our faith!" The Lord replied, "If you had faith the size of a mustard seed, you could say to this mulberry tree, 'Be uprooted and planted in the sea,' and it would obey you. Who among you would say to your slave who has just come in from plowing or tending sheep in the field, 'Come here at once and take your place at the table'? Would you not rather say to him, 'Prepare supper for me, put on your apron and serve me while I eat and drink; later you may eat and drink'? Do you thank the slave for doing what was commanded? So you also, when you have done all that you were ordered to do, say, 'We are worthless slaves; we have done only what we ought to have done!'"

The Gospel of the Lord.

◆ All sit and observe silence.

FOR SILENT REFLECTION

How much faith do I have in God? What are ways that I could increase my faith?

CLOSING PRAYER

Let us stand and bring our hopes and needs to God as we pray, "Lord, hear our prayer."

◆ All may add their own prayers here.

Let us pray: **Our Father . . . Amen.**

Lord God,
you provide us many occasions in this life
where our faith is tested.
Help us to become more willing to
serve you without complaining.
Guide us to always do your will first.
We ask this through Christ our Lord.

Amen.

✛ All make the Sign of the Cross.

OPENING

Today, the feast of Our Lady of the Rosary, serves as a reminder of this traditional Catholic prayer practice that helps us to meditate on the great mysteries of our salvation.

✛ All make the Sign of the Cross.

In the name of the Father, and of the Son, and of the Holy Spirit. Amen.

PSALM (For a longer psalm, see page xi.) Psalm 145:2–3, 4–5, 10–11

I will praise your name for ever.

I will praise your name for ever.

Every day I will bless you,
    and praise your name for ever and ever.
Great is the LORD, and greatly to be praised;
    his greatness is unsearchable.

I will praise your name for ever.

◆ All stand and sing **Alleluia.**

GOSPEL
Luke 10:25, 30–37

A reading from the holy Gospel according to Luke

A lawyer stood up to test Jesus. "Teacher," he said, "what must I do to inherit eternal life?" Jesus replied, "A man was going down from Jerusalem to Jericho, and fell into the hands of robbers, who stripped him, beat him, and went away, leaving him half dead. Now by chance a priest was going down that road; and when he saw him, he passed by on the other side. So likewise a Levite, when he came to the place and saw him, passed by on the other side. But a Samaritan [suh-MEHR-ih-tuhn] while traveling came near him; and when he saw him, he was moved with pity. He went to him and bandaged his wounds, having poured oil and wine on them. Then he put him on his own animal, brought him to an inn, and took care of him. The next day he took out two denarii [dih-NAHR-ee-ī], gave them to the innkeeper, and said, 'Take care of him; and when I come back, I will repay you whatever more you spend.' Which of these three, do you think, was a neighbor to the man who fell into the hands of the robbers?" He said, "The one who showed him mercy." Jesus said to him, "Go and do likewise."

The Gospel of the Lord.

◆ All sit and observe silence.

FOR SILENT REFLECTION

Who are my true neighbors? How is someone we don't know our neighbor?

CLOSING PRAYER

Let us stand and bring our hopes and needs to God as we pray, "Lord, hear our prayer."

◆ All may add their own prayers here.

Let us pray: **Our Father . . . Amen.**

Lord Jesus,
you invite us to enlarge our concept of
"neighborhood."
Give us the courage to forgive others and
to expand our reach
to include all people.
We ask this in your name.

Amen.

✛ All make the Sign of the Cross.

PRAYER FOR **TUESDAY** **OCTOBER 8, 2013**

OPENING

Today's Gospel reminds us that our busyness can distract us from truly important things.

✦ All make the Sign of the Cross.

In the name of the Father, and of the Son, and of the Holy Spirit. Amen.

PSALM (For a longer psalm, see page xi.) Psalm 145:2–3, 4–5, 10–11

I will praise your name for ever.

I will praise your name for ever.

Every day I will bless you,
   and praise your name for ever and ever.
Great is the LORD, and greatly to be praised;
   his greatness is unsearchable.

I will praise your name for ever.

✦ All stand and sing **Alleluia.**

GOSPEL   Luke 10:38–42

A reading from the holy Gospel according to Luke

Now as they went on their way, he entered a certain village, where a woman named Martha welcomed him into her home. She had a sister named Mary, who sat at the Lord's feet and listened to what he was saying. But Martha was distracted by her many tasks; so she came to him and asked, "Lord, do you not care that my sister has left me to do all the work by myself? Tell her then to help me." But the Lord answered her, "Martha, Martha, you are worried and distracted by many things; there is need of only one thing. Mary has chosen the better part, which will not be taken away from her."

The Gospel of the Lord.

✦ All sit and observe silence.

FOR SILENT REFLECTION

When do I set aside time to listen to our Lord?

CLOSING PRAYER

Let us stand and bring our hopes and needs to God as we pray, "Lord, hear our prayer."

✦ All may add their own prayers here.

Let us pray: **Our Father . . . Amen.**

Lord Jesus,
our lives are often packed with
too many activities,
and we get frenzied by
deadlines too.
Help us to remember
to take time to listen to you,
source of all wisdom.
Assist us in our decisions about
priorities
so that we are indeed
setting aside special time for you.
In your name we pray.

Amen.

✦ All make the Sign of the Cross.

OPENING

Today we remember St. Denis and his companions. Denis was bishop of Paris in the third century and was martyred because leaders of that time opposed the Christian faith. Another saint whom we remember today is John Leonardi, who became a priest and encouraged many laymen to become priests as well. In 1579, he developed a book of Christian doctrine that was in use until the 19th century. In today's Gospel, we recognize the essence of the "Our Father," our beloved prayer.

✦ All make the Sign of the Cross.

In the name of the Father, and of the Son, and of the Holy Spirit. Amen.

PSALM   (For a longer psalm, see page xi.) Psalm 145:2–3, 4–5, 10–11

I will praise your name for ever.

I will praise your name for ever.

Every day I will bless you,
  and praise your name for ever and ever.
Great is the LORD, and greatly to be praised;
  his greatness is unsearchable.

I will praise your name for ever.

◆ All stand and sing **Alleluia**.

GOSPEL   Luke 11:1–4

A reading from the holy Gospel according to Luke

Jesus was praying in a certain place, and after he had finished, one of his disciples said to him, "Lord, teach us to pray, as John taught his disciples." He said to them, "When you pray, say: Father, hallowed be your name. Your kingdom come. Give us each day our daily bread. And forgive us our sins, for we ourselves forgive everyone indebted to us. And do not bring us to the time of trial."

The Gospel of the Lord.

◆ All sit and observe silence.

FOR SILENT REFLECTION

What can I discover about prayer and my faith from the Lord's Prayer?

CLOSING PRAYER

Let us stand and bring our hopes and needs to God as we pray, "Lord, hear our prayer."

◆ All may add their own prayers here.

Let us pray: **Our Father . . . Amen.**

Almighty Lord,
your simple prayer says it all:
we praise God,
we desire our Creator's kingdom on earth,
we ask for the basics,
and forgive others as they forgive us.
May we always remember this
majestic prayer and its
impact on our spiritual growth.
We this ask in your name.

Amen.

✦ All make the Sign of the Cross.

PRAYER FOR **THURSDAY** **OCTOBER 10, 2013**

OPENING

In today's Gospel, Jesus highlights how much our Father cares for us by listening to our requests and meeting our needs.

✚ All make the Sign of the Cross.

In the name of the Father, and of the Son, and of the Holy Spirit. Amen.

PSALM   (For a longer psalm, see page xi.) Psalm 145:2–3, 4–5, 10–11

I will praise your name for ever.

I will praise your name for ever.

Every day I will bless you,
  and praise your name for ever and ever.
Great is the LORD, and greatly to be praised;
  his greatness is unsearchable.

I will praise your name for ever.

◆ All stand and sing **Alleluia.**

GOSPEL   Luke 11:5–13

A reading from the holy Gospel according to Luke

Jesus said to his disciples, "Suppose one of you has a friend, and you go to him at midnight and say to him, 'Friend, lend me three loaves of bread; for a friend of mine has arrived, and I have nothing to set before him.' And he answers from within, 'Do not bother me; the door has already been locked, and my children are with me in bed; I cannot get up and give you anything.' I tell you, even though he will not get up and give him anything because he is his friend, at least because of his persistence he will get up and give him whatever he needs.

So I say to you, Ask, and it will be given you; search, and you will find; knock, and the door will be opened for you. For everyone who asks receives, and everyone who searches finds, and for everyone who knocks, the door will be opened. Is there anyone among you who, if your child asks for a fish, will give a snake instead of a fish? Or if the child asks for an egg, will give a scorpion? If you then, who are evil, know how to give good gifts to your children, how much more will the heavenly Father give the Holy Spirit to those who ask him!"

The Gospel of the Lord.

◆ All sit and observe silence.

FOR SILENT REFLECTION

What requests have I made of God? What are my needs?

CLOSING PRAYER

Let us stand and bring our hopes and needs to God as we pray, "Lord, hear our prayer."

◆ All may add their own prayers here.

Let us pray: **Our Father . . . Amen.**

Lord God,
you remind us of how persistence matters.
You know our needs and listen to
all our requests.
Continue to reassure us with the hope
that our prayers will be answered.
We ask this through Christ our Lord.

Amen.

✚ All make the Sign of the Cross.

OPENING

In today's Gospel, Jesus reminds Jewish leaders that his authority to cast out demons comes from God.

✝ All make the Sign of the Cross.

In the name of the Father, and of the Son, and of the Holy Spirit. Amen.

PSALM (For a longer psalm, see page xi.) Psalm 145:2–3, 4–5, 10–11

I will praise your name for ever.

I will praise your name for ever.

Every day I will bless you,
  and praise your name for ever and ever.
Great is the LORD, and greatly to be praised;
  his greatness is unsearchable.

I will praise your name for ever.

◆ All stand and sing **Alleluia.**

GOSPEL   Luke 11:15–20, 23

A reading from the holy Gospel according to Luke

When Jesus had driven out a demon, some of crowd said, "He casts out demons by Beelzebul [bee-EL-zeh-buhl], the ruler of the demons." Others, to test him, kept demanding from him a sign from heaven. But he knew what they were thinking and said to them, "Every kingdom divided against itself becomes a desert, and house falls on house. If Satan also is divided against himself, how will his kingdom stand?—for you say that I cast out the demons by Beelzebul. Now if I cast out the demons by Beelzebul, by whom do your exorcists cast them out? Therefore they will be your judges. But if it is by the finger of God that I cast out the demons, then the kingdom of God has come to you. Whoever is not with me is against me, and whoever does not gather with me scatters."

The Gospel of the Lord.

◆ All sit and observe silence.

FOR SILENT REFLECTION

How do I nurture my heart and mind so that I point to Jesus as the leader of my life?

CLOSING PRAYER

Let us stand and bring our hopes and needs to God as we pray, "Lord, hear our prayer."

◆ All may add their own prayers here.

Let us pray: **Our Father . . . Amen.**

Lord Jesus,
you cast out demons with
God's authority.
You point the way to the
power of our Creator
even as people slandered you.
Help us to be true to God
as the source of all healing.
We ask this in your name.

Amen.

✝ All make the Sign of the Cross.

PRAYER FOR THE WEEK

OPENING

In today's Gospel, we see an example of someone showing thankfulness. Why do you think only one person showed their gratitude?

✛ All make the Sign of the Cross.

In the name of the Father, and of the Son, and of the Holy Spirit. Amen.

PSALM (For a longer psalm, see page xi.) Psalm 145:2–3, 4–5, 10–11

I will praise your name for ever.

I will praise your name for ever.

Every day I will bless you,
   and praise your name for ever and ever.
Great is the LORD, and greatly to be praised;
   his greatness is unsearchable.

I will praise your name for ever.

◆ All stand and sing **Alleluia.**

GOSPEL   Luke 17:11–19

A reading from the holy Gospel according to Luke

On the way to Jerusalem Jesus was going through the region between Samaria [suh-MAYR-ee-uh] and Galilee [GAL-ih-lee]. As he entered a village, ten lepers approached him. Keeping their distance, they called out, saying, "Jesus, Master, have mercy on us!" When he saw them, he said to them, "Go and show yourselves to the priests." And as they went, they were made clean. Then one of them, when he saw that he was healed, turned back, praising God with a loud voice. He prostrated himself at Jesus's feet and thanked him. And he was a Samaritan. Then Jesus asked, "Were not ten made clean? But the other nine, where are they? Was none of them found to return and give praise to God except this foreigner?" Then he said to him, "Get up and go on your way; your faith has made you well."

The Gospel of the Lord.

◆ All sit and observe silence.

FOR SILENT REFLECTION

Why is it important to show our gratitude and to say thank you?

CLOSING PRAYER

Let us stand and bring our hopes and needs to God as we pray, "Lord, hear our prayer."

◆ All may add their own prayers here.

Let us pray: **Our Father . . . Amen.**

Lord Jesus,
your healing powers cure
any ailment, even as we forget
to recognize your holiness.
We praise you for your
blessings in our lives.
Help us to show gratitude
to all who help others in your name.
We ask this in your name.

Amen.

✛ All make the Sign of the Cross.

OPENING

Today is Columbus Day, a public holiday in the United States that celebrates the arrival of Christopher Columbus to the Americas in 1492. Today we also remember St. Callistus, who was a slave in imperial Rome. Over time he worked his way to managing burial grounds, and was later named a deacon and adviser to the pope.

✜ All make the Sign of the Cross.

In the name of the Father, and of the Son, and of the Holy Spirit. Amen.

PSALM (For a longer psalm, see page xi.) Psalm 145:2–3, 4–5, 10–11

I will praise your name for ever.

I will praise your name for ever.

Every day I will bless you,
 and praise your name for ever and ever.
Great is the LORD, and greatly to be praised;
 his greatness is unsearchable.

I will praise your name for ever.

◆ All stand and sing **Alleluia.**

GOSPEL   Luke 11:29–30, 32

A reading from the holy Gospel according to Luke

When the crowds were increasing, Jesus began to say, "This generation is an evil generation; it asks for a sign, but no sign will be given to it except the sign of Jonah. For just as Jonah became a sign to the people of Nineveh [NIN-uh-vuh], so the Son of Man will be to this generation. The people of Nineveh will rise up at the judgment with this generation and condemn it, because they repented at the proclamation of Jonah, and see, something greater than Jonah is here!"

The Gospel of the Lord.

◆ All sit and observe silence.

FOR SILENT REFLECTION

How can I be a witness to signs of the living Christ?

CLOSING PRAYER

Let us stand and bring our hopes and needs to God as we pray, "Lord, hear our prayer."

◆ All may add their own prayers here.

Let us pray: **Our Father . . . Amen.**

Lord Jesus,
you are the sign of new life.
Through your words and actions
you revealed your power over death
for all of us.
Guide us as we see your presence
all around us:
in myself, in others, and in the
circumstances of our days.
We ask this in your name.

Amen.

✜ All make the Sign of the Cross.

PRAYER FOR **TUESDAY**
OCTOBER 15, 2013

OPENING

Today we remember St. Teresa of Avila, Spain, who was born in 1515. As a Carmelite nun, she devoted herself to intense prayer, even while suffering from headaches and other ailments. She became known for helping her sisters in Christ to better embrace the values of poverty and simplicity. She also wrote books describing how to deepen times of prayer. She was named a Doctor of the Church. In today's Gospel, Jesus was invited to dinner by a Pharisee [FAYR-uh-see] and chose not to do the ceremonial washing before the meal. Jesus delivers a bitter lesson on how our appearances need to match a pure heart.

✢ All make the Sign of the Cross.

In the name of the Father, and of the Son, and of the Holy Spirit. Amen.

PSALM (For a longer psalm, see page xi.) Psalm 145:2–3, 4–5, 10–11

I will praise your name for ever.

I will praise your name for ever.

Every day I will bless you,
    and praise your name for ever and ever.
Great is the LORD, and greatly to be praised;
    his greatness is unsearchable.

I will praise your name for ever.

◆ All stand and sing **Alleluia.**

GOSPEL   Luke 11:37–41

A reading from the holy Gospel according to Luke

While he was speaking, a Pharisee [FAYR-uh-see] invited him to dine with him; so he went in and took his place at the table. The Pharisee was amazed to see that he did not first wash before dinner. Then the Lord said to him, "Now you Pharisees clean the outside of the cup and of the dish, but inside you are full of greed and wickedness. You fools! Did not the one who made the outside make the inside also? So give for alms those things that are within; and see, everything will be clean for you."

The Gospel of the Lord.

◆ All sit and observe silence.

FOR SILENT REFLECTION

Why are our thoughts as important as our action?

CLOSING PRAYER

Let us stand and bring our hopes and needs to God as we pray, "Lord, hear our prayer."

◆ All may add their own prayers here.

Let us pray: **Our Father . . . Amen.**

Lord Jesus,
you taught the Pharisee
a tough lesson about being authentic.
Guide us as we remain genuine
in our devotion to you
in word and deed.
We ask this in your name.

Amen.

✢ All make the Sign of the Cross.

OPENING

Today we remember St. Margaret Mary Alacoque from the 17th century, who was a nun and mystic from France. In her prayer, she had visions of Christ, who directed her to establish a devotion to the Sacred Heart. We also remember St. Hedwig, from the 12th century, who used her wealth to establish hospitals and monasteries. In today's Gospel, Jesus reveals how leaders have paid too much attention to the details of law, forgetting about its intent.

✤ All make the Sign of the Cross.

In the name of the Father, and of the Son, and of the Holy Spirit. Amen.

PSALM (For a longer psalm, see page xi.) Psalm 145:2–3, 4–5, 10–11

I will praise your name for ever.

I will praise your name for ever.

Every day I will bless you,
and praise your name for ever and ever.
Great is the LORD, and greatly to be praised;
his greatness is unsearchable.

I will praise your name for ever.

◆ All stand and sing **Alleluia.**

GOSPEL Luke 11:42–46

A reading from the holy Gospel according to Luke

The Lord said: "But woe to you Pharisees [FAYR-uh-seez]! For you tithe [tīth] mint and rue and herbs of all kinds, and neglect justice and the love of God; it is these you ought to have practiced, without neglecting the others. Woe to you Pharisees! For you love to have the seat of honor in the synagogues and to be greeted with respect in the marketplaces. Woe to you! For you are like unmarked graves, and people walk over them without realizing it." One of the lawyers answered him, "Teacher, when you say these things, you insult us too." And he said, "Woe also to you lawyers! For you load people with burdens hard to bear, and you yourselves do not lift a finger to ease them."

The Gospel of the Lord.

◆ All sit and observe silence.

FOR SILENT REFLECTION

Do I fully contribute my talents and skills at school or on teams?

CLOSING PRAYER

Let us stand and bring our hopes and needs to God as we pray, "Lord, hear our prayer."

◆ All may add their own prayers here.

Let us pray: **Our Father . . . Amen.**

Lord Jesus,
your strong words revealed
the actions of these leaders
behind the scenes.
May we have the courage to be
kind and merciful in
all that we do and say.
We ask this in your name.

Amen.

✤ All make the Sign of the Cross.

PRAYER FOR **THURSDAY** OCTOBER 17, 2013

OPENING

Today we remember St. Ignatius of Antioch, bishop and martyr, who was among the earliest group of church leaders after the Apostles. He was sentenced to death in Rome. While being transported there, he hastily wrote letters to regional churches and friends. These letters are considered to be accurate historical accounts of the early Church.

✦ All make the Sign of the Cross.

In the name of the Father, and of the Son, and of the Holy Spirit. Amen.

PSALM (For a longer psalm, see page xi.) Psalm 145:2–3, 4–5, 10–11

I will praise your name for ever.

I will praise your name for ever.

Every day I will bless you,
 and praise your name for ever and ever.
Great is the LORD, and greatly to be praised;
 his greatness is unsearchable.

I will praise your name for ever.

◆ All stand and sing **Alleluia.**

GOSPEL   Luke 11:47–54

A reading from the holy Gospel according to Luke

The Lord said: "Woe to you! For you build the tombs of the prophets whom your ancestors killed. So you are witnesses and approve of the deeds of your ancestors; for they killed them, and you build their tombs. Therefore also the Wisdom of God said, 'I will send them prophets and apostles, some of whom they will kill and persecute,' so that this generation may be charged with the blood of all the prophets shed since the foundation of the world, from the blood of Abel to the blood of Zechariah [zek-uh-RĪ-uh], who perished between the altar and the sanctuary." When he went outside, the scribes and the Pharisees began to be very hostile toward him and to cross-examine him about many things, lying in wait for him, to catch him in something he might say.

The Gospel of the Lord.

◆ All sit and observe silence.

FOR SILENT REFLECTION

When rules seem to get too complicated, how can I simplify them using Jesus's loving guides for living?

CLOSING PRAYER

Let us stand and bring our hopes and needs to God as we pray, "Lord, hear our prayer."

◆ All may add their own prayers here.

Let us pray: **Our Father . . . Amen.**

Lord Jesus,
you angered many in
positions of power because
you spoke the truth.
Help us to remain focused on
your simple rules of truth and love.
We ask this in your name.

Amen.

✦ All make the Sign of the Cross.

78

OPENING

Today we remember St. Luke, who was a key author of the New Testament, not only for writing the third Gospel, but also the Acts of the Apostles. He traveled with St. Paul and interviewed people who had known Jesus. As a Gentile, Luke wrote primarily for an audience who were not Christ's Jewish followers.

✚ All make the Sign of the Cross.

In the name of the Father, and of the Son, and of the Holy Spirit. Amen.

PSALM (For a longer psalm, see page xi.) Psalm 145:2–3, 4–5, 10–11

I will praise your name for ever.

I will praise your name for ever.

Every day I will bless you,
 and praise your name for ever and ever.
Great is the LORD, and greatly to be praised;
 his greatness is unsearchable.

I will praise your name for ever.

◆ All stand and sing **Alleluia.**

GOSPEL   Luke 12:1–7

A reading from the holy Gospel according to Luke

After the Lord appointed seventy others and sent them on ahead of him in pairs to every town and place where he himself intended to go. He said to them, "The harvest is plentiful, but the laborers are few; therefore ask the Lord of the harvest to send out his laborers into the harvest. Go on your way. See I am sending you out like lambs into the midst of wolves. Carry no purse, no bag, no sandals; and greet no one on the road. Whatever house you enter, first say, 'Peace to this house.'"

The Gospel of the Lord.

◆ All sit and observe silence.

FOR SILENT REFLECTION

How can I bring peace to places I visit and people I encounter?

CLOSING PRAYER

Let us stand and bring our hopes and needs to God as we pray, "Lord, hear our prayer."

◆ All may add their own prayers here.

Let us pray: **Our Father . . . Amen.**

Holy God,
you desire us to be bearers of
your peace and your love to all.
Help us to trust that you will guide
and be with us always.
We ask this in the name of your Son, Jesus.

Amen.

✚ All make the Sign of the Cross.

PRAYER FOR THE WEEK

WITH A READING FROM THE GOSPEL FOR **SUNDAY, OCTOBER 20, 2013**

OPENING

Today's Gospel leads us to gain confidence in prayer. Jesus gives us hope that what we need will be granted.

✝ All make the Sign of the Cross.

In the name of the Father, and of the Son, and of the Holy Spirit. Amen.

PSALM

(For a longer psalm, see page xii.) Psalm 98: 1bcde, 2–3ab, 3cd–4

The LORD has made known his victory.

The LORD has made known his victory.

O sing to the LORD a new song,
   for he has done marvelous things.
His right hand and his holy arm
   have gained him victory.

The LORD has made known his victory.

◆ All stand and sing **Alleluia.**

GOSPEL

Luke 18:1–8

A reading from the holy Gospel according to Luke

Then Jesus told them a parable about their need to pray always and not to lose heart. He said, "In a certain city there was a judge who neither feared God nor had respect for people. In that city there was a widow who kept coming to him and saying, 'Grant me justice against my opponent.' For a while he refused; but later he said to himself, 'Though I have no fear of God and no respect for anyone, yet because this widow keeps bothering me, I will grant her justice, so that she may not wear me out by continually coming.'" And the Lord said, "Listen to what the unjust judge says. And will not God grant justice to his chosen ones who cry to him day and night? Will he delay long in helping them? I tell you, he will quickly grant justice to them. And yet, when the Son of Man comes, will he find faith on earth?"

The Gospel of the Lord.

◆ All sit and observe silence.

FOR SILENT REFLECTION

Am I persistent with my prayer requests? For what do I need God's help?

CLOSING PRAYER

Let us stand and bring our hopes and needs to God as we pray, "Lord, hear our prayer."

◆ All may add their own prayers here.

Let us pray: **Our Father . . . Amen.**

Lord Jesus,
you reassure us of your answers
to our needs,
for we are your beloved children.
Our persistence in prayer,
our communication with you,
needs to be ongoing.
Keep us, Lord, in your
continual care.
We thank you for your
ever-present grace.
In your name we pray.

Amen.

✝ All make the Sign of the Cross.

OPENING

In today's Gospel, Jesus reminds us to guard against becoming greedy with our possessions and the money we earn.

✚ All make the Sign of the Cross.

In the name of the Father, and of the Son, and of the Holy Spirit. Amen.

PSALM

(For a longer psalm, see page xii.) Psalm 98:1bcde, 2–3ab, 3cd–4

The LORD has made known his victory.

The LORD has made known his victory.

O sing to the LORD a new song,
    for he has done marvelous things.
His right hand and his holy arm
    have gained him victory.

The LORD has made known his victory.

◆ All stand and sing **Alleluia.**

GOSPEL

Luke 12:13–21

A reading from the holy Gospel according to Luke

Someone in the crowd said to Jesus, "Teacher, tell my brother to divide the family inheritance with me." But he said to him, "Friend, who set me to be a judge or arbitrator over you?" And he said to them, "Take care! Be on your guard against all kinds of greed; for one's life does not consist in the abundance of possessions." Then he told them a parable: "The land of a rich man produced abundantly. And he thought to himself, 'What should I do, for I have no place to store my crops?' Then he said, 'I will do this: I will pull down my barns and build larger ones, and there I will store all my grain and my goods. And I will say to my soul, 'Soul, you have ample goods laid up for many years; relax, eat, drink, be merry.' But God said to him, 'You fool! This very night your life is being demanded of you. And the things you have prepared, whose will they be?' So it is with those who store up treasures for themselves but are not rich toward God."

The Gospel of the Lord.

◆ All sit and observe silence.

FOR SILENT REFLECTION

How do I contribute my time and talents for building God's kingdom?

CLOSING PRAYER

Let us stand and bring our hopes and needs to God as we pray, "Lord, hear our prayer."

◆ All may add their own prayers here.

Let us pray: **Our Father . . . Amen.**

Lord Jesus,
you teach us that acquiring wealth
is pointless unless we
share it with others.
You ask us to channel our energy
in meeting our needs and
accomplishing good for the world.
Give us the courage to match our
desires in faith with how we
use our resources.
We ask this in your name.

Amen.

✚ All make the Sign of the Cross.

PRAYER FOR **TUESDAY** **OCTOBER 22, 2013**

OPENING

In today's reading, from St. Paul to the Romans, he explains the purpose of Jesus, the Son of God, in our world and what Christ means for our salvation.

✚ All make the Sign of the Cross.

In the name of the Father, and of the Son, and of the Holy Spirit. Amen.

PSALM

(For a longer psalm, see page xii.) Psalm 98:1bcde, 2–3ab, 3cd–4

The LORD has made known his victory.

The LORD has made known his victory.

O sing to the LORD a new song,
   for he has done marvelous things.
His right hand and his holy arm
   have gained him victory.

The LORD has made known his victory.

READING

Romans 5:12, 15b, 17–19, 20b–21

Therefore, just as sin came into the world through one man, and death came through sin, and so death spread to all because all have sinned. But the free gift is not like the trespass. For if the many died through the one man's trespass, much more surely have the grace of God and the free gift in the grace of the one man, Jesus Christ, abounded for the many. If, because of the one man's trespass, death exercised dominion through that one, much more surely will those who receive the abundance of grace and the free gift of righteousness exercise dominion in life through the one man, Jesus Christ. Therefore just as one man's trespass led to condemnation for all, so one man's act of righteousness leads to justification and life for all. For just as by the one man's disobedience the many were made sinners, so by the one man's obedience the many will be made righteous. But law came in, with the result that the trespass multiplied; but where sin increased, grace abounded all the more, so that, just as sin exercised dominion in death, so grace might also exercise dominion through justification leading to eternal life through Jesus Christ our Lord.

The Word of the Lord.

◆ All observe silence.

FOR SILENT REFLECTION

What does God's gift of Jesus mean to me?

CLOSING PRAYER

Let us stand and bring our hopes and needs to God as we pray, "Lord, hear our prayer."

◆ All may add their own prayers here.

Let us pray: **Our Father . . . Amen.**

Almighty God,
you sent your Son to save the world.
You sent Jesus to show us the way,
to give us hope over the threat of death.
Through Christ, we know
there is life everlasting.
We thank you and praise you.
In Christ's name we pray.

Amen.

✚ All make the Sign of the Cross.

OPENING

Today we remember St. John of Capistrano, born in Italy in 1386, and who became a Franciscan friar and priest. He was a fiery preacher, calling for reforms in both Christian and governmental realms.

✚ All make the Sign of the Cross.

In the name of the Father, and of the Son, and of the Holy Spirit. Amen.

PSALM

(For a longer psalm, see page xii.) Psalm 98:1bcde, 2–3ab, 3cd–4

The LORD has made known his victory.

The LORD has made known his victory.

O sing to the LORD a new song,
    for he has done marvelous things.
His right hand and his holy arm
    have gained him victory.

The LORD has made known his victory.

◆ All stand and sing **Alleluia.**

GOSPEL

Luke 12:39–44, 48b

A reading from the holy Gospel according to Luke

Jesus said to his disciples: "But know this: if the owner of the house had known at what hour the thief was coming, he would not have let his house be broken into. You also must be ready, for the Son of Man is coming at an unexpected hour."

Peter said, "Lord, are you telling this parable for us or for everyone?" And the Lord said, "Who then is the faithful and prudent manager whom his master will put in charge of his slaves, to give them their allowance of food at the proper time? Blessed is that slave whom his master will find at work when he arrives. Truly I tell you, he will put that one in charge of all his possessions. From everyone to whom much has been given, much will be required; and from the one to whom much has been entrusted, even more will be demanded."

The Gospel of the Lord.

◆ All sit and observe silence.

FOR SILENT REFLECTION

Do my responsibilities at home grow as I mature? How can I be more helpful at school and with my parents and all those who care for me?

CLOSING PRAYER

Let us stand and bring our hopes and needs to God as we pray, "Lord, hear our prayer."

◆ All may add their own prayers here.

Let us pray: **Our Father . . . Amen.**

Lord Jesus,
our time on this earth is short
compared to the glorious time
we'll spend with you in heaven.
Help us to tell the world about you
through our daily actions of love.
We ask this in your name.

Amen.

✚ All make the Sign of the Cross.

PRAYER FOR **THURSDAY** **OCTOBER 24, 2013**

OPENING

Today we remember St. Anthony Mary Claret, born near Barcelona, Spain, in 1807, and who became a priest, missionary, and writer. As an energetic reformer, he established libraries, hospitals, schools, and religious orders. The Claretians are named after this saint, and serve in parishes, foreign missions, and inner city campuses, as well as in publishing. In today's Gospel, Jesus tells us that conflict is inevitable for his followers, just as people sometimes squabble within families and teams about important issues, or even small tasks.

✚ All make the Sign of the Cross.

In the name of the Father, and of the Son, and of the Holy Spirit. Amen.

PSALM
(For a longer psalm, see page xii.) Psalm 98:1bcde, 2–3ab, 3cd–4

The LORD has made known his victory.

The LORD has made known his victory.

O sing to the LORD a new song,
for he has done marvelous things.
His right hand and his holy arm
have gained him victory.

The LORD has made known his victory.

◆ All stand and sing **Alleluia.**

GOSPEL
Luke 12:49–53

A reading from the holy Gospel according to Luke

"I came to bring fire to the earth, and how I wish it were already kindled! I have a baptism with which to be baptized, and what stress I am under until it is completed! Do you think that I have come to bring peace to the earth? No, I tell you, but rather division! From now on five in one household will be divided, three against two and two against three; they will be divided: father against son and son against father, mother against daughter and daughter against mother, mother-in-law against her daughter-in-law and daughter-in-law against mother-in-law."

The Gospel of the Lord.

◆ All sit and observe silence.

FOR SILENT REFLECTION

How can I help at home or at school when there is tension or anger?

CLOSING PRAYER

Let us stand and bring our hopes and needs to God as we pray, "Lord, hear our prayer."

◆ All may add their own prayers here.

Let us pray: **Our Father . . . Amen.**

God almighty,
you sent your Son to show us
how to spread your
message of truth.
Sometimes people resist your Word
and there is conflict and strife.
Guide us toward finding solutions as
your children of peace.
In Christ's name we pray.

Amen.

✚ All make the Sign of the Cross.

OPENING

In today's Gospel, Jesus reminds us to take opportunities to forgive one another sooner rather than later.

✦ All make the Sign of the Cross.

In the name of the Father, and of the Son, and of the Holy Spirit. Amen.

PSALM
(For a longer psalm, see page xii.) Psalm 98:1bcde, 2–3ab, 3cd–4

The LORD has made known his victory.

The LORD has made known his victory.

O sing to the LORD a new song,
   for he has done marvelous things.
His right hand and his holy arm
   have gained him victory.

The LORD has made known his victory.

◆ All stand and sing **Alleluia.**

GOSPEL
Luke 12:54–59

A reading from the holy Gospel according to Luke

Jesus said to the crowds, "When you see a cloud rising in the west, you immediately say, 'It is going to rain'; and so it happens. And when you see the south wind blowing, you say, 'There will be scorching heat'; and it happens. You hypocrites! You know how to interpret the appearance of earth and sky, but why do you not know how to interpret the present time? "And why do you not judge for yourselves what is right? Thus, when you go with your accuser before a magistrate, on the way make an effort to settle the case, or you may be dragged before the judge, and the judge hand you over to the officer, and the officer throw you in prison. I tell you, you will never get out until you have paid the very last penny."

The Gospel of the Lord.

◆ All sit and observe silence.

FOR SILENT REFLECTION

Do I let anger grow for a while before I talk about it with my parents and friends? Have I forgiven others?

CLOSING PRAYER

Let us stand and bring our hopes and needs to God as we pray, "Lord, hear our prayer."

◆ All may add their own prayers here.

Let us pray: **Our Father . . . Amen.**

God our Creator,
you gave us the gift of our
bodies and minds to
act on your behalf and to
solve problems together.
Your Word tells us
to ease the burden of arguments
by talking about issues now
instead of later.
Help us to heed your signs of peace and
forgiveness in the present time.
We ask this in the name of Christ Jesus,
our Lord and Savior.

Amen.

✦ All make the Sign of the Cross.

PRAYER FOR THE WEEK

OPENING

In today's Gospel, Jesus reminds us that the humble of heart will be with him in heaven.

✠ All make the Sign of the Cross.

In the name of the Father, and of the Son, and of the Holy Spirit. Amen.

PSALM
(For a longer psalm, see page xii.) Psalm 98:1bcde, 2–3ab, 3cd–4

The LORD has made known his victory.

The LORD has made known his victory.

O sing to the LORD a new song,
    for he has done marvelous things.
His right hand and his holy arm
    have gained him victory.

The LORD has made known his victory.

◆ All stand and sing **Alleluia.**

GOSPEL
Luke 18:9–14

A reading from the holy Gospel according to Luke

Jesus told this parable to some who trusted in themselves that they were righteous and regarded others with contempt: "Two men went up to the temple to pray, one a Pharisee and the other a tax collector. The Pharisee [FAYR-uh-seez], standing by himself, was praying thus, 'God, I thank you that I am not like other people: thieves, rogues, adulterers, or even like this tax collector. I fast twice a week; I give a tenth of all my income.' But the tax collector, standing far off, would not even look up to heaven, but was beating his breast and saying, 'God, be merciful to me, a sinner!' I tell you, this man went down to his home justified rather than the other; for all who exalt themselves will be humbled, but all who humble themselves will be exalted."

The Gospel of the Lord.

◆ All sit and observe silence.

FOR SILENT REFLECTION

Have I talked and listened to God today in prayer? What does it mean to be humbled?

CLOSING PRAYER

Let us stand and bring our hopes and needs to God as we pray, "Lord, hear our prayer."

◆ All may add their own prayers here.

Let us pray: **Our Father . . . Amen.**

Lord Jesus,
we are mindful of how much we
depend on you.
You see us as we really are.
Our daily prayer should include
a look within and a humble heart.
Guide us as we examine our own actions
before judging others.
In your name we pray.

Amen.

✠ All make the Sign of the Cross.

OPENING

Today we remember Sts. Simon and Jude, two of the Twelve Apostles, both from Galilee, but who preached in lands far from their homeland. Some scholars claim they were distant relatives of Jesus. Both were martyred together in the first century. As we reflect on today's reading, we can be thankful that Sts. Simon and Jude comprise part of our Church's "foundation."

✦ All make the Sign of the Cross.

In the name of the Father, and of the Son, and of the Holy Spirit. Amen.

PSALM

(For a longer psalm, see page xii.) Psalm 98:1bcde, 2–3ab, 3cd–4

The LORD has made known his victory.

The LORD has made known his victory.

O sing to the LORD a new song,
   for he has done marvelous things.
His right hand and his holy arm
   have gained him victory.

The LORD has made known his victory.

READING

Ephesians 2:19–22

A reading from the Letter of St. Paul to the Ephesians

Brothers and sisters: You are no longer strangers and aliens, but you are citizens with saints and also members of the household of God, built upon the foundation of the apostles and prophets, with Christ Jesus himself as the cornerstone. In him the whole structure is joined together and grows into a holy temple in the Lord; in whom you also are built together spiritually into a dwelling place for God.

The Word of the Lord.

◆ All observe silence.

FOR SILENT REFLECTION

Who are the strong people in my life who serve as a cornerstone and foundation of faith? What are their qualities that influence me?

CLOSING PRAYER

Let us stand and bring our hopes and needs to God as we pray, "Lord, hear our prayer."

◆ All may add their own prayers here.

Let us pray: **Our Father . . . Amen.**

God almighty,
thank you for helping us to understand
that we are the Church,
a holy structure built upon
the foundation of the Apostles and
the prophets, with Christ as
our cornerstone.
Our faith in you is strong.
We praise you for your gift of Jesus,
his disciples, and all the saints
throughout the ages.
We pray in the name of Jesus, your Son.

Amen.

✦ All make the Sign of the Cross.

PRAYER FOR **TUESDAY** OCTOBER 29, 2013

OPENING

Today's Gospel is filled with images of expansion and new life. What other examples of growth contribute to building God's kingdom?

✚ All make the Sign of the Cross.

In the name of the Father, and of the Son, and of the Holy Spirit. Amen.

PSALM

(For a longer psalm, see page xii.) Psalm 98:1bcde, 2–3ab, 3cd–4

The Lord has made known his victory.

The Lord has made known his victory.

O sing to the Lord a new song,
    for he has done marvelous things.
His right hand and his holy arm
    have gotten him victory.

The Lord has made known his victory.

◆ All stand and sing **Alleluia.**

GOSPEL

Luke 13:18–21

A reading from the holy Gospel according to Luke

Jesus said, "What is the kingdom of God like? And to what should I compare it? It is like a mustard seed that someone took and sowed in the garden; it grew and became a tree, and the birds of the air made nests in its branches." And again he said, "To what should I compare the kingdom of God? It is like yeast that a woman took and mixed in with three measures of flour until all of it was leavened."

The Gospel of the Lord.

◆ All sit and observe silence.

FOR SILENT REFLECTION

What do you think helps the kingdom of God to grow?

CLOSING PRAYER

Let us stand and bring our hopes and needs to God as we pray, "Lord, hear our prayer."

◆ All may add their own prayers here.

Let us pray: **Our Father . . . Amen.**

God almighty,
you take the smallest of seeds
and grow them to maturity in love.
Help us to be like yeast that
expands your kingdom.
Nurture us as we discern
how your gifts of our talents and skills
can spread the joy of your goodness.
We ask this through Christ our Lord.

Amen.

✚ All make the Sign of the Cross.

HOME PRAYER
CELEBRATING THE SAINTS, REMEMBERING THE DEAD

Find the reading (1 Thessalonians 4:13–18) in your Bible, ask for a volunteer to read it, and encourage the reader to practice reading it a few times. Then gather the household in one room. You may want to light a candle to create an even more prayerful environment.

LEADER:
Saints live among us today as well as with Christ in heaven. These heroes of our faith persevere in troubled times as they follow the path of Jesus. Their unselfish actions, as well as their talents, skills, and virtuous living inspire us as they pray for us.

✦ All make the Sign of the Cross.

ALL: In the name of the Father, and of the Son, and of the Holy Spirit. Amen.

LEADER: Psalm 112: 1–6
Let us pray the Psalm response:
Happy are those who fear the Lord.

ALL: Happy are those who fear the Lord.

LEADER:
Praise the LORD!
   Happy are those who fear the LORD,
   who greatly delight in his commandments.
Their descendants will be mighty in the land;
   the generation of the upright will be
      blessed.

ALL: Happy are those who fear the Lord.

LEADER:
Wealth and riches are in their houses,
   and their righteousness endures forever.
They rise in the darkness as a light for the
      upright;
   they are gracious, merciful, and righteous.

ALL: Happy are those who fear the Lord.

LEADER: 1 Thessalonians 4:13–18
A reading from the First Letter of St. Paul to the Thessalonians

✦ Read the Scripture passage from the Bible.

The Word of the Lord.

◆ All observe a brief silence.

LEADER:
And now let us remember family members and friends who have died:

◆ The leader begins, then pauses so others may add names too.

LEADER:
Lord God,
we ask you to bring these and all
those who have gone before us
into your beloved presence.

◆ Leader pauses, then continues.

Jesus, our Savior,
you are the Source of all being.
We are grateful for our leaders in faith,
as well as our family members and friends
who are with you now in heaven.
Their goodness reveals your holy truth.
Help us to honor your Spirit within us in
everything we do.
We ask this in your name.

ALL: Amen.

✦ All make the Sign of the Cross.

CHILDREN'S DAILY PRAYER 2013–2014 © 2013 Archdiocese of Chicago: Liturgy Training Publications, 3949 South Racine Avenue, Chicago IL 60609. All rights reserved. Orders: 1-800-933-1800 or www.LTP.org. Scripture excerpts are taken from *The New Revised Standard Version Bible: Catholic Edition*, © 1989, Division of Christian Education of the National Council of the Churches of Christ in the United States of America. Used with permission. All rights reserved.

PRAYER SERVICE
FOR ALL SAINTS DAY

Prepare eight leaders for this service. The third leader will need a Bible for the scripture passages and may need help practicing the reading. You may wish to begin by singing "We Are Called," and end with "On Eagle's Wings." If the group will sing, prepare a song leader.

FIRST LEADER:
May the grace and peace of our Lord Jesus Christ be with us, now and forever.

Amen.

SECOND LEADER:
Let us pray:
Creator God,
you inspired many men and women
to serve the poor and to be your witnesses
throughout the ages.
May we be led by your great Spirit
to be your loving hands.
We ask this through Christ, our Lord.

Amen.

◆ All stand and sing **Alleluia.**

THIRD LEADER: Matthew 7:24–29
A reading from the holy Gospel according to Matthew

The Gospel of the Lord.

◆ All sit and observe silence.

FOURTH LEADER:
Lord Jesus,
help us to learn more about
the lives of saints,
our heroes,

CHILDREN'S DAILY PRAYER 2013–2014, © 2013 Archdiocese of Chicago: Liturgy Training Publications. All rights reserved. Orders: 1-800-933-1800 or www.LTP.org.

who listened and devoted their lives
to building your kingdom
here and beyond.
We pray this in your name.

Amen.

FIFTH LEADER:
Let us pray a very ancient prayer called the
Litany of the Saints,
many of whom we've learned about
in these past few months. Let us all respond
"Pray for us" after each name.

Holy Mary, Mother of God,
Queen of the Universe,

ALL: Pray for us.

SIXTH LEADER:
St. Cajetan,
saint of the unemployed,

ALL: Pray for us.

St. Dominic,
who inspired many people to
study Scripture,

ALL: Pray for us.

St. Teresa Benedicta,
also known as Edith Stein,
brilliant professor and author,

ALL: Pray for us.

St. Maximilian Kolbe,
who, while in a Nazi concentration camp,
gave his life to save another prisoner,

ALL: Pray for us.

St. Rose of Lima,
who established social services
for the poor in Peru,

ALL: Pray for us.

St. Monica,
the patient mother of Augustine,
who prayed for him to become Christian,
who later became a saint himself,

ALL: Pray for us.

St. Augustine,
who became a great writer for
the Church, and helped shape
Catholic teaching,

ALL: Pray for us.

SEVENTH LEADER:
Almighty God,
source of all that is holy;
we thank you for our heroes in faith.
May their lives continue to
inspire us to
journey toward your light.
We ask this through Christ our Lord.

Amen.

EIGHTH LEADER:
May the love of God,

✠ All make the Sign of the Cross.

Father, Son, and Holy Spirit,
draw us closer to you in this
family of faith,
now and forever.

Amen.

PRAYER FOR **WEDNESDAY** **OCTOBER 30, 2013**

OPENING

Today's reading from the Letter of St. Paul to the Romans reminds us of the power of the Holy Spirit. Even when we see negative news on TV or the Internet, we can be assured that sooner or later, "all things work together for good."

✝ All make the Sign of the Cross.

In the name of the Father, and of the Son, and of the Holy Spirit. Amen.

PSALM
(For a longer psalm, see page xii.) Psalm 98:1bcde, 2–3ab, 3cd–4

The LORD has made known his victory.

The LORD has made known his victory.

O sing to the LORD a new song,
  for he has done marvelous things.
His right hand and his holy arm
  have gained him victory.

The LORD has made known his victory.

READING
Romans 8:26–30

A reading from the Letter of St. Paul to the Romans

Brothers and sisters: Likewise the Spirit helps us in our weakness; for we do not know how to pray as we ought, but that very Spirit intercedes with sighs too deep for words. And God, who searches the heart, knows what is the mind of the Spirit, because the Spirit intercedes for the saints according to the will of God. We know that all things work together for good for those who love God, who are called according to his purpose.

For those whom he foreknew he also predestined to be conformed to the image of his Son, in order that he might be the firstborn within a large family. And those whom he predestined he also called; and those whom he called he also justified; and those whom he justified he also glorified.

The Word of the Lord.

◆ All observe silence.

FOR SILENT REFLECTION

We know that God is three persons in one: the Father, Son, and Holy Spirit. To whom in the Trinity do I pray the most? Is one easier to visualize or picture than another?

CLOSING PRAYER

Let us stand and bring our hopes and needs to God as we pray, "Lord, hear our prayer."

◆ All may add their own prayers here.

Let us pray: **Our Father . . . Amen.**

God almighty,
you are Father, Son, and Spirit,
and all things created by you are good.
You know all our thoughts and dreams.
You love us as your children and friends.
Help us to trust in this mystery as we
grow in love for the gift of
your divine being.
We ask this in your blessed name.

Amen.

✝ All make the Sign of the Cross.

OPENING

Today's reading serves as a reminder that there is no reason to worry about anything. God loves each of us so much that nothing could ever interfere in this unbelievable gift.

✤ All make the Sign of the Cross.

In the name of the Father, and of the Son, and of the Holy Spirit. Amen.

PSALM

(For a longer psalm, see page xii.) Psalm 98:1bcde, 2–3ab, 3cd–4

The LORD has made known his victory.

The LORD has made known his victory.

O sing to the LORD a new song,
  for he has done marvelous things.
His right hand and his holy arm
  have gained him victory.

The LORD has made known his victory.

READING

Romans 8:31b–35, 37–39

A reading from the Letter of St. Paul to the Romans

Brothers and sisters: If God is for us, who is against us? He who did not withhold his own Son, but gave him up for all of us, will he not with him also give us everything else? Who will bring any charge against God's elect? It is God who justifies. Who is to condemn? It is Christ Jesus, who died, yes, who was raised, who is at the right hand of God, who indeed intercedes for us. Who will separate us from the love of Christ? Will hardship, or distress, or persecution, or famine, or nakedness, or peril, or sword? No, in all these things we are more than conquerors through him who loved us. For I am convinced that neither death, nor life, nor angels, nor rulers, nor things present, nor things to come, nor powers, nor height, nor depth, nor anything else in all creation, will be able to separate us from the love of God in Christ Jesus our Lord.

The Word of the Lord.

◆ All observe silence.

FOR SILENT REFLECTION

Do I really believe that nothing could "separate us from the love of God in Christ Jesus our Lord"?

CLOSING PRAYER

Let us stand and bring our hopes and needs to God as we pray, "Lord, hear our prayer."

◆ All may add their own prayers here.

Let us pray: **Our Father . . . Amen.**

Loving Creator,
almighty God,
you are with us at all times.
May we remember that
nothing can lessen
the love that you have for us.
Guide us Lord as we attempt
to love others with the same
depth and commitment.
We ask this in the name of your Son, Jesus.

Amen.

✤ All make the Sign of the Cross.

PRAYER FOR **FRIDAY** NOVEMBER 1, 2013

OPENING

Today is the Solemnity of All Saints, when we remember all holy men and women who devoted their lives to Christ in extraordinary ways. The Church began honoring those who died for their faith as early as the fourth century.

✝ All make the Sign of the Cross.

In the name of the Father, and of the Son, and of the Holy Spirit. Amen.

PSALM

(For a longer psalm, see page xii.) Psalm 98:1bcde, 2–3ab, 3cd–4

The LORD has made known his victory.

The LORD has made known his victory.

O sing to the LORD a new song,
  for he has done marvelous things.
His right hand and his holy arm
  have gained him victory.

The LORD has made known his victory.

◆ All stand and sing **Alleluia.**

GOSPEL

Matthew 5:1–12a

A reading from the holy Gospel according to Matthew

When Jesus saw the crowds, he went up the mountain; and after he sat down, his disciples came to him. Then he began to speak, and taught them, saying: "Blessed are the poor in spirit, for theirs is the kingdom of heaven. Blessed are those who mourn, for they will be comforted. Blessed are the meek, for they will inherit the earth. Blessed are those who hunger and thirst for righteousness, for they will be filled. Blessed are the merciful, for they will receive mercy. Blessed are the pure in heart, for they will see God. Blessed are the peacemakers, for they will be called children of God. Blessed are those who are persecuted for righteousness' sake, for theirs is the kingdom of heaven. Blessed are you when people revile you and persecute you and utter all kinds of evil against you falsely on my account. Rejoice and be glad, for your reward is great in heaven, for in the same way they persecuted the prophets who were before you."

The Gospel of the Lord.

◆ All sit and observe silence.

FOR SILENT REFLECTION

Who do I know who could be considered a modern-day saint? What are their qualities?

CLOSING PRAYER

Let us stand and bring our hopes and needs to God as we pray, "Lord, hear our prayer."

◆ All may add their own prayers here.

Let us pray: **Our Father . . . Amen.**

Lord of all creation,
you give us the saints to be
our heroes of the faith.
We can learn from their example.
Help us to be merciful, humble,
and committed to serve others.
In Jesus's name we pray.

Amen.

✝ All make the Sign of the Cross.

94

OPENING

Today's Gospel highlights the story of Zacchaeus [zak-KEE-uhs], the experienced, rich tax collector, who realized he needed Jesus to be saved from his vices.

✚ All make the Sign of the Cross.

In the name of the Father, and of the Son, and of the Holy Spirit. Amen.

PSALM
(For a longer psalm, see page xii.) Psalm 98:1bcde, 2–3ab, 3cd–4

The LORD has made known his victory.

The LORD has made known his victory.

O sing to the LORD a new song,
for he has done marvelous things.
His right hand and his holy arm
have gained him victory.

The LORD has made known his victory.

◆ All stand and sing **Alleluia.**

GOSPEL
Luke 19:1–10

A reading from the holy Gospel according to Luke

Jesus entered Jericho and was passing through it. A man was there named Zacchaeus [zak-KEE-uhs]; he was a chief tax collector and was rich. He was trying to see who Jesus was, but on account of the crowd he could not, because he was short in stature. So he ran ahead and climbed a sycamore tree to see him, because he was going to pass that way. When Jesus came to the place, he looked up and said to him, "Zacchaeus, hurry and come down; for I must stay at your house today." So he hurried down and was happy to welcome him. All who saw it began to grumble and said, "He has gone to be the guest of one who is a sinner." Zacchaeus stood there and said to the Lord, "Look, half of my possessions, Lord, I will give to the poor; and if I have defrauded anyone of anything, I will pay back four times as much." Then Jesus said to him, "Today salvation has come to this house, because he too is a son of Abraham. For the Son of Man came to seek out and to save the lost."

The Gospel of the Lord.

◆ All sit and observe silence.

FOR SILENT REFLECTION

How do you imagine Zacchaeus felt when Jesus asked to come to his house?

CLOSING PRAYER

Let us stand and bring our hopes and needs to God as we pray, "Lord, hear our prayer."

◆ All may add their own prayers here.

Let us pray: **Our Father . . . Amen.**

Lord Jesus,
you show us that we cannot earn salvation.
We rely on your mercy.
Help us to surrender our lives
to you alone.
In your name we pray.

Amen.

✚ All make the Sign of the Cross.

ALSO ON THIS DAY: Diwali (Hindu festival of lights) begins

PRAYER FOR **MONDAY** NOVEMBER 4, 2013

OPENING

We remember St. Charles Borromeo, a bishop who lived in the 16th century, who helped reform the Church during the Council of Trent. He was a member of a prominent Italian family, but gave up his wealth to assist the poor and sick. During the plague and famine in 1576, he helped feed over sixty thousand people every day. Today's Gospel serves as a reminder that our gifts are not our own but are to be used for heavenly gain.

✚ All make the Sign of the Cross.

In the name of the Father, and of the Son, and of the Holy Spirit. Amen.

PSALM
(For a longer psalm, see page xii.) Psalm 98:1bcde, 2–3ab, 3cd–4

The LORD has made known his victory.

The LORD has made known his victory.

O sing to the LORD a new song,
　for he has done marvelous things.
His right hand and his holy arm
　have gained him victory.

The LORD has made known his victory.

◆ All stand and sing **Alleluia.**

GOSPEL
Luke 14:12–14

A reading from the holy Gospel according to Luke

He said also to the one who had invited him, "When you give a luncheon or a dinner, do not invite your friends or your brothers or your relatives or rich neighbors, in case they may invite you in return, and you would be repaid. But when you give a banquet, invite the poor, the crippled, the lame, and the blind. And you will be blessed, because they cannot repay you, for you will be repaid at the resurrection of the righteous."

The Gospel of the Lord.

◆ All sit and observe silence.

FOR SILENT REFLECTION

In what ways am I blessed? How am I generous with others?

CLOSING PRAYER

Let us stand and bring our hopes and needs to God as we pray, "Lord, hear our prayer."

◆ All may add their own prayers here.

Let us pray: **Our Father . . . Amen.**

Lord Jesus,
you encourage us to live our faith
as a response to your love.
We need to be hospitable with others
because we are your followers and friends,
not to gain riches in heaven.
Help us to be generous
with your gifts as we give in your name.
We ask this through Christ our Lord.

Amen.

✚ All make the Sign of the Cross.

OPENING

Today's reading provides a compelling list of qualities for living a Christian life.

✦ All make the Sign of the Cross.

In the name of the Father, and of the Son, and of the Holy Spirit. Amen.

PSALM

(For a longer psalm, see page xii.) Psalm 98:1bcde, 2–3ab, 3cd–4

The LORD has made known his victory.

The LORD has made known his victory.

O sing to the LORD a new song,
for he has done marvelous things.
His right hand and his holy arm
have gained him victory.

The LORD has made known his victory.

READING

Romans 12:5–16b

A reading from the letter of St. Paul to the Romans

Brothers and sisters: We, who are many, are one body in Christ, and individually we are members one of another. We have gifts that differ according to the grace given to us: prophecy, in proportion to faith; ministry, in ministering; the teacher, in teaching; the exhorter, in exhortation; the giver, in generosity; the leader, in diligence; the compassionate, in cheerfulness. Let love be genuine; hate what is evil, hold fast to what is good; love one another with mutual affection; outdo one another in showing honor. Do not lag in zeal, be ardent in spirit, serve the Lord. Rejoice in hope, be patient in suffering, persevere in prayer. Contribute to the needs of the saints; extend hospitality to strangers. Bless those who persecute you; bless and do not curse them. Rejoice with those who rejoice, weep with those who weep. Live in harmony with one another; do not be haughty, but associate with the lowly; do not claim to be wiser than you are.

The Word of the Lord.

◆ All observe silence.

FOR SILENT REFLECTION

How do I rejoice and weep with others? What does it mean to "outdo one another in showing honor"?

CLOSING PRAYER

Let us stand and bring our hopes and needs to God as we pray, "Lord, hear our prayer."

◆ All may add their own prayers here.

Let us pray: **Our Father . . . Amen.**

Lord Jesus,
through your servant Paul,
you ask us to live fully with
zeal and love for others.
Our talents and skills are a
reflection of your grace.
Help us to be true to these ideals
to give you all glory and honor.
We ask this in your name.

Amen.

✦ All make the Sign of the Cross.

PRAYER FOR **WEDNESDAY** NOVEMBER 6, 2013

OPENING

Today's reading challenges us to summarize all laws into one. If we follow it, we will follow all the other commandments.

✚ All make the Sign of the Cross.

In the name of the Father, and of the Son, and of the Holy Spirit. Amen.

PSALM

(For a longer psalm, see page xii.) Psalm 98:1bcde, 2–3ab, 3cd–4

The LORD has made known his victory.

The LORD has made known his victory.

O sing to the LORD a new song,
    for he has done marvelous things.
His right hand and his holy arm
    have gained him victory.

The LORD has made known his victory.

READING

Romans 13:8–10

A reading from the Letter of St. Paul to the Romans

Brothers and sisters: Owe no one anything, except to love one another; for the one who loves another has fulfilled the law. The commandments, "You shall not commit adultery; You shall not murder; You shall not steal; You shall not covet"; and any other commandment, are summed up in this word, "Love your neighbor as yourself." Love does no wrong to a neighbor; therefore, love is the fulfilling of the law.

The Word of the Lord.

◆ All observe silence.

FOR SILENT REFLECTION

When is it difficult to love my neighbor? How can I help make it easier?

CLOSING PRAYER

Let us stand and bring our hopes and needs to God as we pray, "Lord, hear our prayer."

◆ All may add their own prayers here.

Let us pray: **Our Father . . . Amen.**

Lord Jesus,
many times we're faced with
tough situations
as people say or do things that
make us mad.
Sometimes we just don't know
what to do.
You remind us to love one another,
no matter what.
Guide us to do just that,
even when we don't know how.
We ask this in your name.

Amen.

✚ All make the Sign of the Cross.

OPENING

In today's reading, St. Paul helps us to remember that Jesus is our Savor for our lives here and beyond.

✚ All make the Sign of the Cross.

In the name of the Father, and of the Son, and of the Holy Spirit. Amen.

PSALM

(For a longer psalm, see page xii.) Psalm 98:1bcde, 2–3ab, 3cd–4

The LORD has made known his victory.

The LORD has made known his victory.

O sing to the LORD a new song,
    for he has done marvelous things.
His right hand and his holy arm
    have gained him victory.

The LORD has made known his victory.

READING

Romans 14:7–12

A reading from the Letter of St. Paul to the Romans

Brothers and sisters: We do not live to ourselves, and we do not die to ourselves. If we live, we live to the Lord, and if we die, we die to the Lord; so then, whether we live or whether we die, we are the Lord's. For to this end Christ died and lived again, so that he might be Lord of both the dead and the living. Why do you pass judgment on your brother or sister? Or you, why do you despise your brother or sister? For we will all stand before the judgment seat of God. For it is written, "As I live, says the Lord, every knee shall bow to me, and every tongue shall give praise to God." So then, each of us will be accountable to God.

The Word of the Lord.

◆ All observe silence.

FOR SILENT REFLECTION

Eternity is such a perplexing thing to understand. Do I think about my life beyond my time here on earth?

CLOSING PRAYER

Let us stand and bring our hopes and needs to God as we pray, "Lord, hear our prayer."

◆ All may add their own prayers here.

Let us pray: **Our Father . . . Amen.**

Jesus Christ,
you are Son of our living God.
You are Lord of all.
Help us to not judge one another harshly,
for we are your sons and daughters,
both here and in our lives beyond
our time on earth.
We ask this in your name.

Amen.

✚ All make the Sign of the Cross.

OPENING

Today's reading fills us with wonder as we remember all the times that the Holy Spirit works through us.

✠ All make the Sign of the Cross.

In the name of the Father, and of the Son, and of the Holy Spirit. Amen.

PSALM

(For a longer psalm, see page xii.) Psalm 98:1bcde, 2–3ab, 3cd–4

The LORD has made known his victory.

The LORD has made known his victory.

O sing to the LORD a new song,
  for he has done marvelous things.
His right hand and his holy arm
  have gained him victory.

The LORD has made known his victory.

READING

Romans 15:19

A reading from the Letter of St. Paul to the Romans

I myself feel confident about you, my brothers and sisters, that you yourselves are full of goodness, filled with all knowledge, and able to instruct one another. Nevertheless on some points I have written to you rather boldly by way of reminder, because of the grace given me by God to be a minister of Christ Jesus to the Gentiles in the priestly service of the gospel of God, so that the offering of the Gentiles may be acceptable, sanctified by the Holy Spirit.

In Christ Jesus, then, I have reason to boast of my work for God. For I will not venture to speak of anything except what Christ has accomplished through me to win obedience from the Gentiles, by word and deed, by the power of signs and wonders, by the power of the Spirit of God, so that from Jerusalem and as far around as Illyricum [il-LEAR-ih-cum] I have fully proclaimed the good news of Christ.

The Word of the Lord.

◆ All observe silence.

FOR SILENT REFLECTION

When do I feel God's Spirit moving through me? With whom will I talk about these experiences?

CLOSING PRAYER

Let us stand and bring our hopes and needs to God as we pray, "Lord, hear our prayer."

◆ All may add their own prayers here.

Let us pray: **Our Father . . . Amen.**

Lord Jesus,
your Spirit moves through us,
just as it flowed through the Apostles.
Help us to proclaim your love and goodness
in words and deeds.
We ask this in your name.

Amen.

✠ All make the Sign of the Cross.

OPENING

Today's Gospel shows how Jesus was challenged by the leaders of his day to explain details about eternal life, using a situation mired with problems.

✚ All make the Sign of the Cross.

In the name of the Father, and of the Son, and of the Holy Spirit. Amen.

PSALM

(For a longer psalm, see page xii.) Psalm 98:1bcde, 2–3ab, 3cd–4

The LORD has made known his victory.

The LORD has made known his victory.

O sing to the LORD a new song,
    for he has done marvelous things.
His right hand and his holy arm
    have gained him victory.

The LORD has made known his victory.

◆ All stand and sing **Alleluia.**

GOSPEL

Luke 20:17–36

A reading from the holy Gospel according to Luke

Some Sadducees [SAD-yoo-seez], those who say there is no resurrection, came to him and asked him a question, "Teacher, Moses wrote for us that if a man's brother dies, leaving a wife but no children, the man shall marry the widow and raise up children for his brother. Now there were seven brothers; the first married, and died childless; then the second and the third married her, and so in the same way all seven died childless. Finally the woman also died. In the resurrection, therefore, whose wife will the woman be? For the seven had married her." Jesus said to them, "Those who belong to this age marry and are given in marriage; but those who are considered worthy of a place in that age and in the resurrection of the dead neither marry nor are given in marriage. Indeed they cannot die anymore, because they are like angels and are children of God, being children of the resurrection."

The Gospel of the Lord.

◆ All sit and observe silence.

FOR SILENT REFLECTION

Where do I see God in our world today? God's appearance may not be as dramatic as what Moses saw in the burning bush, but do you see signs of our Creator at work?

CLOSING PRAYER

Let us stand and bring our hopes and needs to God as we pray, "Lord, hear our prayer."

◆ All may add their own prayers here.

Let us pray: **Our Father . . . Amen.**

God almighty,
we marvel at how
Jesus spoke your truth on matters of
everyday life.
Guide us in our complicated lives,
when we don't know where to go,
when it seems there are no easy answers.
We ask this through Christ our Lord.

Amen.

✚ All make the Sign of the Cross.

PRAYER FOR **MONDAY** NOVEMBER 11, 2013

OPENING

Today we remember St. Martin of Tours, who was born of pagan parents and raised in Italy. His father forced him to serve in the army at the age of 15. He expressed a deep desire to become a Christian and was baptized three years later.

✛ All make the Sign of the Cross.

In the name of the Father, and of the Son, and of the Holy Spirit. Amen.

PSALM

(For a longer psalm, see page xii.) Psalm 98:1bcde, 2–3ab, 3cd–4

The LORD has made known his victory.

The LORD has made known his victory.

O sing to the LORD a new song,
 for he has done marvelous things.
His right hand and his holy arm
 have gained him victory.

The LORD has made known his victory.

◆ All stand and sing **Alleluia.**

GOSPEL

Luke 17:1–6

A reading from the holy Gospel according to Luke

Jesus said to his disciples, "Occasions for stumbling are bound to come, but woe to anyone by whom they come! It would be better for you if a millstone were hung around your neck and you were thrown into the sea than for you to cause one of these little ones to stumble. Be on your guard! If another disciple sins, you must rebuke the offender, and if there is repentance, you must forgive. And if the same person sins against you seven times a day, and turns back to you seven times and says, 'I repent,' you must forgive." The apostles said to the Lord, "Increase our faith!" The Lord replied, "If you had faith the size of a mustard seed, you could say to this mulberry tree, 'Be uprooted and planted in the sea,' and it would obey you."

The Gospel of the Lord.

◆ All sit and observe silence.

FOR SILENT REFLECTION

Why do you think that even a little faith can be so powerful?

CLOSING PRAYER

Let us stand and bring our hopes and needs to God as we pray, "Lord, hear our prayer."

◆ All may add their own prayers here.

Let us pray: **Our Father . . . Amen.**

Jesus, Son of our eternal Father,
help us to take care to
nurture our faith,
just as we exercise our bodies and minds.
Help us to enrich our prayer life
to give honor to your power on earth.
We ask this in your name.

Amen.

✛ All make the Sign of the Cross.

ALSO ON THIS DAY: Veterans Day (U.S.A.); Remembrance Day (Canada)

102

OPENING

Today we remember St. Josaphat, who lived during a turbulent time in Church history. Today's reading, often proclaimed at funeral Masses, gives us hope in eternal life with our Savior.

✝ All make the Sign of the Cross.

In the name of the Father, and of the Son, and of the Holy Spirit. Amen.

PSALM

(For a longer psalm, see page xii.) Psalm 98:1bcde, 2–3ab, 3cd–4

The LORD has made known his victory.

The LORD has made known his victory.

O sing to the LORD a new song,
    for he has done marvelous things.
His right hand and his holy arm
    have gained him victory.

The LORD has made known his victory.

READING

Wisdom 2:23–24; 3:1–6, 9

A reading from the Book of Wisdom

God created us for incorruption, and made us in the image of his own eternity, but through the devil's envy death entered the world, and those who belong to his company experience it. But the souls of the righteous are in the hand of God, and no torment will ever touch them. In the eyes of the foolish they seemed to have died, and their departure was thought to be a disaster, and their going from us to be there destruction; but they are at peace. For though in the sight of others they were punished, their hope is full of immortality. Having been disciplined a little, they will receive great good, because God tested them and found them worthy of himself; like gold in the furnace he tried them and like a sacrificial burnt offering he accepted them. In the time of their visitation they will shine forth. Those who trust in him will understand truth, and the faithful will abide with him in love, because grace and mercy are upon his holy ones, and he watches over his elect.

The Word of the Lord.

◆ All observe silence.

FOR SILENT REFLECTION

How does this reading inspire me with its comforting words?

CLOSING PRAYER

Let us stand and bring our hopes and needs to God as we pray, "Lord, hear our prayer."

◆ All may add their own prayers here.

Let us pray: **Our Father . . . Amen.**

God almighty,
you rule over all
the living and the dead.
We desire to be with you in heaven,
and we know that your justice will prevail.
You give us hope in the Resurrection
and in life everlasting.
We pray in the name of Jesus, your son.

Amen.

✝ All make the Sign of the Cross.

PRAYER FOR **WEDNESDAY** NOVEMBER 13, 2013

OPENING

Today we remember St. Frances Xavier [ZAY-vee-uhr] Cabrini, the first United States citizen to be canonized. She grew up in Italy in the 1850s, ministered in orphanages, and later became a religious sister. She was named prioress of the Missionary Sisters of the Sacred Heart and was asked to go to the United States to set up an orphanage. After many struggles, she founded 67 institutions that serve the poor and the abandoned, many in inner cities. In today's reading, we learn about warnings for those in power. We're challenged to consider how those in positions of authority may have no influence in the next life.

✜ All make the Sign of the Cross.

In the name of the Father, and of the Son, and of the Holy Spirit. Amen.

PSALM

(For a longer psalm, see page xii.) Psalm 98:1bcde, 2–3ab, 3cd–4

The LORD has made known his victory.

The LORD has made known his victory.

O sing to the LORD a new song,
  for he has done marvelous things.
His right hand and his holy arm
  have gained him victory.

The LORD has made known his victory.

READING

Wisdom 6:1–3, 10–11

A reading from the Book of Wisdom

Listen there, O kings, and understand; learn, O judges of the ends of the earth. Give ear, you that rule over multitudes, and boast of many nations. For your dominion was given you from the Lord, and your sovereignty from the Most High; he will search out your works and inquire into your plans. For they will be made holy who observe holy things in holiness, and those who have been taught them will find a defense. Therefore set your desire on my words; long for them, and you will be instructed.

The Word of the Lord.

◆ All observe silence.

FOR SILENT REFLECTION

Who are the powerful in our world? Are there examples of how those in high places may work for God's glory and not their own?

CLOSING PRAYER

Let us stand and bring our hopes and needs to God as we pray, "Lord, hear our prayer."

◆ All may add their own prayers here.

Let us pray: **Our Father . . . Amen.**

God almighty,
you advise the powerful
to direct their strength to
your purpose.
Help us Lord
to know your supreme laws of love.
Guide us with your
loving holiness.
We ask this through Christ our Lord.

Amen.

✜ All make the Sign of the Cross.

OPENING

Today's Gospel is a challenge to look no further than inward to discover where God dwells.

✛ All make the Sign of the Cross.

In the name of the Father, and of the Son, and of the Holy Spirit. Amen.

PSALM

(For a longer psalm, see page xii.) Psalm 98:1bcde, 2–3ab, 3cd–4

The LORD has made known his victory.

The LORD has made known his victory.

O sing to the LORD a new song,
    for he has done marvelous things.
His right hand and his holy arm
    have gained him victory.

The LORD has made known his victory.

◆ All stand and sing **Alleluia.**

GOSPEL

Luke 17:20–25

A reading from the holy Gospel according to Luke

Once Jesus was asked by the Pharisees when the kingdom of God was coming, and he answered, "The kingdom of God is not coming with things that can be observed; nor will they say, 'Look, here it is!' or 'There it is!' For, in fact, the kingdom of God is among you." Then he said to the disciples, "The days are coming when you will long to see one of the days of the Son of Man, and you will not see it. They will say to you, 'Look there!' or 'Look here!' Do not go, do not set off in pursuit. For as the lightning flashes and lights up the sky from one side to the other, so will the Son of Man be in his day. But first he must endure much suffering and be rejected by this generation."

The Gospel of the Lord.

◆ All sit and observe silence.

FOR SILENT REFLECTION

What do I see when I look inward to find God?

CLOSING PRAYER

Let us stand and bring our hopes and needs to God as we pray, "Lord, hear our prayer."

◆ All may add their own prayers here.

Let us pray: **Our Father . . . Amen.**

Lord Jesus,
you tells us that the
"kingdom of God is among you,"
that it is within each of us.
Help us to look within
to discover your love.
May we find kindness,
gentleness, understanding,
prayer, forgiveness, and peace.
Guide us to be your presence
here and now.
We ask this in your name.

Amen.

✛ All make the Sign of the Cross.

PRAYER FOR **FRIDAY** NOVEMBER 15, 2013

OPENING

Today we remember St. Albert the Great, a Doctor of the Church, who is the patron saint of scientists and philosophers. He was born in Germany in the 13th century. He wrote several books on a variety of subjects such as natural science, logic, mathematics, astronomy, and politics. Thomas Aquinas was one of his cherished students. Today's Gospel asks us to seek first God's kingdom, rather than the ideals of this world.

✚ All make the Sign of the Cross.

In the name of the Father, and of the Son, and of the Holy Spirit. Amen.

PSALM
(For a longer psalm, see page xii.) Psalm 98:1bcde, 2–3ab, 3cd–4

The LORD has made known his victory.

The LORD has made known his victory.

O sing to the LORD a new song,
  for he has done marvelous things.
His right hand and his holy arm
  have gained him victory.

The LORD has made known his victory.

◆ All stand and sing **Alleluia.**

GOSPEL
Luke 17:26–27, 31–35

A reading from the holy Gospel according to Luke

Jesus said to his disciples: "Just as it was in the days of Noah, so too it will be in the days of the Son of Man. They were eating and drinking, and marrying and being given in marriage, until the day Noah entered the ark, and the flood came and destroyed all of them. On that day, anyone on the housetop who has belongings in the house must not come down to take them away; and likewise anyone in the field must not turn back. Remember Lot's wife. Those who try to make their life secure will lose it, but those who lose their life will keep it. I tell you, on that night there will be two in one bed; one will be taken and the other left. There will be two women grinding meal together; one will be taken and the other left."

The Gospel of the Lord.

◆ All sit and observe silence.

FOR SILENT REFLECTION

How can I take care of my health, studies, and spiritual life so that I can reflect the life of Jesus among my family and friends?

CLOSING PRAYER

Let us stand and bring our hopes and needs to God as we pray, "Lord, hear our prayer."

◆ All may add their own prayers here.

Let us pray: **Our Father . . . Amen.**

Jesus, Son of God,
you remind us
that we need to focus on your will.
Keep us humble, Lord,
as we make our way to you
with a servant heart.
We ask this in your name.

Amen.

✚ All make the Sign of the Cross.

106

OPENING

Today's Gospel is filled with images of calamity and destruction, but Jesus instills in us a reason for hope and life everlasting.

✝ All make the Sign of the Cross.

In the name of the Father, and of the Son, and of the Holy Spirit. Amen.

PSALM

(For a longer psalm, see page xii.) Psalm 98:1bcde, 2–3ab, 3cd–4

The LORD has made known his victory.

The LORD has made known his victory.

O sing to the LORD a new song,
    for he has done marvelous things.
His right hand and his holy arm
    have gained him victory.

The LORD has made known his victory.

◆ All stand and sing **Alleluia.**

GOSPEL

Luke 21:5–9, 18–19

A reading from the holy Gospel according to Luke

When some were speaking about the temple, how it was adorned with beautiful stones and gifts dedicated to God, Jesus said, "As for these things that you see, the days will come when not one stone will be left upon another; all will be thrown down." They asked him, "Teacher, when will this be, and what will be the sign that this is about to take place?" And he said, "Beware that you are not led astray; for many will come in my name and say, 'I am he!' and,

'The time is near!' Do not go after them. When you hear of wars and insurrections, do not be terrified; for these things must take place first, but the end will not follow immediately. But not a hair of your head will perish. By your endurance you will gain your souls."

The Gospel of the Lord.

◆ All sit and observe silence.

FOR SILENT REFLECTION

Did you hear how Jesus asks us to trust that he will care for us? How do we trust in Jesus?

CLOSING PRAYER

Let us stand and bring our hopes and needs to God as we pray, "Lord, hear our prayer."

◆ All may add their own prayers here.

Let us pray: **Our Father . . . Amen.**

Lord of the universe,
you tell us not to fear.
You remind us of how we will face
tough times in our lives.
You will fill us with wisdom that
stands up against enemies.
May we be courageous with our faith.
May we remember that "not a hair"
on our heads will perish.
In your name we pray.

Amen.

✝ All make the Sign of the Cross.

PRAYER FOR **MONDAY**
NOVEMBER 18, 2013

OPENING

Today we remember the Dedication of the Basilicas of Sts. Peter and Paul in Rome. Both of these sites stand over the place where each of the Apostles was martyred.

✚ All make the Sign of the Cross.

> **In the name of the Father, and of the Son, and of the Holy Spirit. Amen.**

PSALM
(For a longer psalm, see page xii.) Psalm 98:1bcde, 2–3ab, 3cd–4

The LORD has made known his victory.

The LORD has made known his victory.

O sing to the LORD a new song,
   for he has done marvelous things.
His right hand and his holy arm
   have gained him victory.

The LORD has made known his victory.

◆ All stand and sing **Alleluia.**

GOSPEL
Matthew 14:22–27

A reading from the holy Gospel according to Matthew

Jesus made the disciples get into the boat and go on ahead to the other side, while he dismissed the crowds. And after he had dismissed the crowds, he went up the mountain by himself to pray. When evening came, he was there alone, but by this time the boat, battered by the waves, was far from the land, for the wind was against them. And early in the morning he came walking toward them on the sea. But when the disciples saw him walking on the sea, they were terrified, saying, "It is a ghost!" And they cried out in fear. But immediately Jesus spoke to them and said, "Take heart, it is I; do not be afraid."

The Gospel of the Lord.

◆ All sit and observe silence.

FOR SILENT REFLECTION

How does trusting in God help us when we face stormy seas or difficult times?

CLOSING PRAYER

Let us stand and bring our hopes and needs to God as we pray, "Lord, hear our prayer."

◆ All may add their own prayers here.

Let us pray: **Our Father . . . Amen.**

Lord Jesus,
your friends were astounded as
they saw you walking on water.
When Peter focused on you,
he was able to do astounding things.
May we recognize you
in the waves of our lives.
May we have faith strong enough
to join you in the storm,
wherever it may lead.
We ask this in your name.

Amen.

✚ All make the Sign of the Cross.

OPENING

In today's Gospel, we see Zacchaeus [zak-KEE-uhs]. His reputation was not the best, yet Jesus chose to spend time with him.

✝ All make the Sign of the Cross.

In the name of the Father, and of the Son, and of the Holy Spirit. Amen.

PSALM

(For a longer psalm, see page xii.) Psalm 98:1bcde, 2–3ab, 3cd–4

The LORD has made known his victory.

The LORD has made known his victory.

O sing to the LORD a new song,
   for he has done marvelous things.
His right hand and his holy arm
   have gained him victory.

The LORD has made known his victory.

◆ All stand and sing **Alleluia.**

GOSPEL

Luke 19:1–10

A reading from the holy Gospel according to Luke

He entered Jericho and was passing through it. A man was there named Zacchaeus [zak-KEE-uhs]; he was a chief tax collector and was rich. He was trying to see who Jesus was, but on account of the crowd he could not, because he was short in stature. So he ran ahead and climbed a sycamore tree to see him, because he was going to pass that way. When Jesus came to the place, he looked up and said to him, "Zacchaeus, hurry and come down; for I must stay at your house today." So he hurried down and was happy to welcome him. All who saw it began to grumble and said, "He has gone to be the guest of one who is a sinner." Zacchaeus stood there and said to the Lord, "Look, half of my possessions, Lord, I will give to the poor; and if I have defrauded anyone of anything, I will pay back four times as much." Then Jesus said to him, "Today salvation has come to this house, because he too is a son of Abraham. For the Son of Man came to seek out and to save the lost."

The Gospel of the Lord.

◆ All sit and observe silence.

FOR SILENT REFLECTION

Why do you think the people were surprised when Jesus asked to stay with Zacchaeus?

CLOSING PRAYER

Let us stand and bring our hopes and needs to God as we pray, "Lord, hear our prayer."

◆ All may add their own prayers here.

Let us pray: **Our Father . . . Amen.**

Lord almighty,
you chose to share a meal with
the ones whom others shunned.
Help us to recognize that
you love all people.
Help us to learn from your example.
We ask this in your name.

Amen.

✝ All make the Sign of the Cross.

PRAYER FOR **WEDNESDAY** NOVEMBER 20, 2013

OPENING

Today's Gospel asks us to consider how best to use our resources of talents, skills, time, and money.

✚ All make the Sign of the Cross.

In the name of the Father, and of the Son, and of the Holy Spirit. Amen.

PSALM

(For a longer psalm, see page xii.) Psalm 98:1bcde, 2–3ab, 3cd–4

The LORD has made known his victory.

The LORD has made known his victory.

O sing to the LORD a new song,
for he has done marvelous things.
His right hand and his holy arm
have gained him victory.

The LORD has made known his victory.

◆ All stand and sing **Alleluia.**

GOSPEL

Luke 19:12–13, 15–26

A reading from the holy Gospel according to Luke

So Jesus said, "A nobleman went to a distant country to get royal power for himself and then return. He summoned ten of his slaves, and gave them ten pounds, and said to them, 'Do business with these until I come back.' When he returned, he ordered these slaves, to be summoned. The first came forward and said, 'Lord, your pound has made ten more pounds.' He said to him, 'Well done, good slave! Because you have been trustworthy in a

very small thing, take charge of ten cities.' Then the second came, saying, 'Lord, your pound has made five pounds.' He said to him, 'And you, rule over five cities.' Then the other came, saying, 'Lord, here is your pound. I wrapped it up in a piece of cloth, for I was afraid of you, because you are a harsh man. He said to him, 'Why then did you not put my money into the bank? Then when I returned, I could have collected it with interest.' He said to the bystanders, 'Take the pound from him and give it to the one who has ten pounds.' I tell you, to all those who have, more will be given; but from those who have nothing, even what they have will be taken away."

The Gospel of the Lord.

◆ All sit and observe silence.

FOR SILENT REFLECTION

Why should we develop our talents?

CLOSING PRAYER

Let us stand and bring our hopes and needs to God as we pray, "Lord, hear our prayer."

◆ All may add their own prayers here.

Let us pray: **Our Father . . . Amen.**

Lord Jesus,
guide us to make wise choices.
Help us to decide
to grow your kingdom of believers.
We ask this in your name.

Amen.

✚ All make the Sign of the Cross.

OPENING

Today we remember the Presentation of the Blessed Virgin Mary. This is a feast that honors the time when Mary's parents, Anna and Joachim [JOH-uh-kim], offered Mary to God in the temple when she was a child. This fulfilled a promise Anna made to God when she was unable to bear children for a time. Today's Gospel reveals Jesus's feelings about an entire community. Listen as he predicts what will happen to more than one generation.

◆ All make the Sign of the Cross.

In the name of the Father, and of the Son, and of the Holy Spirit. Amen.

PSALM
(For a longer psalm, see page xii.) Psalm 98:1bcde, 2–3ab, 3cd–4

The Lord has made known his victory.

The Lord has made known his victory.

O sing to the Lord a new song,
 for he has done marvelous things.
His right hand and his holy arm
 have gained him victory.

The Lord has made known his victory.

◆ All stand and sing **Alleluia.**

GOSPEL
Luke 19:41–44

A reading from the holy Gospel according to Luke

As Jesus came near and saw the city, he wept over it, saying, "If you, even you, had only recognized on this day the things that make for peace! But now they are hidden from your eyes. Indeed, the days will come upon you, when your enemies will set up ramparts around you and surround you, and hem you in on every side. They will crush you to the ground, you and your children within you, and they will not leave within you one stone upon another; because you did not recognize the time of your visitation from God."

The Gospel of the Lord.

◆ All sit and observe silence.

FOR SILENT REFLECTION

How can we recognize the "things that make for peace"? What makes for peace in my life?

CLOSING PRAYER

Let us stand and bring our hopes and needs to God as we pray, "Lord, hear our prayer."

◆ All may add their own prayers here.

Let us pray: **Our Father . . . Amen.**

Lord Jesus,
you wept over
an entire city that neglected to
recognize the Son of God in their midst.
May we appreciate
your presence all around us
and within us.
May we pray for those who
need the guidance of your Spirit.
We ask this in your name.

Amen.

◆ All make the Sign of the Cross.

PRAYER FOR **FRIDAY**
NOVEMBER 22, 2013

OPENING

Today we remember St. Cecilia, born in Rome in the second century, and who is the patron saint of musicians and Church music. Some scholars have written that she sang to God as she was martyred with her husband and his brother. Today's Gospel shows Jesus protecting his house of worship while leaders plotted to kill him.

◆ All make the Sign of the Cross.

In the name of the Father, and of the Son, and of the Holy Spirit. Amen.

PSALM
(For a longer psalm, see page xii.) Psalm 98:1bcde, 2–3ab, 3cd–4

The LORD has made known his victory.

The LORD has made known his victory.

O sing to the LORD a new song,
    for he has done marvelous things.
His right hand and his holy arm
    have gained him victory.

The LORD has made known his victory.

◆ All stand and sing **Alleluia.**

GOSPEL
Luke 19:45–48

A reading from the holy Gospel according to Luke

Then Jesus entered the temple and began to drive out those who were selling things there; and he said, "It is written, 'My house shall be a house of prayer'; but you have made it a den of robbers." Every day he was teaching in the temple. The chief priests, the scribes, and the leaders of the people kept looking for a way to kill him; but they did not find anything they could do, for all the people were spellbound by what they heard.

The Gospel of the Lord.

◆ All sit and observe silence.

FOR SILENT REFLECTION

Do you see injustice happening within your community? What can you do to help solve the problem(s)?

CLOSING PRAYER

Let us stand and bring our hopes and needs to God as we pray, "Lord, hear our prayer."

◆ All may add their own prayers here.

Let us pray: **Our Father . . . Amen.**

Lord Jesus,
your house was meant for prayer,
for worshiping our Creator.
Help us to be just as committed to
keeping sacred your creation,
and all that you have
deemed to be good.
Keep us true to your teaching
of loving God above all things,
and loving our neighbors as ourselves.
We ask this in your name.

Amen.

✚ All make the Sign of the Cross.

OPENING

Today is the Solemnity of Our Lord Jesus Christ, King of the Universe.

✝ All make the Sign of the Cross.

In the name of the Father, and of the Son, and of the Holy Spirit. Amen.

PSALM

(For a longer psalm, see page xii.) Psalm 98:1bcde, 2–3ab, 3cd–4

The LORD has made known his victory.

The LORD has made known his victory.

O sing to the LORD a new song,
  for he has done marvelous things.
His right hand and his holy arm
  have gained him victory.

The LORD has made known his victory.

◆ All stand and sing **Alleluia.**

GOSPEL

Luke 23:35–43

A reading from the holy Gospel according to Luke

And the people stood by, watching; but the leaders scoffed at him, saying, "He saved others; let him save himself if he is the Messiah of God, his chosen one!" The soldiers also mocked him, coming up and offering him sour wine, and saying, "If you are the King of the Jews, save yourself!" There was also an inscription over him, "This is the King of the Jews." One of the criminals who were hanged there kept deriding him and saying, "Are you not the Messiah? Save yourself and us!" But the other rebuked him, saying, "Do you not fear God, since you are under the same sentence of condemnation? And we indeed have been condemned justly, for we are getting what we deserve for our deeds, but this man has done nothing wrong." Then he said, "Jesus, remember me when you come into your kingdom." He replied, "Truly I tell you, today you will be with me in Paradise."

The Gospel of the Lord.

◆ All sit and observe silence.

FOR SILENT REFLECTION

How do you think the criminal felt when Jesus promised him that he would be in Paradise? What Kind of king is Jesus?

CLOSING PRAYER

Let us stand and bring our hopes and needs to God as we pray, "Lord, hear our prayer."

◆ All may add their own prayers here.

Let us pray: **Our Father . . . Amen.**

Lord Jesus,
you suffered unjustly
even though you were the
Son of God and the King of the Universe.
Guide us toward your presence
in Paradise, your eternal kingdom.
We ask this in your name.

Amen.

✝ All make the Sign of the Cross.

PRAYER FOR **MONDAY** NOVEMBER 25, 2013

OPENING

Today we remember St. Catherine of Alexandria, who was the beautiful daughter of a pagan king and queen in the early fourth century. As a young adult, she convinced leaders to become Christian, which angered the emperor Maxentius [max-EN-ti-us]. He put her in prison and eventually to death. In today's Gospel, Jesus describes how a poor widow contributed more generously than others who were rich. As you hear this Scripture reading proclaimed, think about whether Jesus is only talking about financial abundance.

✢ All make the Sign of the Cross.

In the name of the Father, and of the Son, and of the Holy Spirit. Amen.

PSALM (For a longer psalm, see page xii.) Psalm 98:1bcde, 2–3ab, 3cd–4

The LORD has made known his victory.

The LORD has made known his victory.

O sing to the LORD a new song,
    for he has done marvelous things.
His right hand and his holy arm
    have gained him victory.

The LORD has made known his victory.

◆ All stand and sing **Alleluia.**

GOSPEL Luke 21:1–4

A reading from the holy Gospel according to Luke

Jesus looked up and saw rich people putting their gifts into the treasury; he also saw a poor widow put in two small copper coins. He said, "Truly I tell you, this poor widow has put in more than all of them; for all of them have contributed out of their abundance, but she out of her poverty has put in all she had to live on."

The Gospel of the Lord.

◆ All sit and observe silence.

FOR SILENT REFLECTION

Why is the poor woman's contribution so important? What does she teach us about giving or sharing our resources?

CLOSING PRAYER

Let us stand and bring our hopes and needs to God as we pray, "Lord, hear our prayer."

◆ All may add their own prayers here.

Let us pray: **Our Father . . . Amen.**

Lord Jesus,
help us to appreciate
the gifts you have given to us
and to share them with others.
Help us to remember that even the smallest
of gifts can be a great
offering to you.
We ask this in your name.

Amen.

✢ All make the Sign of the Cross.

OPENING

Today's reading shows a dream that the prophet Daniel interprets for a king who wants to conquer many lands and people. See what happens to the king's plans to build his own empire of glory.

✚ All make the Sign of the Cross.

In the name of the Father, and of the Son, and of the Holy Spirit. Amen.

PSALM

(For a longer psalm, see page xii.) Psalm 98:1bcde, 2–3ab, 3cd–4

The LORD has made known his victory.

The LORD has made known his victory.

O sing to the LORD a new song,
  for he has done marvelous things.
His right hand and his holy arm
  have gained him victory.

The LORD has made known his victory.

READING

Daniel 2:31–35

A reading from the Book of Daniel

"You were looking, O king, and lo! there was a great statue. This statue was huge, its brilliance extraordinary; it was standing before you, and its appearance was frightening. The head of that statue was of fine gold, its chest and arms of silver, its middle and thighs of bronze, its legs of iron, its feet partly of iron and partly of clay. As you looked on, a stone was cut out, not by human hands, and it struck the statue on its feet of iron and clay and broke them in pieces. Then the iron, the clay, the bronze, the silver, and the gold, were all broken in pieces and became like the chaff of the summer threshing floors; and the wind carried them away, so that not a trace of them could be found. But the stone that struck the statue became a great mountain and filled the whole earth."

The Word of the Lord.

◆ All observe silence.

FOR SILENT REFLECTION

What happens when people try to control everything in their lives without keeping God in their plans?

CLOSING PRAYER

Let us stand and bring our hopes and needs to God as we pray, "Lord, hear our prayer."

◆ All may add their own prayers here.

Let us pray: **Our Father . . . Amen.**

God, King of the universe,
throughout all of time, you are the one
who has been Lord over all.
All of creation was made
to serve you.
May we continue to pray to you
to learn more about your will.
May we look to the life of your Son Jesus
as a guide for living.
We ask this through Christ our Lord.

Amen.

✚ All make the Sign of the Cross.

PRAYER SERVICE
FOR THANKSGIVING

Prepare seven leaders for this service. The fourth leader will need a Bible to read the Gospel passage and may need help finding and practicing the reading. You may want to begin by singing "One Bread, One Body," and end with "Table of Plenty." If the group will sing, prepare a song leader.

FIRST LEADER:

✚ All make the Sign of the Cross.

In the name of the Father, and of the Son, and of the Holy Spirit. Amen.

Let us pray:
Almighty God,
you bless us every day with the
signs and wonders of your creation.
We thank you for the fresh air,
trees, stars, and planets, as well as
all the animals and creatures that live on
land and in the sea.
We are grateful that you have entrusted us
with care of your environment.

SECOND LEADER: Psalm 136:1–9

Our refrain is: For his steadfast love endures forever.

ALL: For his steadfast love endures forever.

LEADER: O give thanks to the Lord, for he is good,

ALL: For his steadfast love endures forever;

LEADER: Who alone does great wonders,

ALL: For his steadfast love endures forever;

LEADER: Who by understanding made the heavens,

ALL: For his steadfast love endures forever;

CHILDREN'S DAILY PRAYER 2013–2014, © 2013 Archdiocese of Chicago: Liturgy Training Publications. All rights reserved. Orders: 1-800-933-1800 or www.LTP.org.

LEADER: Who spread out the earth on the waters,

ALL: For his steadfast love endures forever;

LEADER: Who made the great lights,

ALL: For his steadfast love endures forever;

LEADER: The sun to rule over the day,

ALL: For his steadfast love endures forever;

LEADER: The moon and stars to rule over the night,

ALL: For his steadfast love endures forever.

THIRD LEADER:
Creator God,
your presence is with us
today and always.
We are grateful for the
gift of your Son Jesus,
who lived and walked among us,
and whose Spirit fills our hearts
with gratitude and joy.

ALL: Amen.

FOURTH LEADER: 1 John 4:7–16
A reading from the First Letter of John

◆ Read the Scripture passage from the Bible.

The Word of the Lord

FIFTH LEADER: Psalm 100:1–5
Our refrain is: Make a joyful noise to the Lord.

ALL: Make a joyful noise to the Lord.

LEADER: Make a joyful noise to the Lord, all the earth,
Worship the Lord with gladness;
Come into his presence with singing.

ALL: Make a joyful noise to the Lord.

LEADER: Know that the Lord is God.
It is he that made us, and we are his;
We are his people, and the sheep of his pasture.

ALL: Make a joyful noise to the Lord.

LEADER: Enter his gates with thanksgiving,
and his courts with praise.
Give thanks to him, bless his name.

ALL: Make a joyful noise to the Lord.

SIXTH LEADER:
Loving God,
we thank you for all that you
provide for us.
We are grateful for all the loved ones
in our lives now,
and those who have gone before us.
You nurture us in so many ways.
May we always remember to praise you
and love others as you love us.
We ask this through Christ our Lord.

SEVENTH LEADER:
May the love of God,

✝ All make the Sign of the Cross.

Father, Son, and Holy Spirit,
always surround us in faith,
now and forever.

ALL: Amen.

HOME PRAYER
MEAL PRAYER FOR THANKSGIVING

Find the reading (John 15:12–17) in your Bible, ask for a volunteer to read the Scripture passage, and encourage the reader to practice reading it a few times. If practical, light candles for your Thanksgiving table. You may wish to begin with a simple song of thanksgiving or a favorite "Alleluia." Then an older child or an adult reads the leader parts.

LEADER:
Almighty God,
look at the abundance here before us!
It fills us with joy and gratitude.
Let us begin our prayer with the Sign of the
    Cross.

✝ All make the Sign of the Cross.

**In the name of the Father, and of the
Son, and of the Holy Spirit. Amen.**

◆ All stand and sing **Alleluia.**

READER: John 15:12–17
A reading from the holy Gospel according to
John

◆ Read the Gospel passage from the Bible.

The Gospel of the Lord.

◆ All sit and observe silence.

LEADER:
We come to this table,
grateful for the delicious meal we're about to
share,
as well as the family and friends who
surround us here.
Let us pray:
Heavenly Father,
we thank you for the love and friendship
that envelops us today.
Help us to nurture one another
with your peace and serenity in the
midst of our busy lives.
We thank all those who helped prepare
this meal.
We are mindful of people in our community
and
in other regions who may not have enough to
eat today.
May we appreciate all that you provide for us
now, and
we look forward to our heavenly banquet
with you.
We ask this through our Lord Jesus Christ,
your Son, who lives and reigns with you
in the unity of the Holy Spirit, one God,
for ever and ever.

ALL: Amen.

✝ All make the Sign of the Cross.

118 CHILDREN'S DAILY PRAYER 2013–2014, © 2013 Archdiocese of Chicago: Liturgy Training Publications, 3949 South Racine Avenue, Chicago IL 60609. All rights reserved. Orders: 1-800-933-1800 or www.LTP.org. Scripture excerpts are taken from *The New Revised Standard Version Bible: Catholic Edition*, copyright © 1989, Division of Christian Education of the National Council of the Churches of Christ in the United States of America. Used with permission. All rights reserved.

HOME PRAYER

GATHERING AROUND AN ADVENT WREATH FOR PRAYER

Saturday evening before the First Sunday of Advent, gather the household around the wreath. Point out that the wreath is circular, with no beginning or end, like God's love. Explain that there are four candles, one for each Sunday of Advent. The third candle is rose because on the third Sunday we celebrate the joy of waiting for Christmas.

Use this service the first time you light your wreath and then on the following three Sundays when you light each new candle after the Psalm Response.

During the first week of Advent, light the first violet candle. During the second week of Advent, light two violet candles. For the third week, light two violet candles and one rose candle. During the final week of Advent, light all four candles. For your weekday celebration, simply light the candle(s), read one verse from Isaiah 40: 1–5 and 9–11 (choose a different verse each time), and then say grace.

Before you begin, find the reading (John 1:1–5) in your Bible, ask a volunteer to read it, and encourage the reader to practice reading it a few times.

You may wish to begin with a simple Advent song, such as "O Come, O Come, Emmanuel," or "Soon and Very Soon." Then an older child or adult reads the leader parts.

LEADER:

Since ancient times, people have marked the passage of time with the light of the sun. In this holy season of Advent, we observe the passage of time through the light of this wreath, for each candle represents another week closer to the radiance of the newborn Son Jesus. Our anticipation for his glorious arrival can teach us much about patience as well as sharing the flame of our faith. So let us begin our time of prayer with the Sign of the Cross:

✦ All make the Sign of the Cross.

ALL: In the name of the Father, and of the Son, and of the Holy Spirit. Amen.

◆ Light the candle(s). Then all stand and sing Alleluia.

READER: John 1:1–5

A reading from the holy Gospel according to John

✦ Read the Gospel passage from the Bible.

The Gospel of the Lord.

◆ All sit and observe silence.

LEADER:

God our Creator,
bless us as we gather around this Advent wreath,
ever anxious for the arrival of your Son, Jesus.
Renew us with your patience and
the light of your promise.
Help us to prepare our hearts
so that we are open to
your coming into our lives.
We ask this through Jesus Christ, our Lord.

ALL: Amen.

✦ All make the Sign of the Cross.

CHILDREN'S DAILY PRAYER 2013–2014 © 2013 Archdiocese of Chicago: Liturgy Training Publications, 3949 South Racine Avenue, Chicago IL 60609. All rights reserved. Orders: 1-800-933-1800 or www.LTP.org. Scripture excerpts are taken from *The New Revised Standard Version Bible: Catholic Edition*, ©1989, Division of Christian Education of the National Council of the Churches of Christ in the United States of America. Used with permission. All rights reserved.

PRAYER FOR **WEDNESDAY** NOVEMBER 27, 2013

OPENING

Today's reading shows how the prophet Daniel interpreted a frightening handwriting experience for a king who defiled the temple's sacred vessels.

✝ All make the Sign of the Cross.

In the name of the Father, and of the Son, and of the Holy Spirit. Amen.

PSALM

(For a longer psalm, see page xii.) Psalm 98:1bcde, 2–3ab, 3cd–4

The LORD has made known his victory.

The LORD has made known his victory.

O sing to the LORD a new song,
    for he has done marvelous things.
His right hand and his holy arm
    have gained him victory.

The LORD has made known his victory.

READING

Daniel 5:1–6, 13–14, 16–17, 23–28

A reading from the book of Daniel

Daniel was brought in before the king. The king said to Daniel, "So you are Daniel, one of the exiles of Judah, whom my father the king brought from Judah? I have heard of you that a spirit of the gods is in you, and that enlightenment, understanding, and excellent wisdom are found in you. But I have heard that you can give interpretations and solve problems. Now if you are able to read the writing and tell me its interpretation, you shall be clothed in purple, have a chain of gold around your neck, and rank third in the kingdom." Then Daniel

answered in the presence of the king, "Let your gifts be for yourself, or give your rewards to someone else! Nevertheless I will read the writing to the king and let him know the interpretation. This is the interpretation of the matter: God has numbered the days of your kingdom and brought it to an end."

The Word of the Lord.

◆ All observe silence.

FOR SILENT REFLECTION

What does it mean that God is the "power of our very breath"?

CLOSING PRAYER

Let us stand and bring our hopes and needs to God as we pray, "Lord, hear our prayer."

◆ All may add their own prayers here.

Let us pray: **Our Father . . . Amen.**

Almighty God,
Help us to remember
that you are as close to us
as our very breath.
We ask this in the name of Christ your Son.

Amen.

✝ All make the Sign of the Cross.

ALSO ON THIS DAY: Hanukkah (Jewish Festival of Lights) begins at sundown

120

ADVENT

SUNDAY, DECEMBER 1, 2013, TO SUNDAY, DECEMBER 22, 2013

ADVENT

2013

THE MEANING OF ADVENT

"A shoot shall come out from the stump of Jesse, and a branch shall grow out of his roots" (Isaiah 11:1).

Jesse was the father of King David, a great leader of the Jewish people. His family tree gave rise to the greatest kings the world had ever known. But then Jesse's family became weak and scattered. The Jewish people no longer had a strong ruler and they suffered many periods of darkness, misery, and despair. The people of Israel had become like a great tree cut down to its stump. Yet God did not forsake his people.

God, Israel's faithful protector, promised to make a new plant sprout. The people waited and prayed and hoped for many years. They knew that God would keep his promise, just as he had kept his promise to Abraham to give him children and a land—and just as he had brought the Israelites out of slavery into the freedom of living God's holy commandments.

We, too, are a people to whom God has made a solemn promise. During Advent, we read in the Bible about God's promise to send a great Light in the darkness, to give sight to the blind, to fill us with comfort and hope, to put an end to sin and death, to give us more than we could ever hope for or imagine, and to fill us with his joy and peace.

We believe that God's plan of promise took flesh when his Son was conceived in Mary's womb. We believe that Christ is a Light for the world. When all people share in this Light, which is the fullness of God's life and love, then the ancient promises will come to fulfillment. Then the wolf will be the guest of the lamb, the lion will lie down with the calf, and there will be no more death or suffering on all God's holy mountain.

Advent is a time of quiet, joyful preparation for the celebration of Jesus's birth and also a time to remember that we wait for Christ to come again at the end of time. It is a time to enjoy the hope that Christ's Resurrection points to. The first Sunday of Advent is also a time of new beginnings—it is the official start of the Church's calendar. Happy New Year!

PREPARING TO CELEBRATE ADVENT IN THE CLASSROOM

Consider organizing an Advent procession. Children of all ages love solemn processions. Take some time to speak with the children about the time of Advent, sharing the material in "The Meaning of Advent" with them. Explain that Advent has a new color, violet. Then suggest to the children that you have a procession to change the color of your prayer table cloth.

You will want to speak with the children about processions they have participated in or have seen in church. Explain that a procession is a prayerful way to walk, and stress the importance of silence (or singing along if you plan to sing in the procession). You may want to demonstrate a slow, careful walk. Then give each child an object from the prayer table to carry in the procession, and remember to include an Advent wreath with three violet candles and one rose-colored candle (if you need more objects, have some spare candles handy so that everyone has something to hold). The child at the head of the procession should carry the violet cloth. You may simply process in a circle around your classroom, or you may lead your procession through the school. Be bold! Other classes will benefit from witnessing your procession. Just make certain to discuss your plans with your principal or Religious Education Director first. If you wish to sing, you might try the first verse of "Creator of the Stars of Night," or the Taizé canon "Prepare the Way of the Lord."

In this book you will find special prayer services that may be used in the classroom or with a larger group. One is a service for Advent, pages 126–127, which could be used at any time; the other is for the Solemnity of the Immaculate Conception of Mary on December 8, pages 134–135. A "Home Prayer" has been created for Advent. This can be photocopied and sent home with the students so that their households can pray together at special times: Gathering around an Advent Wreath for Prayer appeared at the end of Ordinary Time in Autumn on page 119 so that you would send it home before the First Sunday of Advent.

SACRED SPACE

During Advent there are several ways you can create a mood of anticipation in the classroom. You can place the empty manger from a Christmas Nativity scene on your classroom prayer table. Set a large white pillar candle in a prominent place and explain to the children that you are waiting for Christmas before you light it. You can also use an Advent wreath.

The Advent wreath is a circular candleholder, usually decorated with pine branches. It contains four candles: three violet and one rose-colored. When you first introduce the wreath to your class, wonder together with the children about its circular shape, why we use pine boughs, and the significance of the four candles. Children will often come up with beautiful answers to these questions: the wreath is round because God's love has no beginning and no end; the pine branches never lose their leaves just as God cannot die; and the four candles represent the four Sundays of Advent, the four points of the compass, the four branches of the cross, the four Gospels, the four rivers in Eden, and so on. Explain that you will light one candle for each week in Advent; when all the candles are lit, then Christmas will be right around the corner! The children may be curious about the rose-colored candle. Explain that it is the third one that we light, for the third Sunday in Advent, which is called Gaudete [Gow-DAY-tay] Sunday, on which we celebrate the joy of waiting on the Lord. Here is a prayer to use before lighting your Advent wreath:

"The people who walked in darkness have seen a great light" (Isaiah 9:2a).

Lord God, you promise to send us joy beyond all telling. Let your blessing come upon us as we wait for your promised Light to dispel the darkness of our minds and hearts. Send your peace into the world, and may the fire of your love fill our hearts and make us one with you and with each other. We ask this through the Great Light, *Jesus Christ, who enlightens and encourages us always. Amen.*

Please consider saving your celebration of Christmas until true Christmas Time, after December 25. The time of Advent is a great spiritual gift that helps us grow in the beautiful theological virtue of hope. Also, if you wait until you return from Christmas break to celebrate Christmas in the classroom, the children will have settled down and may be more able to listen to the glad tidings of great joy that you have to share with them.

SACRED MUSIC

Discover which songs your parish will be singing during Advent. Sometimes the setting for the sung parts of the Mass will change with the liturgical time. Other Advent songs that children love include "The King of Glory Comes," "People Look East," "O Come, O Come Emmanuel," and "Savior of the Nations Come."

PRAYERS FOR ADVENT

A wonderful prayer to learn during Advent is the Magnificat of Mary (Luke 1:46–55). All those who faithfully pray the Liturgy of the Hours recite this beautiful prayer each evening, to remember to relive Mary's joy as she prayed to God, the Mighty One. It has been set to various tunes and may be sung. Two lovely settings are the Taizé canon, "Magnificat," and "And Holy Is Your Name."

A NOTE TO CATECHISTS

Make arrangements with your Religious Education Director to store your Advent wreath somewhere in the classroom during the week so that you don't need to carry it back and forth between school and home.

GRACE BEFORE MEALS

ADVENT

LEADER:
Let the clouds rain down the Just One,
and the earth bring forth a Savior.

✛ All make the Sign of the Cross.

**In the name of the Father, and of the
Son, and of the Holy Spirit. Amen.**

LEADER:
Lord God,
you provide for us in so many ways.
You have given us the earth,
full of so much goodness.
You have blessed us with water to drink
and food to nourish our bodies.
As we look forward to your gift of the
Christ child,
we also think about the day
when we will be with you in heaven,
where everyone is filled with the joy
of your glorious presence.
We ask this through Jesus Christ our Lord.

Amen.

✛ All make the Sign of the Cross.

**In the name of the Father, and of the
Son, and of the Holy Spirit. Amen.**

124

LEADER:

O Wisdom of our God Most High,
guiding creation with power and love,
come to teach us the path of knowledge!

✠ All make the Sign of the Cross.

In the name of the Father, and of the Son, and of the Holy Spirit. Amen.

LEADER:

Holy God,
we thank you for this day
with all of its adventures, big and small.
May our days continue to be filled
with the light of your Son, our Lord,
your gift to us,
who shows us the way of
patience and forgiveness and love.
We ask this in his name.

Amen.

✠ All make the Sign of the Cross.

In the name of the Father, and of the Son, and of the Holy Spirit. Amen.

PRAYER SERVICE
FOR ADVENT

Prepare seven leaders for this service. The fourth leader will need a Bible for the Scripture passages and may need help practicing the reading. You might want to ask members of the group to write petitions to be read during the service as well. You may wish to begin by singing "O Come, O Come Emmanuel" and end with "Soon and Very Soon." If the group will sing, prepare a song leader.

FIRST LEADER:

◆ Gesture for all to stand.

◆ All make the sign of the Cross.

In the name of the Father, and of the Son, and of the Holy Spirit. Amen.

May the grace and peace of our Lord Jesus Christ be with us.

Amen.

SECOND LEADER:
Let us pray:
Almighty God,
help us to prepare
our hearts for Jesus, your Son
in this season of busyness and
glittering decorations.
We are grateful
for your simple words of hope
and the gift of new life
through the Christ child.
May we always follow the
one true light of Jesus
who shines for all people
through the darkness.
We ask this through Christ our Lord.
Amen.

CHILDREN'S DAILY PRAYER 2013–2014, © 2013 Archdiocese of Chicago: Liturgy Training Publications. All rights reserved. Orders: 1-800-933-1800 or www.LTP.org.

◆ Gesture for all to sit. An adult lights the appropriate number of candles on the Advent wreath. Allow a moment of silence to enjoy the beauty of the lit wreath. (For a discussion of the significance of the Advent wreath and a prayer for blessing it, see Preparing to Celebrate Advent in the Classroom, the section on Sacred Space on page 123)

THIRD LEADER: Isaiah 40:5a, 11

Let us pray the Psalm Response:
The glory of the Lord shall be revealed.

ALL: The glory of the Lord shall be revealed.

THIRD LEADER:

He will feed his flock like a shepherd;
   he will gather the lambs in his arms,
and carry them in his bosom,
   and gently lead the mother sheep.

ALL: The glory of the Lord shall be revealed.

FOURTH LEADER: Isaiah 11:1–10

A reading from the Book of the Prophet Isaiah

◆ Read the Scripture passage from a Bible.

The Word of the Lord.

◆ All observe silence.

FIFTH LEADER:

Let us bring our hopes and needs to God as we pray, "Lord, hear our prayer."

◆ Read the petitions prepared by the class, pausing after each for the response.

SIXTH LEADER:
Come, Lord Jesus!
May we always remember
how you gave us
your Word made flesh
through Jesus, your Son.
Guide us with his truth
that brings justice and peace
to all the earth.
Fill us with your gentle love
as we look forward to celebrating
your presence this Christmas
with our friends and family.
You are our light and joy!

Amen.

SEVENTH LEADER:
May the Lord bless us,

◆ All make the sign of the Cross.

protect us from all evil,
and bring us to everlasting life.

ALL: Amen.

◆ After the service, an adult extinguishes the candles on the Advent wreath.

OPENING

In today's Gospel, Jesus warns his disciples about his sudden appearance sometime in the future, when he will bring all who have loved God to heaven.

✚ All make the Sign of the Cross.

> **In the name of the Father, and of the Son, and of the Holy Spirit. Amen.**

PSALM

(For a longer psalm, see page xii.) Psalm 85:4a, 8, 10–11, 12–13

Restore us again, O God of our salvation!

Restore us again, O God of our salvation!

Let me hear what God the LORD will speak,
  for he will speak peace to his people,
to his faithful, to those who turn to him in
  their hearts.

Restore us again, O God of our salvation!

◆ All stand and sing **Alleluia.**

GOSPEL

Matthew 24:37–44

A reading from the holy Gospel according to Matthew

"For as the days of Noah were, so will be the coming of the Son of Man. For as in those days before the flood they were eating and drinking, marrying and giving in marriage, until the day Noah entered the ark, and they knew nothing until the flood came and swept them all away, so too will be the coming of the Son of Man. Then two will be in the field; one will be taken and one will be left. Two women will be grinding meal together; one will be taken and one will be left. Keep awake therefore, for you do not know on what day your Lord is coming. But understand this: if the owner of the house had known in what part of the night the thief was coming, he would have stayed awake and would not have let his house be broken into. Therefore you also must be ready, for the Son of Man is coming at an unexpected hour."

The Gospel of the Lord.

◆ All sit and observe silence.

FOR SILENT REFLECTION

Have you experienced times of sudden change? Did you talk about this with God and others?

CLOSING PRAYER

Let us stand and bring our hopes and needs to God as we pray, "Lord, hear our prayer."

◆ All may add their own prayers here.

Let us pray: **Our Father . . . Amen.**

Almighty God,
you have given us the gift
of free will—
the ability to make choices
for right or wrong.
Help us to be ready
when you come again.
We ask this through Christ our Lord.

Amen.

✚ All make the Sign of the Cross.

OPENING

In today's Gospel, we see Jesus amazed at someone's faith. A Roman officer believed in Jesus's authority to heal without even being physically present with the sick person.

✠ All make the Sign of the Cross.

In the name of the Father, and of the Son, and of the Holy Spirit. Amen.

PSALM (For a longer psalm, see page xii.) Psalm 85:4a, 8, 10–11, 12–13

Restore us again, O God of our salvation!

Restore us again, O God of our salvation!

Let me hear what God the LORD will speak,
  for he will speak peace to his people,
to his faithful, to those who turn to him in
    their hearts.

Restore us again, O God of our salvation!

◆ All stand and sing **Alleluia.**

GOSPEL   Matthew 8:5–11

A reading from the holy Gospel according to Matthew

When he entered Capernaum, a centurion came to him, appealing to him and saying, "Lord, my servant is lying at home paralyzed, in terrible distress." And he said to him, "I will come and cure him." The centurion answered, "Lord, I am not worthy to have you come under my roof; but only speak the word, and my servant will be healed. For I also am a man under authority, with soldiers under me; and I say to one, 'Go,' and he goes, and to another, 'Come,' and he comes, and to my slave, 'Do this,' and the slave does it." When Jesus heard him, he was amazed and said to those who followed him, "Truly I tell you, in no one in Israel have I found such faith. I tell you, many will come from east and west and will eat with Abraham and Isaac and Jacob in the kingdom of heaven."

The Gospel of the Lord.

◆ All sit and observe silence.

FOR SILENT REFLECTION

Do I trust that Jesus will respond to my needs? Do I believe in Jesus's authority to heal?

CLOSING PRAYER

Let us stand and bring our hopes and needs to God as we pray, "Lord, hear our prayer."

◆ All may add their own prayers here.

Let us pray: **Our Father . . . Amen.**

Jesus our healer,
you found hope in the faith
of a centurion
who knew you would help
with the power of your spoken word,
even from afar.
Help us to have such solid faith
that we can trust in your good authority
to provide what we need.
We ask this in your name.

Amen.

✠ All make the Sign of the Cross.

PRAYER FOR TUESDAY DECEMBER 3, 2013

OPENING

Today we remember St. Francis Xavier [ZAY-vee-er], who became a priest at the urging of his friend Ignatius of Loyola. In 1537, he sailed to the East Indies, and spread the Gospel to the people of Malaysia, Japan, and India. He lived and worked with the poor and sick, particularly those stricken with leprosy. In today's Gospel, Jesus talks about his relationship with God the Father, and his authority to act on his behalf.

✠ All make the Sign of the Cross.

In the name of the Father, and of the Son, and of the Holy Spirit. Amen.

PSALM (For a longer psalm, see page xii.) Psalm 85:4a, 8, 10–11, 12–13

Restore us again, O God of our salvation!

Restore us again, O God of our salvation!

Let me hear what God the LORD will speak,
  for he will speak peace to his people,
to his faithful, to those who turn to him in
  their hearts.

Restore us again, O God of our salvation!

◆ All stand and sing **Alleluia.**

GOSPEL Luke 10:21–24

A reading from the holy Gospel according to Luke

At that same hour Jesus rejoiced in the Holy Spirit and said, "I thank you, Father, Lord of heaven and earth, because you have hidden these things from the wise and the intelligent and have revealed them to infants; yes, Father, for such was your gracious will. All things have been handed over to me by my Father; and no one knows who the Son is except the Father, or who the Father is except the Son and anyone to whom the Son chooses to reveal him." Then turning to the disciples, Jesus said to them privately, "Blessed are the eyes that see what you see! For I tell you that many prophets and kings desired to see what you see, but did not see it, and to hear what you hear, but did not hear it."

The Gospel of the Lord.

◆ All sit and observe silence.

FOR SILENT REFLECTION

In what ways are we blessed just as Jesus's disciples were blessed?

CLOSING PRAYER

Let us stand and bring our hopes and needs to God as we pray, "Lord, hear our prayer."

◆ All may add their own prayers here.

Let us pray: **Our Father . . . Amen.**

Lord Jesus,
you reveal again how our
trusting hearts of faith
are most important.
Keep us close to you and
your words of truth.
Guide us in this life to be
with you in the next.
We ask this in your name.

Amen.

✠ All make the Sign of the Cross.

130

OPENING

Today we remember St. John Damascene, who was born in Damascus in the seventh century, and who lived under Muslim rule. He is known for his writings about the Eastern Church (of the Greek Fathers) of the Catholic Church.

✚ All make the Sign of the Cross.

In the name of the Father, and of the Son, and of the Holy Spirit. Amen.

PSALM   (For a longer psalm, see page xii.) Psalm 85:4a, 8, 10–11, 12–13

Restore us again, O God of our salvation!

Restore us again, O God of our salvation!

Let me hear what God the LORD will speak,
   for he will speak peace to his people,
to his faithful, to those who turn to him in
      their hearts.

Restore us again, O God of our salvation!

◆ All stand and sing **Alleluia.**

GOSPEL   Matthew 15:29–37

A reading from the holy Gospel according to Matthew

After Jesus had left that place, he passed along the Sea of Galilee, and he went up the mountain, where he sat down. Great crowds came to him, bringing with them the lame, the maimed, the blind, the mute, and many others. Then Jesus called his disciples to him and said, "I have compassion for the crowd, because they have been with me now for three days and have nothing to eat; and I do not want to send them away hungry, for they might faint on the way." The disciples said to him, "Where are we to get enough bread in the desert to feed so great a crowd?" Jesus asked them, "How many loaves have you?" They said, "Seven, and a few small fish." Then ordering the crowd to sit down on the ground, he took the seven loaves and the fish; and after giving thanks he broke them and gave them to the disciples, and the disciples gave them to the crowds. And all of them ate and were filled; and they took up the broken pieces left over, seven baskets full.

The Gospel of the Lord.

◆ All sit and observe silence.

FOR SILENT REFLECTION

When do you feel really well cared for?

CLOSING PRAYER

Let us stand and bring our hopes and needs to God as we pray, "Lord, hear our prayer."

◆ All may add their own prayers here.

Let us pray: **Our Father . . . Amen.**

Lord Jesus,
you know our every need.
You are with us now
through your Spirit and through
the goodness of others.
Guide us as we help our
brothers and sisters in Christ.
In your name we pray.

Amen.

✚ All make the Sign of the Cross.

PRAYER FOR **THURSDAY** **DECEMBER 5, 2013**

OPENING

In today's Gospel, Jesus suggests that we not let his words go in one ear and out the other.

✚ All make the Sign of the Cross.

> **In the name of the Father, and of the Son, and of the Holy Spirit. Amen.**

PSALM   (For a longer psalm, see page xii.) Psalm 85:4a, 8, 10–11, 12–13

Restore us again, O God of our salvation!

Restore us again, O God of our salvation!

Let me hear what God the LORD will speak,
   for he will speak peace to his people,
to his faithful, to those who turn to him in
      their hearts.

Restore us again, O God of our salvation!

◆ All stand and sing **Alleluia.**

GOSPEL   Matthew 7:21, 24–27

A reading from the holy Gospel according to Matthew

Jesus said to his disciples: "Not everyone who says to me, 'Lord, Lord,' will enter the kingdom of heaven, but only the one who does the will of my Father in heaven. Everyone then who hears these words of mine and acts on them will be like a wise man who built his house on rock. The rain fell, the floods came, and the winds blew and beat on that house, but it did not fall, because it had been founded on rock. And everyone who hears these words of mine and does not act on them will be like a foolish man who built his house on sand. The rain fell, and the floods came, and the winds blew and beat against that house, and it fell—and great was its fall!"

The Gospel of the Lord.

◆ All sit and observe silence.

FOR SILENT REFLECTION

What are the potential storms in your life? How do you know that you are building your house of faith on rock?

CLOSING PRAYER

Let us stand and bring our hopes and needs to God as we pray, "Lord, hear our prayer."

◆ All may add their own prayers here.

Let us pray: **Our Father . . . Amen.**

Lord Jesus,
it's true that the mishaps of life
can make us feel unsettled.
You desire us to act on your words
so that our faith can withstand
the errors of our ways
or the mistakes of others.
Keep us anchored on your rock, Lord.
Help us to become one with you—
our granite for a lifetime,
here and beyond.
We ask this in your name.

Amen.

✚ All make the Sign of the Cross.

ALSO ON THIS DAY: Hanukkah (Jewish Festival of Lights ends)

132

OPENING

We remember St. Nicholas today, maybe one of the most beloved of our spiritual heroes, who lived in the fourth century in Myra [MY-ruh], a city in Asia Minor. One of the best known stories about Nicholas concerns his gift bags filled with gold, tossed three times through a poor man's window to help him find suitable husbands for his three daughters. This generosity spawned the custom of giving gifts and providing for the poor at Christmas time. Today's Gospel invites us to discard our insecurities and ask Jesus to cure our blindness.

✚ All make the Sign of the Cross.

In the name of the Father, and of the Son, and of the Holy Spirit. Amen.

PSALM
(For a longer psalm, see page xii.) Psalm 85:4a, 8, 10–11, 12–13

Restore us again, O God of our salvation!

Restore us again, O God of our salvation!

Let me hear what God the LORD will speak,
　　for he will speak peace to his people,
to his faithful, to those who turn to him in
　　their hearts.

Restore us again, O God of our salvation!

◆ All stand and sing **Alleluia.**

GOSPEL
Matthew 9:27–31

A reading from the holy Gospel according to Matthew

As Jesus went on from there, two blind men followed him, crying loudly, "Have mercy on us, Son of David!" When he entered the house, the blind men came to him; and Jesus said to them, "Do you believe that I am able to do this?" They said to him, "Yes, Lord." Then he touched their eyes and said, "According to your faith let it be done to you." And their eyes were opened. Then Jesus sternly ordered them, "See that no one knows of this." But they went away and spread the news about him throughout that district.

The Gospel of the Lord.

◆ All sit and observe silence.

FOR SILENT REFLECTION

What beautiful things have you seen lately? When was the last time you looked in a mirror and thanked God for who you are?

CLOSING PRAYER

Let us stand and bring our hopes and needs to God as we pray, "Lord, hear our prayer."

◆ All may add their own prayers here.

Let us pray: **Our Father . . . Amen.**

Loving God,
as we observe this Advent season
keep us mindful of holy men and women
who have shown their love for you
by their actions toward others.
We ask this through Christ our Lord.

Amen.

✚ All make the Sign of the Cross.

PRAYER SERVICE
SOLEMNITY OF THE IMMACULATE CONCEPTION OF MARY

Prepare six leaders for this service. The third leader will need a Bible for the passages from Luke. Take time to help the third leader practice the readings. You may wish to sing "Sing of Mary" as the opening song. If the group will sing, prepare someone to lead it.

FIRST LEADER:

We remember Mary, the Mother of Jesus on this special day. We celebrate her Immaculate Conception because of her special role. We believe she was conceived with God's special grace in her mother's womb so that one day she would bear Jesus, her Son, our Lord and Savior. She was filled with God's grace and the guidance of the Holy Spirit as she continually followed God's will. She nurtured Jesus in her womb, guided her Son in his youth, and stood by him in his ministry, even through his Death and Resurrection. She is the patroness of the United States because of her constant courage. Let us begin our prayer service in her honor by singing the opening song.

SONG LEADER:

◆ Gesture for all to stand, and lead the first few verses of the song.

SECOND LEADER:

✚ All make the Sign of the Cross.

In the name of the Father, and of the Son, and of the Holy Spirit. Amen.

Let us pray:
Almighty Father,
you gave Mary special grace
when she was conceived
in her mother's womb.
You chose for her a unique role

SOLEMNITY OF THE IMMACULATE CONCEPTION OF MARY

to bring salvation to the world.
She is a sign of hope
for her courage to say, "yes" to you,
every moment of her life.
We pray with her to your Son Jesus,
our Lord and Savior,
in union with the Holy Spirit.

Amen.

◆ Remain standing and sing **Alleluia.**

THIRD LEADER: Luke 1:26–38
A reading from the holy Gospel according to
Luke

◆ Read the Gospel passage from the Bible.

The Gospel of the Lord.

◆ All sit and observe silence.

FOURTH LEADER:

◆ Gesture for all to stand.

Let us bring our hopes and needs to God as
we pray, Lord, hear our prayer.

For the courage to say, "yes" to God
as Mary did throughout her life,
we pray to the Lord.
For all who are struggling with
tough decisions in life,
may they look to Mary as
a true friend on their journey,
we pray to the Lord.
For all married people;
may they continue to be an example
of the love and devotion that
Mary and Joseph shared,
we pray to the Lord.
For all mothers

and those who nurture others,
help us to respect and protect life
from conception until natural death,
we pray to the Lord.
For those throughout the world
who are suffering from
hunger, lack of shelter or disease,
for those who have died,
may we have the compassion of Mary
to give us hope and the promise
of new life through Jesus,
we pray to the Lord.

FIFTH LEADER:
Let us Pray the Hail Mary:

ALL: Hail Mary, full of grace . . .

◆ Pause, and then say:
Let us offer one another the sign of Christ's
peace.

◆ All offer one another a sign of peace.

SIXTH LEADER:
Let us pray Mary's special prayer,
the *Magnificat:*
"My soul magnifies the Lord,
    and my spirit rejoices in God my Savior,
for he has looked with favor on the lowliness
        of his servant.
    Surely, from now on all generations will
        call me blessed;
for the Mighty One has done great things
        for me,
    and holy is his name."

✠ All make the Sign of the Cross.

**In the name of the Father, and of the
Son, and of the Holy Spirit. Amen.**

PRAYER FOR THE WEEK

OPENING

In today's Gospel, we are reminded of the work of John the Baptist, who boldly proclaimed news about our Messiah.

✝ All make the Sign of the Cross.

In the name of the Father, and of the Son, and of the Holy Spirit. Amen.

PSALM (For a longer psalm, see page xii.) Psalm 85:4a, 8, 10–11, 12–13

Restore us again, O God of our salvation!

Restore us again, O God of our salvation!

Let me hear what God the LORD will speak,
   for he will speak peace to his people,
to his faithful, to those who turn to him in
   their hearts.

Restore us again, O God of our salvation!

◆ All stand and sing **Alleluia.**

GOSPEL Matthew 3:1–6

A reading from the holy Gospel according to Matthew

In those days John the Baptist appeared in the wilderness of Judea, proclaiming, "Repent, for the kingdom of heaven has come near." This is the one of whom the prophet Isaiah spoke when he said, "The voice of one crying out in the wilderness: 'Prepare the way of the Lord, make his paths straight.'" Now John wore clothing of camel's hair with a leather belt around his waist, and his food was locusts and wild honey. Then the people of Jerusalem and all Judea were going out to him, and all the region along the Jordan, and they were baptized by him in the river Jordan, confessing their sins.

The Gospel of the Lord.

◆ All sit and observe silence.

FOR SILENT REFLECTION

What other prophets from the Bible spoke about the Savior? Who are today's prophets?

CLOSING PRAYER

Let us stand and bring our hopes and needs to God as we pray, "Lord, hear our prayer."

◆ All may add their own prayers here.

Let us pray: **Our Father . . . Amen.**

Almighty God,
you sent key messengers for centuries
who declared that a Messiah
would be in our midst.
We have hope because of your Word
that Jesus will come again.
May we prepare our hearts and our lives
for your Son's return.
May we live with courage
with help and guidance from
your Spirit.
We ask this through your Son, Jesus Christ.

Amen.

✝ All make the Sign of the Cross.

OPENING

Today we celebrate a special feast day of Mary: the Immaculate Conception. Mary was a person, like each of us, but from the first moment of her conception she was filled with God's grace to be the human vessel for our Lord Jesus.

✛ All make the Sign of the Cross.

In the name of the Father, and of the Son, and of the Holy Spirit. Amen.

PSALM   (For a longer psalm, see page xii.) Psalm 85:4a, 8, 10–11, 12–13

Restore us again, O God of our salvation!

Restore us again, O God of our salvation!

Let me hear what God the LORD will speak,
    for he will speak peace to his people,
to his faithful, to those who turn to him in
    their hearts.

Restore us again, O God of our salvation!

◆ All stand and sing **Alleluia.**

GOSPEL   Luke 1:26–33

A reading from the holy Gospel according to Luke

In the sixth month the angel Gabriel was sent by God to a town in Galilee called Nazareth, to a virgin engaged to a man whose name was Joseph, of the house of David. The virgin's name was Mary. And he came to her and said, "Greetings, favored one! The Lord is with you." But she was much perplexed by his words and pondered what sort of greeting this might be. The angel said to her, "Do not be afraid, Mary, for you have found favor with God. And now, you will conceive in your womb and bear a son, and you will name him Jesus. He will be great, and will be called the Son of the Most High, and the Lord God will give to him the throne of his ancestor David. He will reign over the house of Jacob forever, and of his kingdom there will be no end."

The Gospel of the Lord.

◆ All sit and observe silence.

FOR SILENT REFLECTION

Have you ever experienced a major change in your life? Did you ask God for help?

CLOSING PRAYER

Let us stand and bring our hopes and needs to God as we pray, "Lord, hear our prayer."

◆ All may add their own prayers here.

Let us pray: **Our Father . . . Amen.**

Almighty God,
you sent the angel Gabriel
to ask Mary about
the most important event in her life—
the miracle of Jesus.
With God's power and Spirit,
Jesus was conceived in her womb.
May we be as willing to allow Jesus
in our lives and be filled
with God's Spirit.
Keep us watchful for your
messengers of truth.
We ask this through Christ your Son.

Amen.

✛ All make the Sign of the Cross.

PRAYER FOR **TUESDAY** DECEMBER 10, 2013

OPENING

In today's Gospel, we are reassured of God's love for us. Jesus is our loving shepherd who will never stop looking for those who stray.

✦ All make the Sign of the Cross.

In the name of the Father, and of the Son, and of the Holy Spirit. Amen.

PSALM   (For a longer psalm, see page xii.) Psalm 85:4a, 8, 10–11, 12–13

Restore us again, O God of our salvation!

Restore us again, O God of our salvation!

Let me hear what God the LORD will speak,
    for he will speak peace to his people,
to his faithful, to those who turn to him in
    their hearts.

Restore us again, O God of our salvation!

◆ All stand and sing **Alleluia**.

GOSPEL   Matthew 18:12–14

A reading from the holy Gospel according to Matthew

"What do you think? If a shepherd has a hundred sheep, and one of them has gone astray, does he not leave the ninety-nine on the mountains and go in search of the one that went astray? And if he finds it, truly I tell you, he rejoices over it more than over the ninety-nine that never went astray. So it is not the will of your Father in heaven that one of these little ones should be lost."

The Gospel of the Lord.

◆ All sit and observe silence.

FOR SILENT REFLECTION

What does this Gospel tell us about God's love for each of us? How does this Gospel reassure me?

CLOSING PRAYER

Let us stand and bring our hopes and needs to God as we pray, "Lord, hear our prayer."

◆ All may add their own prayers here.

Let us pray: **Our Father . . . Amen.**

Jesus, our Good Shepherd,
you come looking for us
even when we stray from you.
We are your beloved children,
and you are our shepherd.
Help us to trust
how much you love us,
and that you will search for us
when we are lost.
In your name we pray.

Amen.

✦ All make the Sign of the Cross.

OPENING

Today we remember St. Damasus I [DAM-uh-sus], who served Pope Liberius [Lie-BEER-ee-us] in the fourth century, and was later elected bishop of Rome. Damasus worked amidst church rebellions about leadership and teaching. One of his achievements concerned the support of St. Jerome, whose biblical studies resulted in a respected Latin translation of Scripture known as the Vulgate. Today's Gospel gives us reason to feel confident in our daily sacrifices done in the name of love.

✛ All make the Sign of the Cross.

In the name of the Father, and of the Son, and of the Holy Spirit. Amen.

PSALM (For a longer psalm, see page xii.) Psalm 85:4a, 8, 10–11, 12–13

Restore us again, O God of our salvation!

Restore us again, O God of our salvation!

Let me hear what God the LORD will speak,
    for he will speak peace to his people,
to his faithful, to those who turn to him in
        their hearts.

Restore us again, O God of our salvation!

◆ All stand and sing **Alleluia.**

GOSPEL Matthew 11:28–30

A reading from the holy Gospel according to Matthew

"Come to me, all you that are weary and are carrying heavy burdens, and I will give you rest. Take my yoke upon you, and learn from me; for I am gentle and humble in heart, and you will find rest for your souls. For my yoke is easy, and my burden is light."

The Gospel of the Lord.

◆ All sit and observe silence.

FOR SILENT REFLECTION

What is a yoke? What would be considered my yoke at this phase of my life? What are some heavy burdens being carried by people whom I know?

CLOSING PRAYER

Let us stand and bring our hopes and needs to God as we pray, "Lord, hear our prayer."

◆ All may add their own prayers here.

Let us pray: **Our Father . . . Amen.**

Jesus our redeemer,
you reassure us that our
tough tasks on this earth
can be helped with
your loving care and our
belief in life everlasting.
Your words refresh us
and bring us closer to
celebrating your arrival with us
as a haven and divine healer.
Guide us to your resting place.
In your name we pray.
Amen.

✛ All make the Sign of the Cross.

PRAYER FOR **THURSDAY**
DECEMBER 12, 2013

OPENING

Today we celebrate the Feast of Our Lady of Guadalupe. On December 9, 1531, Mary appeared to Juan Diego. She told him to ask the bishop to build a chapel on the very site of her appearance. When Juan Diego approached the bishop, the bishop asked for a sign. A few days later, Juan Diego returned with his tilma filled with roses and Mary's image emblazoned on his cloak.

✝ All make the Sign of the Cross.

In the name of the Father, and of the Son, and of the Holy Spirit. Amen.

PSALM   (For a longer psalm, see page xii.) Psalm 85:4a, 8, 10–11, 12–13

Restore us again, O God of our salvation!

Restore us again, O God of our salvation!

Let me hear what God the LORD will speak,
   for he will speak peace to his people,
to his faithful, to those who turn to him in
      their hearts.

Restore us again, O God of our salvation!

◆ All stand and sing **Alleluia.**

GOSPEL   Luke 1:39–47

A reading from the holy Gospel according to Luke

In those days Mary set out and went with haste to a Judean town in the hill country, where she entered the house of Zechariah and greeted Elizabeth. When Elizabeth heard Mary's greeting, the child leaped in her womb. And Elizabeth was filled with the Holy Spirit and exclaimed with a loud cry, "Blessed are you among women, and blessed is the fruit of your womb. And why has this happened to me, that the mother of my Lord comes to me? For as soon as I heard the sound of your greeting, the child in my womb leaped for joy. And blessed is she who believed that there would be a fulfillment of what was spoken to her by the Lord." And Mary said, "My soul magnifies the Lord, and my spirit rejoices in God my Savior."

The Gospel of the Lord.

◆ All sit and observe silence.

FOR SILENT REFLECTION

What do you think Mary meant when she said "My soul magnifies the Lord"?

CLOSING PRAYER

Let us stand and bring our hopes and needs to God as we pray, "Lord, hear our prayer."

◆ All may add their own prayers here.

Let us pray: **Our Father . . . Amen.**

Holy Spirit,
your presence is a blessing
and we are often
surprised at how you appear
in unexpected ways.
Keep us aware of how much you
love us and care for us daily.
We ask this through Christ our Lord.

Amen.

✝ All make the Sign of the Cross.

140

OPENING

Today we remember St. Lucy, who lived in Sicily in 300. Even though that region outlawed Christianity, she vowed to devote her life to Christ and was later put to death. She is the patron saint of the blind. In today's reading, God speaks through the prophet Isaiah, reminding people that prosperity and good fortune are the rewards of those who follow God's law.

✚ All make the Sign of the Cross.

In the name of the Father, and of the Son, and of the Holy Spirit. Amen.

PSALM   (For a longer psalm, see page xii.) Psalm 85:4a, 8, 10–11, 12–13

Restore us again, O God of our salvation!

Restore us again, O God of our salvation!

Let me hear what God the LORD will speak,
   for he will speak peace to his people,
to his faithful, to those who turn to him in
   their hearts.

Restore us again, O God of our salvation!

READING   Isaiah 48:17–19

A reading from the Book of the Prophet Isaiah

Thus says the Lord, your Redeemer, the Holy One of Israel: I am the Lord your God, who teaches you for your own good, who leads you in the way you should go. O that you had paid attention to my commandments! Then your prosperity would have been like a river, and your success like the waves of the sea; your offspring would have been like the sand, and your descendants like its grains; their name would never be cut off or destroyed from before me.

The Word of the Lord.

◆ All observe silence.

FOR SILENT REFLECTION

When is it difficult to obey your parents, teachers, or coaches? What are some of the reasons why I should listen to them? How did these people gain their wisdom?

CLOSING PRAYER

Let us stand and bring our hopes and needs to God as we pray, "Lord, hear our prayer."

◆ All may add their own prayers here.

Let us pray: **Our Father . . . Amen.**

Almighty God,
you send people of wisdom and authority
to guide us throughout our lives.
Sometimes it is difficult
to follow their requests
because we want to do things
in our own way,
and at our own time.
Help us to listen and do
what we need to do, and to
learn from their teaching us,
for they have our best interests
in mind, as do you.
We ask this through Christ our Lord.

Amen.

✚ All make the Sign of the Cross.

PRAYER FOR THE WEEK

OPENING

In today's Gospel, we listen to Jesus declare the greatness of John the Baptist, who was a devoted servant to the one who became our Messiah.

✠ All make the Sign of the Cross.

In the name of the Father, and of the Son, and of the Holy Spirit. Amen.

PSALM

(For a longer psalm, see page xii.) Psalm 85:4a, 8, 10–11, 12–13

Restore us again, O God of our salvation!

Restore us again, O God of our salvation!

Let me hear what God the LORD will speak,
    for he will speak peace to his people,
to his faithful, to those who turn to him in
    their hearts.

Restore us again, O God of our salvation!

◆ All stand and sing **Alleluia.**

GOSPEL

Matthew 11:7–11

A reading from the holy Gospel according to Matthew

Jesus began to speak to the crowds about John: "What did you go out into the wilderness to look at? A reed shaken by the wind? What then did you go out to see? Someone dressed in soft robes? Look, those who wear soft robes are in royal palaces. What then did you go out to see? A prophet? Yes, I tell you, and more than a prophet. This is the one about whom it is written, 'See, I am sending my messenger ahead of you, who will prepare your way before you.' Truly I tell you, among those born of women no one has arisen greater than John the Baptist; yet the least in the kingdom of heaven is greater than he."

The Gospel of the Lord.

◆ All sit and observe silence.

FOR SILENT REFLECTION

How did Jesus describe John the Baptist? What does this tell us about the Kingdom of God?

CLOSING PRAYER

Let us stand and bring our hopes and needs to God as we pray, "Lord, hear our prayer."

◆ All may add their own prayers here.

Let us pray: **Our Father . . . Amen.**

Lord Jesus,
you sent John the Baptist
to declare your arrival.
Today we listen to the
prophets among us—
your close followers who
point the way to you.
May we listen to their guidance.
We ask this in your name.

Amen.

✠ All make the Sign of the Cross.

142

OPENING

In today's Gospel, Jesus challenges the chief priests and the elders about their rejection of the baptism of John the Baptist. See how they answer the question that Jesus poses to them.

✝ All make the Sign of the Cross.

In the name of the Father, and of the Son, and of the Holy Spirit. Amen.

PSALM
(For a longer psalm, see page xii.) Psalm 85:4a, 8, 10–11, 12–13

Restore us again, O God of our salvation!

Restore us again, O God of our salvation!

Let me hear what God the LORD will speak,
   for he will speak peace to his people,
to his faithful, to those who turn to him in
   their hearts.

Restore us again, O God of our salvation!

◆ All stand and sing **Alleluia.**

GOSPEL
Matthew 21:23–27

A reading from the holy Gospel according to Matthew

When Jesus entered the temple, the chief priests and the elders of the people came to him as he was teaching, and said, "By what authority are you doing these things, and who gave you this authority?" Jesus said to them, "I will also ask you one question; if you tell me the answer, then I will also tell you by what authority I do these things. Did the baptism of John come from heaven, or was it of human origin?" And they argued with one another, "If we say,

'From heaven,' he will say to us, 'Why then did you not believe him?' But if we say, 'Of human origin,' we are afraid of the crowd; for all regard John as a prophet." So they answered Jesus, "We do not know." And he said to them, "Neither will I tell you by what authority I am doing these things."

The Gospel of the Lord.

◆ All sit and observe silence.

FOR SILENT REFLECTION

Do I carefully consider the guidelines and laws that I follow? Do they value human life and dignity?

CLOSING PRAYER

Let us stand and bring our hopes and needs to God as we pray, "Lord, hear our prayer."

◆ All may add their own prayers here.

Let us pray: **Our Father . . . Amen.**

Lord Jesus,
you challenged the authority
of those who did not believe
you were the Messiah.
They wanted to control the crowds
with their own power.
Help us Lord, as we listen to
people of influence.
Give us courage to challenge leaders
who do not follow God's ways.
We ask this in your name.

Amen.

✝ All make the Sign of the Cross.

PRAYER FOR **TUESDAY**
DECEMBER 17, 2013

OPENING

In today's reading from Genesis, we hear about the tribe of Judah. This tribe will eventually produce King David, from whose family Jesus was descended. Today, in many parts of Mexico and Guatemala, people celebrate the beginning of Las Posadas, which honors the nine months of Mary's pregnancy. For nine days, people process from home to home, dressed as the Holy Family to remember Mary and Joseph's difficult journey from Nazareth to Bethlehem in search of a place to stay. At the last chosen home for the evening, the group continues singing, praying, and sharing food, and they break a piñata at the end.

✚ All make the Sign of the Cross.

In the name of the Father, and of the Son, and of the Holy Spirit. Amen.

PSALM
(For a longer psalm, see page xii.) Psalm 85:4a, 8, 10–11, 12–13

Restore us again, O God of our salvation!

Restore us again, O God of our salvation!

Let me hear what God the LORD will speak,
    for he will speak peace to his people,
to his faithful, to those who turn to him in
    their hearts.

Restore us again, O God of our salvation!

READING
Genesis 49:2, 8–10

A reading from the Book of Genesis

Assemble and hear, O sons of Jacob; listen to Israel your father. Judah, your brothers shall praise you; your hand shall be on the neck of your enemies; your father's sons shall bow down before you. Judah is a lion's whelp; from the prey, my son, you have gone up. He crouches down, he stretches out like a lion, like a lioness—who dares rouse him up? The scepter shall not depart from Judah, nor the ruler's staff from between his feet, until tribute comes to him; and the obedience of the peoples is his.

The Word of the Lord.

◆ All observe silence.

FOR SILENT REFLECTION

In this Advent season, how am I preparing a place in my heart for the child Jesus?

CLOSING PRAYER

Let us stand and bring our hopes and needs to God as we pray, "Lord, hear our prayer."

◆ All may add their own prayers here.

Let us pray: **Our Father . . . Amen.**

God our Father,
you prepared a special people
and a specific time in history
for the birth of Jesus.
May we continue to prepare for
the Christ child in our hearts,
remembering that our Savior is whom
we await at the end of time.
We ask this through Christ our Lord.

Amen.

✚ All make the Sign of the Cross.

ALSO ON THIS DAY: Las Posadas begins

144

OPENING

Today's Gospel reveals the tensions felt by Joseph as he learns that his fiancée Mary is with child before they are married. See how God sends a messenger to explain the divine plan.

✚ All make the Sign of the Cross.

In the name of the Father, and of the Son, and of the Holy Spirit. Amen.

PSALM

(For a longer psalm, see page xii.) Psalm 85:4a, 8, 10–11, 12–13

Restore us again, O God of our salvation!

Restore us again, O God of our salvation!

Let me hear what God the LORD will speak,
    for he will speak peace to his people,
to his faithful, to those who turn to him in
    their hearts.

Restore us again, O God of our salvation!

◆ All stand and sing **Alleluia.**

GOSPEL

Matthew 1:18–23

A reading from the holy Gospel according to Matthew

Now the birth of Jesus the Messiah took place in this way. When his mother Mary had been engaged to Joseph, but before they lived together, she was found to be with child from the Holy Spirit. Her husband Joseph, being a righteous man and unwilling to expose her to public disgrace, planned to dismiss her quietly. But just when he had resolved to do this, an angel of the Lord appeared to him in a dream and said, "Joseph, son of David, do not be afraid to take Mary as your wife, for the child conceived in her is from the Holy Spirit. She will bear a son, and you are to name him Jesus, for he will save his people from their sins." All this took place to fulfill what had been spoken by the Lord through the prophet: "Look, the virgin shall conceive and bear a son, and they shall name him Emmanuel," which means, "God is with us."

The Gospel of the Lord.

◆ All sit and observe silence.

FOR SILENT REFLECTION

Nothing is impossible with God. How does God work in our life?

CLOSING PRAYER

Let us stand and bring our hopes and needs to God as we pray, "Lord, hear our prayer."

◆ All may add their own prayers here.

Let us pray: **Our Father . . . Amen.**

Almighty God,
your Spirit filled the hearts
of Mary and Joseph with courage.
Help us to make room for your Son
in our lives,
even when it doesn't seem possible,
or we feel unworthy.
You fill us with possibilities!
We ask this through Christ our Lord.

Amen.

✚ All make the Sign of the Cross.

ALSO ON THIS DAY: Las Posadas continues

PRAYER FOR **THURSDAY** DECEMBER 19, 2013

OPENING

Today's Gospel illustrates how God works miracles in unusual ways.

✜ All make the Sign of the Cross.

In the name of the Father, and of the Son, and of the Holy Spirit. Amen.

PSALM
(For a longer psalm, see page xii.) Psalm 85:4a, 8, 10–11, 12–13

Restore us again, O God of our salvation!

Restore us again, O God of our salvation!

Let me hear what God the LORD will speak,
for he will speak peace to his people,
to his faithful, to those who turn to him in
their hearts.

Restore us again, O God of our salvation!

◆ All stand and sing **Alleluia.**

GOSPEL
Luke 1:5–15a

A reading from the holy Gospel according to Luke

In the days of King Herod of Judea, there was a priest named Zechariah [zek-uh-RĪ-uh], who belonged to the priestly order of Abijah [uh-BĪ-juh]. His wife was a descendant of Aaron, and her name was Elizabeth. Both of them were righteous before God, living blamelessly according to all the commandments and regulations of the Lord. But they had no children, because Elizabeth was barren, and both were getting on in years. Once when he was serving as priest before God and his section was on duty, he was chosen by lot, according to the custom of the priesthood, to enter the sanctuary of the Lord and offer incense. Then there appeared to him an angel of the Lord, standing at the right side of the altar of incense. When Zechariah saw him, he was terrified; and fear overwhelmed him. But the angel said to him, "Do not be afraid, Zechariah, for your prayer has been heard. Your wife Elizabeth will bear you a son, and you will name him John. You will have joy and gladness, and many will rejoice at his birth, for he will be great in the sight of the Lord."

The Gospel of the Lord.

◆ All sit and observe silence.

FOR SILENT REFLECTION

Have you ever been speechless about one of God's marvels?

CLOSING PRAYER

Let us stand and bring our hopes and needs to God as we pray, "Lord, hear our prayer."

◆ All may add their own prayers here.

Let us pray: **Our Father . . . Amen.**

Heavenly Father,
grant us prophets in our day
so that we may remain focused on
your plan for us.
We ask this through your Son, Jesus.

Amen.

✜ All make the Sign of the Cross.

ALSO ON THIS DAY: Las Posadas continues

146

OPENING

Today's Gospel tells us about the angel Gabriel's visit to Mary, whose "yes" became life-saving news.

✛ All make the Sign of the Cross.

In the name of the Father, and of the Son, and of the Holy Spirit. Amen.

PSALM (For a longer psalm, see page xii.) Psalm 85:4a, 8, 10–11, 12–13

Restore us again, O God of our salvation!

Restore us again, O God of our salvation!

Let me hear what God the LORD will speak,
   for he will speak peace to his people,
to his faithful, to those who turn to him in
      their hearts.

Restore us again, O God of our salvation!

◆ All stand and sing **Alleluia.**

GOSPEL   Luke 1:26–35

A reading from the holy Gospel according to Luke

In the sixth month the angel Gabriel was sent by God to a town in Galilee called Nazareth, to a virgin engaged to a man whose name was Joseph, of the house of David. The virgin's name was Mary. And he came to her and said, "Greetings, favored one! The Lord is with you." But she was much perplexed by his words and pondered what sort of greeting this might be. The angel said to her, "Do not be afraid, Mary, for you have found favor with God. And now, you will conceive in your womb and bear a son, and you will name him Jesus. He will be great, and will be called the Son of the Most High, and the Lord God will give to him the throne of his ancestor David. He will reign over the house of Jacob forever, and of his kingdom there will be no end." Mary said to the angel, "How can this be, since I am a virgin?" The angel said to her, "The Holy Spirit will come upon you, and the power of the Most High will overshadow you; therefore the child to be born will be holy; he will be called Son of God."

The Gospel of the Lord.

◆ All sit and observe silence.

FOR SILENT REFLECTION

Why does the angel tell Mary to not be afraid?

CLOSING PRAYER

Let us stand and bring our hopes and needs to God as we pray, "Lord, hear our prayer."

◆ All may add their own prayers here.

Let us pray: **Our Father . . . Amen.**

God our Father,
help us to be open to
as we say "yes" to Jesus every day.
We ask this through Christ our Lord.

Amen.

✛ All make the Sign of the Cross.

ALSO ON THIS DAY: Las Posadas continues

147

PRAYER FOR THE WEEK

WITH A READING FOR **SUNDAY, DECEMBER 22, 2013**

OPENING

In today's First Reading from the prophet Isaiah, whom we hear often during Advent, see what sign is revealed at the end of the passage. What does the name "Emmanuel" mean?

✚ All make the Sign of the Cross.

In the name of the Father, and of the Son, and of the Holy Spirit. Amen.

PSALM

(For a longer psalm, see page xii.) Psalm 85:4a, 8, 10–11, 12–13

Restore us again, O God of our salvation!

Restore us again, O God of our salvation!

Let me hear what God the LORD will speak,
    for he will speak peace to his people,
to his faithful, to those who turn to him in
        their hearts.

Restore us again, O God of our salvation!

READING

Isaiah 7:10–14

A reading from the Book of the Prophet Isaiah

Again the Lord spoke to Ahaz [AY-haz], saying, Ask a sign of the Lord your God; let it be deep as Sheol or high as heaven. But Ahaz said, I will not ask, and I will not put the Lord to the test. Then Isaiah said: "Hear then, O house of David! Is it too little for you to weary mortals, that you weary my God also? Therefore the Lord himself will give you a sign. Look, the young woman is with child and shall bear a son, and shall name him Emmanuel.

The Word of the Lord.

◆ All observe silence.

FOR SILENT REFLECTION

In the Christmas gifts that I am making, purchasing, or contributing to, how am I reflecting to others that Jesus, our Immanuel, is the main cause for the celebration?

CLOSING PRAYER

Let us stand and bring our hopes and needs to God as we pray, "Lord, hear our prayer."

◆ All may add their own prayers here.

Let us pray: **Our Father . . . Amen.**

God of wisdom,
you spoke to us through
holy people of faith,
and you gave us an
immaculate sign of hope.
May we fill our hearts this Christmas
with your new life
so that others may know
that God is with us.
We ask this through Christ your Son,
our Lord and Savior.

Amen.

✚ All make the Sign of the Cross.

ALSO ON THIS DAY Las Posadas end on December 23

CHRISTMAS

MONDAY, JANUARY 6, 2014, TO FRIDAY, JANUARY 10, 2014

THE MEANING OF CHRISTMAS

"For a child has been born for us,
    a son given to us;
authority rests upon his shoulders;
    and he is named
Wonderful Counselor, Mighty God,
    Everlasting Father, Prince of Peace."
(Isaiah 9:6)

God keeps his promises! He amazes us with gifts we never could have imagined or asked for.

The earth is filled with God's gifts. Think of the solid ground that supports us, gravity that keeps us from floating away, the atmosphere that provides oxygen for breathing and a shield to protect us from the heat of the sun, and water that keeps our cells healthy. We need so many things just to stay alive. And yet the earth contains much more than is necessary to keep us going. Within the earth, precious metals and gems delight us with their shine. Seashells and pinecones amaze us with their geometry. Roses and lilacs fill the air with perfume. Peacocks and panthers and pecans add to the world's great fascination. And every day our friends and family share new thoughts and fresh ways to love. What a world we have been given!

But God wants to give us something even more precious than all these wonders. He wants to share his life with us. One day, in Bethlehem, he placed himself in our hands. He, who was there from the beginning of the universe, who was the Word that spoke every one of us into this world, gave himself to us as a small child who could do nothing for himself.

This gift has changed everything. He has opened his heart for us. He has shown us how to live according to his way. Out of the tree stump of despair, God has brought a flowering branch.

Now we can bloom with the love of Christ if we follow his example and give our whole selves.

Let us stand in front of the manger in Bethlehem and gaze with wonder on Mary and Joseph, the shepherds and angels, and the holy child, Jesus, our Lord.

As we listen to the Gospel readings for the time of Christmas, we can follow the thread of Mary's story: how she listened to God and trusted in his promises, how the Holy Spirit worked in her life and filled Elizabeth and later Simeon, how Mary rejoiced in God's mighty power, how her prayers became prayers of the Church, and how she said "yes" to God's plan. If we walk with Mary through these sacred days, we will deepen our understanding and enjoyment of this holy time.

PREPARING TO CELEBRATE CHRISTMAS IN THE CLASSROOM

It's time to exchange the purple cloth on your prayer table for a white one. If your students enjoyed the Advent procession, you can have another procession to celebrate Christmas (see Preparing to Celebrate Advent in the Classroom on page 123). The last child in the procession can carry a figure of the infant Jesus and place it in the manger that has been waiting empty on your prayer table during Advent.

This book provides a prayer service to celebrate the Solemnity of the Epiphany of the Lord in the classroom or with a larger group (see pages 154–155).

SACRED SPACE

If, during Advent, you kept a big, unlit white pillar candle in your classroom in anticipation of the remembrance of Christ's birth, now is the time to light it! You may wish to sing the joyful hymn, "Let

All Things Now Living," the beautiful "O Radiant Light," or "Many Are the Light Beams."

If you set up a Christmas Nativity scene in your classroom, consider placing the three Magi figures at a distance from the Holy Family. Each day the children can help you bring the Magi closer to Christ until the Epiphany of the Lord, when they arrive. Each time you handle the figures, you can sing "We Three Kings." The prayer service for Epiphany on pages 154–155 provides a beautiful and prayerful way to celebrate the eventual arrival of the Magi in Bethlehem.

Here is a prayer you can use to bless all who pray with your Christmas Nativity scene:

"To you is born this day in the city of David a Savior, who is the Messiah, the Lord" (Luke 2:11).

Loving Father, as we look at this scene, may we remember Mary, the holy Mother of God, who said "yes" to your plan of salvation; may we imitate Saint Joseph, who protected and loved your Son and his blessed mother; and may we adore Jesus forever and ever. We ask this through the same Jesus Christ, our Light and our Life. Amen.

"Silent Night" and "Away in a Manger" are perfect to sing at the conclusion of this prayer.

SACRED MUSIC

Christmas Time is a time of music! There are so many beautiful carols you can sing with the children. Don't forget "Joy to the World," "Angels We Have Heard On High," or "O Come, All Ye Faithful." You may even wish to organize a caroling party and go door to door through your school.

PRAYERS FOR CHRISTMAS

The opening verses of the Gospel according to St. John contain some of the most beautiful poetry in the world:

"In the beginning was the Word, and the Word was with God, and the Word was God. He was in the beginning with God. All things came into being through him, and without him not one thing came into being. What has come into being in him was life, and the life was the light of all people. The light shines in the darkness, and the darkness did not overcome it" (John 1:1–5).

These verses beautifully express the mystery of the Incarnation. You might want to spend some time during religion class reading this beautiful hymn line by line. Ask the children who St. John means when he speaks about the "Word of God." See what they say when you ask them how "all things came into being" through Christ when we know he was born after the creation of the world. How can one person be the "light of all people"? What do the children think St. John means when he says, "the darkness did not overcome" the Light of the World?

A NOTE TO CATECHISTS

See whether you can share a Christmas Nativity scene with the teacher who shares your classroom. If not, perhaps the Religious Education Director can help you find a place to keep a Nativity scene. Or bring your students on a "field trip" to the church and let them pray in front of the parish Nativity scene!

GRACE BEFORE MEALS

CHRISTMAS

LEADER:

"For a child has been born to us . . . "

ALL: "a Son given to us."

✚ All make the Sign of the Cross.

In the name of the Father, and of the Son, and of the Holy Spirit. Amen.

LEADER:

Heavenly Father,
may the food we are about to share
help to nourish our bodies and minds,
just as you nurture us always
with the gift of your Son
and your everlasting Spirit.
May we be a living sign of the
presence of Jesus,
who is hope for the world.
We ask this through Christ our Lord

✚ All make the Sign of the Cross.

In the name of the Father, and of the Son, and of the Holy Spirit. Amen.

152

PRAYER AT DAY'S END
CHRISTMAS

LEADER:
Sing to the Lord a new song,

ALL: for he has done wondrous deeds!

✚ All make the Sign of the Cross.

In the name of the Father, and of the Son, and of the Holy Spirit. Amen.

LEADER:
Heavenly Father,
the gift of your Son
gives us so much joy!
We thank you for this day,
filled with wonder and small adventures.
May we always remember that you
are the source of all goodness
as we praise the miracle of Jesus,
whom you sent to us
to lead the way back to you.
We ask this through Christ our Lord
and Savior.

✚ All make the Sign of the Cross.

In the name of the Father, and of the Son, and of the Holy Spirit. Amen.

PRAYER SERVICE
FOR EPIPHANY

Prepare six leaders and a song leader for this service. The second and fourth leaders will need Bibles to read the Scripture passages and may need help finding and practicing them. Before you begin, remove the figures of shepherds and the three kings from your Nativity scene. Put the shepherds away until next year. Place the kings a short distance from the Nativity scene. Then gather the class near it. This service calls for two songs. Help the song leader prepare to lead the singing.

SONG LEADER:
Please stand and join in singing our opening song, "We Three Kings."

FIRST LEADER:

✚ All make the Sign of the Cross.

May the light of our Creator guide us in this prayer of praise.

ALL: Amen.

Let us pray:
Almighty God,
You are the light of the world!
Guide us with your radiance
as we reflect your goodness in our lives.
We ask this through Christ our Lord.

ALL: Amen.

◆ Gesture for all to sit.

SECOND LEADER: Isaiah 9:2–7
A reading from the Book of the Prophet Isaiah

◆ Read the Scripture passage from the Bible.

The Word of the Lord.

◆ All observe silence.

CHILDREN'S DAILY PRAYER 2013–2014, © 2013 Archdiocese of Chicago: Liturgy Training Publications. All rights reserved. Orders: 1-800-933-1800 or www.LTP.org.

THIRD LEADER: Psalm 148:1–2, 3–4, 9–10, 11–12, 13
Our refrain is: Praise the LORD!

ALL: Praise the LORD!

Praise the LORD from the heavens;
  praise him in the heights!
Praise him, all his angels;
  praise him, all his host!

ALL: Praise the LORD!

Praise him, sun and moon;
  praise him, all you shining stars!
Praise him, you highest heavens,
  and you waters above the heavens!

ALL: Praise the LORD!

Mountains and all hills,
  fruit trees and all cedars!
Wild animals and all cattle,
  creeping things and flying birds!

ALL: Praise the LORD!

Kings of the earth and all peoples,
  princes and all rulers of the earth!
Young men and women alike,
  old and young together!

ALL: Praise the LORD!

◆ All stand and sing **Alleluia.**

FOURTH LEADER: Matthew 2:9b–12
A reading from the holy Gospel according to Matthew

◆ Read the Scripture passage from a Bible.

The Gospel of the Lord

◆ All sit and observe silence.

◆ In silence, an adult slowly moves the three figures of the wise men, one at a time, into the stable.

SONG LEADER:
Let us stand and sing, "Joy to the World."

FIFTH LEADER:
Heavenly Father,
you created the sun, planets,
moon, and stars,
and everything that breathes
to give you glory.
You are almighty and powerful,
yet you are as close to us as our breath,
and you live within our hearts.
Inspire us more with your
gentle Spirit and direction
just as you did the wise men
who traveled far to
see your glory in the Christ child.
We ask this through your Son Jesus.

Amen.

Let us pray: **Our Father . . . Amen.**

SIXTH LEADER:
May God's love, found in the Trinity of
Father, Son, and Spirit,
always surround us on our journey.

ALL: Amen.

✝ All make the Sign of the Cross.

PRAYER FOR **MONDAY**
JANUARY 6, 2014

OPENING

Today we remember St. André Bessette [buh-SET] who experienced a lifetime of sickness and weakness. He was a factory worker during the Civil War and later became a brother in the Congregation of the Holy Cross. As door keeper, sacristan, laundry worker, and messenger, he devoted himself to praying to St. Joseph on behalf of those who were sick. As some people were healed, word spread about his miraculous touch. He was canonized in 2010.

✤ All make the Sign of the Cross.

In the name of the Father, and of the Son, and of the Holy Spirit. Amen.

PSALM

(For a longer psalm, see page xiii.) Psalm 96:1–2a, 2b–3, 5b–6, 11a

Let the heavens be glad and the earth rejoice!

Let the heavens be glad and the earth rejoice!

Sing to the LORD a new song;
  sing to the LORD, all the earth.
Sing to the LORD; bless his name.

Let the heavens be glad and the earth rejoice!

READING

1 John 3:22–24

A reading from the first Letter of St. John

Beloved: We receive from him whatever we ask, because we obey his commandments and do what pleases him.

And this is his commandment, that we should believe in the name of his Son Jesus Christ and love one another, just as he has commanded us. All who obey his commandments abide in him, and he abides in them. And by this we know that he abides in us, by the Spirit that he has given us.

The Word of the Lord.

◆ All observe silence.

FOR SILENT REFLECTION

How do I reflect on my day and ask for guidance from God's Spirit?

CLOSING PRAYER

Let us stand and bring our hopes and needs to God as we pray, "Lord, hear our prayer."

◆ All may add their own prayers here.

Let us pray: **Our Father . . . Amen.**

God our Father,
you gave us the commandments
to help us to live rightly.
Your Spirit guides us.
Help us to look for you
everywhere we are.
We ask this through your Son, Jesus Christ.

Amen.

✤ All make the Sign of the Cross.

OPENING

We remember St. Raymond of Penyafort today, the patron saint of attorneys. Born in 1175, he lived to be 100 years old. He was known for his work in Church law and worked for Pope Gregory IX. He compiled five books called the Decretals, which were the best organized collections of Church law. Later in life, he became the leader of the Dominican order. In today's reading, we hear of the depth of God's love for us with the gift of Jesus.

✚ All make the Sign of the Cross.

In the name of the Father, and of the Son, and of the Holy Spirit. Amen.

PSALM

(For a longer psalm, see page xiii.) Psalm 96:1–2a, 2b–3, 5b–6, 11a

Let the heavens be glad and the earth rejoice!

Let the heavens be glad and the earth rejoice!

Sing to the LORD a new song;
  sing to the LORD, all the earth.
Sing to the LORD; bless his name.

Let the heavens be glad and the earth rejoice!

READING

1 John 4:7–10

A reading from the first Letter of St. John

Beloved, let us love one another, because love is from God; everyone who loves is born of God and knows God. Whoever does not love does not know God, for God is love. God's love was revealed among us in this way: God sent his only Son into the world so that we might live through him. In this is love, not that we loved God but that he loved us and sent his Son to be the atoning sacrifice for our sins.

The Word of the Lord.

◆ All sit and observe silence.

FOR SILENT REFLECTION

How do I show love for my parents and brothers and sisters? How can I do loving acts of kindness for relatives whom I don't see very often?

CLOSING PRAYER

Let us stand and bring our hopes and needs to God as we pray, "Lord, hear our prayer."

◆ All may add their own prayers here.

Let us pray: **Our Father . . . Amen.**

God almighty,
you loved us so much
that you gave us the gift
of your Son
to show us how to live
and to point us
to goodness, truth, and
life everlasting.
Help us to love
even when it isn't easy.
Guide us with your Spirit
as we learn more
about your Son Jesus.
We ask this through Christ our Lord.

Amen.

✚ All make the Sign of the Cross.

PRAYER FOR **WEDNESDAY** JANUARY 8, 2014

OPENING

Today's Gospel shows Jesus as someone who took time to pray and calmed his friends' nerves. How did Jesus get to their boat? How did he cause the winds to stop howling?

✛ All make the Sign of the Cross.

In the name of the Father, and of the Son, and of the Holy Spirit. Amen.

PSALM

(For a longer psalm, see page xiii.) Psalm 96:1–2a, 2b–3, 5b–6, 11a

Let the heavens be glad and the earth rejoice!

Let the heavens be glad and the earth rejoice!

Sing to the LORD a new song;
  sing to the LORD, all the earth.
Sing to the LORD; bless his name.

Let the heavens be glad and the earth rejoice!

◆ All stand and sing **Alleluia.**

GOSPEL

Mark 6:45–52

A reading from the holy Gospel according to Mark

Immediately he made his disciples get into the boat and go on ahead to the other side, to Bethsaida, while he dismissed the crowd. After saying farewell to them, he went up on the mountain to pray.

When evening came, the boat was out on the sea, and he was alone on the land. When he saw that they were straining at the oars against an adverse wind, he came towards them early in the morning, walking on the sea. He intended to pass them by. But when they saw him walking on the sea, they thought it was a ghost and cried out; for they all saw him and were terrified. But immediately he spoke to them and said, "Take heart, it is I; do not be afraid." Then he got into the boat with them and the wind ceased. And they were utterly astounded, for they did not understand about the loaves, but their hearts were hardened.

The Gospel of the Lord.

◆ All sit and observe silence.

FOR SILENT REFLECTION

Have you ever cried out to God when you were afraid? How has God calmed you?

CLOSING PRAYER

Let us stand and bring our hopes and needs to God as we pray, "Lord, hear our prayer."

◆ All may add their own prayers here.

Let us pray: **Our Father . . . Amen.**

Lord Jesus,
you calm the winds of our
busy lives
if we just look to you
and respond to your presence.
God's Spirit worked through you
with the disciples
and it works through us as well.
Help us to remain watchful for
the many miracles that happen
all around us.
We ask this in your name.

Amen.

✛ All make the Sign of the Cross.

OPENING

News about Jesus kept spreading throughout Galilee. The prophet Isaiah foretold that a Messiah would save people, and Jesus merely proclaimed who he was.

✦ All make the Sign of the Cross.

In the name of the Father, and of the Son, and of the Holy Spirit. Amen.

PSALM

(For a longer psalm, see page xiii.) Psalm 96:1–2a, 2b–3, 5b–6, 11a

Let the heavens be glad and the earth rejoice!

Let the heavens be glad and the earth rejoice!

Sing to the LORD a new song;
    sing to the LORD, all the earth.
Sing to the LORD; bless his name.

Let the heavens be glad and the earth rejoice!

◆ All stand and sing **Alleluia.**

GOSPEL

Luke 4:14–21

A reading from the holy Gospel according to Luke

Jesus, filled with the power of the Spirit, returned to Galilee, and a report about him spread through all the surrounding country. He began to teach in their synagogues and was praised by everyone. When he came to Nazareth, where he had been brought up, he went to the synagogue on the sabbath day, as was his custom. He stood up to read, and the scroll of the prophet Isaiah was given to him. He unrolled the scroll and found the place where it was written: "The Spirit of the Lord is upon me, because he has anointed me to bring good news to the poor. He has sent me to proclaim release to the captives and recovery of sight to the blind, to let the oppressed go free, to proclaim the year of the Lord's favor." And he rolled up the scroll, gave it back to the attendant, and sat down. The eyes of all in the synagogue were fixed on him. Then he began to say to them, "Today this scripture has been fulfilled in your hearing."

The Gospel of the Lord.

◆ All sit and observe silence.

FOR SILENT REFLECTION

What do you think Jesus is trying to tell the people in the synagogue?

CLOSING PRAYER

Let us stand and bring our hopes and needs to God as we pray, "Lord, hear our prayer."

◆ All may add their own prayers here.

Let us pray: **Our Father . . . Amen.**

Lord Jesus,
you amazed everyone with the
reading of Isaiah's prophecy.
May we have the courage to
proclaim to others all that we are:
God's children set free by you.
In your name we pray.

Amen.

✦ All make the Sign of the Cross.

PRAYER FOR **FRIDAY** JANUARY 10, 2014

OPENING

In this reading from John, we hear a strong testimony to the power of belief in the One who provides eternal life.

✝ All make the Sign of the Cross.

In the name of the Father, and of the Son, and of the Holy Spirit. Amen.

PSALM   (For a longer psalm, see page xiii.) Psalm 96:1–2a, 2b–3, 5b–6, 11a

Let the heavens be glad and the earth rejoice!

Let the heavens be glad and the earth rejoice!

Sing to the LORD a new song;
    sing to the LORD, all the earth.
Sing to the LORD; bless his name.

Let the heavens be glad and the earth rejoice!

READING   1 John 5:5–13

A reading from the first Letter of St. John

Who is it that conquers the world but the one who believes that Jesus is the Son of God?

This is the one who came by water and blood, Jesus Christ, not with the water only but with the water and the blood. And the Spirit is the one that testifies, for the Spirit is the truth. There are three that testify: the Spirit and the water and the blood, and these three agree. If we receive human testimony, the testimony of God is greater; for this is the testimony of God that he has testified to his Son.

Those who believe in the Son of God have the testimony in their hearts. Those who do not believe in God have made him a liar by not believing in the testimony that God has given

concerning his Son. And this is the testimony: God gave us eternal life, and this life is in his Son. Whoever has the Son has life; whoever does not have the Son of God does not have life. I write these things to you who believe In the name of the Son of God, so that you may know that you have eternal life.

The Word of the Lord.

◆ All observe silence.

FOR SILENT REFLECTION

Do I believe that Jesus, God's Son, came here as a gift to me from our Creator? How do I show my gratitude?

CLOSING PRAYER

Let us stand and bring our hopes and needs to God as we pray, "Lord, hear our prayer."

◆ All may add their own prayers here.

Let us pray: **Our Father . . . Amen.**

God Almighty,
you revealed how we have new life
through the waters of Baptism,
through the life-giving blood
of your Son's sacrifice,
and through your Spirit that
energizes us with new possibilities.
May we spread your
words of hope
so that others may truly live.
We ask this through Christ our Lord.

Amen.

✝ All make the Sign of the Cross.

ORDINARY TIME WINTER

SUNDAY, JANUARY 12, 2014, TO TUESDAY, MARCH 4, 2014

ORDINARY TIME

WINTER

THE MEANING OF ORDINARY TIME

Jesus said, "Again, the kingdom of heaven is like a merchant in search of fine pearls; on finding the one pearl of great value, he went and sold all that he had and bought it" (Matthew 13:45–46).

Advent filled our hearts with quiet hope, and Christmas brought us warmth and light and joy. Now it is Ordinary Time again, but we are not the same people we were during the last Ordinary Time. Our bodies have been growing and changing, we have learned new things, and our friendships have deepened. But even more important than all these things, we are not the same as we were before because we have opened our hearts and minds to God's love.

Remember, everyone who looks for the kingdom of God and lives its promise will change and grow in hidden but miraculous ways. The grace of Advent and the holiness of Christmas are like water and sun for the mustard seed kingdom in our hearts. They cause God's life in us to sprout and grow.

Jesus tells us that the kingdom also has another quality. It is like a pearl, precious beyond everything else. Imagine spending your whole life searching for the most precious pearl. When you finally find it, how would you recognize it? Would searching for pearls help you to learn something about them? What if we were to search in every situation, every moment of our lives, for the precious pearl that is the kingdom of God here on earth? Then, when we finally have eyes to see, what must we "sell" before we can "buy" it? What can selling and buying even mean when we're speaking about the kingdom of God? Surely Jesus doesn't mean that we need money in order to "buy" the kingdom! If that were so, only rich people could be saved!

In the parable of the precious pearl, *selling* means to give up other, lesser pearls. But why would the merchant need to give up something that brings him happiness? Is it possible that spending our attention and love on things that won't last cannot make us truly and deeply happy? How do we then "buy" the kingdom? Can we keep back any little part of ourselves and still enter the kingdom of our God, the one who gives us all?

During Ordinary Time this winter, we will see how the Gospels reflect on the question "When and how did the world first come to see that Jesus Christ is the Son of the Living God?" It seems that God willed that the truth would dawn on us slowly, and that different people would have many different ways of coming to believe in Jesus. Elizabeth felt her baby leap in her womb, angels announced the Good News to the Jewish shepherds, the Magi followed a new star, Simeon somehow "just knew," God spoke from a cloud to those at Jesus's Baptism, and the servants at the wedding in Cana knew when they saw the wine that came from the water jars. Even for us today, our faith in Christ is constantly deepening and strengthening as we recognize his gifts and power with ever-greater understanding.

PREPARING TO CELEBRATE ORDINARY TIME IN THE CLASSROOM

You will need to replace your white cloth with a green one, now that it is Ordinary Time again. Plan another procession with your students if they respond well to them. Otherwise, you might ask them if they have any ideas about how to change the cloths with care and dignity. You might be surprised at the depth of their suggestions.

From January 18 through 25, the Church joins with our Protestant brothers and sisters in the Week of Prayer for Christian Unity. A special prayer service, which may be used anytime during the week, is provided on page 171.

On February 2 we celebrate the feast of the Presentation of the Lord, also known as "Candlemas." This is a beautiful feast to celebrate with

162

children. Before you begin prayer that day, dim the classroom lights and light a candle. Help the student proclaiming the Scripture to practice so that it can be done well, and allow time for the class to ponder the story together. (See more below, under Prayers for Ordinary Time and A Note to Catechists.)

SACRED SPACE

Now would be a good time to bring a potted plant to place on your prayer table. A spider plant or an ivy will withstand long weekends without attention. Give the care and watering over to your students. Make a job chart and allow them to take turns fetching water in a watering can for the plant. Watching the plant grow will provide a concrete sign of the growth that takes place in our hearts during this liturgical season.

SACRED MUSIC

This would be the perfect time to learn how to sing one of the psalms. Psalm 27 ("The Lord Is My Light and My Salvation") and Psalm 23 ("The Lord Is My Shepherd") are two beautiful psalms that have many different musical settings.

Children also love to learn spirituals ("This Little Light of Mine," "Lord, I Want to Be a Christian," and "There Is a Balm in Gilead"). Invite children to share favorite spiritual songs from their ethnic backgrounds and try singing songs from other countries ("We are Marching in the Light," "Pan de Vida," the round "Shalom Chevarim").

Also, don't forget to sing Alleluia often during these days. When Lent arrives, we will have to wait a long time before Easter when we can sing it again. The best Alleluia to sing is the one your parish uses before the Sunday Gospel.

PRAYERS FOR ORDINARY TIME

Each night before going to bed, Catholic men and women around the world pray the Canticle of Simeon, the prayer of the elderly man who met the Holy Family in the temple of Jerusalem when Mary and Joseph brought Jesus there as a baby. God had promised Simeon that he would not die before he saw the Messiah. So when Simeon saw the child Jesus, he took him in his arms and said this prayer:

"Master, now you are dismissing your servant
    in peace,
    according to your word;
for my eyes have seen your salvation,
    which you have prepared in the presence
        of all peoples,
    a light for revelation to the Gentiles
        and for glory to your people Israel"
        (Luke 2:29–32).

Introduce this prayer on February 2, the feast of the Presentation of the Lord. You may want to ask the children about certain key words in the prayer. Possible "wondering" questions could include: Why does Simeon call himself God's "servant"? Does the word *servant* recall anything that Mary once said? How did Simeon know that Jesus was a special baby? How is this small baby a "light" and a "glory"?

A NOTE TO CATECHISTS

Sometimes building codes will not allow school teachers or catechists to burn matches or light candles in the classroom. If possible, for February 2, plan a visit to a room where fire is permitted so that your celebration of the feast of the Presentation of the Lord will be set apart from the days surrounding it.

GRACE BEFORE MEALS

ORDINARY TIME • WINTER

LEADER:

Who is this King of glory?

ALL: The Lord, strong and mighty.

✠ All make the Sign of the Cross.

In the name of the Father, and of the Son, and of the Holy Spirit. Amen.

LEADER:

Heavenly Father,
we thank you for
the food we are about to share.
The abundance of this meal
reflects your goodness,
and how you provide for us
every day, in so many ways.
We ask this through Christ our Lord.

ALL: Amen.

✠ All make the Sign of the Cross.

In the name of the Father, and of the Son, and of the Holy Spirit. Amen.

PRAYER AT DAY'S END
ORDINARY TIME • WINTER

LEADER:
Your word is a light to my feet,

ALL: and a light to my path.

✛ All make the Sign of the Cross.

In the name of the Father, and of the Son, and of the Holy Spirit. Amen.

LEADER:
Heavenly Father,
thank you for this day of learning.
As we make our way home or
to other activities,
help us turn to you
for guidance in everything we do.
Keep us safe as we respond
to your Word in our hearts
as we meet with family and friends.
We ask this through Christ our Lord.

ALL: Amen.

✛ All make the Sign of the Cross.

In the name of the Father, and of the Son, and of the Holy Spirit. Amen.

PRAYER FOR THE WEEK

OPENING

Today's Gospel describes Jesus's baptism. Perhaps those who witnessed this glorious event witnessed Jesus as both human and divine that day, as a holy person entrusted with God's sacred plans.

✚ All make the Sign of the Cross.

In the name of the Father, and of the Son, and of the Holy Spirit. Amen.

PSALM (For a longer psalm, see page xiii.) Psalm 23:1–3a, 3b–4, 5, 6

I shall dwell in the house of the LORD my
whole life long.

**I shall dwell in the house of the LORD my
whole life long.**

The LORD is my shepherd, I shall not want.
   He makes me lie down in green pastures;
he leads me beside still waters;
   he restores my soul.

**I shall dwell in the house of the LORD my
whole life long.**

◆ All stand and sing **Alleluia.**

GOSPEL   Matthew 3:13–17

A reading from the holy Gospel according to Matthew

Then Jesus came from Galilee to John at the Jordan, to be baptized by him. John would have prevented him, saying, "I need to be baptized by you, and do you come to me?" But Jesus answered him, "Let it be so now; for it is proper for us in this way to fulfill all righteousness." Then he consented. And when Jesus had been baptized, just as he came up from the water, suddenly the heavens were opened to him and he saw the Spirit of God descending like a dove and alighting on him. And a voice from heaven said, "This is my Son, the Beloved, with whom I am well pleased."

The Gospel of the Lord.

◆ All sit and observe silence.

FOR SILENT REFLECTION

What is your mission in life? Have you been affirmed by things that you do well? Do you have talents that help reveal God's glory to others?

CLOSING PRAYER

Let us stand and bring our hopes and needs to God as we pray, "Lord, hear our prayer."

◆ All may add their own prayers here.

Let us pray: **Our Father . . . Amen.**

Lord Jesus,
you chose to be baptized that day so that
God could reveal to the world
that you were his Son, the Beloved.
God declared for us
the intent of your mission,
to show us that you were
the Chosen One for our salvation.
Guide us to appreciate
our own Baptism and the call
to be your chosen ones in this world.
We ask this in your name.

Amen.

✚ All make the Sign of the Cross.

166

OPENING

Today's Gospel shows how Jesus was able to lead ordinary people to do extraordinary things.

✝ All make the Sign of the Cross.

In the name of the Father, and of the Son, and of the Holy Spirit. Amen.

PSALM (For a longer psalm, see page xiii.) Psalm 23:1–3a, 3b–4, 5, 6

I shall dwell in the house of the LORD my
  whole life long.

**I shall dwell in the house of the LORD my
  whole life long.**

The LORD is my shepherd, I shall not want.
  He makes me lie down in green pastures;
he leads me beside still waters;
  he restores my soul.

**I shall dwell in the house of the LORD my
  whole life long.**

◆ All stand and sing **Alleluia.**

GOSPEL

Mark 1:14–20

A reading from the holy Gospel according to Mark

After John was arrested, Jesus came to Galilee, proclaiming the good news of God, and saying, "The time is fulfilled, and the kingdom of God has come near; repent, and believe in the good news." As Jesus passed along the Sea of Galilee, he saw Simon and his brother Andrew casting a net into the sea—for they were fishermen. And Jesus said to them, "Follow me and I will make you fish for people." And immediately they left their nets and followed him. As he went a little farther, he saw James son of Zebedee and his brother John, who were in their boat mending the nets. Immediately he called them; and they left their father Zebedee in the boat with the hired men, and followed him.

The Gospel of the Lord.

◆ All sit and observe silence.

FOR SILENT REFLECTION

When have I made a choice to follow Christ? What activities or thoughts did I leave behind?

CLOSING PRAYER

Let us stand and bring our hopes and needs to God as we pray, "Lord, hear our prayer."

◆ All may add their own prayers here.

Let us pray: **Our Father . . . Amen.**

Jesus our leader,
your call to us is captivating,
and we follow you through
difficult times.
Keep us motivated as we
walk in the steps of your Apostles,
whom you also called
to do amazing things with
their simple, yet powerful skills.
We ask this in your name.

Amen.

✝ All make the Sign of the Cross.

PRAYER FOR **TUESDAY**
JANUARY 14, 2014

OPENING

In today's Gospel, Jesus astounds the worshipers when he casts out an "unclean Spirit." His God-given authority amazes everyone for miles around.

✚ All make the Sign of the Cross.

In the name of the Father, and of the Son, and of the Holy Spirit. Amen.

PSALM (For a longer psalm, see page xiii.) Psalm 23:1–3a, 3b–4, 5, 6

I shall dwell in the house of the LORD my
    whole life long.

**I shall dwell in the house of the LORD my
    whole life long.**

The LORD is my shepherd, I shall not want.
    He makes me lie down in green pastures;
he leads me beside still waters;
    he restores my soul.

**I shall dwell in the house of the LORD my
    whole life long.**

◆ All stand and sing **Alleluia.**

GOSPEL   Mark 1:21–28

A reading from the holy Gospel according to Mark

Jesus went to Capernaum; and when the sabbath came, he entered the synagogue and taught. They were astounded at his teaching, for he taught them as one having authority, and not as the scribes. Just then there was in their synagogue a man with an unclean spirit, and he cried out, "What have you to do with us, Jesus of Nazareth? Have you come to destroy us? I know who you are, the Holy One of God." But Jesus rebuked him, saying, "Be silent, and come out of him!" And the unclean spirit, convulsing him and crying with a loud voice, came out of him. They were all amazed, and they kept on asking one another, "What is this? A new teaching—with authority! He commands even the unclean spirits, and they obey him." At once his fame began to spread throughout the surrounding region of Galilee.

The Gospel of the Lord.

◆ All sit and observe silence.

FOR SILENT REFLECTION

What about Jesus's life and work astound you? Where did Jesus's power come from?

CLOSING PRAYER

Let us stand and bring our hopes and needs to God as we pray, "Lord, hear our prayer."

◆ All may add their own prayers here.

Let us pray: **Our Father . . . Amen.**

Lord Jesus,
you had the ultimate source of integrity,
which astounded people everywhere.
Your goodness caused others to wonder
which authority gave you power.
May we choose wisely to whom
positions of authority are given.
Guide us as we grow to become leaders
who make pathways to your truth.
We ask this in your name.

Amen.

✚ All make the Sign of the Cross.

OPENING

Today's reading is a "wake-up call" for Samuel, who was learning about God's persistence.

✚ All make the Sign of the Cross.

In the name of the Father, and of the Son, and of the Holy Spirit. Amen.

PSALM (For a longer psalm, see page xiii.) Psalm 23:1–3a, 3b–4, 5, 6

I shall dwell in the house of the LORD my
      whole life long.

**I shall dwell in the house of the LORD my
      whole life long.**

The LORD is my shepherd, I shall not want.
   He makes me lie down in green pastures;
he leads me beside still waters;
   he restores my soul.

**I shall dwell in the house of the LORD my
      whole life long.**

READING   1 Samuel 3:1–10

A reading from the first Book of Samuel

Now the boy Samuel was ministering to the Lord under Eli. The word of the Lord was rare in those days; visions were not widespread. At that time Eli, whose eyesight had begun to grow dim so that he could not see, was lying down in his room; the lamp of God had not yet gone out, and Samuel was lying down in the temple of the Lord, where the ark of God was. Then the Lord called, "Samuel! Samuel!" and he said, "Here I am!" and ran to Eli, and said, "Here I am, for you called me." But he said, "I did not call; lie down again." So he went and lay down. The Lord called again, "Samuel!"

Samuel got up and went to Eli, and said, "Here I am, for you called me." But he said, "I did not call, my son; lie down again." Now Samuel did not yet know the Lord, and the word of the Lord had not yet been revealed to him. The Lord called Samuel again, a third time. And he got up and went to Eli, and said, "Here I am, for you called me." Then Eli perceived that the Lord was calling the boy. Therefore Eli said to Samuel, "Go, lie down; and if he calls you, you shall say, 'Speak, Lord, for your servant is listening.'" So Samuel went and lay down in his place. Now the Lord came and stood there, calling as before, "Samuel! Samuel!" And Samuel said, "Speak, for your servant is listening."

The Word of the Lord.

◆ All observe silence.

FOR SILENT REFLECTION

How does God speak to you?

CLOSING PRAYER

Let us stand and bring our hopes and needs to God as we pray, "Lord, hear our prayer."

◆ All may add their own prayers here.

Let us pray: **Our Father . . . Amen.**

God our Creator,
you are persistent with your
requests to make known
what we need to do.
Help us to respond to your call.
We ask this through Christ our Lord.

Amen.

✚ All make the Sign of the Cross.

PRAYER FOR **THURSDAY** JANUARY 16, 2014

OPENING

In today's Gospel, we hear about a leper who was always abandoned because of his disease. Then after being cured, he told everyone about the miracle and was ecstatic to be included again in the community.

✛ All make the Sign of the Cross.

In the name of the Father, and of the Son, and of the Holy Spirit. Amen.

PSALM (For a longer psalm, see page xiii.) Psalm 23:1–3a, 3b–4, 5, 6

I shall dwell in the house of the LORD my whole life long.

I shall dwell in the house of the LORD my whole life long.

The LORD is my shepherd, I shall not want.
   He makes me lie down in green pastures;
he leads me beside still waters;
   he restores my soul.

I shall dwell in the house of the LORD my whole life long.

◆ All stand and sing **Alleluia.**

GOSPEL   Mark 1:40–45

A reading from the holy Gospel according to Mark

A leper came to him begging him, and kneeling he said to him, "If you choose, you can make me clean." Moved with pity, Jesus stretched out his hand and touched him, and said to him, "I do choose. Be made clean!" Immediately the leprosy left him, and he was made clean. After sternly warning him he sent him away at once,

saying to him, "See that you say nothing to anyone; but go, show yourself to the priest, and offer for your cleansing what Moses commanded, as a testimony to them." But he went out and began to proclaim it freely, and to spread the word, so that Jesus could no longer go into a town openly, but stayed out in the country; and people came to him from every quarter.

The Gospel of the Lord.

◆ All sit and observe silence.

FOR SILENT REFLECTION

How do I include others who may feel "less than" the popular ones? How can I help make others feel welcomed?

CLOSING PRAYER

Let us stand and bring our hopes and needs to God as we pray, "Lord, hear our prayer."

◆ All may add their own prayers here.

Let us pray: **Our Father . . . Amen.**

Lord Jesus,
it's true that people can't keep
your miracles a secret.
You heal us;
you make us whole again if we ask.
May we always look to you for
new beginnings.
May we strive to love you completely
as you love us.
In your name we pray.

Amen.

✛ All make the Sign of the Cross.

170

PRAYER SERVICE
WEEK OF PRAYER FOR CHRISTIAN UNITY

Prepare four leaders and a song leader for this service. The second leader will need a Bible to read the Scripture passage and may need help finding and practicing it.

FIRST LEADER:
May the peace of Christ, who unites brothers and sisters around the world in his name, be with us, now and for ever.

ALL: Amen.

✛ All make the Sign of the Cross.

Let us pray:
Almighty God,
Creator of all wisdom,
you have made each of us
in your image
to reflect your many gifts.
We have been blessed through the
waters of Baptism,
to join with all Christians in the
loving power of
Father, Son, and Spirit.
Send your Spirit to guide us
as we seek your truth
and become united with Jesus
as our leader in faith.
We ask this through Christ our Lord.

ALL: Amen.

◆ All stand and sing **Alleluia.**

SECOND LEADER: John 15:12–17

A reading from the holy Gospel according to John

◆ Read the Gospel passage from the Bible.

The Gospel of the Lord.

Let us pause and pray in silence for peace and unity among all Christians.

◆ Observe a time of silence.

THIRD LEADER:
Lord God,
you have made yourself known
to all the nations.
We declare your handiwork through
acts of peace and social justice
that assist all in need.
Guide us with your ways of peace.
Give us the courage to seek solutions
that benefit all
and that serve people
to build dignity and respect
for one another.
We ask this through Christ our Lord.

ALL: Amen.

FOURTH LEADER:
Now let us offer to one another a sign of Christ's peace.

◆ All offer one another a sign of peace.

And may the Lord bless us,

✛ All make the Sign of the Cross.

protect us from all evil,
and bring us to everlasting life.

ALL: Amen.

CHILDREN'S DAILY PRAYER 2013–2014 © 2013 Archdiocese of Chicago: Liturgy Training Publications, 3949 South Racine Avenue, Chicago IL 60609. All rights reserved. Orders: 1-800-933-1800 or www.LTP.org. Scripture excerpts are taken from *The New Revised Standard Version Bible: Catholic Edition*, © 1989, Division of Christian Education of the National Council of the Churches of Christ in the United States of America. Used with permission. All rights reserved.

PRAYER FOR **FRIDAY** **JANUARY 17, 2014**

OPENING

In today's Gospel, we can imagine Jesus getting a little irritated at the naysayers in the crowd. He shows them God's power with another dramatic healing of someone who couldn't walk until his friends helped him out.

✚ All make the Sign of the Cross.

In the name of the Father, and of the Son, and of the Holy Spirit. Amen.

PSALM (For a longer psalm, see page xiii.) Psalm 23:1–3a, 3b–4, 5, 6

I shall dwell in the house of the LORD my
  whole life long.

**I shall dwell in the house of the LORD my
  whole life long.**

The LORD is my shepherd, I shall not want.
  He makes me lie down in green pastures;
he leads me beside still waters;
  he restores my soul.

**I shall dwell in the house of the LORD my
  whole life long.**

◆ All stand and sing **Alleluia.**

GOSPEL   Mark 2:1–5

A reading from the holy Gospel according to Mark

When Jesus returned to Capernaum after some days, it was reported that he was at home. So many gathered around that there was no longer room for them, not even in front of the door; and he was speaking the word to them. Then some people came, bringing to him a paralyzed man, carried by four of them. And when they could not bring him to Jesus because of the crowd, they removed the roof above him; and after having dug through it, they let down the mat on which the paralytic lay. When Jesus saw their faith, he said to the paralytic, "Son, your sins are forgiven."

The Gospel of the Lord.

◆ All sit and observe silence.

FOR SILENT REFLECTION

Why is it important to forgive? Do I ask God for forgiveness? Do I forgive others who have hurt me?

CLOSING PRAYER

Let us stand and bring our hopes and needs to God as we pray, "Lord, hear our prayer."

◆ All may add their own prayers here.

Let us pray: **Our Father . . . Amen.**

Jesus, Son of God,
some people went to extraordinary lengths
to be in your powerful presence,
and you rewarded their faith.
Help us to go beyond the easy path
when we need to be one with you.
Help us clear roadblocks
to assist our friends in reaching
your healing touch.
We ask this in your name.

Amen.

✚ All make the Sign of the Cross.

OPENING

Today's reading shows John the Baptist declaring the identity of Jesus. He's a true prophet and has courage and integrity.

✜ All make the Sign of the Cross.

In the name of the Father, and of the Son, and of the Holy Spirit. Amen.

PSALM (For a longer psalm, see page xiii.) Psalm 23:1–3a, 3b–4, 5, 6

I shall dwell in the house of the LORD my
　　whole life long.

**I shall dwell in the house of the LORD my
　　whole life long.**

The LORD is my shepherd, I shall not want.
　He makes me lie down in green pastures;
he leads me beside still waters;
　he restores my soul.

**I shall dwell in the house of the LORD my
　　whole life long.**

◆ All stand and sing **Alleluia.**

GOSPEL   John 1:29–34

A reading from the holy Gospel according to John

John the Baptist saw Jesus coming toward him and declared, "Here is the Lamb of God who takes away the sin of the world! This is he of whom I said, 'After me comes a man who ranks ahead of me because he was before me.' I myself did not know him; but I came baptizing with water for this reason, that he might be revealed to Israel." And John testified, "I saw the Spirit descending from heaven like a dove, and it remained on him. I myself did not know him, but the one who sent me to baptize with water said to me, 'He on whom you see the Spirit descend and remain is the one who baptizes with the Holy Spirit.' And I myself have seen and have testified that this is the Son of God."

The Gospel of the Lord.

◆ All sit and observe silence.

FOR SILENT REFLECTION

Why do you think John the Baptist called Jesus the "Lamb of God"? What does "Lamb of God" mean to you?

CLOSING PRAYER

Let us stand and bring our hopes and needs to God as we pray, "Lord, hear our prayer."

◆ All may add their own prayers here.

Let us pray: **Our Father . . . Amen.**

Jesus our Savior,
you inspired prophets to
declare your name and
your presence everywhere.
They devoted their lives to
spreading the word about your majesty.
They were your witnesses to
God's glorious affirmations
of you as God's Son.
May we be your courageous prophets.
In your name we pray.

Amen.

✜ All make the Sign of the Cross.

OPENING

Today's Gospel speaks of Jesus as a bridegroom and also gives us the image of our faith as something new.

✛ All make the Sign of the Cross.

In the name of the Father, and of the Son, and of the Holy Spirit. Amen.

PSALM (For a longer psalm, see page xiii.) Psalm 23:1–3a, 3b–4, 5, 6

I shall dwell in the house of the LORD my
    whole life long.

**I shall dwell in the house of the LORD my
    whole life long.**

The LORD is my shepherd, I shall not want.
    He makes me lie down in green pastures;
he leads me beside still waters;
    he restores my soul.

**I shall dwell in the house of the LORD my
    whole life long.**

◆ All stand and sing **Alleluia**.

GOSPEL Mark 2:18–22

A reading from the holy Gospel according to Mark

John's disciples and the Pharisees were fasting; and people came and said to him, "Why do John's disciples and the disciples of the Pharisees fast, but your disciples do not fast?" Jesus said to them, "The wedding guests cannot fast while the bridegroom is with them, can they? As long as they have the bridegroom with them, they cannot fast. The days will come when the bridegroom is taken away from them, and then they will fast on that day.

"No one sews a piece of unshrunk cloth on an old cloak; otherwise, the patch pulls away from it, the new from the old, and a worse tear is made. And no one puts new wine into old wineskins; otherwise, the wine will burst the skins, and the wine is lost, and so are the skins; but one puts new wine into fresh wineskins."

The Gospel of the Lord.

◆ All sit and observe silence.

FOR SILENT REFLECTION

How do I nourish my prayer life?

CLOSING PRAYER

Let us stand and bring our hopes and needs to God as we pray, "Lord, hear our prayer."

◆ All may add their own prayers here.

Let us pray: **Our Father . . . Amen.**

Jesus our Redeemer,
you remind us
to make the effort
to renew ourselves.
May we exercise our lives of faith
with your guidance and love.
In your name we pray.

Amen.

✛ All make the Sign of the Cross.

OPENING

Today we remember St. Agnes, a beautiful girl in third-century Rome, who was pursued by several young men for marriage. One of the suitors, whom she rejected, reported her as being a Christian. This was against the law at the time, and she was banished to live in harsh conditions and later martyred.

✛ All make the Sign of the Cross.

In the name of the Father, and of the Son, and of the Holy Spirit. Amen.

PSALM (For a longer psalm, see page xiii.) Psalm 23:1–3a, 3b–4, 5, 6

I shall dwell in the house of the LORD my whole life long.

I shall dwell in the house of the LORD my whole life long.

The LORD is my shepherd, I shall not want.
  He makes me lie down in green pastures;
he leads me beside still waters;
  he restores my soul.

I shall dwell in the house of the LORD my whole life long.

◆ All stand and sing **Alleluia.**

GOSPEL   Mark 2:23–28

A reading from the holy Gospel according to Mark

One sabbath Jesus was going through the grainfields; and as they made their way his disciples began to pluck heads of grain. The Pharisees said to him, "Look, why are they doing what is not lawful on the sabbath?" And he said to them, "Have you never read what David did when he and his companions were hungry and in need of food? He entered the house of God, when Abiathar [uh-BĬ-uh-thahr] was high priest, and ate the bread of the Presence, which it is not lawful for any but the priests to eat, and he gave some to his companions." Then he said to them, "The sabbath was made for humankind, and not humankind for the sabbath; so the Son of Man is lord even of the sabbath."

The Gospel of the Lord.

◆ All sit and observe silence.

FOR SILENT REFLECTION

Do you know why we try to keep the Sabbath holy? How is Sunday different from other days of the week for you?

CLOSING PRAYER

Let us stand and bring our hopes and needs to God as we pray, "Lord, hear our prayer."

◆ All may add their own prayers here.

Let us pray: **Our Father . . . Amen.**

Lord Jesus,
you guide us in our decisions
of how to give you honor.
Help us to never lose sight
of what is really true.
We ask this in your name.

Amen.

✛ All make the Sign of the Cross.

PRAYER FOR **WEDNESDAY** JANUARY 22, 2014

OPENING

Today's Gospel again shows Jesus curing on the Sabbath. Through his actions, he reminds us that love is the greatest of all of the commandments.

✝ All make the Sign of the Cross.

In the name of the Father, and of the Son, and of the Holy Spirit. Amen.

PSALM (For a longer psalm, see page xiii.) Psalm 23:1–3a, 3b–4, 5, 6

I shall dwell in the house of the LORD my
    whole life long.

**I shall dwell in the house of the LORD my
    whole life long.**

The LORD is my shepherd, I shall not want.
    He makes me lie down in green pastures;
he leads me beside still waters;
    he restores my soul.

**I shall dwell in the house of the LORD my
    whole life long.**

◆ All stand and sing **Alleluia.**

GOSPEL   Mark 3:1–5

A reading from the holy Gospel according to Mark

Again he entered the synagogue, and a man was there who had a withered hand. They watched him to see whether he would cure him on the sabbath, so that they might accuse him. And he said to the man who had the withered hand, "Come forward." Then he said to them, "Is it lawful to do good or to do harm on the sabbath, to save life or to kill?" But they were silent. He looked around at them with anger; he was grieved at their hardness of heart and said to the man, "Stretch out your hand." He stretched it out, and his hand was restored.

The Gospel of the Lord.

◆ All sit and observe silence.

FOR SILENT REFLECTION

How do you think the man with the withered hand felt when Jesus cured him?

CLOSING PRAYER

Let us stand and bring our hopes and needs to God as we pray, "Lord, hear our prayer."

◆ All may add their own prayers here.

Let us pray: **Our Father . . . Amen.**

Lord Jesus,
you healed people who
had faith in you.
May we stay focused on
you and what is most important.
Keep us faithful to the guidance
of your gentle Spirit.
We ask this in your name.

Amen.

✝ All make the Sign of the Cross.

ALSO ON THIS DAY: Day of Prayer for the Legal Protection of Unborn Children

176

OPENING

Today we remember St. Vincent, who was ordained a deacon by his friend St. Valerius of Zaragossa in Spain. Even though he was imprisoned for his faith, he remained courageous.

✝ All make the Sign of the Cross.

In the name of the Father, and of the Son, and of the Holy Spirit. Amen.

PSALM (For a longer psalm, see page xiii.) Psalm 23:1–3a, 3b–4, 5, 6

I shall dwell in the house of the LORD my
   whole life long.

**I shall dwell in the house of the LORD my
   whole life long.**

The LORD is my shepherd, I shall not want.
   He makes me lie down in green pastures;
he leads me beside still waters;
   he restores my soul.

**I shall dwell in the house of the LORD my
   whole life long.**

◆ All stand and sing **Alleluia.**

GOSPEL
Mark 3:7–12

A reading from the holy Gospel according to Mark

Jesus departed with his disciples to the sea, and a great multitude from Galilee followed him; hearing all that he was doing, they came to him in great numbers from Judea, Jerusalem, Idumea, beyond the Jordan, and the region around Tyre [tīr] and Sidon [STĪ-duhn]. He told his disciples to have a boat ready for him because of the crowd, so that they would not crush him; for he had cured many, so that all who had diseases pressed upon him to touch him. Whenever the unclean spirits saw him, they fell down before him and shouted, "You are the Son of God!" But he sternly ordered them not to make him known.

The Gospel of the Lord.

◆ All sit and observe silence.

FOR SILENT REFLECTION

Who among my family members or friends are suffering from physical, mental, or emotional pain? How can I be a comfort to them?

CLOSING PRAYER

Let us stand and bring our hopes and needs to God as we pray, "Lord, hear our prayer."

◆ All may add their own prayers here.

Let us pray: **Our Father . . . Amen.**

Lord Jesus,
news about your divine power
spread throughout the land.
People everywhere wanted to be
healed by your glorious presence.
Help us to be your healing hands
within our circle of family and friends.
May we be compassionate with
all people who are struggling with
physical, mental, or emotional pain.
In your name we pray.

Amen.

✝ All make the Sign of the Cross.

PRAYER FOR **FRIDAY**
JANUARY 24, 2014

OPENING

Today we remember St. Francis de Sales who convinced his parents that he should become a priest even though he had studied for years to be a lawyer. He later became bishop of Geneva, and became known for his many pamphlets and books that explained the faith.

✠ All make the Sign of the Cross.

In the name of the Father, and of the Son, and of the Holy Spirit. Amen.

PSALM (For a longer psalm, see page xiii.) Psalm 23:1–3a, 3b–4, 5, 6

I shall dwell in the house of the LORD my
   whole life long.

**I shall dwell in the house of the LORD my
   whole life long.**

The LORD is my shepherd, I shall not want.
   He makes me lie down in green pastures;
he leads me beside still waters;
   he restores my soul.

**I shall dwell in the house of the LORD my
   whole life long.**

◆ All stand and sing **Alleluia.**

GOSPEL
Mark 3:13–19

A reading from the holy Gospel according to Mark

Jesus went up the mountain and called to him those whom he wanted, and they came to him. And he appointed twelve, whom he also named apostles, to be with him, and to be sent out to proclaim the message, and to have authority to cast out demons. So he appointed the twelve: Simon (to whom he gave the name Peter); James son of Zebedee and John the brother of James (to whom he gave the name Boanerges [boh-uh-NURH-jeez], that is, Sons of Thunder); and Andrew, and Philip, and Bartholomew, and Matthew, and Thomas, and James son of Alphaeus [AL-fee-uhs], and Thaddaeus [THAD-ee-uhs], and Simon the Cananaean [KAY-nuh-nee-un], and Judas Iscariot [ih-SKAYR-ee-uht], who betrayed him.

The Gospel of the Lord.

◆ All sit and observe silence.

FOR SILENT REFLECTION

Why do you think Jesus wanted to have a group of special Apostles? Who are Jesus's disciples today?

CLOSING PRAYER

Let us stand and bring our hopes and needs to God as we pray, "Lord, hear our prayer."

◆ All may add their own prayers here.

Let us pray: **Our Father . . . Amen.**

Jesus, our leader,
may we, like the Twelve, respond fully
to your call to follow you.
We ask this in your name.

Amen.

✠ All make the Sign of the Cross.

PRAYER FOR THE WEEK

OPENING

Today's Gospel highlights how Jesus moved in the region of Galilee and called more people to follow him.

✚ All make the Sign of the Cross.

> **In the name of the Father, and of the Son, and of the Holy Spirit. Amen.**

PSALM (For a longer psalm, see page xiii.) Psalm 23:1–3a, 3b–4, 5, 6

I shall dwell in the house of the LORD my
    whole life long.

**I shall dwell in the house of the LORD my
    whole life long.**

The LORD is my shepherd, I shall not want.
    He makes me lie down in green pastures;
he leads me beside still waters;
    he restores my soul.

**I shall dwell in the house of the LORD my
    whole life long.**

◆ All stand and sing **Alleluia.**

GOSPEL
Matthew 4:18–23

A reading from the holy Gospel according to Matthew

As he walked by the Sea of Galilee, he saw two brothers, Simon, who is called Peter, and Andrew his brother, casting a net into the sea—for they were fishermen. And he said to them, "Follow me, and I will make you fish for people." Immediately they left their nets and followed him. As he went from there, he saw two other brothers, James son of Zebedee [ZEB-uh-dee] and his brother John, in the boat with their father Zebedee, mending their nets, and he called them. Immediately they left the boat and their father, and followed him.

Jesus went throughout Galilee, teaching in their synagogues and proclaiming the good news of the kingdom and curing every disease and every sickness among the people.

The Gospel of the Lord.

◆ All sit and observe silence.

FOR SILENT REFLECTION

How do I focus my energy to accomplish what Jesus wants of me?

CLOSING PRAYER

Let us stand and bring our hopes and needs to God as we pray, "Lord, hear our prayer."

◆ All may add their own prayers here.

Let us pray: **Our Father . . . Amen.**

Lord Jesus,
you called on specific people who were
in the midst of their daily living.
You empowered them to do
amazing things.
May we allow ourselves to be
guided by your Spirit of vocation
that brings us closer to your will for us.
We ask this in your name.

Amen.

✚ All make the Sign of the Cross.

PRAYER FOR **MONDAY** JANUARY 27, 2014

OPENING

Today's Gospel illustrates how strong we need to be in our faith to prevent other forces from tearing it down.

✝ All make the Sign of the Cross.

In the name of the Father, and of the Son, and of the Holy Spirit. Amen.

PSALM (For a longer psalm, see page xiii.) Psalm 23:1–3a, 3b–4, 5, 6

I shall dwell in the house of the LORD my
　whole life long.

**I shall dwell in the house of the LORD my
　whole life long.**

The LORD is my shepherd, I shall not want.
　He makes me lie down in green pastures;
he leads me beside still waters;
　he restores my soul.

**I shall dwell in the house of the LORD my
　whole life long.**

◆ All stand and sing **Alleluia.**

GOSPEL   Mark 3:22–30

A reading from the holy Gospel according to Mark

The scribes who came down from Jerusalem said, "He has Beelzebul [bee-EL-zeh-buhl], and by the ruler of the demons he casts out demons." And he called them to him, and spoke to them in parables, "How can Satan cast out Satan? If a kingdom is divided against itself, that kingdom cannot stand. And if a house is divided against itself, that house will not be able to stand. And if Satan has risen up against himself and is divided, he cannot stand, but his end has come. But no one can enter a strong man's house and plunder his property without first tying up the strong man; then indeed the house can be plundered.

"Truly I tell you, people will be forgiven for their sins and whatever blasphemies they utter; but whoever blasphemes against the Holy Spirit can never have forgiveness, but is guilty of an eternal sin"— for they had said, "He has an unclean spirit."

The Gospel of the Lord.

◆ All sit and observe silence.

FOR SILENT REFLECTION

What are some of the temptations that I face? How can I withstand these invasions to my "house" of faith?

CLOSING PRAYER

Let us stand and bring our hopes and needs to God as we pray, "Lord, hear our prayer."

◆ All may add their own prayers here.

Let us pray: **Our Father . . . Amen.**

Lord Jesus,
may we remain strong as the
temptations of our world
sometimes cause us to
lose sight of our faith in you.
In your name we pray.

Amen.

✝ All make the Sign of the Cross.

OPENING

Today we remember St. Thomas Aquinas, a great teacher of the Catholic faith, known for his writings about faith, human reason, and divine revelation. He was named a Doctor of the Church and died in 1274. He is the patron saint of Catholic schools and students.

✚ All make the Sign of the Cross.

In the name of the Father, and of the Son, and of the Holy Spirit. Amen.

PSALM (For a longer psalm, see page xiii.) Psalm 23:1–3a, 3b–4, 5, 6

I shall dwell in the house of the LORD my whole life long.

I shall dwell in the house of the LORD my whole life long.

The LORD is my shepherd, I shall not want.
He makes me lie down in green pastures;
he leads me beside still waters;
he restores my soul.

I shall dwell in the house of the LORD my whole life long.

READING   2 Samuel 6:12–14a

A reading from the Second Book of Samuel

It was told King David, "The Lord has blessed the household of Obed-edom and all that belongs to him, because of the ark of God." So David went and brought up the ark of God from the house of Obed-edom to the city of David with rejoicing; and when those who bore the ark of the Lord had gone six paces, he sacrificed an ox and a fatling. David danced before the Lord with all his might.

The Word of the Lord.

◆ All observe silence.

FOR SILENT REFLECTION

When was the last time that I thanked God for his presence in my life?

CLOSING PRAYER

Let us stand and bring our hopes and needs to God as we pray, "Lord, hear our prayer."

◆ All may add their own prayers here.

Let us pray: **Our Father . . . Amen.**

Almighty God,
we praise you for
all of your creation, and
all of your history with
prophets and kings
who celebrated you too.
We honor you today and always
for being a key presence in our lives.
May we remember
your great achievements in glory
until the end of time.
We ask this through Christ our Lord.

Amen.

✚ All make the Sign of the Cross.

PRAYER FOR **WEDNESDAY** JANUARY 29, 2014

OPENING

In today's Gospel, Jesus tells the story about seeds of Good News being sown on a path, on rock, and then in good soil.

✦ All make the Sign of the Cross.

In the name of the Father, and of the Son, and of the Holy Spirit. Amen.

PSALM (For a longer psalm, see page xiii.) Psalm 23:1–3a, 3b–4, 5, 6

I shall dwell in the house of the LORD my whole life long.

I shall dwell in the house of the LORD my whole life long.

The LORD is my shepherd, I shall not want.
　He makes me lie down in green pastures;
he leads me beside still waters;
　he restores my soul.

I shall dwell in the house of the LORD my whole life long.

◆ All stand and sing **Alleluia.**

GOSPEL   Mark 4:3–9

A reading from the holy Gospel according to Mark

Jesus said to them: "Listen! A sower went out to sow. And as he sowed, some seed fell on the path, and the birds came and ate it up. Other seed fell on rocky ground, where it did not have much soil, and it sprang up quickly, since it had no depth of soil. And when the sun rose, it was scorched; and since it had no root, it withered away. Other seed fell among thorns, and the thorns grew up and choked it, and it yielded no grain. Other seed fell into good soil and brought forth grain, growing up and increasing and yielding thirty and sixty and a hundredfold." And he said, "Let anyone with ears to hear listen!"

The Gospel of the Lord.

◆ All sit and observe silence.

FOR SILENT REFLECTION

Where are seeds of Jesus's Good News planted in your life?

CLOSING PRAYER

Let us stand and bring our hopes and needs to God as we pray, "Lord, hear our prayer."

◆ All may add their own prayers here.

Let us pray: **Our Father . . . Amen.**

Lord Jesus,
you can enrich our lives so much
with your words of life,
but we have a choice
of what to do with your wisdom.
May we become the rich soil for
your Good News of hope.
May we produce grains of faith
that feed others and inspire them
to do the same.
We ask this in your name.

Amen.

✦ All make the Sign of the Cross.

OPENING

Today's Gospel gives a simple message about human relationships. After you hear this Scripture proclaimed, think about whether keeping secrets is a healthy way to build relationships.

✚ All make the Sign of the Cross.

In the name of the Father, and of the Son, and of the Holy Spirit. Amen.

PSALM (For a longer psalm, see page xiii.) Psalm 23:1–3a, 3b–4, 5, 6

I shall dwell in the house of the LORD my whole life long.

I shall dwell in the house of the LORD my whole life long.

The LORD is my shepherd, I shall not want.
   He makes me lie down in green pastures;
he leads me beside still waters;
   he restores my soul.

I shall dwell in the house of the LORD my whole life long.

◆ All stand and sing **Alleluia.**

GOSPEL   Mark 4:21–25

A reading from the holy Gospel according to Mark

Jesus said to his disciples, "Is a lamp brought in to be put under the bushel basket, or under the bed, and not on the lampstand? For there is nothing hidden, except to be disclosed; nor is anything secret, except to come to light. Let anyone with ears to hear listen!" And he said to them, "Pay attention to what you hear; the measure you give will be the measure you get, and still more will be given you. For to those who have, more will be given; and from those who have nothing, even what they have will be taken away."

The Gospel of the Lord.

◆ All sit and observe silence.

FOR SILENT REFLECTION

Is the light of your faith covered up or placed on a stand so that others can see? Do you treat others as you want to be treated?

CLOSING PRAYER

Let us stand and bring our hopes and needs to God as we pray, "Lord, hear our prayer."

◆ All may add their own prayers here.

Let us pray: **Our Father . . . Amen.**

Lord Jesus,
your simple truths
steer us on the right path of
honesty and positive living.
May we honor each other
with your grace-filled light
for all to see.
In your name we pray.

Amen.

✚ All make the Sign of the Cross.

PRAYER FOR **FRIDAY**
JANUARY 31, 2014

OPENING

Today we remember St. John Bosco, who worked with the youth after being ordained in 1841. He started an institution that trained young people to be printers, shoemakers, and tailors.

✛ All make the Sign of the Cross.

In the name of the Father, and of the Son, and of the Holy Spirit. Amen.

PSALM (For a longer psalm, see page xiii.) Psalm 23:1–3a, 3b–4, 5, 6

I shall dwell in the house of the LORD my
     whole life long.

**I shall dwell in the house of the LORD my
     whole life long.**

The LORD is my shepherd, I shall not want.
     He makes me lie down in green pastures;
he leads me beside still waters;
     he restores my soul.

**I shall dwell in the house of the LORD my
     whole life long.**

◆ All stand and sing **Alleluia.**

GOSPEL   Mark 4:30–34

A reading from the holy Gospel according to Mark

Jesus said, "With what can we compare the kingdom of God, or what parable will we use for it? It is like a mustard seed, which, when sown upon the ground, is the smallest of all the seeds on earth; yet when it is sown it grows up and becomes the greatest of all shrubs, and puts forth large branches, so that the birds of the air can make nests in its shade."

With many such parables he spoke the word to them, as they were able to hear it; he did not speak to them except in parables, but he explained everything in private to his disciples.

The Gospel of the Lord.

◆ All sit and observe silence.

FOR SILENT REFLECTION

How do I nurture my prayer life and relationship with Jesus? What are the sun, water, and nutrients that I need for my faith to flourish?

CLOSING PRAYER

Let us stand and bring our hopes and needs to God as we pray, "Lord, hear our prayer."

◆ All may add their own prayers here.

Let us pray: **Our Father . . . Amen.**

Lord Jesus,
we are the smallest of seeds,
yet we grow if we heed your
words of love.
May we continue to be nourished
with your truth
so that we can produce abundantly.
In your name we pray.

Amen.

✛ All make the Sign of the Cross.

PRAYER FOR THE WEEK

OPENING

In this Gospel, Simeon is overjoyed at seeing the Christ child: a sign of salvation for all people.

✠ All make the Sign of the Cross.

In the name of the Father, and of the Son, and of the Holy Spirit. Amen.

PSALM (For a longer psalm, see page xiii.) Psalm 23:1–3a, 3b–4, 5, 6

I shall dwell in the house of the LORD my
whole life long.

**I shall dwell in the house of the LORD my
whole life long.**

The LORD is my shepherd, I shall not want.
He makes me lie down in green pastures;
he leads me beside still waters;
he restores my soul.

**I shall dwell in the house of the LORD my
whole life long.**

◆ All stand and sing **Alleluia.**

GOSPEL   Luke 2:22, 24–32

A reading from the holy Gospel according to Luke

When the time came for their purification according to the law of Moses, they brought him up to Jerusalem to present him to the Lord (as it is written in the law of the Lord).

Now there was a man in Jerusalem whose name was Simeon; this man was righteous and devout, looking forward to the consolation of Israel, and the Holy Spirit rested on him. It had been revealed to him by the Holy Spirit that he would not see death before he had seen the Lord's Messiah. Guided by the Spirit, Simeon came into the temple; and when the parents brought in the child Jesus, to do for him what was customary under the law, Simeon took him in his arms and praised God, saying, "Master, now you are dismissing your servant in peace, according to your word; for my eyes have seen your salvation, which you have prepared in the presence of all peoples, a light for revelation to the Gentiles and for glory to your people Israel."

The Gospel of the Lord.

◆ All sit and observe silence.

FOR SILENT REFLECTION

Simeon was led by the Holy Spirit to see the Messiah. How does God's Spirit reveal truth to me?

CLOSING PRAYER

Let us stand and bring our hopes and needs to God as we pray, "Lord, hear our prayer."

◆ All may add their own prayers here.

Let us pray: **Our Father . . . Amen.**

Father, Son, and Spirit,
keep us watchful for your
divine signs among us.
May we be faithful to
Jesus who was a vulnerable baby
and yet Savior of the world.
We ask this through Christ our Lord.

Amen.

✠ All make the Sign of the Cross.

OPENING

Today we remember St. Blaise, a bishop in Armenia in the early 300s. According to legend, as he was being hauled to prison, he healed a child who had a fish bone lodged in his throat.

✚ All make the Sign of the Cross.

In the name of the Father, and of the Son, and of the Holy Spirit. Amen.

PSALM (For a longer psalm, see page xiii.) Psalm 23:1–3a, 3b–4, 5, 6

I shall dwell in the house of the LORD my
　　whole life long.

**I shall dwell in the house of the LORD my
　　whole life long.**

The LORD is my shepherd, I shall not want.
　He makes me lie down in green pastures;
he leads me beside still waters;
　he restores my soul.

**I shall dwell in the house of the LORD my
　　whole life long.**

◆ All stand and sing **Alleluia.**

GOSPEL   Mark 5:1–2, 5–9

A reading from the holy Gospel according to Mark

Jesus and his disciples came to the other side of the sea, to the country of the Gerasenes [GER-uh-seenz]. And when he had stepped out of the boat, immediately a man out of the tombs with an unclean spirit met him. Night and day among the tombs and on the mountains he was always howling and bruising himself with stones. When he saw Jesus from a distance, he ran and bowed down before him; and he shouted at the top of his voice, "What have you to do with me, Jesus, Son of the Most High God? I adjure you by God, do not torment me." For he had said to him, "Come out of the man, you unclean spirit!" Then Jesus asked him, "What is your name?" He replied, "My name is Legion; for we are many."

The Gospel of the Lord.

◆ All sit and observe silence.

FOR SILENT REFLECTION

Again, we see Jesus helping a man who is suffering. Let us pray for people we know who are struggling in some way.

CLOSING PRAYER

Let us stand and bring our hopes and needs to God as we pray, "Lord, hear our prayer."

◆ All may add their own prayers here.

Let us pray: **Our Father . . . Amen.**

Lord Jesus,
your power to do good is awesome.
May we always remember
your mighty works and to
thank you for the energy of the
Holy Spirit who is such a
positive force in our lives.
We ask this in your name.

Amen.

✚ All make the Sign of the Cross.

OPENING

In today's Gospel, we learn more about Jesus living out his ministry of healing.

✝ All make the Sign of the Cross.

> **In the name of the Father, and of the Son, and of the Holy Spirit. Amen.**

PSALM (For a longer psalm, see page xiii.) Psalm 23:1–3a, 3b–4, 5, 6

I shall dwell in the house of the LORD my
   whole life long.

**I shall dwell in the house of the LORD my
   whole life long.**

The LORD is my shepherd, I shall not want.
   He makes me lie down in green pastures;
he leads me beside still waters;
   he restores my soul.

**I shall dwell in the house of the LORD my
   whole life long.**

◆ All stand and sing **Alleluia.**

GOSPEL   Mark 5:22–23, 35–42

A reading from the holy Gospel according to Mark

One of the leaders of the synagogue named Jairus [JĪ-ruhs] came and, when he saw Jesus, fell at his feet and begged him repeatedly, "My little daughter is at the point of death. Come and lay your hands on her, so that she may be made well, and live."

Some people came from the leader's house to say, "Your daughter is dead. Why trouble the teacher any further?" But overhearing what they said, Jesus said to the leader of the synagogue, "Do not fear, only believe." He allowed no one to follow him except Peter, James, and John, the brother of James. When they came to the house of the leader of the synagogue, he saw a commotion, people weeping and wailing loudly. When he had entered, he said to them, "Why do you make a commotion and weep? The child is not dead but sleeping." He took her by the hand and said to her, "Talitha cum," which means, "Little girl, get up!" And immediately the girl got up and began to walk about.

The Gospel of the Lord.

◆ All sit and observe silence.

FOR SILENT REFLECTION

When do we pray for healing?

CLOSING PRAYER

Let us stand and bring our hopes and needs to God as we pray, "Lord, hear our prayer."

◆ All may add their own prayers here.

Let us pray: **Our Father . . . Amen.**

Jesus, our Savior,
may we continue to call on you
for healing and strength.
We ask this in your name.

Amen.

✝ All make the Sign of the Cross.

PRAYER FOR **WEDNESDAY** FEBRUARY 5, 2014

OPENING

Today we remember St. Agatha who was martyred in Italy in the third century because she was a Christian.

✦ All make the Sign of the Cross.

In the name of the Father, and of the Son, and of the Holy Spirit. Amen.

PSALM (For a longer psalm, see page xiii.) Psalm 23:1–3a, 3b–4, 5, 6

I shall dwell in the house of the LORD my
    whole life long.

**I shall dwell in the house of the LORD my
    whole life long.**

The LORD is my shepherd, I shall not want.
    He makes me lie down in green pastures;
he leads me beside still waters;
    he restores my soul.

**I shall dwell in the house of the LORD my
    whole life long.**

◆ All stand and sing **Alleluia.**

GOSPEL
Mark 6:1–5

A reading from the holy Gospel according to Mark

Jesus left that place and came to his hometown, and his disciples followed him. On the sabbath he began to teach in the synagogue, and many who heard him were astounded. They said, "Where did this man get all this? What is this wisdom that has been given to him? What deeds of power are being done by his hands! Is not this the carpenter, the son of Mary and brother of James and Joses and Judas and Simon, and are not his sisters here with us?" And they took offense at him. Then Jesus said to them, "Prophets are not without honor, except in their hometown, and among their own kin, and in their own house."

The Gospel of the Lord.

◆ All sit and observe silence.

FOR SILENT REFLECTION

The people who saw Jesus work many miracles wondered where his power came from. Why do you think they were suprised?

CLOSING PRAYER

Let us stand and bring our hopes and needs to God as we pray, "Lord, hear our prayer."

◆ All may add their own prayers here.

Let us pray: **Our Father . . . Amen.**

Lord Jesus,
you were not understood
within your own community.
Help us to recognize
your presence among our
family and friends.
We ask this in your name.

Amen.

✦ All make the Sign of the Cross.

OPENING

Today we remember St. Paul Miki and his companions: priests, brothers, and laypeople, even children—all crucified on a hill in Nagasaki, Japan, in 1597 because of their Christian faith.

✝ All make the Sign of the Cross.

In the name of the Father, and of the Son, and of the Holy Spirit. Amen.

PSALM (For a longer psalm, see page xiii.) Psalm 23:1–3a, 3b–4, 5, 6

I shall dwell in the house of the LORD my
whole life long.

**I shall dwell in the house of the LORD my
whole life long.**

The LORD is my shepherd, I shall not want.
He makes me lie down in green pastures;
he leads me beside still waters;
he restores my soul.

**I shall dwell in the house of the LORD my
whole life long.**

◆ All stand and sing **Alleluia.**

GOSPEL   Mark 6:7–13

A reading from the holy Gospel according to Mark

Jesus called the twelve and began to send them out two by two, and gave them authority over the unclean spirits. He ordered them to take nothing for their journey except a staff; no bread, no bag, no money in their belts; but to wear sandals and not to put on two tunics. He said to them, "Wherever you enter a house, stay there until you leave the place. If any place will not welcome you and they refuse to hear you, as you leave, shake off the dust that is on your feet as a testimony against them." So they went out and proclaimed that all should repent. They cast out many demons, and anointed with oil many who were sick and cured them.

The Gospel of the Lord.

◆ All sit and observe silence.

FOR SILENT REFLECTION

When have you needed to "shake off the dust" because your Good News was rejected?

CLOSING PRAYER

Let us stand and bring our hopes and needs to God as we pray, "Lord, hear our prayer."

◆ All may add their own prayers here.

Let us pray: **Our Father . . . Amen.**

Jesus our leader,
those who listened and heeded
the Good News
found new life in Christ.
May we embrace your leaders
who abide by your Spirit of goodness
and who bring us your Word.
In your name we pray.

Amen.

✝ All make the Sign of the Cross.

PRAYER FOR **FRIDAY**
FEBRUARY 7, 2014

OPENING FRIDAY

Today's Gospel is about the death of John the Baptist. He confronted an evil leader and was imprisoned and later sacrificed because of someone else's anger.

✝ All make the Sign of the Cross.

In the name of the Father, and of the Son, and of the Holy Spirit. Amen.

PSALM (For a longer psalm, see page xiii.) Psalm 23:1–3a, 3b–4, 5, 6

I shall dwell in the house of the LORD my
　whole life long.

**I shall dwell in the house of the LORD my
　whole life long.**

The LORD is my shepherd, I shall not want.
　He makes me lie down in green pastures;
he leads me beside still waters;
　he restores my soul.

**I shall dwell in the house of the LORD my
　whole life long.**

◆ All stand and sing **Alleluia.**

GOSPEL
Mark 6:21–29

A reading from the holy Gospel according to Mark

On his birthday Herod gave a banquet. When his daughter Herodias came in and danced, she pleased Herod and his guests; and the king said to the girl, "Ask me for whatever you wish, and I will give it." And he solemnly swore to her, "Whatever you ask me, I will give you, even half of my kingdom." She went out and said to her mother, "What should I ask for?" She replied, "The head of John the baptizer." Immediately she rushed back to the king and requested, "I want you to give me at once the head of John the Baptist on a platter." The king was deeply grieved; yet out of regard for his oaths and for the guests, he did not want to refuse her. Immediately the king sent a soldier of the guard with orders to bring John's head. He went and beheaded him in the prison, brought his head on a platter, and gave it to the girl. Then the girl gave it to her mother. When his disciples heard about it, they came and took his body, and laid it in a tomb.

The Gospel of the Lord.

◆ All sit and observe silence.

FOR SILENT REFLECTION

Why is the truth sometimes hard for us to hear?

CLOSING PRAYER

Let us stand and bring our hopes and needs to God as we pray, "Lord, hear our prayer."

◆ All may add their own prayers here.

Let us pray: **Our Father . . . Amen.**

Jesus our guide,
you remind us that the
Christian life is never easy.
Keep us safe as we do your work.
May our burdens be lifted
with the help of your gentle Spirit.
We ask this in your name.

Amen.

✝ All make the Sign of the Cross.

190

PRAYER FOR THE WEEK

OPENING

In today's Gospel, Jesus calls us to be salt for the earth and a light for others to see God's glory.

✦ All make the Sign of the Cross.

In the name of the Father, and of the Son, and of the Holy Spirit. Amen.

PSALM (For a longer psalm, see page xiii.) Psalm 23:1–3a, 3b–4, 5, 6

I shall dwell in the house of the LORD my
　　whole life long.

**I shall dwell in the house of the LORD my
　　whole life long.**

The LORD is my shepherd, I shall not want.
　He makes me lie down in green pastures;
he leads me beside still waters;
　he restores my soul.

**I shall dwell in the house of the LORD my
　　whole life long.**

◆ All stand and sing **Alleluia.**

GOSPEL   Matthew 5:13–16

A reading from the holy Gospel according to Matthew

Jesus said to his disciples: "You are the salt of the earth; but if salt has lost its taste, how can its saltiness be restored? It is no longer good for anything, but is thrown out and trampled under foot. You are the light of the world. A city built on a hill cannot be hid. No one after lighting a lamp puts it under the bushel basket, but on the lampstand, and it gives light to all in the house. In the same way, let your light shine before others, so that they may see your good works and give glory to your Father in heaven."

The Gospel of the Lord.

◆ All sit and observe silence.

FOR SILENT REFLECTION

What does salt do for our food? How am I salt for Christ in this world? Where is the lamp of my faith placed?

CLOSING PRAYER

Let us stand and bring our hopes and needs to God as we pray, "Lord, hear our prayer."

◆ All may add their own prayers here.

Let us pray: **Our Father . . . Amen.**

Christ our Lord,
you remind us of our role
as your disciples:
to be flavor
to the dullness of the world
and to give light
for God's majesty to shine.
Help us to have courage
to be salt and light,
for their functions reveal
our goodness that comes from you.
In your name we pray.

Amen.

✦ All make the Sign of the Cross.

PRAYER FOR **MONDAY FEBRUARY 10, 2014**

OPENING

Today we remember St. Scholastica, who was the twin sister of St. Benedict. They were born in 480 in central Italy. She founded a religious community for women near a monastery that Benedict managed.

✛ All make the Sign of the Cross.

In the name of the Father, and of the Son, and of the Holy Spirit. Amen.

PSALM (For a longer psalm, see page xiii.) Psalm 23:1–3a, 3b–4, 5, 6

I shall dwell in the house of the LORD my
    whole life long.

**I shall dwell in the house of the LORD my
    whole life long.**

The LORD is my shepherd, I shall not want.
    He makes me lie down in green pastures;
he leads me beside still waters;
    he restores my soul.

**I shall dwell in the house of the LORD my
    whole life long.**

READING   1 Kings 8:1, 6–11

A reading from the First Book of Kings

Then Solomon assembled the elders of Israel and all the heads of the tribes, the leaders of the ancestral houses of the Israelites, before King Solomon in Jerusalem, to bring up the ark of the covenant of the LORD out of the city of David, which is Zion. Then the priests brought the ark of the covenant of the LORD to its place, in the inner sanctuary of the house, in the most holy place, underneath the wings of the cherubim. For the cherubim spread out their wings over the place of the ark, so that the cherubim made a covering above the ark and its poles. There was nothing in the ark except the two tablets of stone that Moses had placed there at Horeb, where the LORD made a covenant with the Israelites, when they came out of the land of Egypt. And when the priests came out of the holy place, a cloud filled the house of the Lord, so that the priests could not stand to minister because of the cloud; for the glory of the LORD filled the house of the LORD.

The Word of the Lord.

◆ All sit and observe silence.

FOR SILENT REFLECTION

How often do I set aside time to pray?

CLOSING PRAYER

Let us stand and bring our hopes and needs to God as we pray, "Lord, hear our prayer."

◆ All may add their own prayers here.

Let us pray: **Our Father . . . Amen.**

Almighty God,
you make your presence known
in so many ways.
May we make time
to recognize your presence within us
and all around us.
We ask this through Christ our Lord.

Amen.

✛ All make the Sign of the Cross.

OPENING

Today's feast, the Feast of Our Lady of Lourdes, began in 1907 to remember the apparitions of the Virgin Mary to a young girl, St. Bernadette.

✝ All make the Sign of the Cross.

In the name of the Father, and of the Son, and of the Holy Spirit. Amen.

PSALM (For a longer psalm, see page xiii.) Psalm 23:1–3a, 3b–4, 5, 6

I shall dwell in the house of the LORD my
   whole life long.

**I shall dwell in the house of the LORD my
   whole life long.**

The LORD is my shepherd, I shall not want.
   He makes me lie down in green pastures;
he leads me beside still waters;
   he restores my soul.

**I shall dwell in the house of the LORD my
   whole life long.**

◆ All stand and sing **Alleluia.**

GOSPEL   Mark 7:1–2, 5–8

A reading from the holy Gospel according to Mark

Now when the Pharisees and some of the scribes who had come from Jerusalem gathered around him, they noticed that some of his disciples were eating with defiled hands, that is, without washing them. So the Pharisees and the scribes asked him, "Why do your disciples not live according to the tradition of the elders, but eat with defiled hands?" He said to them,

"Isaiah prophesied rightly about you hypocrites, as it is written,
   'This people honors me with their lips,
      but their hearts are far from me;
   in vain do they worship me,
      teaching human precepts as doctrines.'
You abandon the commandment of God and hold to human tradition."

The Gospel of the Lord.

◆ All sit and observe silence.

FOR SILENT REFLECTION

What are some of our faith traditions that help us keep God's commandments of love?

CLOSING PRAYER

Let us stand and bring our hopes and needs to God as we pray, "Lord, hear our prayer."

◆ All may add their own prayers here.

Let us pray: **Our Father . . . Amen.**

Jesus our leader,
you help us to understand
what is truly essential.
Guide us in our living
so that we keep your
commandments of love.
We ask this in your name.

Amen.

✝ All make the Sign of the Cross.

PRAYER FOR **WEDNESDAY** FEBRUARY 12, 2014

OPENING

In today's Gospel, Jesus gives us a sobering look at life without God's Spirit within us.

✠ All make the Sign of the Cross.

In the name of the Father, and of the Son, and of the Holy Spirit. Amen.

PSALM (For a longer psalm, see page xiii.) Psalm 23:1–3a, 3b–4, 5, 6

I shall dwell in the house of the LORD my
   whole life long.

**I shall dwell in the house of the LORD my
   whole life long.**

The LORD is my shepherd, I shall not want.
   He makes me lie down in green pastures;
he leads me beside still waters;
   he restores my soul.

**I shall dwell in the house of the LORD my
   whole life long.**

◆ All stand and sing **Alleluia.**

GOSPEL
Mark 7:14–23

A reading from the holy Gospel according to Mark

Jesus called the crowd again and said to them, "Listen to me, all of you, and understand: there is nothing outside a person that by going in can defile, but the things that come out are what defile."

When he had left the crowd and entered the house, his disciples asked him about the parable. He said to them, "Then do you also fail to understand? Do you not see that whatever goes into a person from outside cannot defile, since it enters, not the heart but the stomach, and goes out into the sewer?" (Thus he declared all foods clean.) And he said, "It is what comes out of a person that defiles. For it is from within, from the human heart, that evil intentions come: fornication, theft, murder, adultery, avarice, wickedness, deceit, licentiousness, envy, slander, pride, folly. All these evil things come from within, and they defile a person."

The Gospel of the Lord.

◆ All sit and observe silence.

FOR SILENT REFLECTION

How can I be filled more with God's Spirit?

CLOSING PRAYER

Let us stand and bring our hopes and needs to God as we pray, "Lord, hear our prayer."

◆ All may add their own prayers here.

Let us pray: **Our Father . . . Amen.**

Lord Jesus,
we rely on you so much
to help us remain full
of your goodness and truth.
God created us in his image,
yet we sometimes lean toward
our own ways that are not yours.
Guide us as
we love you more each day and
reflect all that you are.
In your name we pray.

Amen.

✠ All make the Sign of the Cross.

194

OPENING

Today's Gospel shows Jesus testing a woman's faith, who surprised him with its depth.

✚ All make the Sign of the Cross.

In the name of the Father, and of the Son, and of the Holy Spirit. Amen.

PSALM (For a longer psalm, see page xiii.) Psalm 23:1–3a, 3b–4, 5, 6

I shall dwell in the house of the LORD my
  whole life long.

**I shall dwell in the house of the LORD my
  whole life long.**

The LORD is my shepherd, I shall not want.
  He makes me lie down in green pastures;
he leads me beside still waters;
  he restores my soul.

**I shall dwell in the house of the LORD my
  whole life long.**

◆ All stand and sing **Alleluia.**

GOSPEL
Mark 7:24–30

A reading from the holy Gospel according to Mark

Jesus set out and went away to the region of Tyre [tīr]. He entered a house and did not want anyone to know he was there. Yet he could not escape notice, but a woman whose little daughter had an unclean spirit immediately heard about him, and she came and bowed down at his feet. Now the woman was a Gentile, of Syrophoenician [sī-roh-fuh-NEE-shun] origin. She begged him to cast the demon out of her daughter. He said to her, "Let the children be fed first, for it is not fair to take the children's food and throw it to the dogs." But she answered him, "Sir, even the dogs under the table eat the children's crumbs." Then he said to her, "For saying that, you may go—the demon has left your daughter." So she went home, found the child lying on the bed, and the demon gone.

The Gospel of the Lord.

◆ All sit and observe silence.

FOR SILENT REFLECTION

How do I welcome others who have different beliefs than me?

CLOSING PRAYER

Let us stand and bring our hopes and needs to God as we pray, "Lord, hear our prayer."

◆ All may add their own prayers here.

Let us pray: **Our Father . . . Amen.**

Lord Jesus,
you had no boundaries
on your healing touch.
May we be mindful of
how much God loves every person
regardless of their spiritual tradition
or level of faith.
We ask this in your name.

Amen.

✚ All make the Sign of the Cross.

PRAYER FOR **FRIDAY** **FEBRUARY 14, 2014**

OPENING

Today is St. Valentine's Day, a day that has its roots in Rome, where it was a tradition to give handwritten messages of admiration that included Valentine's name. Today we also remember Sts. Cyril and Methodius [muh-THOH-dee-uhs], two brothers who became missionaries and teachers for the Slavic people in the ninth century.

✛ All make the Sign of the Cross.

In the name of the Father, and of the Son, and of the Holy Spirit. Amen.

PSALM (For a longer psalm, see page xiii.) Psalm 23:1–3a, 3b–4, 5, 6

I shall dwell in the house of the LORD my
　　whole life long.

**I shall dwell in the house of the LORD my
　　whole life long.**

The LORD is my shepherd, I shall not want.
　He makes me lie down in green pastures;
he leads me beside still waters;
　he restores my soul.

**I shall dwell in the house of the LORD my
　　whole life long.**

◆ All stand and sing **Alleluia.**

GOSPEL   Mark 7:32–37

A reading from the holy Gospel according to Mark

They brought to Jesus a deaf man who had an impediment in his speech; and they begged him to lay his hand on him. He took him aside in private, away from the crowd, and put his fingers into his ears, and he spat and touched his tongue. Then looking up to heaven, he sighed and said to him, "Ephphatha [EF-uh-thuh]," that is, "Be opened." And immediately his ears were opened, his tongue was released, and he spoke plainly. Then Jesus ordered them to tell no one; but the more he ordered them, the more zealously they proclaimed it. They were astounded beyond measure, saying, "He has done everything well; he even makes the deaf to hear and the mute to speak."

The Gospel of the Lord.

◆ All sit and observe silence.

FOR SILENT REFLECTION

How do I ask God to "open" my heart to those who seem deaf to my needs? How can I offer a healing touch in communicating with them?

CLOSING PRAYER

Let us stand and bring our hopes and needs to God as we pray, "Lord, hear our prayer."

◆ All may add their own prayers here.

Let us pray: **Our Father . . . Amen.**

Jesus our healer,
you touch us with your
healing words and power today,
just as you felt the needs of the deaf man.
May we be bold in
asking for your
guidance and healing.
We ask this through Christ our Lord.

Amen.

✛ All make the Sign of the Cross.

PRAYER FOR THE WEEK

OPENING

Today's Gospel reminds us that our thoughts and feelings have the power to bring good or evil into the world.

✚ All make the Sign of the Cross.

In the name of the Father, and of the Son, and of the Holy Spirit. Amen.

PSALM (For a longer psalm, see page xiii.) Psalm 23:1–3a, 3b–4, 5, 6

I shall dwell in the house of the LORD my
    whole life long.

**I shall dwell in the house of the LORD my
    whole life long.**

The LORD is my shepherd, I shall not want.
    He makes me lie down in green pastures;
he leads me beside still waters;
    he restores my soul.

**I shall dwell in the house of the LORD my
    whole life long.**

◆ All stand and sing **Alleluia.**

GOSPEL   Matthew 5:21–22, 27–28, 33–34, 37

A reading from the holy Gospel according to Matthew

Jesus said, "You have heard that it was said to those of ancient times, 'You shall not murder'; and 'whoever murders shall be liable to judgment.' But I say to you that if you are angry with a brother or sister, you will be liable to judgment; and if you insult a brother or sister, you will be liable to the council; and if you say, 'You fool,' you will be liable to the hell of fire.

You have heard that it was said, 'You shall not commit adultery.' But I say to you that everyone who looks at a woman with lust has already committed adultery with her in his heart.

"Again, you have heard that it was said to those of ancient times, 'You shall not swear falsely, but carry out the vows you have made to the Lord.' But I say to you, Do not swear at all, either by heaven, for it is the throne of God, Let your word be 'Yes, Yes' or 'No, No'; anything more than this comes from the evil one."

The Gospel of the Lord.

◆ All sit and observe silence.

FOR SILENT REFLECTION

Why do you think Jesus tells us to mean it when we say "Yes" or say "No"?

CLOSING PRAYER

Let us stand and bring our hopes and needs to God as we pray, "Lord, hear our prayer."

◆ All may add their own prayers here.

Let us pray: **Our Father . . . Amen.**

Lord Jesus,
you tell us in straightforward terms
how difficult it is to
enter the kingdom of heaven.
Help us to be kind and merciful with others
as we study, work, and play today.
We ask this through Christ our Lord.

Amen.

✚ All make the Sign of the Cross.

PRAYER FOR **MONDAY** **FEBRUARY 17, 2014**

OPENING

Today we remember the Seven Founders of the Servite Order. In 1240, seven noblemen of Florence made the decision to lead a life of solitude, prayer, and service to God. Their order grew and some members eventually settled in the United States (in New York and Philadelphia).

✠ All make the Sign of the Cross.

In the name of the Father, and of the Son, and of the Holy Spirit. Amen.

PSALM (For a longer psalm, see page xiii.) Psalm 23:1–3a, 3b–4, 5, 6

I shall dwell in the house of the LORD my
    whole life long.

**I shall dwell in the house of the LORD my
    whole life long.**

The LORD is my shepherd, I shall not want.
  He makes me lie down in green pastures;
he leads me beside still waters;
    he restores my soul.

**I shall dwell in the house of the LORD my
    whole life long.**

READING
James 1:2–5

A reading from the beginning of the Letter of St. James

My brothers and sisters, whenever you face trials of any kind, consider it nothing but joy, because you know that the testing of your faith produces endurance; and let endurance have its full effect, so that you may be mature and complete, lacking in nothing. If any of you is lacking in wisdom, ask God, who gives to all generously and ungrudgingly, and it will be given you.

The Word of the Lord.

◆ All observe silence.

FOR SILENT REFLECTION

How do I regard difficulties in my life? How are they tests of courage for growing my faith?

CLOSING PRAYER

Let us stand and bring our hopes and needs to God as we pray, "Lord, hear our prayer."

◆ All may add their own prayers here.

Let us pray: **Our Father . . . Amen.**

Almighty God,
you remind us that we can ask you
with confidence for what we need.
We will have times of difficulty,
yet you tell us how much
we will learn and become stronger.
Guide us, Creator, as we mature
with your grace.
Help us to seek your will alone
for that is all we need.
We ask this through Christ our Lord.

Amen.

✠ All make the Sign of the Cross.

OPENING

In today's Gospel, Jesus cautions his followers about becoming like the Pharisees or Herod. He wants us to follow the God-sent One who feeds with life-giving bread.

✜ All make the Sign of the Cross.

In the name of the Father, and of the Son, and of the Holy Spirit. Amen.

PSALM (For a longer psalm, see page xiii.) Psalm 23:1–3a, 3b–4, 5, 6

I shall dwell in the house of the LORD my whole life long.

I shall dwell in the house of the LORD my whole life long.

The LORD is my shepherd, I shall not want.
  He makes me lie down in green pastures;
he leads me beside still waters;
  he restores my soul.

I shall dwell in the house of the LORD my whole life long.

◆ All stand and sing **Alleluia**.

GOSPEL
Mark 8:14–21

A reading from the holy Gospel according to Mark

The disciples had forgotten to bring any bread; and they had only one loaf with them in the boat. And he cautioned them, saying, "Watch out—beware of the yeast of the Pharisees and the yeast of Herod." They said to one another, "It is because we have no bread." And becoming aware of it, Jesus said to them, "Why are you talking about having no bread? Do you still not perceive or understand? Are your hearts hardened? Do you have eyes, and fail to see? Do you have ears, and fail to hear? And do you not remember? When I broke the five loaves for the five thousand, how many baskets full of broken pieces did you collect?" They said to him, "Twelve." "And the seven for the four thousand, how many baskets full of broken pieces did you collect?" And they said to him, "Seven." Then he said to them, "Do you not yet understand?"

The Gospel of the Lord.

◆ All sit and observe silence.

FOR SILENT REFLECTION

Do I get absorbed sometimes with my fear that my basic needs might not be met? How can I allow God to supply what is truly essential?

CLOSING PRAYER

Let us stand and bring our hopes and needs to God as we pray, "Lord, hear our prayer."

◆ All may add their own prayers here.

Let us pray: **Our Father . . . Amen.**

Lord Jesus,
you provide real food for me.
I don't need to fear;
you will always be near me
and keep me safe
as I follow your path of life.
We ask this in your name.

Amen.

✜ All make the Sign of the Cross.

PRAYER FOR **WEDNESDAY** **FEBRUARY 19, 2014**

OPENING

Today's reading from James gives us practical advice on how to live the Christian life.

✠ All make the Sign of the Cross.

In the name of the Father, and of the Son, and of the Holy Spirit. Amen.

PSALM (For a longer psalm, see page xiii.) Psalm 23:1–3a, 3b–4, 5, 6

I shall dwell in the house of the LORD my
   whole life long.

I shall dwell in the house of the LORD my
   whole life long.

The LORD is my shepherd, I shall not want.
   He makes me lie down in green pastures;
he leads me beside still waters;
   he restores my soul.

I shall dwell in the house of the LORD my
   whole life long.

READING   James 1:19–25

A reading from the Letter of St. James

You must understand this, my beloved: let everyone be quick to listen, slow to speak, slow to anger; for your anger does not produce God's righteousness. Therefore rid yourselves of all sordidness and rank growth of wickedness, and welcome with meekness the implanted word that has the power to save your souls. But be doers of the word, and not merely hearers who deceive themselves. For if any are hearers of the word and not doers, they are like those who look at themselves in a mirror; for they look at themselves and, on going away, immediately forget what they were like. But those who look into the perfect law, the law of liberty, and persevere, being not hearers who forget but doers who act—they will be blessed in their doing.

The Word of the Lord.

◆ All observe silence.

FOR SILENT REFLECTION

Why is it important to be "quick to listen" and "slow to anger"?

CLOSING PRAYER

Let us stand and bring our hopes and needs to God as we pray, "Lord, hear our prayer."

◆ All may add their own prayers here.

Let us pray: **Our Father . . . Amen.**

Lord Jesus,
you tell us to be
"doers of the Word,"
and not merely "hearers."
You ask us to
focus on the difficult task at hand
and to not react with anger
when we are provoked.
Help us to be your servants
as we act on your behalf
with positive actions instead of with
some of the negative ways of the world.
In your name we pray.

Amen.

✠ All make the Sign of the Cross.

OPENING

Today's Gospel concerns identity and personal mission. Jesus tells his disciples about his role in this world, a role that many of them rejected because it was too painful to hear.

✚ All make the Sign of the Cross.

In the name of the Father, and of the Son, and of the Holy Spirit. Amen.

PSALM (For a longer psalm, see page xiii.) Psalm 23:1–3a, 3b–4, 5, 6

I shall dwell in the house of the LORD my
    whole life long.

**I shall dwell in the house of the LORD my
    whole life long.**

The LORD is my shepherd, I shall not want.
    He makes me lie down in green pastures;
he leads me beside still waters;
    he restores my soul.

**I shall dwell in the house of the LORD my
    whole life long.**

◆ All stand and sing **Alleluia.**

GOSPEL   Mark 8:27–30

A reading from the holy Gospel according to Mark

Jesus went on with his disciples to the villages of Caesarea [sez-uh-REE-uh] Philippi [fih-LIP-ī]; and on the way he asked his disciples, "Who do people say that I am?" And they answered him, "John the Baptist; and others, Elijah; and still others, one of the prophets." He asked them, "But who do you say that I am?" Peter answered him, "You are the Messiah." And he sternly ordered them not to tell anyone about him.

The Gospel of the Lord.

◆ All sit and observe silence.

FOR SILENT REFLECTION

What do you think the disciples felt when they heard Jesus's answer? Have you experienced a time in your life when the truth was very difficult to accept?

CLOSING PRAYER

Let us stand and bring our hopes and needs to God as we pray, "Lord, hear our prayer."

◆ All may add their own prayers here.

Let us pray: **Our Father . . . Amen.**

Lord Jesus,
you revealed to your friends
your true mission from God,
which was difficult for them to accept.
Help us to be loving to others
who don't understand the
meaning of your cross.
Guide us to understand the full meaning
of your name, Messiah.
We ask this in your name.

Amen.

✚ All make the Sign of the Cross.

PRAYER FOR **FRIDAY**
FEBRUARY 21, 2014

OPENING

Today's reading reminds us that we do good works for the Lord because of our faith, not to be rewarded in heaven. Our love for Christ gives us reason to love others.

✝ All make the Sign of the Cross.

In the name of the Father, and of the Son, and of the Holy Spirit. Amen.

PSALM (For a longer psalm, see page xiii.) Psalm 23:1–3a, 3b–4, 5, 6

I shall dwell in the house of the LORD my
    whole life long.

**I shall dwell in the house of the LORD my
    whole life long.**

The LORD is my shepherd, I shall not want.
    He makes me lie down in green pastures;
he leads me beside still waters;
    he restores my soul.

**I shall dwell in the house of the LORD my
    whole life long.**

READING
James 2:14–18, 26

A reading from the Letter of St. James

What good is it, my brothers and sisters, if you say you have faith but do not have works? Can faith save you? If a brother or sister is naked and lacks daily food, and one of you says to them, "Go in peace; keep warm and eat your fill," and yet you do not supply their bodily needs, what is the good of that? So faith by itself, if it has no works, is dead. But someone will say, "You have faith and I have works." Show me your faith apart from your works,

and I by my works will show you my faith. You see that a person is justified by works and not by faith alone. For just as the body without the spirit is dead, so faith without works is also dead.

The Word of the Lord.

◆ All observe silence.

FOR SILENT REFLECTION

How do I respond to God's generous love for me? What are my "works" of faith?

CLOSING PRAYER

Let us stand and bring our hopes and needs to God as we pray, "Lord, hear our prayer."

◆ All may add their own prayers here.

Let us pray: **Our Father . . . Amen.**

Almighty God,
you give us so much grace
that we respond with grace
for others.
Our works of charity and love
give you glory.
Help us to stay true to you
and not accomplish works
for our own glory.
We ask this through Jesus,
our Savior and Redeemer.

Amen.

✝ All make the Sign of the Cross.

OPENING

Today's Gospel is a lesson in right living, and one that is difficult to accomplish. We hope and pray that prayer and practice will help us to love our enemies.

✦ All make the Sign of the Cross.

In the name of the Father, and of the Son, and of the Holy Spirit. Amen.

PSALM (For a longer psalm, see page xiii.) Psalm 23:1–3a, 3b–4, 5, 6

I shall dwell in the house of the LORD my
    whole life long.

**I shall dwell in the house of the LORD my
    whole life long.**

The LORD is my shepherd, I shall not want.
    He makes me lie down in green pastures;
he leads me beside still waters;
    he restores my soul.

**I shall dwell in the house of the LORD my
    whole life long.**

◆ All stand and sing **Alleluia.**

GOSPEL
Matthew 5:38–42

A reading from the holy Gospel according to Matthew

Jesus said to his disciples: "You have heard that it was said, 'An eye for an eye and a tooth for a tooth.' But I say to you, Do not resist an evildoer. But if anyone strikes you on the right cheek, turn the other also; and if anyone wants to sue you and take your coat, give your cloak as well; and if anyone forces you to go one mile, go also the second mile. Give to everyone who begs from you, and do not refuse anyone who wants to borrow from you."

The Gospel of the Lord.

◆ All sit and observe silence.

FOR SILENT REFLECTION

Who are the difficult people in my life? How do I deal with them? What could I do differently?

CLOSING PRAYER

Let us stand and bring our hopes and needs to God as we pray, "Lord, hear our prayer."

◆ All may add their own prayers here.

Let us pray: **Our Father . . . Amen.**

Lord Jesus,
your laws of love are
sometimes difficult to hear.
You ask us to turn the other cheek
and to love those who
persecute us.
Help us to try to understand
your ways of right living.
Keep us mindful of how
we respond to those who bother us,
for we must be generous with
our love as you are with us.
We ask this in your name.

Amen.

✦ All make the Sign of the Cross.

PRAYER FOR **MONDAY** **FEBRUARY 24, 2014**

OPENING

Today's reading from St. James is a lesson in living well for God's glory. It reminds us to check our motives for our goals. Listen to what kind of harvest will be sown if we heed these words.

✚ All make the Sign of the Cross.

In the name of the Father, and of the Son, and of the Holy Spirit. Amen.

PSALM (For a longer psalm, see page xiii.) Psalm 23:1–3a, 3b–4, 5, 6

I shall dwell in the house of the LORD my
 whole life long.

**I shall dwell in the house of the LORD my
 whole life long.**

The LORD is my shepherd, I shall not want.
 He makes me lie down in green pastures;
he leads me beside still waters;
 he restores my soul.

**I shall dwell in the house of the LORD my
 whole life long.**

READING

James 3:13–18

A reading from the Letter of St. James

Beloved: Who is wise and understanding among you? Show by your good life that your works are done with gentleness born of wisdom. But if you have bitter envy and selfish ambition in your hearts, do not be boastful and false to the truth. Such wisdom does not come down from above, but is earthly, unspiritual, devilish. For where there is envy and selfish ambition, there will also be disorder and wickedness of every kind. But the wisdom from above is first pure, then peaceable, gentle, willing to yield, full of mercy and good fruits, without a trace of partiality or hypocrisy. And a harvest of righteousness is sown in peace for those who make peace.

The Word of the Lord.

◆ All observe silence.

FOR SILENT REFLECTION

What is our motivation for doing well in our studies, sports, and personal goals? How can we make God first in our lives?

CLOSING PRAYER

Let us stand and bring our hopes and needs to God as we pray, "Lord, hear our prayer."

◆ All may add their own prayers here.

Let us pray: **Our Father . . . Amen.**

Lord Jesus,
you help us understand how
our ambition cannot be selfish.
To be your faithful servants,
we must have wisdom that is
pure, gentle, willing to yield, and
full of mercy.
Help us to be filled with your Spirit
who can lead us to
righteous living in your name.
We ask this in your name.

Amen.

✚ All make the Sign of the Cross.

OPENING

In today's Gospel Jesus takes a child in his arms to describe how we should welcome one another.

✦ All make the Sign of the Cross.

In the name of the Father, and of the Son, and of the Holy Spirit. Amen.

PSALM (For a longer psalm, see page xiii.) Psalm 23:1–3a, 3b–4, 5, 6

I shall dwell in the house of the LORD my
   whole life long.

**I shall dwell in the house of the LORD my
   whole life long.**

The LORD is my shepherd, I shall not want.
   He makes me lie down in green pastures;
he leads me beside still waters;
   he restores my soul.

**I shall dwell in the house of the LORD my
   whole life long.**

◆ All stand and sing **Alleluia.**

GOSPEL   Mark 9:30, 32–37

A reading from the holy Gospel according to Mark

Jesus and his disciples went on from there and passed through Galilee.

   Then they came to Capernaum [kuh-PER-nee-*m]; and when he was in the house he asked them, "What were you arguing about on the way?" But they were silent, for on the way they had argued with one another who was the greatest. He sat down, called the twelve, and said to them, "Whoever wants to be first must be last of all and servant of all." Then he took a little child and put it among them; and taking it in his arms, he said to them, "Whoever welcomes one such child in my name welcomes me, and whoever welcomes me welcomes not me but the one who sent me."

The Gospel of the Lord.

◆ All sit and observe silence.

FOR SILENT REFLECTION

Who have you welcomed recently? Were these people excluded by others? How did you help build friendships?

CLOSING PRAYER

Let us stand and bring our hopes and needs to God as we pray, "Lord, hear our prayer."

◆ All may add their own prayers here.

Let us pray: **Our Father . . . Amen.**

Jesus our teacher,
you welcomed the children.
You surprised the Apostles
who argued over
who was the greatest.
Help us to embrace those who
are not easy to include in our groups.
Guide us in discovering the
essence of servant leadership.
We ask this in your name.

Amen.

✦ All make the Sign of the Cross.

PRAYER FOR **WEDNESDAY** **FEBRUARY 26, 2014**

OPENING

In today's Gospel, we see Jesus explaining to John that God's Spirit works in mysterious ways. Have you ever heard the saying, "God writes straight with crooked lines"? Think about how this expression applies to Jesus's message for today.

✚ All make the Sign of the Cross.

In the name of the Father, and of the Son, and of the Holy Spirit. Amen.

PSALM (For a longer psalm, see page xiii.) Psalm 23:1–3a, 3b–4, 5, 6

I shall dwell in the house of the LORD my
whole life long.

**I shall dwell in the house of the LORD my
whole life long.**

The LORD is my shepherd, I shall not want.
He makes me lie down in green pastures;
he leads me beside still waters;
he restores my soul.

**I shall dwell in the house of the LORD my
whole life long.**

◆ All stand and sing **Alleluia.**

GOSPEL   Mark 9:38–40

A reading from the holy Gospel according to Mark

John said to Jesus, "Teacher, we saw someone casting out demons in your name, and we tried to stop him, because he was not following us." But Jesus said, "Do not stop him; for no one who does a deed of power in my name will be able soon afterward to speak evil of me. Whoever is not against us is for us."

The Gospel of the Lord.

◆ All sit and observe silence.

FOR SILENT REFLECTION

Have you ever been surprised to see something good arising out of a negative situation? Why do you think it occurred?

CLOSING PRAYER

Let us stand and bring our hopes and needs to God as we pray, "Lord, hear our prayer."

◆ All may add their own prayers here.

Let us pray: **Our Father . . . Amen.**

Loving Father,
you sent your Son to
teach us to love all people,
even those who may appear to be
working against good.
Grant us the ability
to accept people who are
different than we are but who may be
fighting for the same cause of Christ
in a different way.
We ask this through your Son Jesus.

Amen.

✚ All make the Sign of the Cross.

OPENING

In the Gospel today, we listen to the commitment that Jesus requires all of his followers.

✛ All make the Sign of the Cross.

In the name of the Father, and of the Son, and of the Holy Spirit. Amen.

PSALM (For a longer psalm, see page xiii.) Psalm 23:1–3a, 3b–4, 5, 6

I shall dwell in the house of the LORD my
　　whole life long.

**I shall dwell in the house of the LORD my
　　whole life long.**

The LORD is my shepherd, I shall not want.
　He makes me lie down in green pastures;
he leads me beside still waters;
　he restores my soul.

**I shall dwell in the house of the LORD my
　　whole life long.**

◆ All stand and sing **Alleluia.**

GOSPEL
Mark 9:41–48, 50

A reading from the holy Gospel according to Mark

Jesus said to his disciples: "For truly I tell you, whoever gives you a cup of water to drink because you bear the name of Christ will by no means lose the reward.

　"If any of you put a stumbling block before one of these little ones who believe in me, it would be better for you if a great millstone were hung around your neck and you were thrown into the sea. If your hand causes you to stumble, cut it off; it is better for you to enter life maimed than to have two hands and to go to hell, to the unquenchable fire. And if your foot causes you to stumble, cut it off; it is better for you to enter life lame than to have two feet and to be thrown into hell.

　"For everyone will be salted with fire. Salt is good; but if salt has lost its saltiness, how can you season it? Have salt in yourselves, and be at peace with one another."

The Gospel of the Lord.

◆ All sit and observe silence.

FOR SILENT REFLECTION

Do you think Jesus is asking us to literally cut off our hands or feet? What could he mean?

CLOSING PRAYER

Let us stand and bring our hopes and needs to God as we pray, "Lord, hear our prayer."

◆ All may add their own prayers here.

Let us pray: **Our Father . . . Amen.**

Jesus our Redeemer,
you ask us to commit to
remaining your beloved sons and daughters.
Help us to follow your lead
about giving up activities, plans, and people
who lead us away
from your goodness, truth, and beauty.
Give us strength to
resist what may cause us
to fall from your grace.
In your name we pray.

Amen.

✛ All make the Sign of the Cross.

PRAYER FOR **FRIDAY** **FEBRUARY 28, 2014**

OPENING

Today's reading guides us in the verbal commitments we make. We also need to look to our faith heroes—the prophets—who were tested many times. They asked God for help and were assisted by the Spirit in their decisions and actions.

✦ All make the Sign of the Cross.

In the name of the Father, and of the Son, and of the Holy Spirit. Amen.

PSALM (For a longer psalm, see page xiii.) Psalm 23:1–3a, 3b–4, 5, 6

I shall dwell in the house of the LORD my
  whole life long.

**I shall dwell in the house of the LORD my
  whole life long.**

The LORD is my shepherd, I shall not want.
  He makes me lie down in green pastures;
he leads me beside still waters;
  he restores my soul.

**I shall dwell in the house of the LORD my
  whole life long.**

READING
James 5:9–12

A reading from the Letter of St. James

Beloved, do not grumble against one another, so that you may not be judged. See, the Judge is standing at the doors! As an example of suffering and patience, beloved, take the prophets who spoke In the name of the Lord. Indeed we call blessed those who showed endurance. You have heard of the endurance of Job, and you have seen the purpose of the Lord, how the Lord is compassionate and merciful.

Above all, my beloved, do not swear, either by heaven or by earth or by any other oath, but let your "Yes" be yes and your "No" be no, so that you may not fall under condemnation.

The Word of the Lord.

◆ All observe silence.

FOR SILENT REFLECTION

Do I look to others with experience when I need to make a decision? Which of God's prophets and saints do I look to for inspiration and guidance?

CLOSING PRAYER

Let us stand and bring our hopes and needs to God as we pray, "Lord, hear our prayer."

◆ All may add their own prayers here.

Let us pray: **Our Father . . . Amen.**

God our guide,
you entrust us with the ability
to follow you and your Son Jesus,
even though we sometimes
move the opposite way.
Assist us as we
discern your will.
Help us to realize
what we really need
in our heart of hearts so that
our "yes" is always
for you.
We ask this through Christ our Lord.
Amen.

✦ All make the Sign of the Cross.

PRAYER FOR THE WEEK

OPENING

In today's Gospel Jesus points to nature—to the birds in the air and the lilies in the field—to teach us a lesson on how we should live.

✝ All make the Sign of the Cross.

In the name of the Father, and of the Son, and of the Holy Spirit. Amen.

PSALM (For a longer psalm, see page xiii.) Psalm 23:1–3a, 3b–4, 5, 6

I shall dwell in the house of the LORD my
    whole life long.

**I shall dwell in the house of the LORD my
    whole life long.**

The LORD is my shepherd, I shall not want.
    He makes me lie down in green pastures;
he leads me beside still waters;
    he restores my soul.

**I shall dwell in the house of the LORD my
    whole life long.**

◆ All stand and sing **Alleluia.**

GOSPEL
Matthew 6:25–32

A reading from the holy Gospel according to Matthew

Jesus said to his disciples: "Look at the birds of the air; they neither sow nor reap nor gather into barns, and yet your heavenly Father feeds them. Are you not of more value than they? And can any of you by worrying add a single hour to your span of life? And why do you worry about clothing? Consider the lilies of the field, how they grow; they neither toil nor spin, yet I tell you, even Solomon in all his glory was not clothed like one of these. But if God so clothes the grass of the field, which is alive today and tomorrow is thrown into the oven, will he not much more clothe you—you of little faith? Therefore do not worry, saying, 'What will we eat?' or 'What will we drink?' or 'What will we wear?' For it is the Gentiles who strive for all these things; and indeed your heavenly Father knows that you need all these things."

The Gospel of the Lord.

◆ All sit and observe silence.

FOR SILENT REFLECTION

According to Jesus, for what should we worry? What should be our goal?

CLOSING PRAYER

Let us stand and bring our hopes and needs to God as we pray, "Lord, hear our prayer."

◆ All may add their own prayers here.

Let us pray: **Our Father . . . Amen.**

Lord Jesus,
lead us to serenity
and to trust in your care for us.
Reassure us of your kingdom
and of eternal existence with
our Creator.
In your name we pray.

Amen.

✝ All make the Sign of the Cross.

PRAYER FOR **MONDAY** **MARCH 3, 2014**

OPENING

Today we remember St. Katharine Drexel, who left her privileged, rich lifestyle to become a missionary for Native and Black Americans.

✚ All make the Sign of the Cross.

In the name of the Father, and of the Son, and of the Holy Spirit. Amen.

PSALM (For a longer psalm, see page xiii.) Psalm 23:1–3a, 3b–4, 5, 6

I shall dwell in the house of the LORD my
　　whole life long.

**I shall dwell in the house of the LORD my
　　whole life long.**

The LORD is my shepherd, I shall not want.
　He makes me lie down in green pastures;
he leads me beside still waters;
　he restores my soul.

**I shall dwell in the house of the LORD my
　　whole life long.**

◆ All stand and sing **Alleluia.**

GOSPEL   Mark 10:17–22

A reading from the holy Gospel according to Mark

As Jesus was setting out on a journey, a man ran up and knelt before him, and asked him, "Good Teacher, what must I do to inherit eternal life?" Jesus said to him, "Why do you call me good? No one is good but God alone. You know the commandments: 'You shall not murder; You shall not commit adultery; You shall not steal; You shall not bear false witness; You shall not defraud; Honor your father and mother.'" He said to him, "Teacher, I have kept all these since my youth." Jesus, looking at him, loved him and said, "You lack one thing; go, sell what you own, and give the money to the poor, and you will have treasure in heaven; then come, follow me." When he heard this, he was shocked and went away grieving, for he had many possessions.

The Gospel of the Lord.

◆ All sit and observe silence.

FOR SILENT REFLECTION

Why do you think Jesus challenges the rich man to share his wealth with the poor?

CLOSING PRAYER

Let us stand and bring our hopes and needs to God as we pray, "Lord, hear our prayer."

◆ All may add their own prayers here.

Let us pray: **Our Father . . . Amen.**

Lord God,
in our culture of abundance,
your requirements can seem difficult.
Keep us alert about
the needs of others so that
our excess can be distributed
to the needs of our family and friends
and those who struggle with finding their own food and shelter.
We ask this through Christ our Lord.

Amen.

✚ All make the Sign of the Cross.

OPENING

Today we remember the patron Saint of Lithuania, Poland, and Russia. St. Casimir was born to be a king in 1458, and attempted to meet his father's royalty standards by leading an army, but failed and returned to a life of prayer and study. He did reign briefly as the king of Poland in his father's absence but died of lung trouble at the age of 23.

✚ All make the Sign of the Cross.

In the name of the Father, and of the Son, and of the Holy Spirit. Amen.

PSALM (For a longer psalm, see page xiii.) Psalm 23:1–3a, 3b–4, 5, 6

I shall dwell in the house of the LORD my
　　whole life long.

**I shall dwell in the house of the LORD my
　　whole life long.**

The LORD is my shepherd, I shall not want.
　　He makes me lie down in green pastures;
he leads me beside still waters;
　　he restores my soul.

**I shall dwell in the house of the LORD my
　　whole life long.**

◆ All stand and sing **Alleluia.**

GOSPEL　　　　　　　　　　　Mark 10:28–31

A reading from the holy Gospel according to Mark

Peter began to say to Jesus, "Look, we have left everything and followed you." Jesus said, "Truly I tell you, there is no one who has left house or brothers or sisters or mother or father or children or fields, for my sake and for the sake of the good news, who will not receive a hundredfold now in this age—houses, brothers and sisters, mothers and children, and fields with persecutions—and in the age to come eternal life. But many who are first will be last, and the last will be first."

The Gospel of the Lord.

◆ All sit and observe silence.

FOR SILENT REFLECTION

What might I need to leave behind to follow Jesus? Why?

CLOSING PRAYER

Let us stand and bring our hopes and needs to God as we pray, "Lord, hear our prayer."

◆ All may add their own prayers here.

Let us pray: **Our Father . . . Amen.**

Jesus our leader,
your words remind us
to keep your truth
front and center in our lives.
Help us to be your leaders
of the faith.
We ask this in your name.

Amen.

✚ All make the Sign of the Cross.

HOME PRAYER
KEEPING LENT

Before you begin, place a candle, an empty bowl, and a jar with a slit cut into the lid (for coins to give to the poor) where the household will gather in prayer. Find the reading (Matthew 7:7–12) in your Bible, ask for a volunteer to read it and encourage him/her to practice reading it a few times. You may wish to begin with a simple song, such as "Jesus, Remember Me," or "Amen" (but not "Alleluia" during Lent). An older child or adult reads the leader parts.

LEADER:
Lent is a time of reflection
and of turning our hearts to God.
We turn our attention to
growing spiritually
so that we can fully cherish the joy of Easter.
Lent helps us to listen more and pray,
just as Jesus did in the desert.

✦ All make the Sign of the Cross.

In the name of the Father, and of the Son, and of the Holy Spirit. Amen.

LEADER: Psalm 37:5a, 3–4, 23–24, 27–28, 30–31
Let us repeat the Psalm Response:
Commit your way to the Lord.

ALL: Commit your way to the Lord.

Trust in the Lord, and do good;
　　so you will live in the land, and enjoy
　　　　security.
Take delight in the Lord,
　　and he will give you the desires of your
　　　　heart.

ALL: Commit your way to the Lord.

Our steps are made firm by the Lord,
　　when he delights in our way;
though we stumble, we shall not fall headlong,
　　for the Lord holds us by the hand.

ALL: Commit your way to the Lord.

✦ All stand and sing **Praise to You, Lord Jesus Christ.**

LEADER: Matthew 7:7–12
A reading from the holy Gospel according to Matthew

✦ Read the Gospel passage from the Bible.

The Gospel of the Lord.

✦ All sit and observe silence. An adult lights the candle.

LEADER:
Heavenly Father,
you sent your Son to us
to light the way back to you.
Guide us in this season of Lent
so that we can focus on you
and on others who may need our help.
We ask this through our Lord Jesus Christ,
your Son, who lives and reigns with you
in the unity of the Holy Spirit, one God, for
ever and ever.

ALL: Amen.

LEADER:
Let us pray as Jesus taught us: **Our Father . . .**

Amen.

✦ All make the Sign of the Cross.

 CHILDREN'S DAILY PRAYER 2013–2014, © 2013 Archdiocese of Chicago: Liturgy Training Publications, 3949 South Racine Avenue, Chicago IL 60609. All rights reserved. Orders: 1-800-933-1800 or www.LTP.org. Scripture excerpts are taken from *The New Revised Standard Version Bible: Catholic Edition*, copyright © 1989, Division of Christian Education of the National Council of the Churches of Christ in the United States of America. Used with permission. All rights reserved.

LENT

WEDNESDAY, MARCH 5, 2014, TO FRIDAY, APRIL 11, 2014

LENT

2014

THE MEANING OF LENT

Jesus said, " 'You shall love the Lord your God with all your heart, and with all your soul, and with all your mind.' This is the greatest and first commandment. And a second is like it: 'You shall love your neighbor as yourself.' On these two commandments hang all the law and the prophets" (Matthew 22:37b–40).

We can't love someone we don't know. If we want to love God, we need to meet him and spend time with him. How do we do that? We can listen to God's words in the Holy Bible. We can speak to him in the freedom and quiet of our hearts. And we can come face to face with God in the sacraments, particularly the Eucharist and the Sacrament of Reconciliation, where we can meet him in the person of Jesus Christ as often as we like.

We also meet Jesus Christ in each other. It is because God first loved us that we are able to love one another. Sometimes it is a challenge to see the face of Christ in our neighbor and to love our Lord Jesus in the person before us.

Coming to know our God more intimately through Jesus Christ is the work of our lives. That work began at our Baptism when we went down into the waters with Christ and rose to new life with him. Each year during Lent and Triduum we ponder this mystery and we pray for the people who are preparing for Baptism at the Easter Vigil.

It is easy to get distracted from our relationship with Jesus. Too often we turn away from God and do our will instead of God's will. This turning back is called *repenting* (turning again). After a time of distraction or willful turning away we feel great sorrow that we have neglected or damaged our relationship with God and we do penance. Repentance and penance are two important works of Lent. Also during Lent we come closer to God by spending more time praying, either with others or when we're alone, by *fasting*, which means eating less or giving up something that distracts us from knowing God, and by *giving*

alms, which means giving money, time, or possessions to help people in need.

Will giving up candy for six weeks help us to love God more? Will putting a few coins aside help us to see and love Christ in the people who stand in front of us every day? Will eating fish on Fridays help us to meet God? Everything depends on our openness to God. God wants us to change the things we do so that our hearts, souls, and minds will overflow with divine love for God, our neighbors, and also for ourselves. Remember, we are to love others as we love ourselves. All of our work during Lent leads to Easter, when we will join in celebrating the Resurrection and the risen life that we receive in Baptism.

TRIDUUM

Lent's purpose—to lead us to the Triduum—becomes more focused as we celebrate Palm Sunday of the Lord's Passion and enter into Holy Week. However, the time of Lent doesn't actually end until the Mass of the Lord's Supper on Holy Thursday evening. At that moment we enter the Triduum, the three holiest days of the Church year. These days are counted from sunset to sunset. So the first day of Triduum begins on Holy Thursday evening and includes Good Friday. The second day runs from Good Friday evening through Holy Saturday. And the third day runs from Holy Saturday evening through Easter Sunday evening. You will find a prayer service to be used on one of the school days of Holy Week (page 261–262), and Home Prayer pages to copy and send home so that families can keep the Three Days of Triduum holy (pages 263–264).

PREPARING TO CELEBRATE LENT IN THE CLASSROOM

Remember that you'll need to change your prayer tablecloth from green to purple.

For the first day of Lent that you meet with the children, place on the prayer table a small glass bowl, a finger towel, and a glass pitcher half-full of water. Copy this prayer on an index card:

Wash me, O Lord, from my iniquity, cleanse me from my sin.

Gather the children around the empty glass bowl. Remind them of the moment during Mass when the priest washes his hands. Explain that this hand washing is silent prayer that the priest does with his hands. Ask a student volunteer to hold his or her fingertips over the bowl and pour a little water over them; dry them with the towel. When you are finished, ask the children what this prayer might mean. What is the priest asking God to do? Why would the priest wash his hands at this moment? After the children have had a chance to reflect on the meaning of the gesture, suggest that the priest is not only asking for clean hands and ask: What else would the priest like God to clean? Then bring out the index card with the prayer. Explain that this is the prayer the priest says as he washes his hands. How can the priest wash away his sins by having someone pour water on his fingers? Finish your reflection by going around the table and practicing the gesture with each other, taking turns being the one who pours the water and being the one whose hands are cleaned. Ask the children if they think that the priest is the only one who needs a clean heart to approach the altar of the Lord.

After you have explored the themes in The Meaning of Lent with the children, open the classroom Bible and read the parable of the good Samaritan (Luke 10:25–37) together. Draw attention to Jesus's final words, "Go and do likewise." Ask the children what they can do that would be like the action of the good Samaritan. Talk together about the needs of people in your area and think of how to respond to them. Perhaps the children could create cards for people in hospitals or nursing homes, collect pennies for disaster relief, or bring canned goods for the local food pantry. If the children are older, consider taking them to prepare and serve a meal at a local soup kitchen. Ask the children how they might "go and do likewise" in their own families as well. Home Prayer is found on page 212.

SACRED SPACE

It's time to remove your living plant from the prayer table and put it near a window. For Lent you could decorate your prayer table with a stalk of dried wheat or some bare branches in a vase.

SACRED MUSIC

Children love to sing "Jesus, Remember Me," and "What Wondrous Love Is This?" Other songs for Lent are "Amazing Grace," the African American spiritual "Somebody's Knockin' at Your Door," and the Latin hymn "Ubi Caritas." We don't sing "Alleluia" during Lent. Tell the children we are saving all our Alleluia joy for Easter. For the Prayer for the Week, where there is a Gospel, we sing an acclamation, such as "Praise to you, Lord Jesus Christ" to whatever tune the parish is using.

PRAYERS FOR LENT

Lent is the perfect time to learn or to review an Act of Contrition. Psalm 51 is also a beautiful prayer for this season of penance and conversion.

A NOTE TO CATECHISTS

If any children in your group are preparing to celebrate the Sacraments of Initiation at the Easter Vigil, gather them to read the following three great accounts from the Gospel of John: 1) Jesus and the woman at the well (John 4:5–15, 19b–26, 39a, 40–42); 2) Jesus and the man born blind (John 9:1, 6–9, 13–17, 34–38); and 3) Jesus raises Lazarus (John 11:3–7, 17, 20–27, 33b–45). These are long passages and may require some time to read and discuss with your students, but fight the temptation to rush through them! After you have read and meditated together, consider inviting the children to act out these highly dramatic accounts. All of us will benefit from these readings as we prepare to celebrate the joy of the Resurrection.

GRACE BEFORE MEALS

LENT

LEADER:

We adore you, O Christ, and we praise you

ALL: because by your holy cross you have redeemed the world.

✝ All make the Sign of the Cross.

In the name of the Father, and of the Son, and of the Holy Spirit. Amen.

LEADER:

God of compassion,
we thank you for this meal
and for those who prepared it.
May we be nourished by this food
and by the love and friendship we share.
Help us to be mindful of people
in our community and other regions
who will remain hungry today.
May we become your true food for others
through gifts of your Spirit and our works of
        charity.
We ask this through Christ our Lord.

Amen.

✝ All make the Sign of the Cross.

In the name of the Father, and of the Son, and of the Holy Spirit. Amen.

PRAYER AT DAY'S END

LEADER:
Blessed be the Lord,

ALL: for he has heard the sound of my pleadings.

✚ All make the Sign of the Cross.

In the name of the Father, and of the Son, and of the Holy Spirit. Amen.

LEADER:
Merciful Lord,
sometimes we fail in what
we say or do.
As our school day ends,
help us to remember that
your mercy and love
are never-ending.
Guide us as we renew our
commitment
to deepen our relationship with you
throughout this season of Lent.
We ask this in your name.

Amen.

✚ All make the Sign of the Cross.

In the name of the Father, and of the Son, and of the Holy Spirit. Amen.

PRAYER SERVICE
ASH WEDNESDAY

Prepare eight leaders for this service. Before you begin, prepare a long piece of butcher-block paper or cloth banner with the word "Alleluia" written on it. The inside of the first three letters, "A-l-l" should be colored in, but you should only be able to see an outline of the rest of the word's letters, "e-l-u-i-a." Hang this banner for all to see, but make it accessible so that an additional letter can be colored each week of Lent. On Fridays during Lent, you may want to incorporate coloring the additional letters when you do Prayer at Day's End for Lent, found on page 217.

The fifth and sixth leaders of this Prayer Service will need Bibles for the Scripture passages and may need help practicing them. You may wish to begin by singing "From Ashes to the Living Font" and end with "Soon and Very Soon." If the group will sing, prepare a song leader.

FIRST LEADER:

◆ All make the sign of the Cross.

In the name of the Father, and of the Son, and of the Holy Spirit. Amen.

May God's grace be with us as we prepare our hearts for the way of Jesus.

Amen.

Today we embark together on a journey through Lent. It is a time for self-discovery as we remember how Jesus went into the desert for 40 days and was tempted by the devil. During our Lenten experience, we pray more, eat less, and give to the poor to prepare ourselves for the biggest event in our Christian faith—Christ's Resurrection at Easter! But we must make ready our hearts

and minds, like an athlete trains for a key game or race. We need to strengthen our good habits as we remain God's sons and daughters through the waters of Baptism.

SECOND LEADER:

Each year, on Ash Wednesday, Catholics are marked with ashes in the Sign of the Cross as a reminder that we are entering into Lent. This ashen sign reminds us of our humanness, and that sometimes we fail. We need God's help to succeed. That's why prayer is so vital in our lives.

THIRD LEADER:

During Lent, we also fast from the word "Alleluia," which means "Praise the Lord" in Hebrew. We've prepared this banner with only three of the letters colored in. But you'll see that on this special day, we are *all* in this together! Lent can be a time for us *all* to get closer to Christ. Just like a team trains for a big game, we *all* can do this through prayer and sacrifice. So at the end of each week in Lent, we will color in 1 more letter to mark another week closer to our declaring this joyous word!

FOURTH LEADER:

Let us pray:
Almighty Father,
through the waters of Baptism,
you claimed us as
your sons and daughters.

CHILDREN'S DAILY PRAYER 2013–2014, © 2013 Archdiocese of Chicago: Liturgy Training Publications. All rights reserved. Orders: 1-800-933-1800 or www.LTP.org.

You love us without condition.
May our prayers, fasting, and
works of charity deepen
our connection with you
as we better understand the suffering of
our brothers and sisters around the world.
May we remember how
Jesus was tempted in the desert
and that *all* of us need to make
you
our priority
in word and deed.
We ask this through Christ our Lord.

ALL: Amen.

◆ All stand and sing **Praise to you, Lord Jesus Christ** . . .

FIFTH LEADER: Matthew 4:1–11
A reading from the holy Gospel according to
Matthew

◆ Read the Scripture passage from a Bible.

The Gospel of the Lord.

◆ All remain standing and observe silence.

SIXTH LEADER: Matthew 6:1–2
A reading from the holy Gospel according to
Matthew

◆ Read the Scripture passage from a Bible.

The Gospel of the Lord.

◆ All sit and observe silence.

SEVENTH LEADER:
Let us pray as Jesus taught us:

ALL: Our Father . . . Amen.

Lord God,
help us to be one with you
during this season of Lent.
Guide us as you led
Jesus through the
trying times in his life.
May we let go of
our negative habits and thoughts
that make us feel distant
from your loving presence.
We look forward to
the joy of Easter,
for our hope is Jesus
in this time of preparation.
We ask this through Christ our Lord.

Amen.

EIGHTH LEADER:
Let us offer to one another a sign of Christ's
peace:

◆ All offer one another a sign of peace.

And may the Lord bless us,

◆ All make the Sign of the Cross.

protect us from all evil,
and bring us to everlasting life.

ALL: Amen.

PRAYER FOR **WEDNESDAY** MARCH 5, 2014

OPENING

Today is Ash Wednesday, the first day of Lent, when we begin 40 days of reflection and renewal to turn our hearts even more to God.

✦ All make the Sign of the Cross.

In the name of the Father, and of the Son, and of the Holy Spirit. Amen.

PSALM   (For a longer psalm, see page xiv.) Psalm 34:4–5, 6–7, 16–17, 18–19

The LORD saves the crushed in spirit.

The LORD saves the crushed in spirit.

I sought the LORD, and he answered me,
   and delivered me from all my fears.
Look to him, and be radiant;
   so your faces shall never be ashamed.

The LORD saves the crushed in spirit.

◆ All stand and sing **Praise to you, Lord Jesus Christ . . .**

GOSPEL   Matthew 6:3–6, 16–18

A reading from the holy Gospel according to Matthew

Jesus said to his disciples: "But when you give alms, do not let your left hand know what your right hand is doing, so that your alms may be done in secret; and your Father who sees in secret will reward you.

"And whenever you pray, do not be like the hypocrites; for they love to stand and pray in the synagogues and at the street corners, so that they may be seen by others. Truly I tell you, they have received their reward. But whenever you pray, go into your room and shut the door and pray to your Father who is in secret; and your Father who sees in secret will reward you.

"And whenever you fast, do not look dismal, like the hypocrites, for they disfigure their faces so as to show others that they are fasting. Truly I tell you, they have received their reward. But when you fast, put oil on your head and wash your face, so that your fasting may be seen not by others but by your Father who is in secret; and your Father who sees in secret will reward you."

The Gospel of the Lord.

◆ All sit and observe silence.

FOR SILENT REFLECTION

How will I deepen my prayer life this Lent?

CLOSING PRAYER

Let us stand and bring our hopes and needs to God as we pray, "Lord, hear our prayer."

◆ All may add their own prayers here.

Let us pray: **Our Father . . . Amen.**

Lord Jesus,
you ask us to focus on prayer from the heart.
Guide us toward doing good for others and praying for them.
We ask this in your name.

Amen.

✦ All make the Sign of the Cross.

220

OPENING

In today's reading, Moses is speaking to his people about their choice to follow God.

✝ All make the Sign of the Cross.

In the name of the Father, and of the Son, and of the Holy Spirit. Amen.

PSALM

(For a longer psalm, see page xiv.) Psalm 34:4–5, 6–7, 16–17, 18–19

The LORD saves the crushed in spirit.

The LORD saves the crushed in spirit.

I sought the LORD, and he answered me,
    and delivered me from all my fears.
Look to him, and be radiant;
    so your faces shall never be ashamed.

The LORD saves the crushed in spirit.

READING

Deuteronomy 30:15–20

A reading from the Book of Deuteronomy

Moses said to the people: "See, I have set before you today life and prosperity, death and adversity. If you obey the commandments of the LORD your God that I am commanding you today, by loving the LORD your God, walking in his ways, and observing his commandments, decrees, and ordinances, then you shall live and become numerous, and the LORD your God will bless you in the land that you are entering to possess. But if your heart turns away and you do not hear, but are led astray to bow down to other gods and serve them, I declare to you today that you shall perish; you shall not live long in the land that you are crossing the Jordan to enter and possess. I call heaven and earth to witness against you today that I have set before you life and death, blessings and curses. Choose life so that you and your descendants may live, loving the LORD your God, obeying him, and holding fast to him; for that means life to you and length of days, so that you may live in the land that the LORD swore to give to your ancestors, to Abraham, to Isaac, and to Jacob."

The Word of the Lord.

◆ All observe silence.

FOR SILENT REFLECTION

How do you include God in helping you make key choices?

CLOSING PRAYER

Let us stand and bring our hopes and needs to God as we pray, "Lord, hear our prayer."

◆ All may add their own prayers here.

Let us pray: **Our Father . . . Amen.**

Almighty God,
you led your chosen people to
their promised land.
Help us to stay committed to
your guiding light and Spirit that
urges us to make right decisions.
We ask this through Christ your Son,
our Lord.

Amen.

✝ All make the Sign of the Cross.

PRAYER FOR **FRIDAY** **MARCH 7, 2014**

OPENING

Today we remember Sts. Perpetua and Felicity, who refused to deny their faith under the persecution of Severus, in the church's early days. Perpetua was a young, well-educated noblewoman of Carthage, and Felicity was a slave.

✚ All make the Sign of the Cross.

In the name of the Father, and of the Son, and of the Holy Spirit. Amen.

PSALM   (For a longer psalm, see page xiv.) Psalm 34:4–5, 6–7, 16–17, 18–19

The LORD saves the crushed in spirit.

The LORD saves the crushed in spirit.

I sought the LORD, and he answered me,
    and delivered me from all my fears.
Look to him, and be radiant;
    so your faces shall never be ashamed.

The LORD saves the crushed in spirit.

READING   Isaiah 58:5a–9a

A reading from the Book of the Prophet Isaiah

"Will you call this a fast, a day acceptable to the LORD? Is not this the fast that I choose: to loose the bonds of injustice, to undo the thongs of the yoke, to let the oppressed go free, and to break every yoke? Is it not to share your bread with the hungry, and bring the homeless poor into your house; when you see the naked, to cover them, and not to hide yourself from your own kin?

Then your light shall break forth like the dawn, and your healing shall spring up quickly;

your vindicator shall go before you, the glory of the LORD shall be your rear guard. Then you shall call, and the LORD will answer; you shall cry for help, and he will say, Here I am."

The Word of the Lord.

◆ All observe silence.

FOR SILENT REFLECTION

In this season of Lent, how can I become more aware of the hungry and the homeless in my own community and in other countries?

CLOSING PRAYER

Let us stand and bring our hopes and needs to God as we pray, "Lord, hear our prayer."

◆ All may add their own prayers here.

Let us pray: **Our Father . . . Amen.**

Almighty God,
your prophets point the way to
our caring for others,
especially those who hunger,
need shelter, or who are sick.
May we be charitable with our
brothers and sisters to
reveal your plan for hope and comfort
in the midst of trials and trouble.
We ask this through Christ our Lord.

Amen.

✚ All make the Sign of the Cross.

OPENING

Today's Gospel shows Jesus in the desert at a very trying time. Listen to all the different ways that Satan tempted him.

✚ All make the Sign of the Cross.

In the name of the Father, and of the Son, and of the Holy Spirit. Amen.

PSALM (For a longer psalm, see page xiv.) Psalm 34:4–5, 6–7, 16–17, 18–19

The LORD saves the crushed in spirit.

The LORD saves the crushed in spirit.

I sought the LORD, and he answered me,
    and delivered me from all my fears.
Look to him, and be radiant;
    so your faces shall never be ashamed.

The LORD saves the crushed in spirit.

◆ All stand and sing **Praise to you, Lord Jesus Christ . . .**

GOSPEL Matthew 4:1–11

A reading from the holy Gospel according to Matthew

Jesus fasted forty days and forty nights, and afterwards he was famished. The tempter came and said to him, "If you are the Son of God, command these stones to become loaves of bread." But he answered, "It is written, 'One does not live by bread alone, but by every word that comes from the mouth of God.'" Then the devil took him to the holy city and placed him on the pinnacle of the temple, saying to him, "If you are the Son of God, throw yourself down; for it is written, 'He will command his angels concerning you,' and 'On their hands they will bear you up, so that you will not dash your foot against a stone.'" Jesus said to him, "Again it is written, 'Do not put the Lord your God to the test.'" Again, the devil took him to a very high mountain and showed him all the kingdoms of the world and their splendor; and he said to him, "All these I will give you, if you will fall down and worship me." Jesus said to him, "Away with you, Satan! for it is written, 'Worship the Lord your God, and serve only him.'" Then the devil left him, and suddenly angels came and waited on him.

The Gospel of the Lord.

◆ All sit and observe silence.

FOR SILENT REFLECTION

How are you tempted?

CLOSING PRAYER

Let us stand and bring our hopes and needs to God as we pray, "Lord, hear our prayer."

◆ All may add their own prayers here.

Let us pray: **Our Father . . . Amen.**

Jesus our teacher,
give us strength to
resist temptation.
Your Way is the way
to everlasting life.
We ask this in your name.

Amen.

✚ All make the Sign of the Cross.

PRAYER FOR **MONDAY** **MARCH 10, 2014**

OPENING

Today's Gospel reminds us that Christ is in each and every person we encounter.

✦ All make the Sign of the Cross.

In the name of the Father, and of the Son, and of the Holy Spirit. Amen.

PSALM

(For a longer psalm, see page xiv.) Psalm 34:4–5, 6–7, 16–17, 18–19

The LORD saves the crushed in spirit.

The LORD saves the crushed in spirit.

I sought the LORD, and he answered me,
  and delivered me from all my fears.
Look to him, and be radiant;
  so your faces shall never be ashamed.

The LORD saves the crushed in spirit.

◆ All stand and sing **Praise to you, Lord Jesus Christ . . .**

GOSPEL

Matthew 25:31–40

A reading from the holy Gospel according to Matthew

Jesus said to his disciples: "When the Son of Man comes in his glory, and all the angels with him, then he will sit on the throne of his glory. All the nations will be gathered before him, and he will separate people one from another as a shepherd separates the sheep from the goats, and he will put the sheep at his right hand and the goats at the left. Then the king will say to those at his right hand, 'Come, you that are blessed by my Father, inherit the kingdom prepared for you from the foundation of the world; for I was hungry and you gave me food, I was thirsty and you gave me something to drink, I was a stranger and you welcomed me, I was naked and you gave me clothing, I was sick and you took care of me, I was in prison and you visited me.' Then the righteous will answer him, 'Lord, when was it that we saw you hungry and gave you food, or thirsty and gave you something to drink? And when was it that we saw you a stranger and welcomed you, or naked and gave you clothing? And when was it that we saw you sick or in prison and visited you?' And the king will answer them, 'Truly I tell you, just as you did it to one of the least of these who are members of my family, you did it to me.'"

The Gospel of the Lord.

◆ All sit and observe silence.

FOR SILENT REFLECTION

What kind gestures have you done for others?

CLOSING PRAYER

Let us stand and bring our hopes and needs to God as we pray, "Lord, hear our prayer."

◆ All may add their own prayers here.

Let us pray: **Our Father . . . Amen.**

Lord Jesus,
help us to be kind and loving to all,
for we are made in your image.
We ask this in your name.

Amen.

✦ All make the Sign of the Cross.

OPENING

Today's Gospel is the Apostle Matthew's version of Jesus's lesson of prayer that later became known as the Lord's Prayer. It's also a reminder that God wants us to be honest in our prayers because our Creator already knows us well.

✝ All make the Sign of the Cross.

In the name of the Father, and of the Son, and of the Holy Spirit. Amen.

PSALM

(For a longer psalm, see page xiv.) Psalm 34:4–5, 6–7, 16–17, 18–19

The LORD saves the crushed in spirit.

The LORD saves the crushed in spirit.

I sought the LORD, and he answered me,
    and delivered me from all my fears.
Look to him, and be radiant;
    so your faces shall never be ashamed.

The LORD saves the crushed in spirit.

◆ All stand and sing **Praise to you, Lord Jesus Christ . . .**

GOSPEL

Matthew 6:7–15

A reading from the holy Gospel according to Matthew

Jesus said to his disciples: "When you are praying, do not heap up empty phrases as the Gentiles do; for they think that they will be heard because of their many words. Do not be like them, for your Father knows what you need before you ask him.

"Pray then in this way: Our Father in heaven, hallowed be your name. Your kingdom come. Your will be done, on earth as it is in heaven. Give us this day our daily bread. And forgive us our debts, as we also have forgiven our debtors. And do not bring us to the time of trial, but rescue us from the evil one. For if you forgive others their trespasses, your heavenly Father will also forgive you; but if you do not forgive others, neither will your Father forgive your trespasses."

The Gospel of the Lord.

◆ All sit and observe silence.

FOR SILENT REFLECTION

What does "daily bread" really mean? What is your "daily bread"?

CLOSING PRAYER

Let us stand and bring our hopes and needs to God as we pray, "Lord, hear our prayer."

◆ All may add their own prayers here.

Let us pray: **Our Father . . . Amen.**

Lord Jesus,
we know that our God is
so loving that he knows
our every need, even before we ask.
Help us to pray your prayer often
so that we put our
minds and hearts with our Creator,
whom we are privileged to call
our Father and friend.
In your name we pray.

Amen.

✝ All make the Sign of the Cross.

PRAYER FOR **WEDNESDAY** MARCH 12, 2014

OPENING

Today's reading involves the prophet Jonah, who was entrusted with declaring to the inhabitants of Nineveh that they needed to change their ways.

✛ All make the Sign of the Cross.

In the name of the Father, and of the Son, and of the Holy Spirit. Amen.

PSALM
(For a longer psalm, see page xiv.) Psalm 34:4–5, 6–7, 16–17, 18–19

The LORD saves the crushed in spirit.

The LORD saves the crushed in spirit.

I sought the LORD, and he answered me,
  and delivered me from all my fears.
Look to him, and be radiant;
  so your faces shall never be ashamed.

The LORD saves the crushed in spirit.

READING
Jonah 3:3–10

A reading from the Book of the Prophet Jonah

So Jonah set out and went to Nineveh, according to the word of the Lord. Now Nineveh was an exceedingly large city, a three days' walk across. Jonah began to go into the city, going a day's walk. And he cried out, "Forty days more, and Nineveh shall be overthrown!"

And the people of Nineveh believed God; they proclaimed a fast, and everyone, great and small, put on sackcloth. When the news reached the king of Nineveh, he rose from his throne, removed his robe, covered himself with sackcloth, and sat in ashes. Then he had a proclamation made in Nineveh: "By the decree of the king and his nobles: No human being or animal, no herd or flock, shall taste anything. They shall not feed, nor shall they drink water. Human beings and animals shall be covered with sackcloth, and they shall cry mightily to God. All shall turn from their evil ways and from the violence that is in their hands. Who knows? God may relent and change his mind; he may turn from his fierce anger, so that we do not perish." When God saw what they did, how they turned from their evil ways, God changed his mind about the calamity that he had said he would bring upon them; and he did not do it.

The Word of the Lord.

◆ All observe silence.

FOR SILENT REFLECTION

How are we challenged to change?

CLOSING PRAYER

Let us stand and bring our hopes and needs to God as we pray, "Lord, hear our prayer."

◆ All may add their own prayers here.

Let us pray: **Our Father . . . Amen.**

Almighty God,
help us to follow your decrees
as they lead us back to you.
We ask this through Christ our Lord.

Amen.

✛ All make the Sign of the Cross.

OPENING

In today's Gospel, we hear again how God listens to everyone, but we must communicate with our Creator regularly.

✙ All make the Sign of the Cross.

In the name of the Father, and of the Son, and of the Holy Spirit. Amen.

PSALM

(For a longer psalm, see page xiv.) Psalm 34:4–5, 6–7, 16–17, 18–19

The LORD saves the crushed in spirit.

The LORD saves the crushed in spirit.

I sought the LORD, and he answered me,
  and delivered me from all my fears.
Look to him, and be radiant;
  so your faces shall never be ashamed.

The LORD saves the crushed in spirit.

◆ All stand and sing **Praise to you, Lord Jesus Christ . . .**

GOSPEL

Matthew 7:7–12

A reading from the holy Gospel according to Matthew

Jesus said to his disciples: "Ask, and it will be given you; search, and you will find; knock, and the door will be opened for you. For everyone who asks receives, and everyone who searches finds, and for everyone who knocks, the door will be opened. Is there anyone among you who, if your child asks for bread, will give a stone? Or if the child asks for a fish, will give a snake? If you then, who are evil, know how to give good gifts to your children, how much more will your Father in heaven give good things to those who ask him!

"In everything do to others as you would have them do to you; for this is the law and the prophets."

The Gospel of the Lord.

◆ All sit and observe silence.

FOR SILENT REFLECTION

What do you need? For what have you asked God? Have you received answers in your prayers or in other ways?

CLOSING PRAYER

Let us stand and bring our hopes and needs to God as we pray, "Lord, hear our prayer."

◆ All may add their own prayers here.

Let us pray: **Our Father . . . Amen.**

Jesus our guide,
you lead us to be persistent
in our prayers and to
ask for what we need.
You know how prayer changes us,
especially when we talk with you like
we talk with our closest friends.
Continue to help us
to stay connected with you,
the source of all good.
In your name we pray.

Amen.

✙ All make the Sign of the Cross.

PRAYER FOR **FRIDAY** MARCH 14, 2014

OPENING

Today's Gospel reminds us that just doing the bare minimum in settling conflict is not enough. Listen to the guidelines that Jesus describes.

✚ All make the Sign of the Cross.

In the name of the Father, and of the Son, and of the Holy Spirit. Amen.

PSALM   (For a longer psalm, see page xiv.) Psalm 34:4–5, 6–7, 16–17, 18–19

The LORD saves the crushed in spirit.

The LORD saves the crushed in spirit.

I sought the LORD, and he answered me,
    and delivered me from all my fears.
Look to him, and be radiant;
    so your faces shall never be ashamed.

The LORD saves the crushed in spirit.

◆ All stand and sing **Praise to you, Lord Jesus Christ . . .**

GOSPEL   Matthew 5:21–24

A reading from the holy Gospel according to Matthew

Jesus said to his disciples: "You have heard that it was said to those of ancient times, 'You shall not murder'; and 'whoever murders shall be liable to judgment.' But I say to you that if you are angry with a brother or sister, you will be liable to judgment; and if you insult a brother or sister, you will be liable to the council; and if you say, 'You fool,' you will be liable to the hell of fire. So when you are offering your gift at the altar, if you remember that your brother or sister has something against you, leave your gift there before the altar and go; first be reconciled to your brother or sister, and then come and offer your gift."

The Gospel of the Lord.

◆ All sit and observe silence.

FOR SILENT REFLECTION

How often do I forgive others? How do I work with friends and family when I have done wrong?

CLOSING PRAYER

Let us stand and bring our hopes and needs to God as we pray, "Lord, hear our prayer."

◆ All may add their own prayers here.

Let us pray: **Our Father . . . Amen.**

Lord Jesus,
you ask us to forgive one another
and to be reconciled.
Help us to have courage to
seek your path to wholeness.
In your name we pray.

Amen.

✚ All make the Sign of the Cross.

228

OPENING

Today's Gospel is Matthew's account of the Transfiguration. Jesus took his closest friends to the place where God spoke to him directly.

✛ All make the Sign of the Cross.

> **In the name of the Father, and of the Son, and of the Holy Spirit. Amen.**

PSALM

(For a longer psalm, see page xiv.) Psalm 34:4–5, 6–7, 16–17, 18–19

The LORD saves the crushed in spirit.

The LORD saves the crushed in spirit.

I sought the LORD, and he answered me,
  and delivered me from all my fears.
Look to him, and be radiant;
  so your faces shall never be ashamed.

The LORD saves the crushed in spirit.

◆ All stand and sing **Praise to you, Lord Jesus Christ . . .**

GOSPEL

Matthew 17:1–9

A reading from the holy Gospel according to Matthew

Jesus took with him Peter and James and his brother John and led them up a high mountain, by themselves. And he was transfigured before them, and his face shone like the sun, and his clothes became dazzling white. Suddenly there appeared to them Moses and Elijah, talking with him. Then Peter said to Jesus, "Lord, it is good for us to be here; if you wish, I will make three dwellings here, one for you, one for Moses, and one for Elijah." While he was still speaking, suddenly a bright cloud overshadowed them, and from the cloud a voice said, "This is my Son, the Beloved; with him I am well pleased; listen to him!" When the disciples heard this, they fell to the ground and were overcome by fear. But Jesus came and touched them, saying, "Get up and do not be afraid." And when they looked up, they saw no one except Jesus himself alone. As they were coming down the mountain, Jesus ordered them, "Tell no one about the vision until after the Son of Man has been raised from the dead."

The Gospel of the Lord.

◆ All sit and observe silence.

FOR SILENT REFLECTION

Why do you think Jesus might have ordered the three apostles not to tell what they saw?

CLOSING PRAYER

Let us stand and bring our hopes and needs to God as we pray, "Lord, hear our prayer."

◆ All may add their own prayers here.

Let us pray: **Our Father . . . Amen.**

Lord Jesus,
you are God's beloved Son.
May we be worthy to be called
your sons and daughters.
In your name we pray.

Amen.

✛ All make the Sign of the Cross.

PRAYER FOR **MONDAY**
MARCH 17, 2014

OPENING

Today we remember St. Patrick, who was born in the fifth century. He felt called to be a missionary in Ireland and worked from one coast to another, establishing monasteries, ordaining priests, and calling all people to live in holiness. Many people became Christian and took up his cause to do missionary work as well. Today's Gospel from Luke reminds us that Jesus's way of living can be difficult at times, especially when we get angry.

✜ All make the Sign of the Cross.

In the name of the Father, and of the Son, and of the Holy Spirit. Amen.

PSALM (For a longer psalm, see page xiv.) Psalm 34:4–5, 6–7, 16–17, 18–19

The LORD saves the crushed in spirit.

The LORD saves the crushed in spirit.

I sought the LORD, and he answered me,
    and delivered me from all my fears.
Look to him, and be radiant;
    so your faces shall never be ashamed.

The LORD saves the crushed in spirit.

◆ All stand and sing **Praise to you, Lord Jesus Christ . . .**

GOSPEL Luke 6:36–38

A reading from the holy Gospel according to Luke

Jesus said to his disciples: "Be merciful, just as your Father is merciful.

"Do not judge, and you will not be judged; do not condemn, and you will not be condemned. Forgive, and you will be forgiven; give, and it will be given to you. A good measure, pressed down, shaken together, running over, will be put into your lap; for the measure you give will be the measure you get back."

The Gospel of the Lord.

◆ All sit and observe silence.

FOR SILENT REFLECTION

Do I judge or condemn others sometimes? Why? If yes, how can I deal with this?

CLOSING PRAYER

Let us stand and bring our hopes and needs to God as we pray, "Lord, hear our prayer."

◆ All may add their own prayers here.

Let us pray: **Our Father . . . Amen.**

Lord Jesus,
you ask us to be merciful
and to not condemn.
We need to forgive,
which can be the
hardest thing to do.
Guide us as we try
to be loving with those
who sometimes anger us.
Help us to be aware
of our emotions
before we act in harmful ways.
In your name we pray.

Amen.

✜ All make the Sign of the Cross.

OPENING

In today's Gospel, Jesus tells his followers about greatness. It is not seen in the actions of many religious people at that time because many of them wanted to appear pious.

✝ All make the Sign of the Cross.

In the name of the Father, and of the Son, and of the Holy Spirit. Amen.

PSALM
(For a longer psalm, see page xiv.) Psalm 34:4–5, 6–7, 16–17, 18–19

The LORD saves the crushed in spirit.

The LORD saves the crushed in spirit.

I sought the LORD, and he answered me,
  and delivered me from all my fears.
Look to him, and be radiant;
  so your faces shall never be ashamed.

The LORD saves the crushed in spirit.

◆ All stand and sing **Praise to you, Lord Jesus Christ . . .**

GOSPEL
Matthew 23:1–12

A reading from the holy Gospel according to Matthew

Jesus said to the crowds and to his disciples, "The scribes and the Pharisees sit on Moses' seat; therefore, do whatever they teach you and follow it; but do not do as they do, for they do not practice what they teach. They tie up heavy burdens, hard to bear, and lay them on the shoulders of others; but they themselves are unwilling to lift a finger to move them. They do all their deeds to be seen by others; for they make their phylacteries broad and their fringes long. They love to have the place of honor at banquets and the best seats in the synagogues, and to be greeted with respect in the marketplaces, and to have people call them rabbi. But you are not to be called rabbi, for you have one teacher, and you are all students. And call no one your father on earth, for you have one Father—the one in heaven. Nor are you to be called instructors, for you have one instructor, the Messiah. The greatest among you will be your servant. All who exalt themselves will be humbled, and all who humble themselves will be exalted."

The Gospel of the Lord.

◆ All sit and observe silence.

FOR SILENT REFLECTION

Who does Jesus mean is the "one teacher"?

CLOSING PRAYER

Let us stand and bring our hopes and needs to God as we pray, "Lord, hear our prayer."

◆ All may add their own prayers here.

Let us pray: **Our Father . . . Amen.**

Lord Jesus,
help us to be
servant leaders today.
Guide us to be honest and helpful
with our family and friends,
coaches, and teachers.
In your name we pray.

Amen.

✝ All make the Sign of the Cross.

PRAYER FOR **WEDNESDAY** MARCH 19, 2014

OPENING

Today we remember St. Joseph, the holy husband of Mary and foster father of Jesus. He cared for his Holy Family with grace and humility.

✦ All make the Sign of the Cross.

In the name of the Father, and of the Son, and of the Holy Spirit. Amen.

PSALM

(For a longer psalm, see page xiv.) Psalm 34:4–5, 6–7, 16–17, 18–19

The LORD saves the crushed in spirit.

The LORD saves the crushed in spirit.

I sought the LORD, and he answered me,
    and delivered me from all my fears.
Look to him, and be radiant;
    so your faces shall never be ashamed.

The LORD saves the crushed in spirit.

◆ All stand and sing **Praise to you, Lord Jesus Christ** . . .

GOSPEL

Luke 2:41–51

A reading from the holy Gospel according to Luke

Now every year his parents went to Jerusalem for the festival of the Passover. And when he was twelve years old, they went up as usual for the festival. When the festival was ended and they started to return, the boy Jesus stayed behind in Jerusalem, but his parents did not know it. Assuming that he was in the group of travelers, they went a day's journey. Then they started to look for him among their relatives and friends. When they did not find him, they returned to Jerusalem to search for him. After three days they found him in the temple, sitting among the teachers, listening to them and asking them questions. And all who heard him were amazed at his understanding and his answers. When his parents saw him they were astonished; and his mother said to him, "Child, why have you treated us like this? Look, your father and I have been searching for you in great anxiety." He said to them, "Why were you searching for me? Did you not know that I must be in my Father's house?" But they did not understand what he said to them. Then he went down with them and came to Nazareth, and was obedient to them.

The Gospel of the Lord.

◆ All sit and observe silence.

FOR SILENT REFLECTION

Why do you think Jesus said to his Mother, "Did you not know that I must be in my Father's house?"

CLOSING PRAYER

Let us stand and bring our hopes and needs to God as we pray, "Lord, hear our prayer."

◆ All may add their own prayers here.

Let us pray: **Our Father . . . Amen.**

Jesus our teacher,
may we learn from
your wisdom and grace.
We ask this in your name.

Amen.

✦ All make the Sign of the Cross.

Prepare six leaders for this service. The third leader will need a Bible for the passage from Matthew. Take time to help the third leader practice the readings. You may wish to sing "You Are the Light of the World," "Blest Are They" or "We Are Called," as opening or closing songs. If the group will sing, prepare someone to lead.

FIRST LEADER:

Today we remember Joseph, the husband of Mary and the foster father of Jesus here on earth. At several key times in his life, Joseph listened and followed special messengers that God directed to this humble carpenter. Joseph's faith led him to marry his fiancée, even though she became pregnant in a divinely inspired way. He courageously took them to Egypt to escape Herod's wrath. And Joseph raised Jesus as his own son, guiding his growth.

✝ All make the Sign of the Cross.

In the name of the Father, and of the Son, and of the Holy Spirit. Amen.

Let us remember Joseph as we begin by singing the opening song.

SONG LEADER:

◆ Gesture for all to stand, and lead the first few verses of the song.

SECOND LEADER:

Let us pray:
Almighty Father,
may we look to Joseph as our guide
as he responded to your call to be
a devoted husband and father.

PRAYER SERVICE
SOLEMNITY OF ST. JOSEPH

We pray with him to your Son Jesus,
our Lord and Savior,
in union with the Holy Spirit.

Amen.

◆ Remain standing and sing **Praise to you, Lord Jesus Christ** . . .

THIRD LEADER: Matthew 2:13–15
A reading from the holy Gospel according to Matthew

◆ Read the Gospel passage from the Bible.

The Gospel of the Lord.

◆ All remain standing and observe silence.

FOURTH LEADER:
Let us bring our hopes and needs to God as
we pray, Lord, hear our prayer.
For the courage to live our faith
through word and action
as Joseph did throughout his days,
we pray to the Lord.

For all who are struggling with
tough decisions in life,
may they look to Joseph as
a brave friend on their journey,
we pray to the Lord.

For all married couples;
may they continue to be an example
of the love and devotion that
Joseph and Mary shared,
we pray to the Lord.

For all fathers
and those who nurture others.
Help us to respect and protect life
from conception until natural death.
We pray to the Lord.

May we have the conviction
to lead the way as Joseph did
to hope and the promise
of new life through Jesus.
We pray to the Lord.

FIFTH LEADER:
Let us pray as Jesus taught us:
Our Father . . . Amen.

◆ Pause, and then say:

Let us offer one another the sign of Christ's
peace.

◆ All offer one another a sign of peace.

SIXTH LEADER:
Let us pray:
Heavenly Father,
your servant Joseph
was a man of great faith.
He listened to you in prayer
and to angels whom you sent
in dreams.
He is a symbol for courage
in following God's will.
May we look to him
in times of trouble or doubt.
We ask this through Christ our Lord.

ALL: Amen.

✝ All make the Sign of the Cross.

**In the name of the Father, and of the
Son, and of the Holy Spirit. Amen.**

 CHILDREN'S DAILY PRAYER 2013–2014, © 2013 Archdiocese of Chicago: Liturgy Training Publications. All rights reserved. Orders: 1-800-933-1800 or www.LTP.org.

HOME PRAYER
LEARNING FROM ST. JOSEPH

Find the reading (Matthew 1:18–24) in your Bible, ask for a volunteer to read it and to practice it a few times. You may wish to begin with a simple song, such as "God Is So Good," or "Amen" (but not "Alleluia" during Lent). An older child or adult reads the leader parts.

LEADER:

St. Joseph was a humble carpenter who listened to God throughout his life. He obeyed God to become the foster father of Jesus and to protect his family on their lifelong journey together.

✚ All make the Sign of the Cross.

In the name of the Father, and of the Son, and of the Holy Spirit. Amen.

LEADER: Psalm 9:1a, 2, 9–10, 13, 18

Let us repeat the Psalm Response:
I will give thanks to the Lord with my whole heart.

ALL: I will give thanks to the Lord with my whole heart.

The Lord is a stronghold for the oppressed,
 a stronghold in times of trouble.
And those who know your name put their
  trust in you,
  for you, O Lord, have not forsaken those
   who seek you.

ALL: I will give thanks to the Lord with my whole heart.

Be gracious to me, O Lord.
 See what I suffer from those who hate me;
 you are the one who lifts me up from the
  gates of death.

ALL: I will give thanks to the Lord with my whole heart.

For the needy shall not always be forgotten,
 nor the hope of the poor perish forever.

ALL: I will give thanks to the Lord with my whole heart.

◆ All stand and sing **Praise to you Lord Jesus Christ . . .**

LEADER: Matthew 1:18–24

A reading from the holy Gospel according to Matthew

◆ Read the Gospel passage from the Bible.

The Gospel of the Lord.

◆ All sit and observe silence.

LEADER:

Let us pray:
Heavenly Father,
we are thankful for Joseph,
who chose to be the earthly father
of your Son, Jesus.
He taught Jesus by his examples of
hard work and faithful integrity.
Help us to turn to Joseph as our guide
as we journey to unknown territory
to follow God's will.
We ask this through our Lord Jesus Christ,
your Son, who lives and reigns with you
in the unity of the Holy Spirit, one God, for
ever and ever.

ALL: Amen.

✚ All make the Sign of the Cross.

CHILDREN'S DAILY PRAYER 2013–2014 © 2013 Archdiocese of Chicago: Liturgy Training Publications, 3949 South Racine Avenue, Chicago IL 60609. All rights reserved. Orders: 1-800-933-1800 or www.LTP.org. Scripture excerpts are taken from *The New Revised Standard Version Bible: Catholic Edition,* © 1989, Division of Christian Education of the National Council of the Churches of Christ in the United States of America. Used with permission. All rights reserved.

PRAYER FOR **THURSDAY** MARCH 20, 2014

OPENING

Today's Gospel concerns all people, rich or poor.

✛ All make the Sign of the Cross.

In the name of the Father, and of the Son, and of the Holy Spirit. Amen.

PSALM

(For a longer psalm, see page xiv.) Psalm 34:4–5, 6–7, 16–17, 18–19

The LORD saves the crushed in spirit.

The LORD saves the crushed in spirit.

I sought the LORD, and he answered me,
　　and delivered me from all my fears.
Look to him, and be radiant;
　　so your faces shall never be ashamed.

The LORD saves the crushed in spirit.

◆ All stand and sing **Praise to you, Lord Jesus Christ . . .**

GOSPEL

Luke 16:19–26

A reading from the holy Gospel according to Luke

Jesus said to the Pharisees: "There was a rich man who was dressed in purple and fine linen and who feasted sumptuously every day. And at his gate lay a poor man named Lazarus, covered with sores, who longed to satisfy his hunger with what fell from the rich man's table; even the dogs would come and lick his sores. The poor man died and was carried away by the angels to be with Abraham. The rich man also died and was buried. In Hades, where he was being tormented, he looked up and saw Abraham far away with Lazarus by his side. He called out, 'Father Abraham, have mercy on me, and send Lazarus to dip the tip of his finger in water and cool my tongue; for I am in agony in these flames.' But Abraham said, 'Child, remember that during your lifetime you received your good things, and Lazarus in like manner evil things; but now he is comforted here, and you are in agony. Besides all this, between you and us a great chasm has been fixed, so that those who might want to pass from here to you cannot do so, and no one can cross from there to us.'"

The Gospel of the Lord.

◆ All sit and observe silence.

FOR SILENT REFLECTION

What could the rich man have done while he was alive?

CLOSING PRAYER

Let us stand and bring our hopes and needs to God as we pray, "Lord, hear our prayer."

◆ All may add their own prayers here.

Let us pray: **Our Father . . . Amen.**

Lord Jesus,
guide us in our decisions
of how we should assist
those in need so that they
can live with dignity.
We ask this in your name.

Amen.

✛ All make the Sign of the Cross.

OPENING

Today's Gospel keeps us aware of our responsibility of being a Christian.

✛ All make the Sign of the Cross.

In the name of the Father, and of the Son, and of the Holy Spirit. Amen.

PSALM

(For a longer psalm, see page xiv.) Psalm 34:4–5, 6–7, 16–17, 18–19

The LORD saves the crushed in spirit.

The LORD saves the crushed in spirit.

I sought the LORD, and he answered me,
    and delivered me from all my fears.
Look to him, and be radiant;
    so your faces shall never be ashamed.

The LORD saves the crushed in spirit.

◆ All stand and sing **Praise to you, Lord Jesus Christ** . . .

GOSPEL

Matthew 21:33–42

A reading from the holy Gospel according to Matthew

Jesus said to the chief priests and the elders of the people: "Listen to another parable. There was a landowner who planted a vineyard, put a fence around it, dug a wine press in it, and built a watchtower. Then he leased it to tenants and went to another country. When the harvest time had come, he sent his slaves to the tenants to collect his produce. But the tenants seized his slaves and beat one, killed another, and stoned another. Again he sent other slaves, more than the first; and they treated them in the same way. Finally he sent his son to them, saying, 'They will respect my son.' But when the tenants saw the son, they said to themselves, 'This is the heir; come, let us kill him and get his inheritance." So they seized him, threw him out of the vineyard, and killed him. Now when the owner of the vineyard comes, what will he do to those tenants?" They said to him, "He will put those wretches to a miserable death, and lease the vineyard to other tenants who will give him the produce at the harvest time." Jesus said to them, "Have you never read in the scriptures: 'The stone that the builders rejected has become the cornerstone; this was the Lord's doing, and it is amazing in our eyes'?"

The Gospel of the Lord.

◆ All sit and observe silence.

FOR SILENT REFLECTION

How do I produce fruit for God's kingdom?

CLOSING PRAYER

Let us stand and bring our hopes and needs to God as we pray, "Lord, hear our prayer."

◆ All may add their own prayers here.

Let us pray: **Our Father . . . Amen.**

Almighty God,
help us to listen to Jesus,
who teaches us with parables of truth.
Help us to act with justice.
We ask this through Christ your Son.

Amen.

✛ All make the Sign of the Cross.

PRAYER FOR THE WEEK

OPENING

In today's Gospel, Jesus stops at a well and reveals more about his identity as the Messiah.

✛ All make the Sign of the Cross.

In the name of the Father, and of the Son, and of the Holy Spirit. Amen.

PSALM

(For a longer psalm, see page xiv.) Psalm 34:4–5, 6–7, 16–17, 18–19

The LORD saves the crushed in spirit.

The LORD saves the crushed in spirit.

I sought the LORD, and he answered me,
   and delivered me from all my fears.
Look to him, and be radiant;
   so your faces shall never be ashamed.

The LORD saves the crushed in spirit.

◆ All stand and sing **Praise to you, Lord Jesus Christ . . .**

GOSPEL

John 4:7–15, 19–26

A reading from the holy Gospel according to John

A Samaritan woman came to the well to draw water, and Jesus said to her, "Give me a drink." The Samaritan woman said to him, "How is it that you, a Jew, ask a drink of me, a woman of Samaria?" Jesus answered her, "If you knew the gift of God, and who it is that is saying to you, 'Give me a drink,' you would have asked him, and he would have given you living water." The woman said to him, "Sir, you have no bucket, and the well is deep. Where do you get that living water? Are you greater than our ancestor Jacob, who gave us the well, and with his sons and his flocks drank from it?" Jesus said to her, "Everyone who drinks of this water will be thirsty again, but those who drink of the water that I will give them will never be thirsty. The water that I will give will become in them a spring of water gushing up to eternal life." The woman said to him, "Sir, give me this water, so that I may never be thirsty or have to keep coming here to draw water. I know that Messiah is coming (who is called Christ). When he comes, he will proclaim all things to us." Jesus said to her, "I am he, the one who is speaking to you."

The Gospel of the Lord.

◆ All sit and observe silence.

FOR SILENT REFLECTION

To what kind of water is Jesus referring?

CLOSING PRAYER

Let us stand and bring our hopes and needs to God as we pray, "Lord, hear our prayer."

◆ All may add their own prayers here.

Let us pray: **Our Father . . . Amen.**

Lord Jesus,
help us to appreciate the
gift of our Baptismal waters to be
your beloved sons and daughters.
In your name we pray.

Amen.

✛ All make the Sign of the Cross.

OPENING

In today's Gospel we hear how the people in Jesus's hometown rejected him.

✝ All make the Sign of the Cross.

In the name of the Father, and of the Son, and of the Holy Spirit. Amen.

PSALM
(For a longer psalm, see page xiv.) Psalm 34:4–5, 6–7, 16–17, 18–19

The LORD saves the crushed in spirit.

The LORD saves the crushed in spirit.

I sought the LORD, and he answered me,
 and delivered me from all my fears.
Look to him, and be radiant;
 so your faces shall never be ashamed.

The LORD saves the crushed in spirit.

◆ All stand and sing **Praise to you, Lord Jesus Christ** . . .

GOSPEL
Luke 4:24–30

A reading from the holy Gospel according to Luke

Jesus said to the people in the synagogue at Nazareth: "Truly I tell you, no prophet is accepted in the prophet's hometown. But the truth is, there were many widows in Israel in the time of Elijah, when the heaven was shut up three years and six months, and there was a severe famine over all the land; yet Elijah was sent to none of them except to a widow at Zarephath in Sidon. There were also many lepers in Israel in the time of the prophet Elisha, and none of them was cleansed except Naaman the Syrian." When they heard this, all in the synagogue were filled with rage. They got up, drove him out of the town, and led him to the brow of the hill on which their town was built, so that they might hurl him off the cliff. But he passed through the midst of them and went on his way.

The Gospel of the Lord.

◆ All sit and observe silence.

FOR SILENT REFLECTION

Why do you think the people in Jesus's hometown rejected him?

CLOSING PRAYER

Let us stand and bring our hopes and needs to God as we pray, "Lord, hear our prayer."

◆ All may add their own prayers here.

Let us pray: **Our Father . . . Amen.**

Lord Jesus,
help us to respond in love
to those who reveal your truth.
We ask this in your name.

Amen.

✝ All make the Sign of the Cross.

PRAYER FOR **TUESDAY** MARCH 25, 2014

OPENING

Today is the Solemnity of the Annunciation of the Lord, when the angel Gabriel appeared to Mary to announce God's plan for her and for our salvation.

✚ All make the Sign of the Cross.

In the name of the Father, and of the Son, and of the Holy Spirit. Amen.

PSALM
(For a longer psalm, see page xiv.) Psalm 34:4–5, 6–7, 16–17, 18–19

The LORD saves the crushed in spirit.

The LORD saves the crushed in spirit.

I sought the LORD, and he answered me,
    and delivered me from all my fears.
Look to him, and be radiant;
    so your faces shall never be ashamed.

The LORD saves the crushed in spirit.

◆ All stand and sing **Praise to you, Lord Jesus Christ . . .**

GOSPEL
Luke 1:26–38

A reading from the holy Gospel according to Luke

In the sixth month the angel Gabriel was sent by God to a town in Galilee called Nazareth, to a virgin engaged to a man whose name was Joseph, of the house of David. The virgin's name was Mary. And he came to her and said, "Greetings, favored one! The Lord is with you." But she was much perplexed by his words. The angel said to her, "Do not be afraid, Mary, for you have found favor with God. And now, you will conceive in your womb and bear a son, and you will name him Jesus. He will be great, and will be called the Son of the Most High, and the Lord God will give to him the throne of his ancestor David. He will reign over the house of Jacob forever, and of his kingdom there will be no end." Mary said to the angel, "How can this be, since I am a virgin?" The angel said to her, "The Holy Spirit will come upon you, and the power of the Most High will overshadow you; therefore the child to be born will be holy; he will be called Son of God." Then Mary said, "Here am I, the servant of the Lord; let it be with me according to your word." Then the angel departed from her.

The Gospel of the Lord.

◆ All sit and observe silence.

FOR SILENT REFLECTION

Nothing is impossible with God. How do you see God's Spirit implanted in your friends and family?

CLOSING PRAYER

Let us stand and bring our hopes and needs to God as we pray, "Lord, hear our prayer."

◆ All may add their own prayers here.

Let us pray: **Our Father . . . Amen.**

Almighty God,
may we say "yes" to your Spirit.
May we be your servants so that
your Son is revealed to all.
We ask this through Christ your Son,
our Lord and Savior.

Amen.

✚ All make the Sign of the Cross.

OPENING

In today's Gospel, Jesus tells his followers about God's mission for him.

✦ All make the Sign of the Cross.

In the name of the Father, and of the Son, and of the Holy Spirit. Amen.

PSALM

(For a longer psalm, see page xiv.) Psalm 34:4–5, 6–7, 16–17, 18–19

The LORD saves the crushed in spirit.

The LORD saves the crushed in spirit.

I sought the LORD, and he answered me,
  and delivered me from all my fears.
Look to him, and be radiant;
  so your faces shall never be ashamed.

The LORD saves the crushed in spirit.

◆ All stand and sing **Praise to you, Lord Jesus Christ . . .**

GOSPEL

Matthew 5:17–19

A reading from the holy Gospel according to Matthew

Jesus said to his disciples: "Do not think that I have come to abolish the law or the prophets; I have come not to abolish but to fulfill. For truly I tell you, until heaven and earth pass away, not one letter, not one stroke of a letter, will pass from the law until all is accomplished. Therefore, whoever breaks one of the least of these commandments, and teaches others to do the same, will be called least in the kingdom of heaven; but whoever does them and teaches them will be called great in the kingdom of heaven."

The Gospel of the Lord.

◆ All sit and observe silence.

FOR SILENT REFLECTION

What do you think was one of the main purposes for God sending Jesus to us?

CLOSING PRAYER

Let us stand and bring our hopes and needs to God as we pray, "Lord, hear our prayer."

◆ All may add their own prayers here.

Let us pray: **Our Father . . . Amen.**

Lord Jesus,
you ask us to strengthen our commitment
to honor the commandments.
Help us to follow your
laws of love.
We ask this in your name.

Amen.

✦ All make the Sign of the Cross.

PRAYER FOR **THURSDAY** **MARCH 27, 2014**

OPENING

Today's reading shows Jesus answering his critics who said he cast out demons in the devil's name. He also warns those who help destroy rather than build God's kingdom.

✚ All make the Sign of the Cross.

In the name of the Father, and of the Son, and of the Holy Spirit. Amen.

PSALM

(For a longer psalm, see page xiv.) Psalm 34:4–5, 6–7, 16–17, 18–19

The LORD saves the crushed in spirit.

The LORD saves the crushed in spirit.

I sought the LORD, and he answered me,
   and delivered me from all my fears.
Look to him, and be radiant;
   so your faces shall never be ashamed.

The LORD saves the crushed in spirit.

◆ All stand and sing **Praise to you, Lord Jesus Christ . . .**

GOSPEL

Luke 11:14–23

A reading from the holy Gospel according to Luke

Jesus was casting out a demon that was mute; when the demon had gone out, the one who had been mute spoke, and the crowds were amazed. But some of them said, "He casts out demons by Beelzebul, the ruler of the demons." Others, to test him, kept demanding from him a sign from heaven. But he knew what they were thinking and said to them, "Every kingdom divided against itself becomes a desert, and house falls on house. If Satan also is divided against himself, how will his kingdom stand? —for you say that I cast out the demons by Beelzebul. Now if I cast out the demons by Beelzebul, by whom do your exorcists cast them out? Therefore they will be your judges. But if it is by the finger of God that I cast out the demons, then the kingdom of God has come to you. When a strong man, fully armed, guards his castle, his property is safe. But when one stronger than he attacks him and over-powers him, he takes away his armor in which he trusted and divides his plunder. Whoever is not with me is against me, and whoever does not gather with me scatters."

The Gospel of the Lord.

◆ All sit and observe silence.

FOR SILENT REFLECTION

Do I sometimes criticize people or things when I don't understand them? Why?

CLOSING PRAYER

Let us stand and bring our hopes and needs to God as we pray, "Lord, hear our prayer."

◆ All may add their own prayers here.

Let us pray: **Our Father . . . Amen.**

Lord Jesus,
your critics did not realize how destructive their words or actions could be.
Help us to build up your kingdom through our words and actions of love.
We ask this in your name.

Amen.

✚ All make the Sign of the Cross.

OPENING

Today's Gospel relays the essence of the commandments.

✦ All make the Sign of the Cross.

In the name of the Father, and of the Son, and of the Holy Spirit. Amen.

PSALM

(For a longer psalm, see page xiv.) Psalm 34:4–5, 6–7, 16–17, 18–19

The LORD saves the crushed in spirit.

The LORD saves the crushed in spirit.

I sought the LORD, and he answered me,
   and delivered me from all my fears.
Look to him, and be radiant;
   so your faces shall never be ashamed.

The LORD saves the crushed in spirit.

◆ All stand and sing **Praise to you, Lord Jesus Christ . . .**

GOSPEL

Mark 12:28–34

A reading from the holy Gospel according to Mark

One of the scribes came near and heard them disputing with one another, and seeing that he answered them well, he asked him, "Which commandment is the first of all?" Jesus answered, "The first is, 'Hear, O Israel: the Lord our God, the Lord is one; you shall love the Lord your God with all your heart, and with all your soul, and with all your mind, and with all your strength.' The second is this, 'You shall love your neighbor as yourself.' There is no other commandment greater than these."

Then the scribe said to him, "You are right, Teacher; you have truly said that 'he is one, and besides him there is no other'; and 'to love him with all the heart, and with all the understanding, and with all the strength,' and 'to love one's neighbor as oneself,' —this is much more important than all whole burnt offerings and sacrifices." When Jesus saw that he answered wisely, he said to him, "You are not far from the kingdom of God." After that no one dared to ask him any question.

The Gospel of the Lord.

◆ All sit and observe silence.

FOR SILENT REFLECTION

How do you grow in your relationship with God?

CLOSING PRAYER

Let us stand and bring our hopes and needs to God as we pray, "Lord, hear our prayer."

◆ All may add their own prayers here.

Let us pray: **Our Father . . . Amen.**

Lord Jesus,
you guide us with your wisdom,
which is the essence of
living with goodness and truth.
May we follow you every day
and everywhere.
In your name we pray.

Amen.

✦ All make the Sign of the Cross.

PRAYER FOR THE WEEK

OPENING

In today's Gospel story we learn what it means to change from misunderstanding to awareness.

✛ All make the Sign of the Cross.

In the name of the Father, and of the Son, and of the Holy Spirit. Amen.

PSALM

(For a longer psalm, see page xiv.) Psalm 34:4–5, 6–7, 16–17, 18–19

The LORD saves the crushed in spirit.

The LORD saves the crushed in spirit.

I sought the LORD, and he answered me,
   and delivered me from all my fears.
Look to him, and be radiant;
   so your faces shall never be ashamed.

The LORD saves the crushed in spirit.

◆ All stand and sing **Praise to you, Lord Jesus Christ . . .**

GOSPEL

John 9:1, 6–9, 13–17

A reading from the holy Gospel according to John

As Jesus walked along, he saw a man blind from birth. He spat on the ground and made mud with the saliva and spread the mud on the man's eyes, saying to him, "Go, wash in the pool of Siloam." Then he went and washed and came back able to see.

The neighbors and those who had seen him before as a beggar began to ask, "Is this not the man who used to sit and beg?" Some were saying, "It is he." Others were saying, "No, but it is someone like him." He kept saying, "I am the man."

They brought to the Pharisees the man who had formerly been blind. Now it was a sabbath day when Jesus made the mud and opened his eyes. Then the Pharisees also began to ask him how he had received his sight. He said to them, "He put mud on my eyes. Then I washed, and now I see." Some of the Pharisees said, "This man is not from God, for he does not observe the sabbath." But others said, "How can a man who is a sinner perform such signs?" And they were divided. So they said again to the blind man, "What do you say about him? It was your eyes he opened." He said, "He is a prophet."

The Gospel of the Lord.

◆ All sit and observe silence.

FOR SILENT REFLECTION

How does my "blindness" keep me from loving others?

CLOSING PRAYER

Let us stand and bring our hopes and needs to God as we pray, "Lord, hear our prayer."

◆ All may add their own prayers here.

Let us pray: **Our Father . . . Amen.**

Lord Jesus,
you increase our awareness
and cure our "blindness."
Help us to see clearly.
We ask this in your name.

Amen.

✛ All make the Sign of the Cross.

OPENING

Today's Gospel shows the faith of a royal official who knew Jesus would save his dying son even though Jesus wasn't even near the boy.

✚ All make the Sign of the Cross.

In the name of the Father, and of the Son, and of the Holy Spirit. Amen.

PSALM

(For a longer psalm, see page xiv.) Psalm 34:4–5, 6–7, 16–17, 18–19

The LORD saves the crushed in spirit.

The LORD saves the crushed in spirit.

I sought the LORD, and he answered me,
    and delivered me from all my fears.
Look to him, and be radiant;
    so your faces shall never be ashamed.

The LORD saves the crushed in spirit.

◆ All stand and sing **Praise to you, Lord Jesus Christ . . .**

GOSPEL

John 4:46–54

A reading from the holy Gospel according to John

Jesus came again to Cana in Galilee where he had changed the water into wine. Now there was a royal official whose son lay ill in Capernaum [kuh-PERR-nee-um]. When he heard that Jesus had come from Judea to Galilee, he went and begged him to come down and heal his son, for he was at the point of death. Then Jesus said to him, "Unless you see signs and wonders you will not believe." The official said to him, "Sir, come down before my little boy dies." Jesus said to him, "Go; your son will live." The man believed the word that Jesus spoke to him and started on his way. As he was going down, his slaves met him and told him that his child was alive. So he asked them the hour when he began to recover, and they said to him, "Yesterday at one in the afternoon the fever left him." The father realized that this was the hour when Jesus had said to him, "Your son will live." So he himself believed, along with his whole household. Now this was the second sign that Jesus did after coming from Judea to Galilee.

The Gospel of the Lord.

◆ All sit and observe silence.

FOR SILENT REFLECTION

What signs of God's Spirit do I see in the world?

CLOSING PRAYER

Let us stand and bring our hopes and needs to God as we pray, "Lord, hear our prayer."

◆ All may add their own prayers here.

Let us pray: **Our Father . . . Amen.**

Almighty God,
you see signs of faith
among your people.
Guide us as we strive
to do your will and to
keep your words of life
in our thoughts.
We ask this through Jesus Christ
your Son, our Lord.

Amen.

✚ All make the Sign of the Cross.

PRAYER FOR **TUESDAY** APRIL 1, 2014

OPENING

Today's Gospel shows more of the pettiness of the officials because Jesus healed people on the Sabbath.

✦ All make the Sign of the Cross.

In the name of the Father, and of the Son, and of the Holy Spirit. Amen.

PSALM

(For a longer psalm, see page xiv.) Psalm 34:4–5, 6–7, 16–17, 18–19

The LORD saves the crushed in spirit.

The LORD saves the crushed in spirit.

I sought the LORD, and he answered me,
and delivered me from all my fears.
Look to him, and be radiant;
so your faces shall never be ashamed.

The LORD saves the crushed in spirit.

◆ All stand and sing **Praise to you, Lord Jesus Christ . . .**

GOSPEL

John 5:2–3, 5–16

A reading from the holy Gospel according to John

Now in Jerusalem by the Sheep Gate there is a pool, called in Hebrew Beth-zatha, which has five porticoes. In these lay many invalids—blind, lame, and paralyzed. One man was there who had been ill for thirty-eight years. When Jesus saw him lying there and knew that he had been there a long time, he said to him, "Do you want to be made well?" The sick man answered him, "Sir, I have no one to put me into the pool when the water is stirred up; and while I am making my way, someone else steps down ahead of me." Jesus said to him, "Stand up, take your mat and walk." At once the man was made well, and he took up his mat and began to walk. Now that day was a sabbath. So the Jews said to the man who had been cured, "It is the sabbath; it is not lawful for you to carry your mat." But he answered them, "The man who made me well said to me, 'Take up your mat and walk.'" Later Jesus found him in the temple and said to him, "See, you have been made well! Do not sin any more, so that nothing worse happens to you." The man went away and told the Jews that it was Jesus who had made him well. Therefore the Jews started persecuting Jesus, because he was doing such things on the sabbath.

The Gospel of the Lord.

◆ All sit and observe silence.

FOR SILENT REFLECTION

What is the intent of the Sabbath?

CLOSING PRAYER

Let us stand and bring our hopes and needs to God as we pray, "Lord, hear our prayer."

◆ All may add their own prayers here.

Let us pray: **Our Father . . . Amen.**

Lord Jesus,
you are the source of our strength.
Help us to be more present
to you and others.
We ask this in your name.

Amen.

✦ All make the Sign of the Cross.

OPENING

Today we remember St. Francis of Paola from the 15th century, who founded an order of brothers devoted to a life of humility, poverty, and chastity.

✚ All make the Sign of the Cross.

In the name of the Father, and of the Son, and of the Holy Spirit. Amen.

PSALM

(For a longer psalm, see page xiv.) Psalm 34:4–5, 6–7, 16–17, 18–19

The LORD saves the crushed in spirit.

The LORD saves the crushed in spirit.

I sought the LORD, and he answered me,
  and delivered me from all my fears.
Look to him, and be radiant;
  so your faces shall never be ashamed.

The LORD saves the crushed in spirit.

◆ All stand and sing **Praise to you, Lord Jesus Christ . . .**

GOSPEL

John 5:19–24

A reading from the holy Gospel according to John

Jesus said to them, "Very truly, I tell you, the Son can do nothing on his own, but only what he sees the Father doing; for whatever the Father does, the Son does likewise. The Father loves the Son and shows him all that he himself is doing; and he will show him greater works than these, so that you will be astonished. Indeed, just as the Father raises the dead and gives them life, so also the Son gives life to whomever he wishes. The Father judges no one but has given all judgment to the Son, so that all may honor the Son just as they honor the Father. Anyone who does not honor the Son does not honor the Father who sent him. Very truly, I tell you, anyone who hears my word and believes him who sent me has eternal life, and does not come under judgment, but has passed from death to life."

The Gospel of the Lord.

◆ All sit and observe silence.

FOR SILENT REFLECTION

What do we learn about God the Father from Jesus's life?

CLOSING PRAYER

Let us stand and bring our hopes and needs to God as we pray, "Lord, hear our prayer."

◆ All may add their own prayers here.

Let us pray: **Our Father . . . Amen.**

God Almighty,
you sent Jesus to us to
reveal more about your
loving presence
and to show us how to live.
May we learn to honor you
by following his example.
We ask this through Christ our Lord
and Savior.

Amen.

✚ All make the Sign of the Cross.

PRAYER FOR **THURSDAY** APRIL 3, 2014

OPENING

In today's Gospel, Jesus speaks the truth to those present about their disbelief in him as God's Son, even though they had witnessed miracles and heard John the Baptist's testimony.

✦ All make the Sign of the Cross.

In the name of the Father, and of the Son, and of the Holy Spirit. Amen.

PSALM
(For a longer psalm, see page xiv.) Psalm 34:4–5, 6–7, 16–17, 18–19

The LORD saves the crushed in spirit.

The LORD saves the crushed in spirit.

I sought the LORD, and he answered me,
    and delivered me from all my fears.
Look to him, and be radiant;
    so your faces shall never be ashamed.

The LORD saves the crushed in spirit.

◆ All stand and sing **Praise to you, Lord Jesus Christ . . .**

GOSPEL
John 5:31–36, 43–47

A reading from the holy Gospel according to John

Jesus said to the Jews: "If I testify about myself, my testimony is not true. There is another who testifies on my behalf, and I know that his testimony to me is true. You sent messengers to John, and he testified to the truth. Not that I accept such human testimony, but I say these things so that you may be saved. He was a burning and shining lamp, and you were willing to rejoice for a while in his light. But I have a testimony greater than John's. I have come in my Father's name, and you do not accept me; if another comes in his own name, you will accept him. How can you believe when you accept glory from one another and do not seek the glory that comes from the one who alone is God? Do not think that I will accuse you before the Father; your accuser is Moses, on whom you have set your hope. If you believed Moses, you would believe me, for he wrote about me. But if you do not believe what he wrote, how will you believe what I say?"

The Gospel of the Lord.

◆ All sit and observe silence.

FOR SILENT REFLECTION

How do I determine what's true or false? What factors help me make this decision?

CLOSING PRAYER

Let us stand and bring our hopes and needs to God as we pray, "Lord, hear our prayer."

◆ All may add their own prayers here.

Let us pray: **Our Father . . . Amen.**

Jesus our light,
help us to recognize your
presence in others
as your Spirit works
through all who follow you.
We ask this in your name.

Amen.

✦ All make the Sign of the Cross.

248

OPENING

Today we remember St. Isadore of Seville, who lived in the 6th century, and is considered the patron saint of the Internet. He was called the "Schoolmaster of the Middle Ages" because he wrote an encyclopedia, dictionary, and histories of the world.

✚ All make the Sign of the Cross.

In the name of the Father, and of the Son, and of the Holy Spirit. Amen.

PSALM   (For a longer psalm, see page xiv.) Psalm 34:4–5, 6–7, 16–17, 18–19

The LORD saves the crushed in spirit.

The LORD saves the crushed in spirit.

I sought the LORD, and he answered me,
    and delivered me from all my fears.
Look to him, and be radiant;
    so your faces shall never be ashamed.

The LORD saves the crushed in spirit.

◆ All stand and sing **Praise to you, Lord Jesus Christ . . .**

GOSPEL   John 7:1–2, 10, 25–30

A reading from the holy Gospel according to John

Jesus went about in Galilee. He did not wish to go about in Judea because the Jews were looking for an opportunity to kill him. Now the Jewish festival of Booths was near. But after his brothers had gone to the festival, then he also went, not publicly but as it were in secret. Now some of the people of Jerusalem were saying, "Is not this the man whom they are trying to kill? And here he is, speaking openly, but they say nothing to him! Can it be that the authorities really know that this is the Messiah? Yet we know where this man is from; but when the Messiah comes, no one will know where he is from." Then Jesus cried out as he was teaching in the temple, "You know me, and you know where I am from. I have not come on my own. But the one who sent me is true, and you do not know him. I know him, because I am from him, and he sent me." Then they tried to arrest him, but no one laid hands on him, because his hour had not yet come.

The Gospel of the Lord.

◆ All sit and observe silence.

FOR SILENT REFLECTION

If I lived at the time of Jesus, would it be difficult for me to believe that Jesus was the Messiah?

CLOSING PRAYER

Let us stand and bring our hopes and needs to God as we pray, "Lord, hear our prayer."

◆ All may add their own prayers here.

Let us pray: **Our Father . . . Amen.**

Lord Jesus,
help us to see clearly
your message from the Father
for us today
so that we might truly live.
We ask this in your name.

Amen.

✚ All make the Sign of the Cross.

PRAYER FOR THE WEEK

OPENING

Today's Gospel is a foreshadowing of Jesus's Resurrection.

✦ All make the Sign of the Cross.

In the name of the Father, and of the Son, and of the Holy Spirit. Amen.

PSALM

(For a longer psalm, see page xiv.) Psalm 34:4–5, 6–7, 16–17, 18–19

The LORD saves the crushed in spirit.

The LORD saves the crushed in spirit.

I sought the LORD, and he answered me,
 and delivered me from all my fears.
Look to him, and be radiant;
 so your faces shall never be ashamed.

The LORD saves the crushed in spirit.

◆ All stand and sing **Praise to you, Lord Jesus Christ . . .**

GOSPEL

John 11:20–21, 23–36, 38, 41–44

A reading from the holy Gospel according to John

When Martha heard that Jesus was coming, she went and met him, while Mary stayed at home. Martha said to Jesus, "Lord, if you had been here, my brother would not have died.

When Jesus saw her weeping, and the Jews who came with her also weeping, he was greatly disturbed in spirit and deeply moved. He said, "Where have you laid him?" They said to him, "Lord, come and see." Jesus began to weep. So the Jews said, "See how he loved him!" Then Jesus, again greatly disturbed, came to the tomb. It was a cave, and a stone was lying against it. Jesus said, "Take away the stone." So they took away the stone. And Jesus looked upward and said, "Father, I thank you for having heard me. I know that you always hear me, but I have said this for the sake of the crowd standing here, so that they may believe that you sent me." When he had said this, he cried with a loud voice, "Lazarus, come out!" The dead man came out, his hands and feet bound with strips of cloth, and his face wrapped in a cloth. Jesus said to them, "Unbind him, and let him go."

The Gospel of the Lord.

◆ All sit and observe silence.

FOR SILENT REFLECTION

What does it tell us about Jesus to know that he too wept?

CLOSING PRAYER

Let us stand and bring our hopes and needs to God as we pray, "Lord, hear our prayer."

◆ All may add their own prayers here.

Let us pray: **Our Father . . . Amen.**

Jesus our redeemer,
in your compassion
you raised Lazarus from the dead.
Help all who grieve the
loss of someone they love.
In your name we pray.

Amen.

✦ All make the Sign of the Cross.

OPENING

Today we remember St. John Baptist de la Salle, who was born in 1651 in France, known for his refined upbringing, good looks, nobility, and sharp mind. He was ordained at 27, and began establishing schools to help deprived youth. He gave away his fortune and devoted himself to helping the poor.

✚ All make the Sign of the Cross.

In the name of the Father, and of the Son, and of the Holy Spirit. Amen.

PSALM

(For a longer psalm, see page xiv.) Psalm 34:4–5, 6–7, 16–17, 18–19

The LORD saves the crushed in spirit.

The LORD saves the crushed in spirit.

I sought the LORD, and he answered me,
   and delivered me from all my fears.
Look to him, and be radiant;
   so your faces shall never be ashamed.

The LORD saves the crushed in spirit.

◆ All stand and sing **Praise to you, Lord Jesus Christ** . . .

GOSPEL

John 8:3–11

A reading from the holy Gospel according to John

The scribes and the Pharisees brought a woman who had been caught in adultery; and making her stand before all of them, they said to him, "Teacher, this woman was caught in the very act of committing adultery. Now in the law Moses commanded us to stone such women.

Now what do you say?" Jesus bent down and wrote with his finger on the ground. When they kept on questioning him, he straightened up and said to them, "Let anyone among you who is without sin be the first to throw a stone at her." And once again he bent down and wrote on the ground. When they heard it, they went away, one by one, beginning with the elders; and Jesus was left alone with the woman standing before him. Jesus straightened up and said to her, "Woman, where are they? Has no one condemned you?" She said, "No one, sir." And Jesus said, "Neither do I condemn you. Go your way, and from now on do not sin again."

The Gospel of the Lord.

◆ All sit and observe silence.

FOR SILENT REFLECTION

What does Jesus's example teach us?

CLOSING PRAYER

Let us stand and bring our hopes and needs to God as we pray, "Lord, hear our prayer."

◆ All may add their own prayers here.

Let us pray: **Our Father . . . Amen.**

Jesus our redeemer,
you continually give us
opportunities to improve our ways.
Guide us as we work and study
as your sons and daughters.
In your name we pray.

Amen.

✚ All make the Sign of the Cross.

PRAYER FOR **TUESDAY**
APRIL 8, 2014

OPENING

In today's Gospel, Jesus seeks to explain his divine identity.

✝ All make the Sign of the Cross.

In the name of the Father, and of the Son, and of the Holy Spirit. Amen.

PSALM

(For a longer psalm, see page xiv.) Psalm 34:4–5, 6–7, 16–17, 18–19

The LORD saves the crushed in spirit.

The LORD saves the crushed in spirit.

I sought the LORD, and he answered me,
 and delivered me from all my fears.
Look to him, and be radiant;
 so your faces shall never be ashamed.

The LORD saves the crushed in spirit.

◆ All stand and sing **Praise to you, Lord Jesus Christ . . .**

GOSPEL

John 8:21–27

A reading from the holy Gospel according to John

Jesus said to the Pharisees: "I am going away, and you will search for me, but you will die in your sin. Where I am going, you cannot come." Then the Jews said, "Is he going to kill himself? Is that what he means by saying, 'Where I am going, you cannot come'?" He said to them, "You are from below, I am from above; you are of this world, I am not of this world. I told you that you would die in your sins, for you will die in your sins unless you believe that I am he." They said to him, "Who are you?"

Jesus said to them, "Why do I speak to you at all? I have much to say about you and much to condemn; but the one who sent me is true, and I declare to the world what I have heard from him." They did not understand that he was speaking to them about the Father.

The Gospel of the Lord.

◆ All sit and observe silence.

FOR SILENT REFLECTION

Who is Jesus for you?

CLOSING PRAYER

Let us stand and bring our hopes and needs to God as we pray, "Lord, hear our prayer."

◆ All may add their own prayers here.

Let us pray: **Our Father . . . Amen.**

Creator of our world,
may we continue to
reach for you and to
listen to your
urgings in prayer.
Guide us as we
learn more about you
through your Son Jesus
and your Spirit.
We ask this through Christ, your Son
and our Lord and Savior.

Amen.

✝ All make the Sign of the Cross.

OPENING

Today's Gospel concerns freedom and truth and our everyday choices to turn toward or away from sin.

✚ All make the Sign of the Cross.

In the name of the Father, and of the Son, and of the Holy Spirit. Amen.

PSALM
(For a longer psalm, see page xiv.) Psalm 34:4–5, 6–7, 16–17, 18–19

The LORD saves the crushed in spirit.

The LORD saves the crushed in spirit.

I sought the LORD, and he answered me,
    and delivered me from all my fears.
Look to him, and be radiant;
    so your faces shall never be ashamed.

The LORD saves the crushed in spirit.

◆ All stand and sing **Praise to you, Lord Jesus Christ** . . .

GOSPEL
John 8:31–36, 38

A reading from the holy Gospel according to John

Jesus said to the Jews who had believed in him, "If you continue in my word, you are truly my disciples; and you will know the truth, and the truth will make you free." They answered him, "We are descendants of Abraham and have never been slaves to anyone. What do you mean by saying, 'You will be made free'?" Jesus answered them, "Very truly, I tell you, everyone who commits sin is a slave to sin. The slave does not have a permanent place in the household; the son has a place there forever. So if the Son makes you free, you will be free indeed. I declare what I have seen in the Father's presence; as for you, you should do what you have heard from the Father."

The Gospel of the Lord.

◆ All sit and observe silence.

FOR SILENT REFLECTION

What does it mean that "the truth will make you free"?

CLOSING PRAYER

Let us stand and bring our hopes and needs to God as we pray, "Lord, hear our prayer."

◆ All may add their own prayers here.

Let us pray: **Our Father . . . Amen.**

Lord Jesus,
you remind us that we are
God's beloved children/, just as you
were the Beloved Son of God.
We know that your truth
will make us free.
We pray this in your name.

Amen.

✚ All make the Sign of the Cross.

PRAYER FOR **THURSDAY** APRIL 10, 2014

OPENING

Today's Gospel is a continuation of Jesus trying to explain to crowds more about his identity as God's Son.

✚ All make the Sign of the Cross.

In the name of the Father, and of the Son, and of the Holy Spirit. Amen.

PSALM

(For a longer psalm, see page xiv.) Psalm 34:4–5, 6–7, 16–17, 18–19

The LORD saves the crushed in spirit.

The LORD saves the crushed in spirit.

I sought the LORD, and he answered me,
　and delivered me from all my fears.
Look to him, and be radiant;
　so your faces shall never be ashamed.

The LORD saves the crushed in spirit.

◆ All stand and sing **Praise to you, Lord Jesus Christ . . .**

GOSPEL

John 8:51–55

A reading from the holy Gospel according to John

Jesus said to the Jews: "Very truly, I tell you, whoever keeps my word will never see death." The Jews said to him, "Now we know that you have a demon. Abraham died, and so did the prophets; yet you say, 'Whoever keeps my word will never taste death.' Are you greater than our father Abraham, who died? The prophets also died. Who do you claim to be?" Jesus answered, "If I glorify myself, my glory is nothing. It is my Father who glorifies me, he of whom you say, 'He is our God,' though you do not know him. But I know him; if I would say that I do not know him, I would be a liar like you. But I do know him and I keep his word."

The Gospel of the Lord.

◆ All sit and observe silence.

FOR SILENT REFLECTION

Who do you say that Jesus is? What words would you use to describe him to your friends?

CLOSING PRAYER

Let us stand and bring our hopes and needs to God as we pray, "Lord, hear our prayer."

◆ All may add their own prayers here.

Let us pray: **Our Father . . . Amen.**

Jesus our hope,
many people of your time
did not understand the
power behind your wisdom.
May we honor your Word
and believe in you.
We ask this in your name.

Amen.

✚ All make the Sign of the Cross.

254

OPENING

Today we remember St. Stanislaus [STAN-is-lahs], the bishop of Krakow, Poland, in 1072. He was known for speaking out about the unjust wars and immoral acts of King Boleslaus II.

✚ All make the Sign of the Cross.

In the name of the Father, and of the Son, and of the Holy Spirit. Amen.

PSALM
(For a longer psalm, see page xiv.) Psalm 34:4–5, 6–7, 16–17, 18–19

The LORD saves the crushed in spirit.

The LORD saves the crushed in spirit.

I sought the LORD, and he answered me,
  and delivered me from all my fears.
Look to him, and be radiant;
  so your faces shall never be ashamed.

The LORD saves the crushed in spirit.

◆ All stand and sing **Praise to you, Lord Jesus Christ** . . .

GOSPEL
John 10:31–38

A reading from the holy Gospel according to John

The Jews took up stones again to stone him. Jesus replied, "I have shown you many good works from the Father. For which of these are you going to stone me?" The Jews answered, "It is not for a good work that we are going to stone you, but for blasphemy, because you, though only a human being, are making yourself God." Jesus answered, "Is it not written in your law, 'I said, you are gods'? If those to whom the word of God came were called 'gods'—and the scripture cannot be annulled—can you say that the one whom the Father has sanctified and sent into the world is blaspheming because I said, 'I am God's Son'? If I am not doing the works of my Father, then do not believe me. But if I do them, even though you do not believe me, believe the works, so that you may know and understand that the Father is in me and I am in the Father."

The Gospel of the Lord.

◆ All sit and observe silence.

FOR SILENT REFLECTION

For what reasons were the Jews trying to arrest Jesus? Had he done anything wrong?

CLOSING PRAYER

Let us stand and bring our hopes and needs to God as we pray, "Lord, hear our prayer."

◆ All may add their own prayers here.

Let us pray: **Our Father . . . Amen.**

Lord Jesus,
we believe you are the
source of all that is holy.
May we strengthen our bond
with you in prayer.
May we see your movement
of the Spirit in others
every day, everywhere.
We ask this in your name.

Amen.

✚ All make the Sign of the Cross.

PRAYER FOR THE WEEK

OPENING

Today's Gospel tells of Jesus's trial before Pilate.

✝ All make the Sign of the Cross.

In the name of the Father, and of the Son, and of the Holy Spirit. Amen.

PSALM

(For a longer psalm, see page xiv.) Psalm 34:4–5, 6–7, 16–17, 18–19

The LORD saves the crushed in spirit.

The LORD saves the crushed in spirit.

I sought the LORD, and he answered me,
   and delivered me from all my fears.
Look to him, and be radiant;
   so your faces shall never be ashamed.

The LORD saves the crushed in spirit.

◆ All stand and sing **Praise to you, Lord Jesus Christ . . .**

GOSPEL

Matthew 27:15–18, 20–24

A reading from the holy Gospel according to Matthew

Now at the festival the governor was accustomed to release a prisoner for the crowd, anyone whom they wanted. At that time they had a notorious prisoner, called Jesus Barabbas. So after they had gathered, Pilate said to them, "Whom do you want me to release for you, Jesus Barabbas or Jesus who is called the Messiah?" For he realized that it was out of jealousy that they had handed him over. Now the chief priests and the elders persuaded the crowds to ask for Barabbas and to have Jesus killed. The governor again said to them, "Which of the two do you want me to release for you?" And they said, "Barabbas." Pilate said to them, "Then what should I do with Jesus who is called the Messiah?" All of them said, "Let him be crucified!" Then he asked, "Why, what evil has he done?" But they shouted all the more, "Let him be crucified!" So when Pilate saw that he could do nothing, but rather that a riot was beginning, he took some water and washed his hands before the crowd, saying, "I am innocent of this man's blood; see to it yourselves."

The Gospel of the Lord.

◆ All sit and observe silence.

FOR SILENT REFLECTION

Why do you think Pilate said he was innocent of Jesus's Death?

CLOSING PRAYER

Let us stand and bring our hopes and needs to God as we pray, "Lord, hear our prayer."

◆ All may add their own prayers here.

Let us pray: **Our Father . . . Amen.**

Holy God,
although he was innocent,
Jesus died that we might live.
During this Holy Week
help us to remember his great love.
We ask this through Christ our Lord.

Amen.

✝ All make the Sign of the Cross.

OPENING

Today's Gospel shows how Jesus was cared for in the home of Mary and Martha.

✚ All make the Sign of the Cross.

In the name of the Father, and of the Son, and of the Holy Spirit. Amen.

PSALM

(For a longer psalm, see page xiv.) Psalm 34:4–5, 6–7, 16–17, 18–19

The LORD saves the crushed in spirit.

The LORD saves the crushed in spirit.

I sought the LORD, and he answered me,
   and delivered me from all my fears.
Look to him, and be radiant;
   so your faces shall never be ashamed.

The LORD saves the crushed in spirit.

◆ All stand and sing **Praise to you, Lord Jesus Christ . . .**

GOSPEL

John 12:1–9

A reading from the holy Gospel according to John

Six days before the Passover Jesus came to Bethany, the home of Lazarus, whom he had raised from the dead. There they gave a dinner for him. Martha served, and Lazarus was one of those at the table with him. Mary took a pound of costly perfume made of pure nard, anointed Jesus' feet, and wiped them with her hair. The house was filled with the fragrance of the perfume. But Judas Iscariot, one of his disciples (the one who was about to betray him), said, "Why was this perfume not sold for three hundred denarii and the money given to the poor?" (He said this not because he cared about the poor, but because he was a thief; he kept the common purse and used to steal what was put into it.) Jesus said, "Leave her alone. She bought it so that she might keep it for the day of my burial. You always have the poor with you, but you do not always have me." When the great crowd of the Jews learned that he was there, they came not only because of Jesus but also to see Lazarus, whom he had raised from the dead.

The Gospel of the Lord.

◆ All sit and observe silence.

FOR SILENT REFLECTION

What does Jesus's response tell us about him?

CLOSING PRAYER

Let us stand and bring our hopes and needs to God as we pray, "Lord, hear our prayer."

◆ All may add their own prayers here.

Let us pray: **Our Father . . . Amen.**

Lord Jesus,
Mary offered her thanks and praise
through her kindness.
May we show others
the same love
through our acts of service and care.
We ask this in your name.

Amen.

✚ All make the Sign of the Cross.

PRAYER FOR **TUESDAY**
APRIL 15, 2014

OPENING

Today's Gospel tells how one of Jesus's friends would betray him.

✤ All make the Sign of the Cross.

In the name of the Father, and of the Son, and of the Holy Spirit. Amen.

PSALM

(For a longer psalm, see page xiv.) Psalm 34:4–5, 6–7, 16–17, 18–19

The LORD saves the crushed in spirit.

The LORD saves the crushed in spirit.

I sought the LORD, and he answered me,
   and delivered me from all my fears.
Look to him, and be radiant;
   so your faces shall never be ashamed.

The LORD saves the crushed in spirit.

◆ All stand and sing **Praise to you, Lord Jesus Christ . . .**

GOSPEL

John 13:21–30

A reading from the holy Gospel according to John

Jesus was troubled in spirit, and declared, "Very truly, I tell you, one of you will betray me." The disciples looked at one another, uncertain of whom he was speaking. One of his disciples—the one whom Jesus loved—was reclining next to him; Simon Peter therefore motioned to him to ask Jesus of whom he was speaking. So while reclining next to Jesus, he asked him, "Lord, who is it?" Jesus answered, "It is the one to whom I give this piece of bread when I have dipped it in the dish." So when he had dipped the piece of bread, he gave it to Judas son of Simon Iscariot. After he received the piece of bread, Satan entered into him. Jesus said to him, "Do quickly what you are going to do." Now no one at the table knew why he said this to him. Some thought that, because Judas had the common purse, Jesus was telling him, "Buy what we need for the festival"; or, that he should give something to the poor. So, after receiving the piece of bread, he immediately went out. And it was night.

The Gospel of the Lord.

◆ All sit and observe silence.

FOR SILENT REFLECTION

Why do you think Judas would betray Jesus?

CLOSING PRAYER

Let us stand and bring our hopes and needs to God as we pray, "Lord, hear our prayer."

◆ All may add their own prayers here.

Let us pray: **Our Father . . . Amen.**

Lord Jesus,
keep us close to you
and give us courage
to do what is right.
We ask this in your name.

Amen.

✤ All make the Sign of the Cross.

ALSO ON THIS DAY: Jewish Passover begins at sunset

OPENING

Today's reading from Isaiah gives us hope that whatever comes from evil will never ultimately succeed.

✚ All make the Sign of the Cross.

In the name of the Father, and of the Son, and of the Holy Spirit. Amen.

PSALM

(For a longer psalm, see page xiv.) Psalm 34:4–5, 6–7, 16–17, 18–19

The LORD saves the crushed in spirit.

The LORD saves the crushed in spirit.

I sought the LORD, and he answered me,
   and delivered me from all my fears.
Look to him, and be radiant;
   so your faces shall never be ashamed.

The LORD saves the crushed in spirit.

READING

Isaiah 50:4–9a

A reading from the Book of the Prophet Isaiah

The Lord God has given me the tongue of a teacher, that I may know how to sustain the weary with a word. Morning by morning he wakens my ear to listen as those who are taught. The Lord God has opened my ear, and I was not rebellious, I did not turn backward. I gave my back to those who struck me, and my cheeks to those who pulled out the beard; I did not hide my face from insult and spitting. The Lord God helps me; therefore I have not been disgraced; therefore I have set my face like flint, and I know that I shall not be put to shame; he who vindicates me is near. Who will contend with me? Let us stand up together. Who are my adversaries? Let them confront me. It is the Lord God who helps me; who will declare me guilty? All of them will wear out like a garment; the moth will eat them up.

The Word of the Lord.

◆ All observe silence.

FOR SILENT REFLECTION

How should we react to those who try to do us harm? What does the prophet Isaiah suggest?

CLOSING PRAYER

Let us stand and bring our hopes and needs to God as we pray, "Lord, hear our prayer."

◆ All may add their own prayers here.

Let us pray: **Our Father . . . Amen.**

God our hope,
you shower us with grace
when we are insulted
or harmed.
We have nothing to fear.
Help us to pray for those
who seek vengeance
or who don't know about
your Son Jesus.
We ask this through Christ our Lord.

Amen.

✚ All make the Sign of the Cross.

PRAYER FOR **THURSDAY**
APRIL 17, 2014

OPENING

Today's reading shows Jesus proclaiming a key reading from the prophet Isaiah. Listen to how he ends his reading of the scroll.

✚ All make the Sign of the Cross.

In the name of the Father, and of the Son, and of the Holy Spirit. Amen.

PSALM
(For a longer psalm, see page xiv.) Psalm 34:4–5, 6–7, 16–17, 18–19

The LORD saves the crushed in spirit.

The LORD saves the crushed in spirit.

I sought the LORD, and he answered me,
    and delivered me from all my fears.
Look to him, and be radiant;
    so your faces shall never be ashamed.

The LORD saves the crushed in spirit.

◆ All stand and sing **Praise to you, Lord Jesus Christ . . .**

GOSPEL
Luke 4:16–21

A reading from the holy Gospel according to Luke

Jesus came to Nazareth, where he had been brought up, he went to the synagogue on the sabbath day, as was his custom. He stood up to read, and the scroll of the prophet Isaiah was given to him. He unrolled the scroll and found the place where it was written: "The Spirit of the Lord is upon me, because he has anointed me to bring good news to the poor. He has sent me to proclaim release to the captives and recovery of sight to the blind, to let the oppressed go free, to proclaim the year of the Lord's favor." And he rolled up the scroll, gave it back to the attendant, and sat down. The eyes of all in the synagogue were fixed on him. Then he began to say to them, "Today this scripture has been fulfilled in your hearing."

The Gospel of the Lord

◆ All sit and observe silence.

FOR SILENT REFLECTION

"Today this scripture has been fulfilled in your hearing." What do you imagine was the reaction in the synagogue to Jesus's statement? Why?

CLOSING PRAYER

Let us stand and bring our hopes and needs to God as we pray, "Lord, hear our prayer."

◆ All may add their own prayers here.

Let us pray: **Our Father . . . Amen.**

Lord Jesus,
you astounded everyone there
with your proclamation of
your true identity.
May we reveal your plan
of salvation and hope to others
in our path today,
for we have the gift
of your Word and our faith.
We ask this in your name.

Amen.

✚ All make the Sign of the Cross.

260

This prayer service may be used on any day of Holy Week. Arrange a simple environment. On a table covered with a violet cloth, place a candle and a Bible. Prepare six leaders for this service. The second and third leaders will need Bibles to read the Scripture passages (John 13:3–5, 12–15 and John 19:16–18, 28–30) and may need help finding and practicing them. You may wish to sing "Jesus, Remember Me" throughout, as indicated, and end with "We Remember." If there will be singing, prepare a song leader. Use deliberate, unhurried movements and a quiet voice to set a reverent tone that will invite the children into this time of reflection and prayer.

◆ All make the sign of the Cross.

In the name of the Father, and of the Son, and of the Holy Spirit. Amen.

FIRST LEADER:

Three days of the Church year stand out from the rest, and they are called one special name: the Triduum [TRID-oo-uhm]. The Triduum begins on the evening of Holy Thursday, when we remember the Last Supper: Jesus took bread and wine, blessed it, broke it, and offered it to his followers. He also washed his disciples' feet to help them realize how they must become servant leaders for all.

The Triduum continues with Good Friday, when we recall how Jesus was abandoned by his friends, suffered through torture, and was brutally crucified. We remember the one "good" thing about this day: Jesus died for our salvation. On this evening and until the evening of Holy Saturday, we reflect on how we sometimes fail to love others. We pray for each other, yet we eagerly await a much better event. At the Easter Vigil and on Easter Sunday, we

PRAYER SERVICE
HOLY WEEK

celebrate Christ's Resurrection! Jesus's rising from the dead proved that death has no power over us!

◆ All stand and sing **Praise to you, Lord Jesus Christ** . . .

SECOND LEADER: John 13:3–5, 12–15
A reading from the holy Gospel according to John

◆ Read the Gospel passage from the Bible. All observe silence. Then all sing "Jesus Remember Me."

THIRD LEADER: John 19:16b–8, 28–30
A reading from the holy Gospel according to John

◆ Read the Gospel passage from the Bible.

The Gospel of the Lord.

◆ All sit and observe silence. Then all sing "Jesus Remember Me."

FOURTH LEADER:
Let us pray the Psalm Response:
Answer me, O Lord, for your steadfast love is good.

ALL: Answer me, O Lord, for your steadfast love is good.

Do not hide your face from your servant,
    for I am in distress—make haste to answer
        me.
Draw near to me, redeem me,
    set me free because of my enemies.

ALL: Answer me, O Lord, for your steadfast love is good.

For the Lord hears the needy,
    and does not despise his own that are
        in bonds.

Let heaven and earth praise him,
    the seas and everything that moves in them.

ALL: Answer me, O Lord, for your steadfast love is good.

FIFTH LEADER:
Let us stand and pray as Jesus taught us:

Our Father . . . Amen.

God our Father,
during these special three days,
help us to honor the gift of your Son,
who showed us how to love.
Guide us to be compassionate with others
as we move toward
the Feast of the Resurrection.
We ask this through Christ our Lord.

ALL: Amen.

SIXTH LEADER:
May the Lord bless us,

✠ All make the Sign of the Cross.

protect us from all evil,
and bring us to everlasting life.

ALL: Amen.

CHILDREN'S DAILY PRAYER 2013–2014, © 2013 Archdiocese of Chicago: Liturgy Training Publications. All rights reserved. Orders: 1-800-933-1800 or www.LTP.org.

Before you begin, find the reading (John 13:3–5) in your Bible, ask for a volunteer to read it, and help the reader to practice reading it a few times. You could begin with a simple song, such as "Jesus, Remember Me," or "Amen." (We don't sing "Alleluia" until the Easter Vigil.) An older child or adult reads the leader parts.

LEADER

Today is Holy Thursday, and this evening we will remember two important things that Jesus did for his disciples and for us. On this night of the Last Supper, Jesus offered himself as bread and wine and said, "Do this in memory of me." Later, he washed the feet of his followers, teaching them by example of how we must be a servant for all.

◆ All make the Sign of the Cross.

In the name of the Father, and of the Son, and of the Holy Spirit. Amen.

LEADER: Psalm 27:1, 4, 5, 11, 13–14

Let us repeat the Psalm Response:
Teach me your way, O Lord.

ALL: Teach me your way, O Lord.

The Lord is my light and my salvation;
　　whom shall I fear?
The Lord is the stronghold of my life;
　　of whom shall I be afraid?

ALL: Teach me your way, O Lord.

One thing I asked of the Lord,
　　that will I seek after:
to live in the house of the Lord
　　all the days of my life,
to behold the beauty of the Lord,
　　and to inquire in his temple.

ALL: Teach me your way, O Lord.

I believe that I shall see the goodness
　　of the Lord
　　in the land of the living.
Wait for the Lord;
　　be strong, and let your heart take courage;
　　wait for the Lord!

ALL: Teach me your way, O Lord.

◆ All stand and sing **Praise to you, Lord Jesus Christ** . . .

LEADER: John 13:3–5

A reading from the holy Gospel according to John

◆ Read the Gospel passage from the Bible.

The Gospel of the Lord.

◆ All sit and observe silence.

FOR SILENT REFLECTION

Why did Jesus, the disciples' leader, wish to be their servant?

LEADER:
Let us pray as Jesus taught us:

Our Father . . . Amen.

LEADER:
Almighty God,
we remember Jesus's
act of service of washing his friends' feet.
May we honor you with
our acts of love today and always.
We ask this through Christ our Lord.

ALL: Amen.

◆ All make the Sign of the Cross.

CHILDREN'S DAILY PRAYER 2013–2014 © 2013 Archdiocese of Chicago: Liturgy Training Publications, 3949 South Racine Avenue, Chicago IL 60609. All rights reserved. Orders: 1-800-933-1800 or www.LTP.org. Scripture excerpts are taken from *The New Revised Standard Version Bible: Catholic Edition*, © 1989, Division of Christian Education of the National Council of the Churches of Christ in the United States of America. Used with permission. All rights reserved.

HOME PRAYER
GOOD FRIDAY

Before you begin, find the reading (John 18:33–37) in your Bible, ask for a volunteer to read it, and help the reader to practice it a few times. You could begin with a simple song, such as "Jesus, Remember Me," or "Amen." (We don't sing "Alleluia" until the Easter Vigil.) An older child or adult reads the leader parts.

LEADER:

Today we remember Jesus's anguish and Death on the cross. It is a sad time we don't understand. But Good Friday is also a day that we recall the goodness of God's Son who chose to die so that he could save us from sin and death. This day gives us so much hope because of the promise of new life!

✚ All make the Sign of the Cross.

In the name of the Father, and of the Son, and of the Holy Spirit. Amen.

LEADER: Psalm 31:1, 2, 5a, 14–16, 21

Let us repeat the Psalm Response:
Into your hand I commit my spirit.

ALL: Into your hand I commit my spirit.

In you, O Lord, I seek refuge;
   do not let me ever be put to shame;
   in your righteousness deliver me.
Incline your ear to me;
   rescue me speedily.
Be a rock of refuge for me,
   a strong fortress to save me.

ALL: Into your hand I commit my spirit.

Blessed be the Lord,
   for he has wondrously shown his steadfast
      love to me
   when I was beset as a city under siege.

ALL: Into your hand I commit my spirit.

◆ All stand and sing **Praise to you, Lord Jesus Christ . . .**

LEADER: John 18:33–37

A reading from the holy Gospel according to John

◆ Read the Gospel passage from the Bible.

The Gospel of the Lord.

◆ All sit and observe silence.

LEADER:

As I reflect on Jesus's love for me, how can I thank him?

LEADER:

Let us pray as Jesus taught us:

Our Father . . . Amen.

LEADER:

Today we remember Jesus's great love. Help us to honor him with our lives. We ask this in the name of the Father, the Son, and the Holy Spirit.

ALL: Amen.

✚ All make the Sign of the Cross.

 CHILDREN'S DAILY PRAYER 2013–2014, © 2013 Archdiocese of Chicago: Liturgy Training Publications, 3949 South Racine Avenue, Chicago IL 60609. All rights reserved. Orders: 1-800-933-1800 or www.LTP.org. Scripture excerpts are taken from *The New Revised Standard Version Bible: Catholic Edition*, copyright © 1989, Division of Christian Education of the National Council of the Churches of Christ in the United States of America. Used with permission. All rights reserved.

EASTER TIME

SUNDAY, APRIL 20, 2014, TO SUNDAY, JUNE 8, 2014

THE MEANING OF EASTER TIME

Three days after his Death on the cross, "Jesus himself stood among the disciples and said to them, 'Peace be with you.' They were startled and terrified, and thought that they were seeing a ghost. He said to them, 'Why are you frightened, and why do doubts arise in your hearts? Look at my hands and my feet; see that it is I myself. Touch me and see' " (Luke 24:36b–39a).

God is love. Out of nothingness, the power of God's love, a divine spark of life, kindled the dawn of creation in an explosion of heat and light. Out of love, God created human beings in the divine image to share in God's life. At all times and among every people, God has welcomed those who do good and seek God in their hearts. Whenever we have turned away from God, God calls us back. When human wickedness might have prevailed, God cleansed creation, choosing Noah and his family to help preserve every species and forge a new life on a renewed earth. God called Abraham to enter into a covenant with God, promising what seemed impossible to make a great nation of Abraham and Sarah's descendents. When God's people were enslaved, God called Moses to lead them into freedom, and when his people needed a king, God sent a shepherd boy named David to become a great king. God's people became a strong and prayerful people.

From the dawn of creation, God has shown the power of divine love. Out of emptiness, God creates a universe. God protects the earth from the wicked, and from a couple too old to have children, makes a great and holy people. He frees his people from slavery and gives a little boy the grace to become a great king. Out of death on a cross, God's Son now conquers death, and invites us to enter into eternal life. And in the midst of their confusion after Jesus's Crucifixion, the Holy Spirit unites the followers of Christ, giving birth to a Church that will spread the news of God's love throughout the world.

After Jesus rose from the dead, the Bible tells us that he stayed with his friends for a little while

to teach them: "Then Jesus said to them, 'These are my words that I spoke to you while I was still with you—that everything written about me in the law of Moses, the prophets, and the psalms must be fulfilled.' Then he opened their minds to understand the scriptures, and he said to them, 'Thus it is written, that the Messiah is to suffer and to rise from the dead on the third day, and that repentance and forgiveness of sins is to be proclaimed in his name to all nations, beginning from Jerusalem' " (Luke 24:44b–47).

Even with the help of Jesus, it was difficult for the disciples to understand what the Resurrection meant. Today, with the help of the Holy Spirit, we are still struggling to understand this amazing wonder: the God who loves us is with us.

PREPARING TO CELEBRATE EASTER IN THE CLASSROOM

The liturgical color for Easter Time is white, so your prayer table cloth will need to change once more. If you plan a procession to change the cloth, consider having the child second in line carry a large white pillar candle (the first child will carry the white cloth). You may use the same white pillar you used during Christmas. Make sure you dim the lights before you begin. Then after all the objects have been returned to the prayer table, light the white pillar and chant the following phrase and response three times:

LEADER: The Light of Christ!

ALL: Thanks be to God!

You may use a chant from your parish hymnal or sing "The Light of Christ" on one note. When you are finished singing, read a Gospel account of the Resurrection (John 20:11–18, for example). Sing Alleluia and then announce the following: "Jesus has risen from the dead; Jesus, the Light of the World, has destroyed death. The light of the Risen Christ will never go out, for he shares his light and life with each of us. Not only that, but his light can spread and grow. Jesus shares his new life with each of us." Then call each child by name, one at a time, inviting them to come forward. For each child, light a small votive candle from the large pillar. As you give it to the child, say, "The Risen Christ shares his light with (child's name)." The child will then put the votive candle on the prayer table and sit down. Don't rush. Wait until the child is seated before you call the next child's name. If you are worried about fire, allow each child to hold his or her votive holder briefly, then you can place the candle on the table beside the lit pillar. Make sure you light a votive for yourself. When all the small candles are lit, sit in silence with the children and enjoy the beauty of the light. End your celebration by singing all the Alleluias that you know!

Three prayer services are provided: Easter, Ascension, and Pentecost.

SACRED SPACE

Place some fresh daisies or lilies in a vase on your prayer table. You might also like to put a small glass bowl with a little water in it on the prayer table. When you introduce the water to your students you may say, "Jesus said, 'Let anyone who is thirsty come to me, and let the one who believes in me drink'" (John 7:37b–38a). Perhaps one of your students, or someone they know, received the Sacrament of Baptism at the Holy Saturday celebration of the Easter Vigil. If so, while standing before the water, you could explain that the water of Baptism recalls the great flood that Noah had to pass through to reach God's promise of peace, the Red Sea that Moses and the Israelites had to pass through to reach freedom, and the death that Jesus had to pass through to reach the life of the Resurrection. When we pass through (are baptized with) the water in the baptismal font, we enter into that same new life of the resurrected Christ.

Easter Time ends with the Solemnity of Pentecost. When you celebrate Pentecost as a group, make sure you exchange your white prayer table cloth for a red one.

SACRED MUSIC

Here are some Easter songs that children love: "Jesus Christ Is Risen Today," "What Wondrous Love Is This," "Alleluia, Sing to Jesus," "Come Down, O Love Divine," and "O Sons and Daughters." For Pentecost you might enjoy singing "Come, Holy Ghost" or "Veni Sancte Spiritus."

PRAYERS FOR EASTER

The following prayer is a beautiful psalm from the Easter Vigil:

Psalm 42:1–2, 43:3–4

As a deer longs for flowing streams,
    so my soul longs for you, O God.
My soul thirsts for God
    for the living God.
When shall I come and behold
    the face of God?
O send out your light and your truth;
    let them lead me;
let them bring me to your holy hill
    and to your dwelling.
Then I will go to the altar of God
    to God my exceeding joy;
and I will praise you with the harp,
    O God, my God.

A NOTE TO CATECHISTS

You may wish to study the prayers of Baptism with your students. The prayer of Blessing the Waters of Baptism is particularly rich in symbolism. With older children you could move from the prayer to the account in the Bible that the prayer mentions, then back to the prayer again. You might want to wonder, along with the children, over the long sacred history of water.

GRACE BEFORE MEALS

EASTER

LEADER:
Jesus Christ is risen! He is truly risen!

ALL: Alleluia! Alleluia!

✝ All make the Sign of the Cross.

In the name of the Father, and of the Son, and of the Holy Spirit. Amen.

LEADER:
God, our Creator,
we are thankful for the
air we breathe and the
nourishment you offer
in our every moment on earth.
We are grateful for the meal
we are about to share,
for its nutrients sustain us and
give us energy for
working and playing for the glory
of Christ our Savior.
We ask this in his name.

ALL: Amen.

✝ All make the Sign of the Cross.

In the name of the Father, and of the Son, and of the Holy Spirit. Amen.

PRAYER AT DAY'S END

EASTER

LEADER:
All the ends of the earth have seen

ALL: the victory of our God.

✝ All make the Sign of the Cross.

In the name of the Father, and of the Son, and of the Holy Spirit. Amen.

LEADER:
Heavenly Father,
we are grateful for
what we've learned today.
We thank you for our
teachers, assistants, coaches,
and friends who guide us
along our path.
Help us through the remainder of this day
as we are renewed by your Spirit
and the promise of an
eternal Easter.
We ask this through Christ our Lord.

ALL: Amen.

✝ All make the Sign of the Cross.

In the name of the Father, and of the Son, and of the Holy Spirit. Amen.

269

PRAYER FOR THE WEEK

OPENING

Today's Easter Sunday Gospel shows the brave Mary Magdalene, who was the first one at Jesus's burial site. She tearfully told the others about Jesus, even though she initially didn't understand what his "disappearance" meant.

✛ All make the Sign of the Cross.

> **In the name of the Father, and of the Son, and of the Holy Spirit. Amen.**

PSALM (For a longer psalm, see page xv.) Psalm 105:1–2, 3–4, 6–7

Let the hearts of those who seek
    the LORD rejoice.

**Let the hearts of those who seek
    the LORD rejoice.**

O give thanks to the LORD, call on his name,
  make known his deeds among the peoples.
Sing to him, sing praises to him;
  tell of all his wonderful works.

**Let the hearts of those who seek
    the LORD rejoice.**

◆ All stand and sing **Alleluia.**

GOSPEL

John 20:1–8

A reading from the holy Gospel according to John

Early on the first day of the week, while it was still dark, Mary Magdalene came to the tomb and saw that the stone had been removed from the tomb. So she ran and went to Simon Peter and the other disciple, the one whom Jesus loved, and said to them, "They have taken the Lord out of the tomb, and we do not know where they have laid him." Then Peter and the other disciple set out and went toward the tomb. The two were running together, but the other disciple outran Peter and reached the tomb first. He bent down to look in and saw the linen wrappings lying there, but he did not go in. Then Simon Peter came, following him, and went into the tomb. He saw the linen wrappings lying there, and the cloth that had been on Jesus' head, not lying with the linen wrappings but rolled up in a place by itself.

The Gospel of the Lord.

◆ All sit and observe silence.

FOR SILENT REFLECTION

Can you imagine how Mary and the disciples felt?

CLOSING PRAYER

Let us stand and bring our hopes and needs to God as we pray, "Lord, hear our prayer."

◆ All may add their own prayers here.

Let us pray: **Our Father . . . Amen.**

Lord Jesus,
help us to tell others about
your victory over death,
and that you are present
when we pray and call upon you.
In your name we pray.

Amen.

✛ All make the Sign of the Cross.

OPENING

In Matthew's account of the discovery at Jesus's tomb, the authorities plan to cover up evidence so that they would not be punished for our Savior's disappearance.

✝ All make the Sign of the Cross.

In the name of the Father, and of the Son, and of the Holy Spirit. Amen.

PSALM   (For a longer psalm, see page xv.) Psalm 105:1–2, 3–4, 6–7

Let the hearts of those who seek
    the LORD rejoice.

**Let the hearts of those who seek
    the LORD rejoice.**

O give thanks to the LORD, call on his name,
    make known his deeds among the peoples.
Sing to him, sing praises to him;
    tell of all his wonderful works.

**Let the hearts of those who seek
    the LORD rejoice.**

◆ All stand and sing **Alleluia.**

GOSPEL   Matthew 28:8, 10–14

A reading from the holy Gospel according to Matthew

So they left the tomb quickly with fear and great joy, and ran to tell his disciples. Suddenly Jesus met them and said, "Greetings!" Then Jesus said to them, "Do not be afraid; go and tell my brothers to go to Galilee; there they will see me."

While they were going, some of the guard went into the city and told the chief priests everything that had happened. After the priests had assembled with the elders, they devised a plan to give a large sum of money to the soldiers, telling them, "You must say, 'His disciples came by night and stole him away while we were asleep.' If this comes to the governor's ears, we will satisfy him and keep you out of trouble."

The Gospel of the Lord.

◆ All sit and observe silence.

FOR SILENT REFLECTION

Jesus tells his disciples to not be afraid. Can you think of other times we have heard this message to not fear?

CLOSING PRAYER

Let us stand and bring our hopes and needs to God as we pray, "Lord, hear our prayer."

◆ All may add their own prayers here.

Let us pray: **Our Father . . . Amen.**

Lord Jesus,
may we be your presence today.
May we be a source of hope to those
whose hearts are full of pain.
We ask this in your name.

Amen.

✝ All make the Sign of the Cross.

271

PRAYER FOR **TUESDAY** APRIL 22, 2014

OPENING

In John's account of the Resurrection, two angels announce what had happened, and Jesus surprises Mary by appearing to her.

✚ All make the Sign of the Cross.

In the name of the Father, and of the Son, and of the Holy Spirit. Amen.

PSALM (For a longer psalm, see page xv.) Psalm 105:1–2, 3–4, 6–7

Let the hearts of those who seek
    the LORD rejoice.

**Let the hearts of those who seek
    the LORD rejoice.**

O give thanks to the LORD, call on his name,
    make known his deeds among the peoples.
Sing to him, sing praises to him;
    tell of all his wonderful works.

**Let the hearts of those who seek
    the LORD rejoice.**

◆ All stand and sing **Alleluia.**

GOSPEL   John 20:11–16

A reading from the holy Gospel according to John

Mary stood weeping outside the tomb. As she wept, she bent over to look into the tomb; and she saw two angels in white, sitting where the body of Jesus had been lying, one at the head and the other at the feet. They said to her, "Woman, why are you weeping?" She said to them, "They have taken away my Lord, and I do not know where they have laid him." When she had said this, she turned around and saw Jesus standing there, but she did not know that it was Jesus. Jesus said to her, "Woman, why are you weeping? Whom are you looking for?" Supposing him to be the gardener, she said to him, "Sir, if you have carried him away, tell me where you have laid him, and I will take him away." Jesus said to her, "Mary!" She turned and said to him in Hebrew, "Rabbouni!" [rab-OO-nī] (which means Teacher).

The Gospel of the Lord.

◆ All sit and observe silence.

FOR SILENT REFLECTION

How did Mary Magdalene recognize Jesus?

CLOSING PRAYER

Let us stand and bring our hopes and needs to God as we pray, "Lord, hear our prayer."

◆ All may add their own prayers here.

Let us pray: **Our Father . . . Amen.**

Lord Jesus,
just as Mary Magdalene
recognized you as teacher,
help us to listen to your words
and to follow your example.
In your name we pray.

Amen.

✚ All make the Sign of the Cross.

ALSO ON THIS DAY: Jewish Passover ends

272

OPENING

Today's reading shows the power of believers who act in the name of Jesus. Miracles continued to happen even after Jesus was not physically present on earth, then and now.

✦ All make the Sign of the Cross.

> **In the name of the Father, and of the Son, and of the Holy Spirit. Amen.**

PSALM (For a longer psalm, see page xv.) Psalm 105:1–2, 3–4, 6–7

Let the hearts of those who seek
   the LORD rejoice.

**Let the hearts of those who seek
   the LORD rejoice.**

O give thanks to the LORD, call on his name,
   make known his deeds among the peoples.
Sing to him, sing praises to him;
   tell of all his wonderful works.

**Let the hearts of those who seek
   the LORD rejoice.**

READING   Acts 3:1–9

A reading from the Acts of the Apostles

One day Peter and John were going up to the temple at the hour of prayer, at three o'clock in the afternoon. And a man lame from birth was being carried in. People would lay him daily at the gate of the temple called the Beautiful Gate so that he could ask for alms from those entering the temple. When he saw Peter and John about to go into the temple, he asked them for alms. Peter looked intently at him, as did John, and said, "Look at us." And he fixed his attention on them, expecting to receive something from them. But Peter said, "I have no silver or gold, but what I have I give you; in the name of Jesus Christ of Nazareth, stand up and walk." And he took him by the right hand and raised him up; and immediately his feet and ankles were made strong. Jumping up, he stood and began to walk, and he entered the temple with them, walking and leaping and praising God.

The Word of the Lord.

◆ All observe silence.

FOR SILENT REFLECTION

From what do I need healing?

CLOSING PRAYER

Let us stand and bring our hopes and needs to God as we pray, "Lord, hear our prayer."

◆ All may add their own prayers here.

Let us pray: **Our Father . . . Amen.**

Loving Creator,
help us to call upon you,
Father, Son, and Spirit,
to ease the suffering of this world.
We ask this through our Lord Jesus Christ,
your Son, who lives and reigns with you
in the unity of the Holy Spirit,
one God, for ever and ever.

Amen.

✦ All make the Sign of the Cross.

PRAYER FOR **THURSDAY** APRIL 24, 2014

OPENING

Today's Gospel shows yet another appearance of Jesus to his closest followers. How joyful they must have felt at seeing their leader again.

✛ All make the Sign of the Cross.

In the name of the Father, and of the Son, and of the Holy Spirit. Amen.

PSALM   (For a longer psalm, see page xv.) Psalm 105:1–2, 3–4, 6–7

Let the hearts of those who seek
    the LORD rejoice.

**Let the hearts of those who seek
    the LORD rejoice.**

O give thanks to the LORD, call on his name,
    make known his deeds among the peoples.
Sing to him, sing praises to him;
    tell of all his wonderful works.

**Let the hearts of those who seek
    the LORD rejoice.**

◆ All stand and sing **Alleluia.**

GOSPEL   Luke 24:35–44

A reading from the holy Gospel according to Luke

The disciples told what had happened on the road, and how he had been made known to them in the breaking of the bread.

While they were talking about this, Jesus himself stood among them and said to them, "Peace be with you." They were startled and terrified, and thought that they were seeing a ghost. He said to them, "Why are you frightened, and why do doubts arise in your hearts? Look at my hands and my feet; see that it is I myself. Touch me and see; for a ghost does not have flesh and bones as you see that I have." And when he had said this, he showed them his hands and his feet. While in their joy they were disbelieving and still wondering, he said to them, "Have you anything here to eat?" They gave him a piece of broiled fish, and he took it and ate in their presence. Then he said to them, "These are my words that I spoke to you while I was still with you—that everything written about me in the law of Moses, the prophets, and the psalms must be fulfilled."

The Gospel of the Lord.

◆ All sit and observe silence.

FOR SILENT REFLECTION

How is Jesus with us today?

CLOSING PRAYER

Let us stand and bring our hopes and needs to God as we pray, "Lord, hear our prayer."

◆ All may add their own prayers here.

Let us pray: **Our Father . . . Amen.**

Lord Jesus,
may we be open to your
messages of hope.
We ask this in your name.

Amen.

✛ All make the Sign of the Cross.

274

OPENING

In today's Gospel, Jesus surprises his disciples and provides even more than they had hoped.

✛ All make the Sign of the Cross.

In the name of the Father, and of the Son, and of the Holy Spirit. Amen.

PSALM (For a longer psalm, see page xv.) Psalm 105:1–2, 3–4, 6–7

Let the hearts of those who seek
the LORD rejoice.

**Let the hearts of those who seek
the LORD rejoice.**

O give thanks to the LORD, call on his name,
    make known his deeds among the peoples.
Sing to him, sing praises to him;
    tell of all his wonderful works.

**Let the hearts of those who seek
the LORD rejoice.**

◆ All stand and sing **Alleluia.**

GOSPEL   John 21: 4–8

A reading from the holy Gospel according to Mark

Just after daybreak, Jesus stood on the beach; but the disciples did not know it was Jesus. Jesus said to them, "Children, you have no fish, have you?" They answered him, "No." He said to them, "Cast the net to the right side of hte boat, and you will find some." So they cast it, and now they were not able to haul it in because there were so many fish. That disciple whom Jesus loved said to Peter, "It is the Lord!" When Simon Peter heard it was the Lord, he put on some clothes, for he was naked, and jumped into the sea. But the other disciples came in the boat, dragging the new full of fish, for they were not far from the land, only about a hundred yards off.

The Gospel of the Lord.

◆ All sit and observe silence.

FOR SILENT REFLECTION

How does Jesus help me when I am in need?

CLOSING PRAYER

Let us stand and bring our hopes and needs to God as we pray, "Lord, hear our prayer."

◆ All may add their own prayers here.

Let us pray: **Our Father . . . Amen.**

Lord Jesus,
just as you loved and cared for your disciples,
you love and care for us.
May we trust in you always.
We ask this in your name.

Amen.

✛ All make the Sign of the Cross.

PRAYER FOR THE WEEK

OPENING

Today is Sunday of Divine Mercy, declared by Pope John Paul II in 2000, to celebrate God's mercy in the forgiveness of our sins.

✝ All make the Sign of the Cross.

In the name of the Father, and of the Son, and of the Holy Spirit. Amen.

PSALM   (For a longer psalm, see page xv.) Psalm 105:1–2, 3–4, 6–7

Let the hearts of those who seek
    the LORD rejoice.

**Let the hearts of those who seek
    the LORD rejoice.**

O give thanks to the LORD, call on his name,
    make known his deeds among the peoples.
Sing to him, sing praises to him;
    tell of all his wonderful works.

**Let the hearts of those who seek
    the LORD rejoice.**

◆ All stand and sing **Alleluia.**

GOSPEL   19–20a, 24–28

A reading from the holy Gospel according to John

When it was evening on that day, the first day of the week, and the doors of the house where the disciples had met were locked for fear of the Jews, Jesus came and stood among them and said, "Peace be with you." After he said this, he showed them his hands and his side. But Thomas (who was called the Twin), one of the twelve, was not with them when Jesus came. So the other disciples told him, "We have seen the Lord." But he said to them, "Unless I see the mark of the nails in his hands, and put my finger in the mark of the nails and my hand in his side, I will not believe."

A week later his disciples were again in the house, and Thomas was with them. Although the doors were shut, Jesus came and stood among them and said, "Peace be with you." Then he said to Thomas, "Put your finger here and see my hands. Reach out your hand and put it in my side. Do not doubt but believe." Thomas answered him, "My Lord and my God!"

The Gospel of the Lord.

◆ All sit and observe silence.

FOR SILENT REFLECTION

Would you have been like Thomas had you not seen Jesus?

CLOSING PRAYER

Let us stand and bring our hopes and needs to God as we pray, "Lord, hear our prayer."

◆ All may add their own prayers here.

Let us pray: **Our Father . . . Amen.**

Most faithful God,
we thank you for your Son Jesus,
source of our faith and our peace.
May we always have faith in him.
We ask this through your Son Jesus.

Amen.

✝ All make the Sign of the Cross.

OPENING

Today we remember St. Peter Chanel, who served as a missionary in Western Oceania. He worked with whalers, traders, and warring natives. Two years after his death, whole communities of people became Catholic.

✝ All make the Sign of the Cross.

In the name of the Father, and of the Son, and of the Holy Spirit. Amen.

PSALM (For a longer psalm, see page xv.) Psalm 105:1–2, 3–4, 6–7

Let the hearts of those who seek
the LORD rejoice.

**Let the hearts of those who seek
the LORD rejoice.**

O give thanks to the LORD, call on his name,
make known his deeds among the peoples.
Sing to him, sing praises to him;
tell of all his wonderful works.

**Let the hearts of those who seek
the LORD rejoice.**

◆ All stand and sing **Alleluia.**

GOSPEL
John 3:1–8

A reading from the holy Gospel according to John

There was a Pharisee [FAYR-uh-see] named Nicodemus, [nik-uh-DEE-muhs] a leader of the Jews. He came to Jesus by night and said to him, "Rabbi, we know that you are a teacher who has come from God; for no one can do these signs that you do apart from the presence of God." Jesus answered him, "Very truly, I tell you, no one can see the kingdom of God without being born from above." Nicodemus said to him, "How can anyone be born after having grown old? Can one enter a second time into the mother's womb and be born?" Jesus answered, "Very truly, I tell you, no one can enter the kingdom of God without being born of water and Spirit. What is born of the flesh is flesh, and what is born of the Spirit is spirit. Do not be astonished that I said to you, 'You must be born from above.' The wind blows where it chooses, and you hear the sound of it, but you do not know where it comes from or where it goes. So it is with everyone who is born of the Spirit."

The Gospel of the Lord.

◆ All sit and observe silence.

FOR SILENT REFLECTION

How am I being led by God's Spirit?

CLOSING PRAYER

Let us stand and bring our hopes and needs to God as we pray, "Lord, hear our prayer."

◆ All may add their own prayers here.

Let us pray: **Our Father . . . Amen.**

Lord God,
help us to be open to
your movement in us.
We ask this through your Son Jesus.

Amen.

✝ All make the Sign of the Cross.

PRAYER FOR **TUESDAY**
APRIL 29, 2014

OPENING

Today we remember St. Catherine of Siena, who was born in 1347. After entering the Dominican Third Order at age 18, she focused on prayer and writing. She later advised and championed the cause of Pope Urban VI during a divided time in Church history.

✠ All make the Sign of the Cross.

In the name of the Father, and of the Son, and of the Holy Spirit. Amen.

PSALM (For a longer psalm, see page xv.) Psalm 105:1–2, 3–4, 6–7

Let the hearts of those who seek
    the LORD rejoice.

**Let the hearts of those who seek
    the LORD rejoice.**

O give thanks to the LORD, call on his name,
    make known his deeds among the peoples.
Sing to him, sing praises to him;
    tell of all his wonderful works.

**Let the hearts of those who seek
    the LORD rejoice.**

◆ All stand and sing **Alleluia.**

GOSPEL   John 3:7–13

A reading from the holy Gospel according to John

Jesus said to Nicodemus [nik-uh-DEE-muhs]: "Do not be astonished that I said to you, 'You must be born from above.' The wind blows where it chooses, and you hear the sound of it, but you do not know where it comes from or where it goes. So it is with everyone who is born of the Spirit." Nicodemus said to him, "How can these things be?" Jesus answered him, "Are you a teacher of Israel, and yet you do not understand these things? "Very truly, I tell you, we speak of what we know and testify to what we have seen; yet you do not receive our testimony. If I have told you about earthly things and you do not believe, how can you believe if I tell you about heavenly things? No one has ascended into heaven except the one who descended from heaven, the Son of Man."

The Gospel of the Lord.

◆ All sit and observe silence.

FOR SILENT REFLECTION

What do you think are some of the "heavenly things" to which Jesus refers?

CLOSING PRAYER

Let us stand and bring our hopes and needs to God as we pray, "Lord, hear our prayer."

◆ All may add their own prayers here.

Let us pray: **Our Father . . . Amen.**

Lord Jesus,
you revealed a difficult image
for Nicodemus and for us to bear.
May we honor your Cross
and Resurrection as our reason for
living with purpose for the one true God.
We ask this in your name.

Amen.

✠ All make the Sign of the Cross.

278

OPENING

Today we remember Pope Pius V who founded seminaries for the proper training of priests, published a new missal and catechism, and started religion classes for the young.

✦ All make the Sign of the Cross.

In the name of the Father, and of the Son, and of the Holy Spirit. Amen.

PSALM (For a longer psalm, see page xv.) Psalm 105:1–2, 3–4, 6–7

Let the hearts of those who seek
the LORD rejoice.

**Let the hearts of those who seek
the LORD rejoice.**

O give thanks to the LORD, call on his name,
make known his deeds among the peoples.
Sing to him, sing praises to him;
tell of all his wonderful works.

**Let the hearts of those who seek
the LORD rejoice.**

READING
Acts 5:17–25

A reading from the Acts of the Apostles

The high priest took action; he and all who were with him (that is, the sect of the Sadducees [SAD-yoo-seez]), being filled with jealousy, arrested the apostles and put them in the public prison. But during the night an angel of the Lord opened the prison doors, brought them out, and said, "Go, stand in the temple and tell the people the whole message about this life." When they heard this, they entered the temple at daybreak and went on with their teaching. When the high priest and those with him arrived, they called together the council and the whole body of the elders of Israel, and sent to the prison to have them brought. But when the temple police went there, they did not find them in the prison; so they returned and reported, "We found the prison securely locked and the guards standing at the doors, but when we opened them, we found no one inside." Now when the captain of the temple and the chief priests heard these words, they were perplexed about them, wondering what might be going on. Then someone arrived and announced, "Look, the men whom you put in prison are standing in the temple and teaching the people!"

The Word of the Lord.

◆ All observe silence.

FOR SILENT REFLECTION

What caused the authorities to become so angry?

CLOSING PRAYER

Let us stand and bring our hopes and needs to God as we pray, "Lord, hear our prayer."

◆ All may add their own prayers here.

Let us pray: **Our Father . . . Amen.**

Almighty God,
your word breaks through prison
walls and hardened hearts.
Help us to listen for your call.
We ask this in the name of your Jesus,
your Son.

Amen.

✦ All make the Sign of the Cross.

PRAYER FOR **THURSDAY**
MAY 1, 2014

OPENING

Today we remember St. Joseph the Worker to emphasize how this foster father of Jesus was a dutiful carpenter who used his hands to make a living for his family. So this day honors all those who work hard to put food on the table and a roof over the heads of loved ones.

✛ All make the Sign of the Cross.

In the name of the Father, and of the Son, and of the Holy Spirit. Amen.

PSALM   (For a longer psalm, see page xv.) Psalm 105:1–2, 3–4, 6–7

Let the hearts of those who seek
    the LORD rejoice.

**Let the hearts of those who seek
    the LORD rejoice.**

O give thanks to the LORD, call on his name,
    make known his deeds among the peoples.
Sing to him, sing praises to him;
    tell of all his wonderful works.

**Let the hearts of those who seek
    the LORD rejoice.**

READING   Colossians 3:14–15, 17, 23–24

A reading from the Letter of St. Paul to the Colossians

Brothers and sisters: Above all, clothe yourselves with love, which binds everything together in perfect harmony. And let the peace of Christ rule in your hearts, to which indeed you were called in the one body. And be thankful. And whatever you do, in word or deed, do everything In the name of the Lord Jesus, giving thanks to God the Father through him. Whatever your task, put yourselves into it, as done for the Lord and not for your masters, since you know that from the Lord you will receive the inheritance as your reward; you serve the Lord Christ.

The Word of the Lord.

◆ All observe silence.

FOR SILENT REFLECTION

What does it mean to "clothe yourselves with love"?

CLOSING PRAYER

Let us stand and bring our hopes and needs to God as we pray, "Lord, hear our prayer."

◆ All may add their own prayers here.

Let us pray: **Our Father . . . Amen.**

Lord Jesus,
you inspired your servant Paul
to advise us to clothe ourselves with love
so that everything will be
bound together in perfect harmony.
Help us to remember this
in our daily work and play today.
We ask this in your name.

Amen.

✛ All make the Sign of the Cross.

OPENING

Today we remember St. Athanasius [ath-uh-NAY-shuhs], who lived in the fourth century, and who dedicated his life to fighting Arianism, the belief that Jesus was not divine.

✠ *All make the Sign of the Cross.*

In the name of the Father, and of the Son, and of the Holy Spirit. Amen.

PSALM (For a longer psalm, see page xv.) Psalm 105:1–2, 3–4, 6–7

Let the hearts of those who seek
the LORD rejoice.

**Let the hearts of those who seek
the LORD rejoice.**

O give thanks to the LORD, call on his name,
make known his deeds among the peoples.
Sing to him, sing praises to him;
tell of all his wonderful works.

**Let the hearts of those who seek
the LORD rejoice.**

◆ *All stand and sing **Alleluia.***

GOSPEL   John 6:3–11

A reading from the holy Gospel according to John

Jesus went up the mountain and sat down there with his disciples. Now the Passover, the festival of the Jews, was near. When he looked up and saw a large crowd coming toward him, Jesus said to Philip, "Where are we to buy bread for these people to eat?" He said this to test him, for he himself knew what he was going to do. Philip answered him, "Six months' wages would not buy enough bread for each of them to get a little." One of his disciples, Andrew, Simon Peter's brother, said to him, "There is a boy here who has five barley loaves and two fish. But what are they among so many people?" Jesus said, "Make the people sit down." Now there was a great deal of grass in the place; so they sat down, about five thousand in all. Then Jesus took the loaves, and when he had given thanks, he distributed them to those who were seated; so also the fish, as much as they wanted.

The Gospel of the Lord.

◆ *All sit and observe silence.*

FOR SILENT REFLECTION

How can we recreate the miracle of generosity every day?

CLOSING PRAYER

Let us stand and bring our hopes and needs to God as we pray, "Lord, hear our prayer."

◆ *All may add their own prayers here.*

Let us pray: **Our Father . . . Amen.**

Lord Jesus,
may we give to others
to help provide those in need
with the basics for living.
In your name we pray.

Amen.

✠ *All make the Sign of the Cross.*

PRAYER SERVICE
TO HONOR MARY IN MAY

Prepare six leaders for this service. The third leader will need a Bible for the passages from Luke. Take time to help the lector practice the readings. You may wish to sing "Sing of Mary" as the opening song. If the group will sing, prepare someone to lead it.

FIRST LEADER:

Throughout the month of May, we remember Mary, the Mother of our Lord Jesus. She was a life-giving caregiver for our Savior, and she remains so for us today. She represents the fullness of holiness, for she was conceived without sin and was assumed into heaven because of her special role in our salvation. She serves as an example for all of us to say, "yes" in practical ways to God's Spirit of goodness. Many Catholics turn to this beloved first disciple of Christ for inspiration and for prayer, particularly as the events of Jesus unfold in Scripture during the Church year.

SONG LEADER:

◆ Gesture for all to stand, and lead the first few verses of the song.

SECOND LEADER:

✜ All make the Sign of the Cross.

In the name of the Father, and of the Son, and of the Holy Spirit. Amen.

Let us pray:
Almighty Father,
we honor Mary as our Mother
because you chose her to be
the human vessel for
your Son Jesus,
who was both human and divine.
Help us to be open to
the same Spirit

PRAYER SERVICE
TO HONOR MARY IN MAY

who appeared to Mary,
guiding her throughout her
challenging life with
the Savior for our world.
We ask this through Christ our Lord.

Amen.

◆ Remain standing and sing Alleluia.

THIRD LEADER: Luke 1:26–38

A reading from the holy Gospel according to
Luke

◆ Read the Gospel passage from the Bible.

The Gospel of the Lord.

◆ All sit and observe silence.

FOURTH LEADER:

◆ Gesture for all to stand.

Let us bring our hopes and needs to God as
we respond, Lord, hear our prayer.
For all mothers,
and those who nurture others
throughout life.
May they be open to
God's creative Spirit to bring
new life into the world.

We pray to the Lord . . .

For those facing difficult decisions.
May they look to Mary
for guidance
in following God's plan.

We pray to the Lord . . .

For all married couples.
May they remain devoted

to God, to each other,
and to their sacrament of marriage,
as Mary and Joseph did.

We pray to the Lord . . .

For the sick and the abandoned.
For those who have passed
to the other side of life.
May they feel the loving arms
of Mary with Jesus.

We pray to the Lord . . .

FIFTH LEADER:

Let us Pray the Hail Mary:

ALL: Hail Mary, full of grace . . .

◆ Pause, and then say:

Let us offer one another the sign of Christ's
peace.

◆ All offer one another a sign of peace.

SIXTH LEADER:

Let us pray Mary's special prayer,
the *Magnificat*:
"My soul magnifies the Lord,
   and my spirit rejoices in God my Savior,
for he has looked with favor on the lowliness
      of his servant.
   Surely, from now on all generations will
      call me blessed;
for the Mighty One has done great things
      for me,
   and holy is his name."

✚ All make the Sign of the Cross.

**In the name of the Father, and of the
Son, and of the Holy Spirit. Amen.**

PRAYER FOR THE WEEK

WITH A READING FROM THE GOSPEL FOR **SUNDAY, MAY 4, 2014**

OPENING

Today's Gospel shows another appearance by Jesus to two disciples on their way to Emmaus. [eh-MAY-uhs].

✝ All make the Sign of the Cross.

In the name of the Father, and of the Son, and of the Holy Spirit. Amen.

PSALM   (For a longer psalm, see page xv.) Psalm 105:1–2, 3–4, 6–7

Let the hearts of those who seek
     the LORD rejoice.

**Let the hearts of those who seek
     the LORD rejoice.**

O give thanks to the LORD, call on his name,
     make known his deeds among the peoples.
Sing to him, sing praises to him;
     tell of all his wonderful works.

**Let the hearts of those who seek
     the LORD rejoice.**

◆ All stand and sing **Alleluia.**

GOSPEL   Luke 24:13, 28–32

A reading from the holy Gospel according to Luke

Now on that same day two of them were going to a village called Emmaus, [eh-MAY-uhs] about seven miles from Jerusalem, and talking with each other about all these things that had happened. As they came near the village to which they were going, he walked ahead as if he were going on. But they urged him strongly, saying, "Stay with us, because it is almost evening and the day is now nearly over." So he went in to stay with them. When he was at the table with them, he took bread, blessed and broke it, and gave it to them. Then their eyes were opened, and they recognized him; and he vanished from their sight. They said to each other, "Were not our hearts burning within us while he was talking to us on the road, while he was opening the scriptures to us?"

The Gospel of the Lord.

◆ All sit and observe silence.

FOR SILENT REFLECTION

Does your heart ever "burn within you"?

CLOSING PRAYER

Let us stand and bring our hopes and needs to God as we pray, "Lord, hear our prayer."

◆ All may add their own prayers here.

Let us pray: **Our Father . . . Amen.**

Lord Jesus,
you revealed yourself
in the breaking of the bread.
Help us to appreciate
your presence in the Eucharist.
We ask this in your name.

Amen.

✝ All make the Sign of the Cross.

OPENING

Today's Gospel shows how far Christ's followers pursued him because of the many miracles and signs they had seen.

✝ All make the Sign of the Cross.

In the name of the Father, and of the Son, and of the Holy Spirit. Amen.

PSALM (For a longer psalm, see page xv.) Psalm 105:1–2, 3–4, 6–7

Let the hearts of those who seek
the LORD rejoice.

**Let the hearts of those who seek
the LORD rejoice.**

O give thanks to the LORD, call on his name,
make known his deeds among the peoples.
Sing to him, sing praises to him;
tell of all his wonderful works.

**Let the hearts of those who seek
the LORD rejoice.**

◆ All stand and sing **Alleluia.**

GOSPEL   John 6:25–29

A reading from the holy Gospel according to John

When they found Jesus on the other side of the sea, they said to him, "Rabbi, when did you come here?" Jesus answered them, "Very truly, I tell you, you are looking for me, not because you saw signs, but because you ate your fill of the loaves. Do not work for the food that perishes, but for the food that endures for eternal life, which the Son of Man will give you. For it is on him that God the Father has set his seal."

Then they said to him, "What must we do to perform the works of God?" Jesus answered them, "This is the work of God, that you believe in him whom he has sent."

The Gospel of the Lord.

◆ All sit and observe silence.

FOR SILENT REFLECTION

For what do you work hard?

CLOSING PRAYER

Let us stand and bring our hopes and needs to God as we pray, "Lord, hear our prayer."

◆ All may add their own prayers here.

Let us pray: **Our Father . . . Amen.**

Almighty God,
you inspire us through
the gift of your Son and
the Eucharistic meal that
we share together.
Give us the grace to
become your living bread.
We ask this through your Son,
Jesus Christ,
who lives and reigns with you
in the unity of the Holy Spirit,
one God, for ever and ever.

Amen.

✝ All make the Sign of the Cross.

PRAYER FOR **TUESDAY** MAY 6, 2014

OPENING

In today's Gospel, the crowd challenges Jesus to perform a miracle right then and there. They demanded a sign to support their belief.

✝ All make the Sign of the Cross.

In the name of the Father, and of the Son, and of the Holy Spirit. Amen.

PSALM (For a longer psalm, see page xv.) Psalm 105:1–2, 3–4, 6–7

Let the hearts of those who seek
the LORD rejoice.

**Let the hearts of those who seek
the LORD rejoice.**

O give thanks to the LORD, call on his name,
make known his deeds among the peoples.
Sing to him, sing praises to him;
tell of all his wonderful works.

**Let the hearts of those who seek
the LORD rejoice.**

◆ All stand and sing **Alleluia.**

GOSPEL   John 6:30–35

A reading from the holy Gospel according to John

The crowd said to Jesus: "What sign are you going to give us then, so that we may see it and believe you? What work are you performing? Our ancestors ate the manna in the wilderness; as it is written, 'He gave them bread from heaven to eat.'" Then Jesus said to them, "Very truly, I tell you, it was not Moses who gave you the bread from heaven, but it is my Father who gives you the true bread from heaven. For the bread of God is that which comes down from heaven and gives life to the world." They said to him, "Sir, give us this bread always." Jesus said to them, "I am the bread of life. Whoever comes to me will never be hungry, and whoever believes in me will never be thirsty."

The Gospel of the Lord.

◆ All sit and observe silence.

FOR SILENT REFLECTION

To what kind of "life" is Jesus referring? What type of "hunger" or "thirst" is he talking about?

CLOSING PRAYER

Let us stand and bring our hopes and needs to God as we pray, "Lord, hear our prayer."

◆ All may add their own prayers here.

Let us pray: **Our Father . . . Amen.**

Lord Jesus,
your Eucharist is our true food.
You nourish us also with
your Word that gives us hope.
Guide us as we take in
your divine presence,
knowing that we become
your strength for others.
We ask this in your name.

Amen.

✝ All make the Sign of the Cross.

OPENING

Today's Gospel provides another look at Jesus's teaching that the bread of life for us all. Jesus also talks about God's will for him and for us, which always leads to everlasting life.

✝ All make the Sign of the Cross.

In the name of the Father, and of the Son, and of the Holy Spirit. Amen.

PSALM   (For a longer psalm, see page xv.) Psalm 105:1–2, 3–4, 6–7

Let the hearts of those who seek
　　the LORD rejoice.

**Let the hearts of those who seek
　　the LORD rejoice.**

O give thanks to the LORD, call on his name,
　　make known his deeds among the peoples.
Sing to him, sing praises to him;
　　tell of all his wonderful works.

**Let the hearts of those who seek
　　the LORD rejoice.**

◆ All stand and sing **Alleluia.**

GOSPEL   John 6:35–40

A reading from the holy Gospel according to John

Jesus said to the crowds, "I am the bread of life. Whoever comes to me will never be hungry, and whoever believes in me will never be thirsty. But I said to you that you have seen me and yet do not believe. Everything that the Father gives me will come to me, and anyone who comes to me I will never drive away; for I have come down from heaven, not to do my own will, but the will of him who sent me. And this is the will of him who sent me, that I should lose nothing of all that he has given me, but raise it up on the last day. This is indeed the will of my Father, that all who see the Son and believe in him may have eternal life; and I will raise them up on the last day."

The Gospel of the Lord.

◆ All sit and observe silence.

FOR SILENT REFLECTION

How will Jesus's bread lead me to life with God?

CLOSING PRAYER

Let us stand and bring our hopes and needs to God as we pray, "Lord, hear our prayer."

◆ All may add their own prayers here.

Let us pray: **Our Father . . . Amen.**

Lord Jesus,
everything you did pointed
to your Father,
who is our Father.
Help us to remain open
to your words of life as well as
your food that nourishes us
completely and
makes us whole.
In your name we pray.

Amen.

✝ All make the Sign of the Cross.

PRAYER FOR **THURSDAY** MAY 8, 2014

OPENING

It's fairly easy to see why some people had difficulty with Jesus talking about himself as the "bread of life." Many neighbors who saw Jesus grow up couldn't understand his words: "I am the living bread that came down from heaven."

✝ All make the Sign of the Cross.

In the name of the Father, and of the Son, and of the Holy Spirit. Amen.

PSALM (For a longer psalm, see page xv.) Psalm 105:1–2, 3–4, 6–7

Let the hearts of those who seek
   the LORD rejoice.

**Let the hearts of those who seek
   the LORD rejoice.**

O give thanks to the LORD, call on his name,
   make known his deeds among the peoples.
Sing to him, sing praises to him;
   tell of all his wonderful works.

**Let the hearts of those who seek
   the LORD rejoice.**

◆ All stand and sing **Alleluia.**

GOSPEL   John 6:44–51

A reading from the holy Gospel according to John

Jesus said to the crowds: "No one can come to me unless drawn by the Father who sent me; and I will raise that person up on the last day. It is written in the prophets, 'And they shall all be taught by God.' Everyone who has heard and learned from the Father comes to me. Not that anyone has seen the Father except the one who is from God; he has seen the Father. Very truly, I tell you, whoever believes has eternal life. I am the bread of life. Your ancestors ate the manna in the wilderness, and they died. This is the bread that comes down from heaven, so that one may eat of it and not die. I am the living bread that came down from heaven. Whoever eats of this bread will live forever; and the bread that I will give for the life of the world is my flesh."

The Gospel of the Lord.

◆ All sit and observe silence.

FOR SILENT REFLECTION

As you listen to these Gospel words, what images of Jesus come to mind? Do you think of Jesus as your real food for life's journey?

CLOSING PRAYER

Let us stand and bring our hopes and needs to God as we pray, "Lord, hear our prayer."

◆ All may add their own prayers here.

Let us pray: **Our Father . . . Amen.**

Lord Jesus,
your food is
all that we truly need.
May we partake of your Eucharist
and know that we are one with you
and our Father
who sent you to us to
teach us how to really live.
We ask this in your name.

Amen.

✝ All make the Sign of the Cross.

OPENING

Today's reading shows the transformation of Saul (who is renamed Paul in a later account). Saul was one of the persecutors of Christians, but God shocked him with a strong message.

✦ All make the Sign of the Cross.

In the name of the Father, and of the Son, and of the Holy Spirit. Amen.

PSALM (For a longer psalm, see page xv.) Psalm 105:1–2, 3–4, 6–7

Let the hearts of those who seek
the LORD rejoice.

**Let the hearts of those who seek
the LORD rejoice.**

O give thanks to the LORD, call on his name,
make known his deeds among the peoples.
Sing to him, sing praises to him;
tell of all his wonderful works.

**Let the hearts of those who seek
the LORD rejoice.**

READING   Acts 9:1–9

A reading from the Acts of the Apostles

Saul, still breathing threats and murder against the disciples of the Lord, went to the high priest and asked him for letters to the synagogues [SIN-uh-gogs] at Damascus [duh-MAS-kuhs], so that if he found any who belonged to the Way, men or women, he might bring them bound to Jerusalem. Now as he was going along and approaching Damascus, suddenly a light from heaven flashed around him. He fell to the ground and heard a voice saying to him, "Saul, Saul, why do you persecute me?" He asked, "Who are you, Lord?" The reply came, "I am Jesus, whom you are persecuting. But get up and enter the city, and you will be told what you are to do." The men who were traveling with him stood speechless because they heard the voice but saw no one. Saul got up from the ground, and though his eyes were open, he could see nothing; so they led him by the hand and brought him into Damascus. For three days he was without sight, and neither ate nor drank.

The Word of the Lord.

◆ All observe silence.

FOR SILENT REFLECTION

Why do you think God chose Saul (St. Paul) to be a disciple?

CLOSING PRAYER

Let us stand and bring our hopes and needs to God as we pray, "Lord, hear our prayer."

◆ All may add their own prayers here.

Let us pray: **Our Father . . . Amen.**

Almighty God,
give us the courage to
be your messenger of
healing and clear vision.
We ask this through our Lord,
Jesus Christ, your Son,
who lives and reigns with you
in the unity of the Holy Spirit,
one God, for ever and ever.

Amen.

✦ All make the Sign of the Cross.

PRAYER FOR THE WEEK

OPENING

In today's Gospel, Jesus talks about a sheep-fold, a place where shepherds gather their flocks for the night under the watchful eye of one caretaker. In the morning, each shepherd calls his sheep and leads them out the gate.

✚ All make the Sign of the Cross.

In the name of the Father, and of the Son, and of the Holy Spirit. Amen.

PSALM (For a longer psalm, see page xv.) Psalm 105:1–2, 3–4, 6–7

Let the hearts of those who seek
the LORD rejoice.

**Let the hearts of those who seek
the LORD rejoice.**

O give thanks to the LORD, call on his name,
make known his deeds among the peoples.
Sing to him, sing praises to him;
tell of all his wonderful works.

**Let the hearts of those who seek
the LORD rejoice.**

◆ All stand and sing **Alleluia.**

GOSPEL   John 10:1–7

A reading from the holy Gospel according to John

Jesus said: "Very truly, I tell you, anyone who does not enter the sheepfold by the gate but climbs in by another way is a thief and a bandit. The one who enters by the gate is the shepherd of the sheep. The gatekeeper opens the gate for him, and the sheep hear his voice. He calls his own sheep by name and leads them out. When he has brought out all his own, he goes ahead of them, and the sheep follow him because they know his voice. They will not follow a stranger, but they will run from him because they do not know the voice of strangers." Jesus used this figure of speech with them, but they did not understand what he was saying to them. So again Jesus said to them, "Very truly, I tell you, I am the gate for the sheep."

The Gospel of the Lord.

◆ All sit and observe silence.

FOR SILENT REFLECTION

When have you followed the voice of the Good Shepherd?

CLOSING PRAYER

Let us stand and bring our hopes and needs to God as we pray, "Lord, hear our prayer."

◆ All may add their own prayers here.

Let us pray: **Our Father . . . Amen.**

Lord Jesus,
help us to follow
your voice,
our Good Shepherd,
who cares for us each day.
In your name we pray.

Amen.

✚ All make the Sign of the Cross.

ALSO ON THIS DAY: Mother's Day

OPENING

We remember Sts. Nereus [NEE-rih-yoos] and Achilleus [uh-KIL-ee-us] today, two martyrs from the first century, who were Roman soldiers who chose to follow Christ rather than persecute believers. We also remember St. Pancras, who was martyred at the age of 14 (in the fourth century) during the persecution of Diocletian.

✚ All make the Sign of the Cross.

In the name of the Father, and of the Son, and of the Holy Spirit. Amen.

PSALM (For a longer psalm, see page xv.) Psalm 105:1–2, 3–4, 6–7

Let the hearts of those who seek
    the LORD rejoice.

**Let the hearts of those who seek
    the LORD rejoice.**

O give thanks to the LORD, call on his name,
    make known his deeds among the peoples.
Sing to him, sing praises to him;
    tell of all his wonderful works.

**Let the hearts of those who seek
    the LORD rejoice.**

◆ All stand and sing **Alleluia.**

GOSPEL   John 10:11–16

A reading from the holy Gospel according to John

Jesus said: "I am the good shepherd. The good shepherd lays down his life for the sheep. The hired hand, who is not the shepherd and does not own the sheep, sees the wolf coming and leaves the sheep and runs away—and the wolf snatches them and scatters them. The hired hand runs away because a hired hand does not care for the sheep. I am the good shepherd. I know my own and my own know me, just as the Father knows me and I know the Father. And I lay down my life for the sheep. I have other sheep that do not belong to this fold. I must bring them also, and they will listen to my voice. So there will be one flock, one shepherd."

The Gospel of the Lord.

◆ All sit and observe silence.

FOR SILENT REFLECTION

What do you think Jesus means when he says that there will be one flock and one shepherd?

CLOSING PRAYER

Let us stand and bring our hopes and needs to God as we pray, "Lord, hear our prayer."

◆ All may add their own prayers here.

Let us pray: **Our Father . . . Amen.**

Lord Jesus,
you came to save all
who believe in you.
Your voice is clear.
Help us to follow you.
We ask this in your name.

Amen.

✚ All make the Sign of the Cross.

291

PRAYER FOR **TUESDAY** MAY 13, 2014

OPENING

Today we celebrate the feast of Our Lady of Fatima. The Church recognizes the appearances of Mary to three children in Portugal in 1917.

✚ All make the Sign of the Cross.

In the name of the Father, and of the Son, and of the Holy Spirit. Amen.

PSALM   (For a longer psalm, see page xv.) Psalm 105:1–2, 3–4, 6–7

Let the hearts of those who seek
    the LORD rejoice.

**Let the hearts of those who seek
    the LORD rejoice.**

O give thanks to the LORD, call on his name,
    make known his deeds among the peoples.
Sing to him, sing praises to him;
    tell of all his wonderful works.

**Let the hearts of those who seek
    the LORD rejoice.**

READING   Acts 11:19–24

A reading from the Acts of the Apostles

Those who were scattered because of the persecution that took place over Stephen traveled as far as Phoenicia [fuh-NEE-shuh], Cyprus [SĪ-pruhs], and Antioch [AN-tee-ahk], and they spoke the word to no one except Jews. But among them were some men of Cyprus and Cyrene, who, on coming to Antioch, spoke to the Hellenists also, proclaiming the Lord Jesus. The hand of the Lord was with them, and a great number became believers and turned to the Lord. News of this came to the ears of the church in Jerusalem, and they sent Barnabas to Antioch. When he came and saw the grace of God, he rejoiced, and he exhorted them all to remain faithful to the Lord with steadfast devotion; for he was a good man, full of the Holy Spirit and of faith. And a great many people were brought to the Lord.

The Word of the Lord.

◆ All observe silence.

FOR SILENT REFLECTION

Who helps us to be good Christians?

CLOSING PRAYER

Let us stand and bring our hopes and needs to God as we pray, "Lord, hear our prayer."

◆ All may add their own prayers here.

Let us pray: **Our Father . . . Amen.**

Lord God,
help us to be courageous
as we assist missionaries
who go to areas
where the story of Jesus
may not be well known.
We ask this through Jesus Christ your Son,
who lives and reigns with you
in unity of the Holy Spirit,
one God, for ever and ever.

Amen.

✚ All make the Sign of the Cross.

OPENING

We remember St. Matthias [muh-THĬ-uhs] today, especially in the reading, which shows the process that the Apostles used to replace Judas, who betrayed Jesus.

✛ All make the Sign of the Cross.

> **In the name of the Father, and of the Son, and of the Holy Spirit. Amen.**

PSALM   (For a longer psalm, see page xv.) Psalm 105:1–2, 3–4, 6–7

Let the hearts of those who seek
    the LORD rejoice.

**Let the hearts of those who seek
    the LORD rejoice.**

O give thanks to the LORD, call on his name,
    make known his deeds among the peoples.
Sing to him, sing praises to him;
    tell of all his wonderful works.

**Let the hearts of those who seek
    the LORD rejoice.**

READING   Acts 1:15–16, 20–26

A reading from the Acts of the Apostles

Peter stood up among the believers and said, "Friends, the scripture had to be fulfilled, which the Holy Spirit through David foretold concerning Judas, who became a guide for those who arrested Jesus. Let another take his position of overseer. So one of the men who have accompanied us during all the time that the Lord Jesus went in and out among us, beginning from the baptism of John until the day when he was taken up from us—one of these must become a witness with us to his resurrection." So they proposed two, Joseph called Barsabbas [bahr-SAH-buhs], who was also known as Justus, and Matthias [muh-THĬ-uhs]. Then they prayed and said, "Lord, you know everyone's heart. Show us which one of these two you have chosen to take the place in this ministry and apostleship from which Judas turned aside to go to his own place." And they cast lots for them, and the lot fell on Matthias; and he was added to the eleven apostles.

The Word of the Lord.

◆ All observe silence.

FOR SILENT REFLECTION

Why do we pray before we make important decisions?

CLOSING PRAYER

Let us stand and bring our hopes and needs to God as we pray, "Lord, hear our prayer."

◆ All may add their own prayers here.

Let us pray: **Our Father . . . Amen.**

Almighty God,
bless us with leaders with integrity
to fill important roles
for your work here on earth.
We ask this in the name of Jesus.

Amen.

✛ All make the Sign of the Cross.

PRAYER FOR **THURSDAY** MAY 15, 2014

OPENING

We remember St. Isidore today, who is the patron saint of farmers and rural communities. He was a deeply religious man who worked on an estate near Madrid, devoted to his farming as well as helping the poor and the proper treatment of animals.

✝ All make the Sign of the Cross.

In the name of the Father, and of the Son, and of the Holy Spirit. Amen.

PSALM   (For a longer psalm, see page xv.) Psalm 105:1–2, 3–4, 6–7

Let the hearts of those who seek
    the LORD rejoice.

**Let the hearts of those who seek
    the LORD rejoice.**

O give thanks to the LORD, call on his name,
    make known his deeds among the peoples.
Sing to him, sing praises to him;
    tell of all his wonderful works.

**Let the hearts of those who seek
    the LORD rejoice.**

◆ All stand and sing **Alleluia.**

GOSPEL   John 13:16–20

A reading from the holy Gospel according to John

Jesus said to his disciples: "Very truly, I tell you, servants are not greater than their master, nor are messengers greater than the one who sent them. If you know these things, you are blessed if you do them.

"I am not speaking of all of you; I know whom I have chosen. But it is to fulfill the scripture, 'The one who ate my bread has lifted his heel against me.' I tell you this now, before it occurs, so that when it does occur, you may believe that I am he. Very truly, I tell you, whoever receives one whom I send receives me; and whoever receives me receives him who sent me."

The Gospel of the Lord.

◆ All sit and observe silence.

FOR SILENT REFLECTION

For whom have you been a servant lately? Why is this important?

CLOSING PRAYER

Let us stand and bring our hopes and needs to God as we pray, "Lord, hear our prayer."

◆ All may add their own prayers here.

Let us pray: **Our Father . . . Amen.**

Lord Jesus,
you remind us to receive those
who receive you.
We are your servants,
and we are blessed
to be of help to others.
Guide us in our mission
of being your messengers of hope.
We ask this in your name.

Amen.

✝ All make the Sign of the Cross.

OPENING

Today's reading shows Paul teaching at a synagogue in a remote part of the Roman empire. He began with details from the Hebrew Scriptures and continued to tell them about the Death and Resurrection of Jesus.

✙ All make the Sign of the Cross.

In the name of the Father, and of the Son, and of the Holy Spirit. Amen.

PSALM (For a longer psalm, see page xv.) Psalm 105:1–2, 3–4, 6–7

Let the hearts of those who seek
    the LORD rejoice.

**Let the hearts of those who seek
    the LORD rejoice.**

O give thanks to the LORD, call on his name,
    make known his deeds among the peoples.
Sing to him, sing praises to him;
    tell of all his wonderful works.

**Let the hearts of those who seek
    the LORD rejoice.**

READING   Acts 13:26–31

A reading from the Acts of the Apostles

When Paul came to Antioch [AN-tee-ahk] in Pisidia [pih-SID-ee-uh], he said in the synagogue: "My brothers, you descendants of Abraham's family, and others who fear God, to us the message of this salvation has been sent. Because the residents of Jerusalem and their leaders did not recognize him or understand the words of the prophets that are read every sabbath, they fulfilled those words by condemning him. Even though they found no cause for a sentence of death, they asked Pilate to have him killed. When they had carried out everything that was written about him, they took him down from the tree and laid him in a tomb. But God raised him from the dead; and for many days he appeared to those who came up with him from Galilee to Jerusalem, and they are now his witnesses to the people."

The Gospel of the Lord.

◆ All observe silence.

FOR SILENT REFLECTION

Are there areas in our communities and around the world that need the Good News?

CLOSING PRAYER

Let us stand and bring our hopes and needs to God as we pray, "Lord, hear our prayer."

◆ All may add their own prayers here.

Let us pray: **Our Father . . . Amen.**

God our Savior,
you sent Paul and his friends
to many areas of the world
to speak of Christ's life,
Death, and Resurrection.
Their hearts were on fire
with your messages of love for everyone.
May we be inspired by
their commitment and courage.
We ask this through your Son Jesus.

Amen.

✙ All make the Sign of the Cross.

PRAYER FOR THE WEEK

WITH A READING FROM THE GOSPEL FOR **SUNDAY, MAY 18, 2014**

OPENING

In today's Gospel, Jesus assures each of us a special place if we live a life of faith.

✚ All make the Sign of the Cross.

In the name of the Father, and of the Son, and of the Holy Spirit. Amen.

PSALM
(For a longer psalm, see page xv.) Psalm 118:1–2 and 4, 22–24, 25–27a

The stone that the builders rejected
  has become the chief cornerstone.

**The stone that the builders rejected
  has become the chief cornerstone.**

O give thanks to the LORD, for he is good;
  his steadfast love endures forever!
Let Israel say,
  "His steadfast love endures forever."
Let those who fear the LORD say,
  "His steadfast love endures forever."

**The stone that the builders rejected
  has become the chief cornerstone.**

◆ All stand and sing **Alleluia.**

GOSPEL
John 14:1–9a

A reading from the holy Gospel according to John

Jesus said to his disciples: "Do not let your hearts be troubled. Believe in God, believe also in me. In my Father's house there are many dwelling places. If it were not so, would I have told you that I go to prepare a place for you? And if I go and prepare a place for you, I will come again and will take you to myself, so that where I am, there you may be also. And you know the way to the place where I am going." Thomas said to him, "Lord, we do not know where you are going. How can we know the way?" Jesus said to him, "I am the way, and the truth, and the life. No one comes to the Father except through me. If you know me, you will know my Father also. From now on you do know him and have seen him." Philip said to him, "Lord, show us the Father, and we will be satisfied." Jesus said to him, "Have I been with you all this time, Philip, and you still do not know me? Whoever has seen me has seen the Father."

The Gospel of the Lord.

◆ All sit and observe silence.

FOR SILENT REFLECTION

How is Jesus "the way, the truth, and the life" for you?

CLOSING PRAYER

Let us stand and bring our hopes and needs to God as we pray, "Lord, hear our prayer."

◆ All may add their own prayers here.

Let us pray: **Our Father . . . Amen.**

Jesus our redeemer,
continue to guide us with
your wisdom:
"I am the way, and the truth,
and the life."
We ask this in your name.

Amen.

✚ All make the Sign of the Cross.

296

OPENING

Today's Gospel shows how we must be committed to following God's commandments of love. Jesus also promises the help of God's Spirit.

✝ All make the Sign of the Cross.

In the name of the Father, and of the Son, and of the Holy Spirit. Amen.

PSALM

(For a longer psalm, see page xv.) Psalm 118:1–2 and 4, 22–24, 25–27a

The stone that the builders rejected
  has become the chief cornerstone.

**The stone that the builders rejected
  has become the chief cornerstone.**

O give thanks to the LORD, for he is good;
  his steadfast love endures forever!
Let Israel say,
  "His steadfast love endures forever."
Let those who fear the LORD say,
  "His steadfast love endures forever."

**The stone that the builders rejected
  has become the chief cornerstone.**

◆ All stand and sing **Alleluia.**

GOSPEL

John 14:21–24

A reading from the holy Gospel according to John

Jesus said to his disciples: "They who have my commandments and keep them are those who love me; and those who love me will be loved by my Father, and I will love them and reveal myself to them." Judas (not Iscariot) said to him, "Lord, how is it that you will reveal yourself to us, and not to the world?" Jesus answered him, "Those who love me will keep my word, and my Father will love them, and we will come to them and make our home with them. Whoever does not love me does not keep my words; and the word that you hear is not mine, but is from the Father who sent me."

The Gospel of the Lord.

◆ All sit and observe silence.

FOR SILENT REFLECTION

What does it mean that God is love? Do you recognize God in the people you love?

CLOSING PRAYER

Let us stand and bring our hopes and needs to God as we pray, "Lord, hear our prayer."

◆ All may add their own prayers here.

Let us pray: **Our Father . . . Amen.**

Lord Jesus,
you ask your friends
then and now to be devoted
to your ways through
love and commitment.
May we allow your Spirit
to always move in us.

Amen.

✝ All make the Sign of the Cross.

PRAYER FOR **TUESDAY** MAY 20, 2014

OPENING

Today we remember St. Bernadine of Siena (1380–1444) who was a gifted preacher, sometimes attracting crowds of 30,000. He ran a hospital to help people suffering from the plague.

✢ All make the Sign of the Cross.

In the name of the Father, and of the Son, and of the Holy Spirit. Amen.

PSALM   (For a longer psalm, see page xv.) Psalm 118:1–2 and 4, 22–24, 25–27a

The stone that the builders rejected has become the chief cornerstone.

The stone that the builders rejected has become the chief cornerstone.

O give thanks to the LORD, for he is good;
his steadfast love endures forever!
Let Israel say,
"His steadfast love endures forever."
Let those who fear the LORD say,
"His steadfast love endures forever."

The stone that the builders rejected has become the chief cornerstone.

READING   Acts 14:19–23

A reading from the Acts of the Apostles

In those days, some Jews came there from Antioch [AN-tee-ahk] and Iconium [Ī-KOH-nee-uhm] and won over the crowds. Then they stoned Paul and dragged him out of the city, supposing that he was dead. But when the disciples surrounded him, he got up and went into the city. The next day he went on with Barnabas to Derbe [DER-bee]. After they had proclaimed the good news to that city and had made many disciples, they returned to Lystra [LĬS-truh], then on to Iconium and Antioch. There they strengthened the souls of the disciples and encouraged them to continue in the faith, saying, "It is through many persecutions that we must enter the kingdom of God." And after they had appointed elders for them in each church, with prayer and fasting they entrusted them to the Lord in whom they had come to believe.

The Word of the Lord.

◆ All observe silence.

FOR SILENT REFLECTION

Have you been inspired by another person's story of faith? How?

CLOSING PRAYER

Let us stand and bring our hopes and needs to God as we pray, "Lord, hear our prayer."

◆ All may add their own prayers here.

Let us pray: **Our Father . . . Amen.**

Lord Jesus,
Paul and his followers were so devoted
to spreading your Word to the Gentiles.
Help us to withstand obstacles and criticisms
that we may hear because of our beliefs.
We ask this in your name.

Amen.

✢ All make the Sign of the Cross.

298

PRAYER FOR **WEDNESDAY**
MAY 21, 2014

OPENING

Today we remember St. Christopher Magallanes and his companions who lived under a very anti-Catholic government in Mexico. These martyrs died in different regions of Mexico in the 1920s.

✦ All make the Sign of the Cross.

In the name of the Father, and of the Son, and of the Holy Spirit. Amen.

PSALM
(For a longer psalm, see page xv.) Psalm 118:1–2 and 4, 22–24, 25–27a

The stone that the builders rejected
  has become the chief cornerstone.

**The stone that the builders rejected
  has become the chief cornerstone.**

O give thanks to the LORD, for he is good;
  his steadfast love endures forever!
Let Israel say,
  "His steadfast love endures forever."
Let those who fear the LORD say,
  "His steadfast love endures forever."

**The stone that the builders rejected
  has become the chief cornerstone.**

◆ All stand and sing **Alleluia.**

GOSPEL
John 15:1–5

A reading from the holy Gospel according to John

Jesus said to his disciples: "I am the true vine, and my Father is the vinegrower. He removes every branch in me that bears no fruit. Every branch that bears fruit he prunes to make it bear more fruit. You have already been cleansed by the word that I have spoken to you. Abide in me as I abide in you. Just as the branch cannot bear fruit by itself unless it abides in the vine, neither can you unless you abide in me. I am the vine, you are the branches. Those who abide in me and I in them bear much fruit, because apart from me you can do nothing."

The Gospel of the Lord.

◆ All sit and observe silence.

FOR SILENT REFLECTION

Why is pruning necessary for healthy growth?

CLOSING PRAYER

Let us stand and bring our hopes and needs to God as we pray, "Lord, hear our prayer."

◆ All may add their own prayers here.

Let us pray: **Our Father . . . Amen.**

Lord Jesus,
you are our true vine,
and we know that
we must stay connected with you
to produce the fruit of our faith.
Help us to stay close through
your sacraments and by
taking to heart all that your Word reveals.
We ask this in your name.

Amen.

✦ All make the Sign of the Cross.

PRAYER FOR **THURSDAY** MAY 22, 2014

OPENING

Today we remember St. Rita of Cascia, who was a wife, mother, widow, and religious sister. Born in Italy in 1381, she wanted to be a nun at a young age, but was pressured to marry a cruel man. After he was killed in a brawl (and her sons had died), she joined a religious order and cared for sick nuns.

✦ All make the Sign of the Cross.

In the name of the Father, and of the Son, and of the Holy Spirit. Amen.

PSALM   (For a longer psalm, see page xv.) Psalm 118:1–2 and 4, 22–24, 25–27a

The stone that the builders rejected
 has become the chief cornerstone.

**The stone that the builders rejected
 has become the chief cornerstone.**

O give thanks to the LORD, for he is good;
 his steadfast love endures forever!
Let Israel say,
 "His steadfast love endures forever."
Let those who fear the LORD say,
 "His steadfast love endures forever."

**The stone that the builders rejected
 has become the chief cornerstone.**

◆ All stand and sing **Alleluia.**

GOSPEL   John 15:9–11

A reading from the holy Gospel according to John

Jesus said to his disciples: "As the Father has loved me, so I have loved you; abide in my love.

If you keep my commandments, you will abide in my love, just as I have kept my Father's commandments and abide in his love. I have said these things to you so that my joy may be in you, and that your joy may be complete."

The Gospel of the Lord.

◆ All sit and observe silence.

FOR SILENT REFLECTION

What is real joy? When have you felt truly joyful?

CLOSING PRAYER

Let us stand and bring our hopes and needs to God as we pray, "Lord, hear our prayer."

◆ All may add their own prayers here.

Let us pray: **Our Father . . . Amen.**

Lord God,
your Son's comforting words
show how close you are with Jesus,
and how close we are to you as well.
We thank you for your everlasting love.
Help us to love others as you love us.
We ask this through Jesus Christ
your Son,
who lives and reigns with you
in unity of the Holy Spirit,
one God, for ever and ever.

Amen.

✦ All make the Sign of the Cross.

300

OPENING

Today's Gospel reveals again how we need to love one another selflessly. This is God's desire for us: total love, complete commitment.

✚ All make the Sign of the Cross.

In the name of the Father, and of the Son, and of the Holy Spirit. Amen.

PSALM

(For a longer psalm, see page xv.) Psalm 118:1–2 and 4, 22–24, 25–27a

The stone that the builders rejected
  has become the chief cornerstone.

**The stone that the builders rejected
  has become the chief cornerstone.**

O give thanks to the LORD, for he is good;
  his steadfast love endures forever!
Let Israel say,
  "His steadfast love endures forever."
Let those who fear the LORD say,
  "His steadfast love endures forever."

**The stone that the builders rejected
  has become the chief cornerstone.**

◆ All stand and sing **Alleluia.**

GOSPEL

John 15:12–16a

A reading from the holy Gospel according to John

Jesus said to his disciples: "This is my commandment, that you love one another as I have loved you. No one has greater love than this, to lay down one's life for one's friends. You are my friends if you do what I command you. I do not call you servants any longer, because the servant does not know what the master is doing; but I have called you friends, because I have made known to you everything that I have heard from my Father. You did not choose me but I chose you."

The Gospel of the Lord.

◆ All sit and observe silence.

FOR SILENT REFLECTION

We can be assured that with God we have a life of abundant love. How can I respond to this gift from my Creator?

CLOSING PRAYER

Let us stand and bring our hopes and needs to God as we pray, "Lord, hear our prayer."

◆ All may add their own prayers here.

Let us pray: **Our Father . . . Amen.**

Lord Jesus,
we are grateful that you
chose us to be your
friends and followers.
May your love continue
to lead us to love others.
We ask this in your name.

Amen.

✚ All make the Sign of the Cross.

PRAYER SERVICE
FOR ASCENSION

Prepare six leaders and a song leader for this service. The second and third leaders will need Bibles to read the Scripture passages and may need help finding and practicing them. You may wish to begin by singing "All Will Be Well" and end with "Sing Out, Earth and Skies." Help the song leader prepare to lead the singing.

SONG LEADER:
Please stand and join in singing our opening song.

FIRST LEADER:
So if you have been raised with Christ, seek the things that are above, where Christ is, seated at the right hand of God.

ALL: Amen.

FIRST LEADER:
Today we celebrate the Feast of the Ascension of the Lord. We are joyful on this 40th day of Easter because Jesus returned to heaven to be with God—his promise to the world so that we could experience his Presence in Spirit forever!

✚ All make the Sign of the Cross.

In the name of the Father, and of the Son, and of the Holy Spirit. Amen.

Let us pray:
Almighty God,
you fulfilled your promise
of sending a Savior
to redeem the world.
Now he sits at your right hand
and your Spirit guides us
with holy Presence.
Help us to listen and act according to
your will

so that we can enter into
your kingdom too.
We ask this through Christ our Lord.

ALL: Amen.

◆ Gesture for all to sit.

SECOND LEADER: Colossians 3:2–4
A reading from the Letter of St. Paul to the
Colossians

◆ Read the Scripture passage from the Bible.

The Word of the Lord.

◆ All observe silence.

THIRD LEADER: Acts 1:6–11
A reading from the Acts of the Apostles

◆ Read the Scripture passage from the Bible.

◆ All observe silence.

FOURTH LEADER:
Let us stand and bring our hopes and needs
to God as we pray, "Lord, hear our prayer."

For our brothers and sisters around the world
who do not know Christ.
May they experience
our Risen Lord in eternity.

We pray to the Lord . . .

For our parents and family members
who care for us.
May we remain grateful for their
acts of sacrificial love
that are a reflection of
God's abundant love for us.

We pray to the Lord . . .

For the teachers, school assistants,
and coaches who
guide us in our school activities.
May they continue to
teach us about God
through their
kindness and generosity.

We pray to the Lord . . .

For those who suffer from
illness, hunger, or political strife.
For those who have died.

We pray to the Lord . . .

FIFTH LEADER:
Let us pray the prayer that Jesus taught us:
Our Father . . . Amen.

◆ Pause and then say the following:

Let us offer one another the sign of Christ's
peace.

◆ All offer one another a sign of peace.

SIXTH LEADER:
Let us pray:
Lord our God,
your immense love for us
shines for all to see
in the glory of your Resurrection
and in your return to God.
We praise you for your Spirit
of truth and light
and the promise of your
return again.
We ask this through Christ our Lord.

ALL: Amen.

PRAYER FOR THE WEEK

SONG LEADER:
Please join in singing our closing song.

OPENING

In today's Gospel, Jesus talks about the Spirit whom Jesus will send to be with us always.

✚ All make the Sign of the Cross.

In the name of the Father, and of the Son, and of the Holy Spirit. Amen.

PSALM
(For a longer psalm, see page xv.) Psalm 118:1–2 and 4, 22–24, 25–27a

The stone that the builders rejected
   has become the chief cornerstone.

**The stone that the builders rejected
   has become the chief cornerstone.**

O give thanks to the LORD, for he is good;
   his steadfast love endures forever!
Let Israel say,
   "His steadfast love endures forever."
Let those who fear the LORD say,
   "His steadfast love endures forever."

**The stone that the builders rejected
   has become the chief cornerstone.**

◆ All stand and sing **Alleluia.**

GOSPEL
John 14:15–20

A reading from the holy Gospel according to John

Jesus said to his disciples: "If you love me, you will keep my commandments. And I will ask the Father, and he will give you another Advocate, to be with you forever. This is the Spirit of truth, whom the world cannot receive, because it neither sees him nor knows him. You know him, because he abides with you, and he will be in you.

"I will not leave you orphaned; I am coming to you. In a little while the world will no longer see me, but you will see me; because I live, you also will live. On that day you will know that I am in my Father, and you in me, and I in you."

The Gospel of the Lord.

◆ All sit and observe silence.

FOR SILENT REFLECTION

When do you see signs of God's Spirit? How is the Holy Spirit an advocate?

CLOSING PRAYER

Let us stand and bring our hopes and needs to God as we pray, "Lord, hear our prayer."

◆ All may add their own prayers here.

Let us pray: **Our Father . . . Amen.**

Lord Jesus,
you reassure us with your Spirit
who will never leave us.
Guide us with your Spirit,
who is as close as our breath.
We ask this in your name.

Amen.

✚ All make the Sign of the Cross.

OPENING

Today we remember St. Philip Neri, an Italian born in 1515, who had a very engaging personality. After ordination, his sense of humor and good nature attracted many people to his prayer meetings, filled with song and informal talks. He was also known for his prayer, "Let me get through today, and I shall not fear tomorrow."

✝ All make the Sign of the Cross.

In the name of the Father, and of the Son, and of the Holy Spirit. Amen.

PSALM   (For a longer psalm, see page xv.) Psalm 118:1–2 and 4, 22–24, 25–27a

The stone that the builders rejected
  has become the chief cornerstone.

**The stone that the builders rejected
  has become the chief cornerstone.**

O give thanks to the LORD, for he is good;
  his steadfast love endures forever!
Let Israel say,
  "His steadfast love endures forever."
Let those who fear the LORD say,
  "His steadfast love endures forever."

**The stone that the builders rejected
  has become the chief cornerstone.**

◆ All stand and sing **Alleluia.**

GOSPEL   John 15:26—16:4a

A reading from the holy Gospel according to John

Jesus said to his disciples: "When the Advocate comes, whom I will send to you from the Father, the Spirit of truth who comes from the Father, he will testify on my behalf. You also are to testify because you have been with me from the beginning.

"I have said these things to you to keep you from stumbling. They will put you out of the synagogues. They will do this because they have not known the Father or me. But I have said these things to you so that when their hour comes you may remember that I told you about them."

The Gospel of the Lord.

◆ All sit and observe silence.

FOR SILENT REFLECTION

Have you ever been criticized for your beliefs? Why? How did you respond?

CLOSING PRAYER

Let us stand and bring our hopes and needs to God as we pray, "Lord, hear our prayer."

◆ All may add their own prayers here.

Let us pray: **Our Father . . . Amen.**

Lord Jesus,
you prepared your friends
who would be rejected by
community leaders.
Help us to be thankful for our
religious freedom and how we can
express our love for you.
In your name we pray.

Amen.

✝ All make the Sign of the Cross.

PRAYER FOR **TUESDAY** **MAY 27, 2014**

OPENING

Today we remember St. Augustine of Canterbury. In the sixth century, he led a group from Rome to do missionary work, constructed churches and monasteries, and worked with Britons with their Celtic rites and feasts.

✦ All make the Sign of the Cross.

In the name of the Father, and of the Son, and of the Holy Spirit. Amen.

PSALM

(For a longer psalm, see page xv.) Psalm 118:1–2 and 4, 22–24, 25–27a

The stone that the builders rejected
has become the chief cornerstone.

**The stone that the builders rejected
has become the chief cornerstone.**

O give thanks to the LORD, for he is good;
his steadfast love endures forever!
Let Israel say,
"His steadfast love endures forever."
Let those who fear the LORD say,
"His steadfast love endures forever."

**The stone that the builders rejected
has become the chief cornerstone.**

READING

Acts 16:25–32

A reading from the Acts of the Apostles

About midnight Paul and Silas were praying and singing hymns to God, and the prisoners were listening to them. Suddenly there was an earthquake, so violent that the foundations of the prison were shaken; and immediately all the doors were opened and everyone's chains were unfastened. When the jailer woke up and saw the prison doors wide open, he drew his sword and was about to kill himself, since he supposed that the prisoners had escaped. But Paul shouted in a loud voice, "Do not harm yourself, for we are all here." The jailer called for lights, and rushing in, he fell down trembling before Paul and Silas. Then he brought them outside and said, "Sirs, what must I do to be saved?" They answered, "Believe on the Lord Jesus, and you will be saved, you and your household."

The Word of the Lord.

◆ All observe silence.

FOR SILENT REFLECTION

What were the surprises in the reading today?

CLOSING PRAYER

Let us stand and bring our hopes and needs to God as we pray, "Lord, hear our prayer."

◆ All may add their own prayers here.

Let us pray: **Our Father . . . Amen.**

Spirit of Wonder,
you open doors and hearts
for strong people of faith.
Help us to call upon your name
in stressful times.
We ask this through Christ our Lord.
Amen.

✦ All make the Sign of the Cross.

OPENING

Today's reading shows Paul preaching about God's creation.

✛ All make the Sign of the Cross.

In the name of the Father, and of the Son, and of the Holy Spirit. Amen.

PSALM

(For a longer psalm, see page xv.) Psalm 118:1–2 and 4, 22–24, 25–27a

The stone that the builders rejected
  has become the chief cornerstone.

**The stone that the builders rejected
  has become the chief cornerstone.**

O give thanks to the LORD, for he is good;
  his steadfast love endures forever!
Let Israel say,
  "His steadfast love endures forever."
Let those who fear the LORD say,
  "His steadfast love endures forever."

**The stone that the builders rejected
  has become the chief cornerstone.**

READING

Acts 17:22–28

A reading from the Acts of the Apostles

Then Paul stood in front of the Areopagus and said, "Athenians, I see how extremely religious you are in every way. For as I went through the city and looked carefully at the objects of your worship, I found among them an altar with the inscription, 'To an unknown god.' What therefore you worship as unknown, this I proclaim to you. The God who made the world and everything in it, he who is Lord of heaven and earth, does not live in shrines made by human hands, nor is he served by human hands, as though he needed anything, since he himself gives to all mortals life and breath and all things. From one ancestor he made all nations to inhabit the whole earth, and he allotted the times of their existence and the boundaries of the places where they would live, so that they would search for God and perhaps grope for him and find him—though indeed he is not far from each one of us. For 'In him we live and move and have our being'; as even some of your own poets have said, 'For we too are his offspring.'"

The Word of the Lord.

◆ All observe silence.

FOR SILENT REFLECTION

What are some of God's greatest creations?

CLOSING PRAYER

Let us stand and bring our hopes and needs to God as we pray, "Lord, hear our prayer."

◆ All may add their own prayers here.

Let us pray: **Our Father . . . Amen.**

Almighty God,
in you we "live and move and have
our being," for apart from you,
life would have no meaning.
Thank you for the gift of your Son,
who gave us the Good News
of our life with you.
In Jesus's name we pray.

Amen.

✛ All make the Sign of the Cross.

PRAYER FOR **THURSDAY** MAY 29, 2014

OPENING

Today we celebrate Ascension Thursday in some parts of the United States. For this prayer service, see pages 302–303.

✚ All make the Sign of the Cross.

In the name of the Father, and of the Son, and of the Holy Spirit. Amen.

PSALM

(For a longer psalm, see page xv.) Psalm 118:1–2 and 4, 22–24, 25–27a

The stone that the builders rejected
  has become the chief cornerstone.

**The stone that the builders rejected
  has become the chief cornerstone.**

O give thanks to the LORD, for he is good;
  his steadfast love endures forever!
Let Israel say,
  "His steadfast love endures forever."
Let those who fear the LORD say,
  "His steadfast love endures forever."

**The stone that the builders rejected
  has become the chief cornerstone.**

READING

Acts 18:1–5

A reading from the Acts of the Apostles

Paul left Athens and went to Corinth. There he found a Jew named Aquila, a native of Pontus, who had recently come from Italy with his wife Priscilla, because Claudius had ordered all Jews to leave Rome. Paul went to see them, and, because he was of the same trade, he stayed with them, and they worked together— by trade they were tentmakers. Every sabbath he would argue in the synagogue and would try to convince Jews and Greeks. When Silas and Timothy arrived from Macedonia, Paul was occupied with proclaiming the word, testifying to the Jews that the Messiah was Jesus.

The Word of the Lord.

◆ All observe silence.

FOR SILENT REFLECTION

Why is it important to be with people who share our faith?

CLOSING PRAYER

Let us stand and bring our hopes and needs to God as we pray, "Lord, hear our prayer."

◆ All may add their own prayers here.

Let us pray: **Our Father . . . Amen.**

God Almighty,
you give us hope when
we are feeling discouraged.
You provide us
opportunities for growth.
Help us to discover
what leads us closer to you.
We ask this through your Son Jesus,
our Lord and Savior.

Amen.

✚ All make the Sign of the Cross.

OPENING

In today's Gospel, Jesus describes some of the anguish of being a Christian as well as the joy of his return on the last day.

✜ All make the Sign of the Cross.

In the name of the Father, and of the Son, and of the Holy Spirit. Amen.

PSALM

(For a longer psalm, see page xv.) Psalm 118:1–2 and 4, 22–24, 25–27a

The stone that the builders rejected
  has become the chief cornerstone.

**The stone that the builders rejected
  has become the chief cornerstone.**

O give thanks to the LORD, for he is good;
  his steadfast love endures forever!
Let Israel say,
  "His steadfast love endures forever."
Let those who fear the LORD say,
  "His steadfast love endures forever."

**The stone that the builders rejected
  has become the chief cornerstone.**

◆ All stand and sing **Alleluia**.

GOSPEL

John 16:20–23

A reading from the holy Gospel according to John

Jesus said to his disciples: "Very truly, I tell you, you will weep and mourn, but the world will rejoice; you will have pain, but your pain will turn into joy. When a woman is in labor, she has pain, because her hour has come. But when her child is born, she no longer remembers the anguish because of the joy of having brought a human being into the world. So you have pain now; but I will see you again, and your hearts will rejoice, and no one will take your joy from you.

"On that day you will ask nothing of me. Very truly, I tell you, if you ask anything of the Father in my name, he will give it to you."

The Gospel of the Lord.

◆ All sit and observe silence.

FOR SILENT REFLECTION

What are some examples of how we work hard for a long-term goal?

CLOSING PRAYER

Let us stand and bring our hopes and needs to God as we pray, "Lord, hear our prayer."

◆ All may add their own prayers here.

Let us pray: **Our Father . . . Amen.**

Lord Jesus,
you reassure us of the joy
we'll experience when
we see you again.
And you remind us to
continue talking with you,
asking you for what we need.
Guide us in our prayer, Lord.
Help us to always
confide in you for
our every desire.
In your name we pray.

Amen.

✜ All make the Sign of the Cross.

PRAYER FOR THE WEEK

OPENING

(For the Ascension of the Lord, use the prayer service on pages 302 and 303.) Today's Gospel shows Jesus giving authority to the Apostles to baptize in the name of the Father, Son, and Spirit, and to leave the comfort of their own community.

✚ All make the Sign of the Cross.

In the name of the Father, and of the Son, and of the Holy Spirit. Amen.

PSALM
(For a longer psalm, see page xv.) Psalm 118:1–2 and 4, 22–24, 25–27a

The stone that the builders rejected
  has become the chief cornerstone.

**The stone that the builders rejected
  has become the chief cornerstone.**

O give thanks to the LORD, for he is good;
  his steadfast love endures forever!
Let Israel say,
  "His steadfast love endures forever."
Let those who fear the LORD say,
  "His steadfast love endures forever."

**The stone that the builders rejected
  has become the chief cornerstone.**

◆ All stand and sing **Alleluia.**

GOSPEL
Matthew 28:16–20

A reading from the holy Gospel according to Matthew

The eleven disciples went to Galilee, to the mountain to which Jesus had directed them. When they saw him, they worshiped him; but some doubted. And Jesus came and said to them, "All authority in heaven and on earth has been given to me. Go therefore and make disciples of all nations, baptizing them In the name of the Father and of the Son and of the Holy Spirit, and teaching them to obey everything that I have commanded you. And remember, I am with you always, to the end of the age."

The Gospel of the Lord.

◆ All sit and observe silence.

FOR SILENT REFLECTION

When have I left my own "comfort zone" to talk about Christ with others?

CLOSING PRAYER

Let us stand and bring our hopes and needs to God as we pray, "Lord, hear our prayer."

◆ All may add their own prayers here.

Let us pray: **Our Father . . . Amen.**

Lord Jesus,
you commissioned your friends
to act in your name
and to go to
all the nations.
Give us the courage to
go beyond our personal borders
to be your disciples.
In your name we pray.

Amen.

✚ All make the Sign of the Cross.

OPENING

Today we remember Sts. Marcellinus and Peter from the Church's early centuries, who were martyred under the persecution of Diocletian.

✚ All make the Sign of the Cross.

In the name of the Father, and of the Son, and of the Holy Spirit. Amen.

PSALM
(For a longer psalm, see page xv.) Psalm 118:1–2 and 4, 22–24, 25–27a

The stone that the builders rejected
   has become the chief cornerstone.

**The stone that the builders rejected
   has become the chief cornerstone.**

O give thanks to the LORD, for he is good;
   his steadfast love endures forever!
Let Israel say,
   "His steadfast love endures forever."
Let those who fear the LORD say,
   "His steadfast love endures forever."

**The stone that the builders rejected
   has become the chief cornerstone.**

READING
Acts 19:1–7

A reading from the Acts of the Apostles

While Apollos was in Corinth, Paul passed through the interior regions and came to Ephesus [EF-uh-suhs], where he found some disciples. He said to them, "Did you receive the Holy Spirit when you became believers?" They replied, "No, we have not even heard that there is a Holy Spirit." Then he said, "Into what then were you baptized?" They answered, "Into John's baptism." Paul said, "John baptized with the baptism of repentance, telling the people to believe in the one who was to come after him, that is, in Jesus." On hearing this, they were baptized in the name of the Lord Jesus. When Paul had laid his hands on them, the Holy Spirit came upon them, and they spoke in tongues and prophesied—altogether there were about twelve of them.

The Word of the Lord.

◆ All observe silence.

FOR SILENT REFLECTION

Do you know the words of Baptism? Why are these words important?

CLOSING PRAYER

Let us stand and bring our hopes and needs to God as we pray, "Lord, hear our prayer."

◆ All may add their own prayers here.

Let us pray: **Our Father . . . Amen.**

Almighty God,
the flowing water of our Baptism
makes us a new creation
and gives us strength for our journey.
Guide us in our own travels
as we act in Christ's name.
We ask this in the name of your Son,
who lives and reigns with you
in the unity of the Holy Spirit,
one God, for ever and ever.

Amen.

✚ All make the Sign of the Cross.

PRAYER FOR **TUESDAY** JUNE 3, 2014

OPENING

Today we remember St. Charles Lwanga and his companions who were martyred in 1886 in Africa. Charles assisted several helpers to remain chaste and faithful as they were forced to serve under an abusive leader.

✝ All make the Sign of the Cross.

In the name of the Father, and of the Son, and of the Holy Spirit. Amen.

PSALM

(For a longer psalm, see page xv.) Psalm 118:1–2 and 4, 22–24, 25–27a

The stone that the builders rejected has become the chief cornerstone.

The stone that the builders rejected has become the chief cornerstone.

O give thanks to the LORD, for he is good;
  his steadfast love endures forever!
Let Israel say,
  "His steadfast love endures forever."
Let those who fear the LORD say,
  "His steadfast love endures forever."

The stone that the builders rejected has become the chief cornerstone.

◆ All stand and sing **Alleluia.**

GOSPEL

John 17:1–5

A reading from the holy Gospel according to John

Jesus looked up to heaven and said, "Father, the hour has come; glorify your Son so that the Son may glorify you, since you have given him authority over all people, to give eternal life to all whom you have given him. And this is eternal life, that they may know you, the only true God, and Jesus Christ whom you have sent. I glorified you on earth by finishing the work that you gave me to do. So now, Father, glorify me in your own presence with the glory that I had in your presence before the world existed."

The Gospel of the Lord.

◆ All sit and observe silence.

FOR SILENT REFLECTION

Why do you think Jesus asks his Father to glorify him?

CLOSING PRAYER

Let us stand and bring our hopes and needs to God as we pray, "Lord, hear our prayer."

◆ All may add their own prayers here.

Let us pray: **Our Father . . . Amen.**

Lord Jesus,
you were with God from all eternity.
Help us to glorify you with our lives
so that we may also be with you forever.
We ask this in your name.

Amen.

✝ All make the Sign of the Cross.

OPENING

Today's reading reflects Paul's tearful farewell to church leaders in Ephesus. He warns them to beware of teachers who distort the truth.

✤ All make the Sign of the Cross.

In the name of the Father, and of the Son, and of the Holy Spirit. Amen.

PSALM

(For a longer psalm, see page xv.) Psalm 118:1–2 and 4, 22–24, 25–27a

The stone that the builders rejected
  has become the chief cornerstone.

**The stone that the builders rejected
  has become the chief cornerstone.**

O give thanks to the LORD, for he is good;
  his steadfast love endures forever!
Let Israel say,
  "His steadfast love endures forever."
Let those who fear the LORD say,
  "His steadfast love endures forever."

**The stone that the builders rejected
  has become the chief cornerstone.**

READING

Acts 20:32–37

A reading from the Acts of the Apostles

At Miletus, Paul spoke to the presbyters of the Church of Ephesus: "And now I commend you to God and to the message of his grace, a message that is able to build you up and to give you the inheritance among all who are sanctified. I coveted no one's silver or gold or clothing. You know for yourselves that I worked with my own hands to support myself and my companions. In all this I have given you an example that by such work we must support the weak, remembering the words of the Lord Jesus, for he himself said, 'It is more blessed to give than to receive.'"

When he had finished speaking, he knelt down with them all and prayed.

The Word of the Lord.

◆ All observe silence.

FOR SILENT REFLECTION

What do you think Paul means when he says "It is more blessed to give than receive"?

CLOSING PRAYER

Let us stand and bring our hopes and needs to God as we pray, "Lord, hear our prayer."

◆ All may add their own prayers here.

Let us pray: **Our Father . . . Amen.**

Almighty God,
your servant Paul inspired
church leaders in Ephesus
to spread your Word.
Help us to be ready to
carry your message
in our words and actions.
We ask this through Jesus Christ
your Son, who lives and reigns with you
in the unity of the Holy Spirit,
one God, for ever and ever.

Amen.

✤ All make the Sign of the Cross.

PRAYER FOR **THURSDAY** JUNE 5, 2014

OPENING

Today we remember St. Boniface (672–754) who was known as the "apostle of the Germans." Boniface also established monasteries where several monks and nuns followed him from other regions to help with religious education.

✛ All make the Sign of the Cross.

In the name of the Father, and of the Son, and of the Holy Spirit. Amen.

PSALM (For a longer psalm, see page xv.) Psalm 118:1–2 and 4, 22–24, 25–27a

The stone that the builders rejected
  has become the chief cornerstone.

**The stone that the builders rejected
  has become the chief cornerstone.**

O give thanks to the LORD, for he is good;
  his steadfast love endures forever!
Let Israel say,
  "His steadfast love endures forever."
Let those who fear the LORD say,
  "His steadfast love endures forever."

**The stone that the builders rejected
  has become the chief cornerstone.**

READING Acts 23:6–11

A reading from the Acts of the Apostles

When Paul noticed that some were Sadducees [SAD-you-seez] and others were Pharisees [FAYR-uh-seez], he called out in the council, "Brothers, I am a Pharisee, a son of Pharisees. I am on trial concerning the hope of the resurrection of the dead." When he said this, a dissension began between the Pharisees and the Sadducees, and the assembly was divided. (The Sadducees say that there is no resurrection, or angel, or spirit; but the Pharisees acknowledge all three.) Then a great clamor arose, and certain scribes of the Pharisees' group stood up and contended, "We find nothing wrong with this man. What if a spirit or an angel has spoken to him?" When the dissension became violent, the tribune, fearing that they would tear Paul to pieces, ordered the soldiers to go down, take him by force, and bring him into the barracks. That night the Lord stood near him and said, "Keep up your courage! For just as you have testified for me in Jerusalem, so you must bear witness also in Rome."

The Word of the Lord.

◆ All observe silence.

FOR SILENT REFLECTION

What gives us courage to speak the truth?

CLOSING PRAYER

Let us stand and bring our hopes and needs to God as we pray, "Lord, hear our prayer."

◆ All may add their own prayers here.

Let us pray: **Our Father . . . Amen.**

Lord Jesus,
give us the courage to stand up
for what is good and true.
In your name we pray.

Amen.

✛ All make the Sign of the Cross.

OPENING

Today we remember St. Norbert, who founded religious orders in France in the 12th century. He also felt called to revitalize many of the faithful who had become lukewarm about their beliefs.

✚ All make the Sign of the Cross.

In the name of the Father, and of the Son, and of the Holy Spirit. Amen.

PPSALM (For a longer psalm, see page xv.) Psalm 118:1–2 and 4, 22–24, 25–27a

The stone that the builders rejected
  has become the chief cornerstone.

**The stone that the builders rejected
  has become the chief cornerstone.**

O give thanks to the LORD, for he is good;
  his steadfast love endures forever!
Let Israel say,
  "His steadfast love endures forever."
Let those who fear the LORD say,
  "His steadfast love endures forever."

**The stone that the builders rejected
  has become the chief cornerstone.**

◆ All stand and sing **Alleluia.**

GOSPEL   John 21:15–17

A reading from the holy Gospel according to John

When they had finished breakfast, Jesus said to Simon Peter, "Simon son of John, do you love me more than these?" He said to him, "Yes, Lord; you know that I love you." Jesus said to him, "Feed my lambs." A second time he said to him, "Simon son of John, do you love me?" He said to him, "Yes, Lord; you know that I love you." Jesus said to him, "Tend my sheep." He said to him the third time, "Simon son of John, do you love me?" Peter felt hurt because he said to him the third time, "Do you love me?" And he said to him, "Lord, you know everything; you know that I love you." Jesus said to him, "Feed my sheep."

The Gospel of the Lord.

◆ All sit and observe silence.

FOR SILENT REFLECTION

Why did Jesus ask Peter to show his love by tending his sheep?

CLOSING PRAYER

Let us stand and bring our hopes and needs to God as we pray, "Lord, hear our prayer."

◆ All may add their own prayers here.

Let us pray: **Our Father . . . Amen.**

Lord Jesus,
you asked Peter three times
about his devotion to you.
Help us to love you completely
with our lives,
always committed to new life
because of your Resurrection.
We ask this in your name.

Amen.

✚ All make the Sign of the Cross.

PRAYER FOR THE WEEK

OPENING

On this day of Pentecost (50 days after Easter), we celebrate the birth of the Church. God sends his Holy Spirit upon the Apostles and gives them many gifts. In today's Gospel, listen to Jesus as he entrusts some of God's power to his friends.

✦ All make the Sign of the Cross.

In the name of the Father, and of the Son, and of the Holy Spirit. Amen.

PSALM   (For a longer psalm, see page xv.) Psalm 118:1–2 and 4, 22–24, 25–27a

The stone that the builders rejected
   has become the chief cornerstone.

**The stone that the builders rejected
   has become the chief cornerstone.**

O give thanks to the LORD, for he is good;
   his steadfast love endures forever!
Let Israel say,
   "His steadfast love endures forever."
Let those who fear the LORD say,
   "His steadfast love endures forever."

**The stone that the builders rejected
   has become the chief cornerstone.**

◆ All stand and sing **Alleluia.**

GOSPEL   John 20:19–23

A reading from the holy Gospel according to John

When it was evening on that day, the first day of the week, and the doors of the house where the disciples had met were locked for fear of the Jews, Jesus came and stood among them and said, "Peace be with you." After he said this, he showed them his hands and his side. Then the disciples rejoiced when they saw the Lord. Jesus said to them again, "Peace be with you. As the Father has sent me, so I send you." When he had said this, he breathed on them and said to them, "Receive the Holy Spirit. If you forgive the sins of any, they are forgiven them; if you retain the sins of any, they are retained."

The Gospel of the Lord.

◆ All sit and observe silence.

FOR SILENT REFLECTION

How have you been inspired by God's Spirit to be Christ for the world?

CLOSING PRAYER

Let us stand and bring our hopes and needs to God as we pray, "Lord, hear our prayer."

◆ All may add their own prayers here.

Let us pray: **Our Father . . . Amen.**

Almighty God,
we thank you for your Spirit
who guides us in the
way of peace and reconciliation.
May we always be open to
receiving this great gift.
We ask this through Christ our Lord.

Amen.

✦ All make the Sign of the Cross.

ORDINARY TIME SUMMER

MONDAY JUNE 9, 2014, TO FRIDAY, JUNE 27, 2014

ORDINARY TIME

SUMMER

THE MEANING OF ORDINARY TIME

Jesus said, "I am the vine, you are the branches. Those who abide in me and I in them bear much fruit, because apart from me you can do nothing" (John 15:5).

A vine begins as a single branch. As it grows, new branches begin to grow from the first one. Then more branches form. The whole vine is made up of many branches that spread and grow. A vine must have roots. Jesus is the vine rooted in the eternal love of the Father. The Holy Spirit helps the branches to grow strong and beautiful. The whole vine is made up of many branches that spread and grow as God's love grows in them.

In the parable of the true vine, Jesus tells us that he is the whole vine, while each of us is a branch on that one plant. Although it may seem as though each of us is separate and alone, Jesus says that we need each other just as each branch of the vine depends on all the others.

During Lent we studied the great commandment (see The Meaning of Lent, page 214). When we love God and love our neighbor the way that Jesus taught, that love draws us closer to the ones we love. Through our love for one another, we begin to share in a life that is stronger and bigger than we are by ourselves.

Did you know that right after people are baptized, we call them *neophytes* [NEE-oh-fites], a word that means "new, young plants"? People who have just been baptized are brand-new branches sprouting on the True Vine that is the body of Christ. When a new branch sprouts on a vine, we can see that the vine is growing.

Remember that Ordinary Time is a time of precious growth and change. Each of us grows in holiness during Ordinary Time, but we do not just grow by ourselves apart from other people. Because God's love is the source of our growth, as we grow in holiness, we also grow closer together.

Jesus tells us to "abide" in him. *To abide* means to stay or to remain. When the branches remain attached to the vine, they continue to receive God's life and love. There are many ways we can remain in Jesus. For example, how does Holy Communion help us to stay part of Christ's Body, the Vine of Life? What do we receive from God at Mass? And what do we offer back to God? When we pray, we turn to God and open our hearts to him. When we lift our thoughts and hopes to God, our souls rest in him. We also come closer to God by doing loving acts. Whenever we open our hearts to God in prayer, and make room in our hearts for others, God's love abides in us.

Jesus promises that when we *abide* in his love, we will "bear fruit." What is this marvelous fruit that grows from us, the branches of the True Vine? Can it be sweet, life-giving, and satisfying like fruit from a tree? Or is it something even more wonderful?

People have been thinking and praying over the words of Jesus for hundreds of years. When we ponder these words in our study, turn to them in our prayer, and celebrate them in our worship, we will discover something wonderful. Our study, prayer, and worship will bear fruit. Jesus himself tells us, "I have said these things to you so that my joy may be in you, and that your joy may be complete" (John 15:11).

PREPARING TO CELEBRATE ORDINARY TIME IN THE CLASSROOM

This will be your last time changing the prayer table cloth this year. Even if you haven't had a procession each time the cloth changes, try to have one now. As the school year winds down, it is good to bring the students' focus squarely on the prayer life of your classroom community. You may wish to invite the students to choose something to carry in the procession that has helped

318

their spiritual growth this year. Clear an area near the prayer table, spread it with a green cloth, and let the children place their objects there. As a final project, ask them to write a short essay or poem about the significance of the object they chose. Suggest that they illustrate their work. Invite them to share their writings aloud during one of your final prayer times together. (Some students might feel uncomfortable sharing private thoughts in front of a group. Don't force them to participate in this aspect of your celebration.) You might even consider collecting all the papers into a booklet, which you can photocopy for each student to keep as a memento of the year.

SACRED SPACE

Bring your potted plant back to the prayer table. You may want to discuss how it might be different from how it looked when you first placed it on the prayer table. Some plants, such as spider plants, send out shoots with new plants on them. If your spider plant is sufficiently mature, you may even have enough "spider babies" to clip and give to each of your students in a paper cup with a little soil in it.

SACRED MUSIC

If you have been singing with your students all year, they will probably be quite comfortable with at least one or two of their favorite hymns. Consider scheduling a visit to one of the other classrooms to offer a small concert or sing-along (an older classroom could visit a younger grade; smaller children could sing for the "big kids"). If your students are particularly confident, you may even suggest that they volunteer to sing for an all-school Mass or end-of-the-year prayer service. If you invite parents to the class for one of your final sessions, don't be shy about including them in your prayer. And by all means, sing for them! Some songs that work well in this season are "Christ for the World We Sing," "Lord, I Want

to Be a Christian," and "The King of Love My Shepherd Is."

PRAYERS FOR ORDINARY TIME

There are only a few precious places in the Gospel where we have the chance to listen to Jesus as he prays to his Father in heaven. In these moments, we can see clearly what it is Jesus wants for the world. The following prayer taken from the Gospel according to John shows how much Jesus wants us to abide in his love and to live with each other in the love and peace shared by the Father, Son, and Holy Spirit. Now after meditating with the children on Christ's parable of the true vine, this would be an ideal time to introduce this prayer for unity and love.

"As you, Father, are in me and I am in you, may my followers also be in us, so that the world may believe that you have sent me. The glory that you have given me I have given them, so that they may be one, as we are one, I in them and you in me, that they may become completely one, so that the world may know that you have sent me and have loved them even as you have loved me" (John 17:21b–23).

A NOTE TO CATECHISTS

You may wish to write the names of your students into your personal calendar during the summer months so that you will remember to pray for them even when your group is no longer meeting. Prayer is the most useful and effective way we have to be of service to those about whom we care.

GRACE BEFORE MEALS
ORDINARY TIME • Summer

LEADER:

O give thanks to the Lord, for he is good;

ALL: for his steadfast love endures forever.

✚ All make the Sign of the Cross.

In the name of the Father, and of the Son, and of the Holy Spirit. Amen.

LEADER:

God of abundance,
your grace fills the hearts of
all those who call you Lord,
and even those who may not
know you yet.
Thank you for the gift of this meal
and the nourishment it will provide.
We are grateful for this time to
share it with each other.
May we work together to fill the plates
of those in our community and around the
world who may experience
extreme hunger or thirst today.
We ask this through Christ our Lord.

Amen.

✚ All make the Sign of the Cross.

In the name of the Father, and of the Son, and of the Holy Spirit. Amen.

PRAYER AT DAY'S END

ORDINARY TIME • Summer

LEADER:

See what love the Father has given us,

ALL: that we should be called children of God.

✚ All make the Sign of the Cross.

> **In the name of the Father, and of the Son, and of the Holy Spirit. Amen.**

LEADER:

Almighty Father,
you created us in your image
of goodness and light.
Grant that we may offer you
all that we are in thanksgiving,
here at the end of our school day,
and this night, when we close our eyes
for restful sleep.
May the peace of Christ remain with us
now and forever.
We ask this in Jesus's name.

ALL: Amen.

✚ All make the Sign of the Cross.

> **In the name of the Father, and of the Son, and of the Holy Spirit. Amen.**

321

PRAYER FOR **MONDAY** JUNE 9, 2014

OPENING

Today we remember St. Ephrem, who became known as the "Harp of the Holy Spirit." He lived in the fourth century in Syria, and was a poet and composer of hymns that instructed Christians about their faith.

✝ All make the Sign of the Cross.

In the name of the Father, and of the Son, and of the Holy Spirit. Amen.

PSALM (For a longer psalm, see page xvi.) Psalm 85:8–9, 10–11, 12–13

The LORD speaks of peace to his people.

The LORD speaks of peace to his people.

Let me hear what God the LORD will speak,
   for he will speak peace to his people,
   to his faithful, to those who turn to him in
      their hearts.
Surely his salvation is at hand for those who
      fear him,
   that his glory may dwell in our land.

The LORD speaks of peace to his people.

◆ All stand and sing **Alleluia.**

GOSPEL Matthew 5:2–12a

A reading from the holy Gospel according to Matthew

Jesus began to speak, and taught them, saying: "Blessed are the poor in spirit, for theirs is the kingdom of heaven. Blessed are those who mourn, for they will be comforted. Blessed are the meek, for they will inherit the earth. Blessed are those who hunger and thirst for righteousness, for they will be filled. Blessed are the merciful, for they will receive mercy. Blessed are the pure in heart, for they will see God. Blessed are the peacemakers, for they will be called children of God. Blessed are those who are persecuted for righteousness' sake, for theirs is the kingdom of heaven. Blessed are you when people revile you and persecute you and utter all kinds of evil against you falsely on my account. Rejoice and be glad, for your reward is great in heaven."

The Gospel of the Lord.

◆ All sit and observe silence.

FOR SILENT REFLECTION

What does it mean to be "poor in spirit" or "meek"?

CLOSING PRAYER

Let us stand and bring our hopes and needs to God as we pray, "Lord, hear our prayer."

◆ All may add their own prayers here.

Let us pray: **Our Father . . . Amen.**

Lord Jesus,
comfort those
who live through trying times.
Help us to stay focused
on your message
and seek to be blessed by you.
In your name we pray.

Amen.

✝ All make the Sign of the Cross.

OPENING

Today's reading is about listening to God's Word and finding strength.

✤ All make the Sign of the Cross.

In the name of the Father, and of the Son, and of the Holy Spirit. Amen.

PSALM

(For a longer psalm, see page xvi.) Psalm 85:8–9, 10–11, 12–13

The LORD speaks of peace to his people.

The LORD speaks of peace to his people.

Let me hear what God the LORD will speak,
　for he will speak peace to his people,
　　to his faithful, to those who turn to him in
　　　their hearts.
Surely his salvation is at hand for those who
　　fear him,
　that his glory may dwell in our land.

The LORD speaks of peace to his people.

READING

1 Kings 17:7–14

A reading from the first Book of Kings

Then the word of the LORD came to Elijah, saying, "Go now to Zarephath [ZAYR-uh-fath], which belongs to Sidon [SĪ-duhn], and live there; for I have commanded a widow there to feed you." So he set out and went to Zarephath. When he came to the gate of the town, a widow was there gathering sticks; he called to her and said, "Bring me a little water in a vessel, so that I may drink." As she was going to bring it, he called to her and said, "Bring me a morsel of bread in your hand." But she said, "As the LORD your God lives, I have nothing baked, only a handful of meal in a jar, and a little oil in a jug; I am now gathering a couple of sticks, so that I may go home and prepare it for myself and my son, that we may eat it, and die." Elijah said to her, "Do not be afraid; go and do as you have said; but first make me a little cake of it and bring it to me, and afterwards make something for yourself and your son. For thus says the LORD the God of Israel: The jar of meal will not be emptied and the jug of oil will not fail until the day that the LORD sends rain on the earth."

The Word of the Lord.

◆ All observe silence.

FOR SILENT REFLECTION

Have you trusted God with an outcome?

CLOSING PRAYER

Let us stand and bring our hopes and needs to God as we pray, "Lord, hear our prayer."

◆ All may add their own prayers here.

Let us pray: **Our Father . . . Amen.**

Almighty God,
may we learn to rely on you
for what we need.
We ask this in the name of
Jesus Christ your Son,
who lives and reigns with you,
in the unity of the Holy Spirit,
one God, for ever and ever.

Amen.

✤ All make the Sign of the Cross.

PRAYER FOR **WEDNESDAY** **JUNE 11, 2014**

OPENING

Today we remember St. Barnabas, who preached to communities with St. Paul, drawing many people to follow Christ's way.

✚ All make the Sign of the Cross.

In the name of the Father, and of the Son, and of the Holy Spirit. Amen.

PSALM

(For a longer psalm, see page xvi.) Psalm 85:8–9, 10–11, 12–13

The LORD speaks of peace to his people.

The LORD speaks of peace to his people.

Let me hear what God the LORD will speak,
   for he will speak peace to his people,
   to his faithful, to those who turn to him in
      their hearts.
Surely his salvation is at hand for those who
      fear him,
   that his glory may dwell in our land.

The LORD speaks of peace to his people.

READING

Acts 11:21–26

A reading from the Acts of the Apostles

The hand of the Lord was with them, and a great number became believers and turned to the Lord. News of this came to the ears of the church in Jerusalem, and they sent Barnabas to Antioch. When he came and saw the grace of God, he rejoiced, and he exhorted them all to remain faithful to the Lord with steadfast devotion; for he was a good man, full of the Holy Spirit and of faith. And a great many people were brought to the Lord. Then

Barnabas went to Tarsus to look for Saul, and when he had found him, he brought him to Antioch. So it was that for an entire year they met with the church and taught a great many people, and it was in Antioch that the disciples were first called "Christians."

The Word of the Lord.

◆ All observe silence.

FOR SILENT REFLECTION

Each person in the early church fulfilled a function. What do you think yours is today?

CLOSING PRAYER

Let us stand and bring our hopes and needs to God as we pray, "Lord, hear our prayer."

◆ All may add their own prayers here.

Let us pray: **Our Father . . . Amen.**

Jesus our Lord,
your churches grew
because your first believers
answered your call.
Help us to listen to your
gentle Spirit, urging us forward
to accomplish great things
even with small steps.
In your name we pray.

Amen.

✚ All make the Sign of the Cross.

OPENING

Today's Gospel is a reminder that we shouldn't wait to reconcile with another person. Forgiveness is vital to our spiritual health.

✚ *All make the Sign of the Cross.*

In the name of the Father, and of the Son, and of the Holy Spirit. Amen.

PSALM

(For a longer psalm, see page xvi.) Psalm 85:8–9, 10–11, 12–13

The LORD speaks of peace to his people.

The LORD speaks of peace to his people.

Let me hear what God the LORD will speak,
　for he will speak peace to his people,
　　to his faithful, to those who turn to him in
　　　their hearts.
Surely his salvation is at hand for those who
　　fear him,
　　that his glory may dwell in our land.

The LORD speaks of peace to his people.

◆ *All stand and sing* **Alleluia.**

GOSPEL

Matthew 5:20–24

A reading from the holy Gospel according to Matthew

Jesus said to his disciples: "For I tell you, unless your righteousness exceeds that of the scribes and Pharisees, you will never enter the kingdom of heaven.

"You have heard that it was said to those of ancient times, 'You shall not murder'; and 'whoever murders shall be liable to judgment.'

But I say to you that if you are angry with a brother or sister, you will be liable to judgment; and if you insult a brother or sister, you will be liable to the council; and if you say, 'You fool,' you will be liable to the hell of fire. So when you are offering your gift at the altar, if you remember that your brother or sister has something against you, leave your gift there before the altar and go; first be reconciled to your brother or sister, and then come and offer your gift."

The Gospel of the Lord.

◆ *All sit and observe silence.*

FOR SILENT REFLECTION

What is true reconciliation?

CLOSING PRAYER

Let us stand and bring our hopes and needs to God as we pray, "Lord, hear our prayer."

◆ *All may add their own prayers here.*

Let us pray: **Our Father . . . Amen.**

Lord Jesus,
we need to be in good relationship
with one another.
Help us to reconcile with others
in your name.
We ask this through the power of
your Spirit.

Amen.

✚ *All make the Sign of the Cross.*

PRAYER FOR **FRIDAY**
JUNE 13, 2014

OPENING

Today we remember St. Anthony of Padua from the 13th century, who was recognized as a great man of prayer as well as a Scripture and theology scholar. He answered God's Spirit many times by changing his plans to teach friars and preachers in different regions.

✚ All make the Sign of the Cross.

In the name of the Father, and of the Son, and of the Holy Spirit. Amen.

PSALM

(For a longer psalm, see page xvi.) Psalm 85:8–9, 10–11, 12–13

The LORD speaks of peace to his people.

The LORD speaks of peace to his people.

Let me hear what God the LORD will speak,
　for he will speak peace to his people,
　　to his faithful, to those who turn to him in
　　　their hearts.
Surely his salvation is at hand for those who
　　fear him,
　that his glory may dwell in our land.

The LORD speaks of peace to his people.

READING

1 Kings 19:9, 11–12

A reading from the first Book of Kings

At that place Elijah came to a cave, and spent the night there. Then the word of the LORD came to him, saying, "What are you doing here, Elijah?" He said, "Go out and stand on the mountain before the LORD, for the LORD is about to pass by." Now there was a great wind, so strong that it was splitting mountains

and breaking rocks in pieces before the Lord, but the Lord was not in the wind; and after the wind an earthquake, but the LORD was not in the earthquake; and after the earthquake a fire, but the LORD was not in the fire; and after the fire a sound of sheer silence. When Elijah heard it, he wrapped his face in his mantle and went out and stood at the entrance of the cave.

The Word of the Lord.

◆ All observe silence.

FOR SILENT REFLECTION

How do you see or hear God's voice in nature?

CLOSING PRAYER

Let us stand and bring our hopes and needs to God as we pray, "Lord, hear our prayer."

◆ All may add their own prayers here.

Let us pray: **Our Father . . . Amen.**

God of all creation,
your voice can be heard
in wind, storm, and fire,
as well as in the quiet of
our hearts.
Help us to be still
long enough to hear you.
We ask this through Christ
our Lord and Savior.

Amen.

✚ All make the Sign of the Cross.

OPENING

Today is Holy Trinity Sunday, when we celebrate the power and relationship of God the Father, Jesus, and the Holy Spirit. We see this reflected in today's Gospel, which is a familiar passage for many believers, even for those who have not fully committed to the Christian life.

✦ All make the Sign of the Cross.

In the name of the Father, and of the Son, and of the Holy Spirit. Amen.

PSALM

(For a longer psalm, see page xvi.) Psalm 85:8–9, 10–11, 12–13

The LORD speaks of peace to his people.

The LORD speaks of peace to his people.

Let me hear what God the LORD will speak,
　for he will speak peace to his people,
　　to his faithful, to those who turn to him in
　　　their hearts.
Surely his salvation is at hand for those who
　　fear him,
　　that his glory may dwell in our land.

The LORD speaks of peace to his people.

◆ All stand and sing **Alleluia.**

GOSPEL

John 3:16–18

A reading from the holy Gospel according to John

"For God so loved the world that he gave his only Son, so that everyone who believes in him may not perish but may have eternal life. Indeed, God did not send the Son into the world to condemn the world, but in order that the world might be saved through him. Those who believe in him are not condemned; but those who do not believe are condemned already, because they have not believed in the name of the only Son of God."

The Gospel of the Lord.

◆ All sit and observe silence.

FOR SILENT REFLECTION

Can you imagine what our world would be like without Christ and the Holy Spirit? How much hope would there be?

CLOSING PRAYER

Let us stand and bring our hopes and needs to God as we pray, "Lord, hear our prayer."

◆ All may add their own prayers here.

Let us pray: **Our Father . . . Amen.**

Almighty God,
all around the world
people repeat this Scripture passage
as the hope-filled reason why
God sent his Son.
May we continue to
be thankful for the
tremendous gift of Christ.
May we celebrate the
life, Death, and Resurrection of
our Savior with our own acts
of truth and goodness.
We ask this through Christ our Lord.

Amen.

✦ All make the Sign of the Cross.

ALSO ON THIS DAY: Father's Day (U.S.A.)

OPENING

Today's Gospel is a difficult one to hear and to follow. Listen to what Jesus says about "going the extra mile."

✝ All make the Sign of the Cross.

In the name of the Father, and of the Son, and of the Holy Spirit. Amen.

PSALM

(For a longer psalm, see page xvi.) Psalm 85:8–9, 10–11, 12–13

The LORD speaks of peace to his people.

The LORD speaks of peace to his people.

Let me hear what God the LORD will speak,
    for he will speak peace to his people,
    to his faithful, to those who turn to him in
        their hearts.
Surely his salvation is at hand for those who
        fear him,
    that his glory may dwell in our land.

The LORD speaks of peace to his people.

◆ All stand and sing **Alleluia.**

GOSPEL

Matthew 5:38–42

A reading from the holy Gospel according to Matthew

Jesus said to his disciples: "You have heard that it was said, 'An eye for an eye and a tooth for a tooth.' But I say to you, Do not resist an evil-doer. But if anyone strikes you on the right cheek, turn the other also; and if anyone wants to sue you and take your coat, give your cloak as well; and if anyone forces you to go one mile, go also the second mile. Give to everyone who begs from you, and do not refuse anyone who wants to borrow from you."

The Gospel of the Lord.

◆ All sit and observe silence.

FOR SILENT REFLECTION

What do you think our communities would be like if we followed Jesus's commands?

CLOSING PRAYER

Let us stand and bring our hopes and needs to God as we pray, "Lord, hear our prayer."

◆ All may add their own prayers here.

Let us pray: **Our Father . . . Amen.**

Lord God,
you ask us to
turn the other cheek
and to give our cloak
to those who
wish to do us harm.
We know that our rewards
are not here on earth,
but with you in eternity.
Give us courage to be
forgiving with
our actions and intentions.
We ask this through Christ our Lord.

Amen.

✝ All make the Sign of the Cross.

PRAYER FOR **TUESDAY** **JUNE 17, 2014**

OPENING

Today's Gospel shows how we need to treat those who may disagree with us. It also gives us direction to live rightly in the midst of wrong.

✚ All make the Sign of the Cross.

In the name of the Father, and of the Son, and of the Holy Spirit. Amen.

PSALM
(For a longer psalm, see page xvi.) Psalm 85:8–9, 10–11, 12–13

The LORD speaks of peace to his people.

The LORD speaks of peace to his people.

Let me hear what God the LORD will speak,
    for he will speak peace to his people,
    to his faithful, to those who turn to him in
        their hearts.
Surely his salvation is at hand for those who
        fear him,
    that his glory may dwell in our land.

The LORD speaks of peace to his people.

◆ All stand and sing **Alleluia.**

GOSPEL
Matthew 5:43–48

A reading from the holy Gospel according to Matthew

Jesus said to his disciples: "You have heard that it was said, 'You shall love your neighbor and hate your enemy.' But I say to you, Love your enemies and pray for those who persecute you, so that you may be children of your Father in heaven; for he makes his sun rise on the evil and on the good, and sends rain on the righteous and on the unrighteous. For if you love those who love you, what reward do you have? Do not even the tax collectors do the same? And if you greet only your brothers and sisters, what more are you doing than others? Do not even the Gentiles do the same? Be perfect, therefore, as your heavenly Father is perfect."

The Gospel of the Lord.

◆ All sit and observe silence.

FOR SILENT REFLECTION

Is there someone with whom you disagree? Can you pray for them?

CLOSING PRAYER

Let us stand and bring our hopes and needs to God as we pray, "Lord, hear our prayer."

◆ All may add their own prayers here.

Let us pray: **Our Father . . . Amen.**

Lord Jesus,
loving those with whom we disagree
is a difficult challenge for us.
Give us the motivation
to seek forgiveness
and to pray for those
with whom we struggle.
We ask this in your name.

Amen.

✚ All make the Sign of the Cross.

PRAYER FOR **WEDNESDAY**
JUNE 18, 2014

OPENING

Today's reading is the dramatic story of Elijah's death, and what happens to his son Elisha.

✝ All make the Sign of the Cross.

In the name of the Father, and of the Son, and of the Holy Spirit. Amen.

PSALM

(For a longer psalm, see page xvi.) Psalm 85:8–9, 10–11, 12–13

The LORD speaks of peace to his people.

The LORD speaks of peace to his people.

Let me hear what God the LORD will speak,
    for he will speak peace to his people,
    to his faithful, to those who turn to him in
        their hearts.
Surely his salvation is at hand for those who
        fear him,
    that his glory may dwell in our land.

The LORD speaks of peace to his people.

READING

2 Kings 2:1, 6, 11–14

A reading from the second Book of Kings

Now when the LORD was about to take Elijah up to heaven by a whirlwind, Elijah and Elisha were on their way from Gilgal. Then Elijah said to him, "Stay here; for the Lord has sent me to the Jordan." But he said, "As the LORD lives, and as you yourself live, I will not leave you." So the two of them went on. As they continued walking and talking, a chariot of fire and horses of fire separated the two of them, and Elijah ascended in a whirlwind into heaven. Elisha kept watching and crying out,

"Father, father! The chariots of Israel and its horsemen!" But when he could no longer see him, he grasped his own clothes and tore them in two pieces.

He picked up the mantle of Elijah that had fallen from him, and went back and stood on the bank of the Jordan. He took the mantle of Elijah that had fallen from him, and struck the water, saying, "Where is the LORD, the God of Elijah?" When he had struck the water, the water was parted to the one side and to the other, and Elisha went over.

The Word of the Lord.

◆ All observe silence.

FOR SILENT REFLECTION

What gifts do you need to do God's work?

CLOSING PRAYER

Let us stand and bring our hopes and needs to God as we pray, "Lord, hear our prayer."

◆ All may add their own prayers here.

Let us pray: **Our Father . . . Amen.**

Almighty God,
may we trust you as did your prophet Elijah.
We ask this through your Son Jesus,
our Savior,
who lives and reigns with you
in the unity of the Holy Spirit,
one God, for ever and ever.

Amen.

✝ All make the Sign of the Cross.

OPENING

Today we remember St. Romuald (950–1027), who was known for founding monasteries and hermitages throughout Italy. He encouraged others, even when he faced many roadblocks, even from his fellow monks.

✝ All make the Sign of the Cross.

In the name of the Father, and of the Son, and of the Holy Spirit. Amen.

PSALM

(For a longer psalm, see page xvi.) Psalm 85:8–9, 10–11, 12–13

The LORD speaks of peace to his people.

The LORD speaks of peace to his people.

Let me hear what God the LORD will speak,
   for he will speak peace to his people,
   to his faithful, to those who turn to him in
      their hearts.
Surely his salvation is at hand for those who
      fear him,
   that his glory may dwell in our land.

The LORD speaks of peace to his people.

◆ All stand and sing **Alleluia.**

GOSPEL

Matthew 6:9–15

A reading from the holy Gospel according to Matthew

Jesus said to his disciples: "Pray then in this way: Our Father in heaven, hallowed be your name. Your kingdom come. Your will be done, on earth as it is in heaven. Give us this day our daily bread. And forgive us our debts, as we also have forgiven our debtors. And do not bring us to the time of trial, but rescue us from the evil one. For if you forgive others their trespasses, your heavenly Father will also forgive you; but if you do not forgive others, neither will your Father forgive your trespasses."

The Gospel of the Lord.

◆ All sit and observe silence.

FOR SILENT REFLECTION

What kind of kingdom do you envision of which we all might be a part?

CLOSING PRAYER

Let us stand and bring our hopes and needs to God as we pray, "Lord, hear our prayer."

◆ All may add their own prayers here.

Let us pray: **Our Father . . . Amen.**

Lord Jesus,
you taught us to pray
for your kingdom to come.
Give us the courage to help others
so that we can build your
kingdom together,
here and beyond our life
on earth.

Amen.

✝ All make the Sign of the Cross.

PRAYER FOR **FRIDAY** JUNE 20, 2014

OPENING

Today's Gospel concerns our awareness and what motivates us. The "eye" in this passage signifies our conscience.

✝ All make the Sign of the Cross.

In the name of the Father, and of the Son, and of the Holy Spirit. Amen.

PSALM

(For a longer psalm, see page xvi.) Psalm 85:8–9, 10–11, 12–13

The LORD speaks of peace to his people.

The LORD speaks of peace to his people.

Let me hear what God the LORD will speak,
for he will speak peace to his people,
to his faithful, to those who turn to him in their hearts.
Surely his salvation is at hand for those who fear him,
that his glory may dwell in our land.

The LORD speaks of peace to his people.

◆ All stand and sing **Alleluia.**

GOSPEL

Matthew 6:19–23

A reading from the holy Gospel according to Matthew

Jesus said to his disciples: "Do not store up for yourselves treasures on earth, where moth and rust consume and where thieves break in and steal; but store up for yourselves treasures in heaven, where neither moth nor rust consumes and where thieves do not break in and steal. For where your treasure is, there your heart will be also. The eye is the lamp of the body. So, if your eye is healthy, your whole body will be full of light; but if your eye is unhealthy, your whole body will be full of darkness. If then the light in you is darkness, how great is the darkness!"

The Gospel of the Lord.

◆ All sit and observe silence.

FOR SILENT REFLECTION

For what reason do I work hard in school and/or sports? Where is my treasure?

CLOSING PRAYER

Let us stand and bring our hopes and needs to God as we pray, "Lord, hear our prayer."

◆ All may add their own prayers here.

Let us pray: **Our Father . . . Amen.**

Lord Jesus,
you know our every thought
and ask that we be mindful
of what is most important.
Keep us aware
of what draws us
closer to you,
for you are our
one true Lord.
We ask this in your name.

Amen.

✝ All make the Sign of the Cross.

PRAYER FOR THE WEEK

OPENING

Today is the Solemnity of the Most Holy Body and Blood of Christ, and the Gospel serves as a reminder that we need to rely on God's nourishment throughout our lives.

✚ All make the Sign of the Cross.

In the name of the Father, and of the Son, and of the Holy Spirit. Amen.

PSALM

(For a longer psalm, see page xvi.) Psalm 85:8–9, 10–11, 12–13

The LORD speaks of peace to his people.

The LORD speaks of peace to his people.

Let me hear what God the LORD will speak,
  for he will speak peace to his people,
    to his faithful, to those who turn to him in
      their hearts.
Surely his salvation is at hand for those who
      fear him,
  that his glory may dwell in our land.

The LORD speaks of peace to his people.

◆ All stand and sing **Alleluia.**

GOSPEL

John 6:51–57

A reading from the holy Gospel according to John

Jesus said to his disciples: "I am the living bread that came down from heaven. Whoever eats of this bread will live forever; and the bread that I will give for the life of the world is my flesh." The Jews then disputed among themselves, saying, "How can this man give us his flesh to eat?" So Jesus said to them, "Very truly, I tell you, unless you eat the flesh of the Son of Man and drink his blood, you have no life in you. Those who eat my flesh and drink my blood have eternal life, and I will raise them up on the last day; for my flesh is true food and my blood is true drink. Those who eat my flesh and drink my blood abide in me, and I in them. Just as the living Father sent me, and I live because of the Father, so whoever eats me will live because of me."

The Gospel of the Lord.

◆ All sit and observe silence.

FOR SILENT REFLECTION

When do we eat the "bread from heaven"? How does it help us to live with Jesus and with the Father?

CLOSING PRAYER

Let us stand and bring our hopes and needs to God as we pray, "Lord, hear our prayer."

◆ All may add their own prayers here.

Let us pray: **Our Father . . . Amen.**

Lord Jesus,
we believe in your Real Presence
with us in the Eucharist.
Help us to be one with you
in the breaking of the bread.
In your name we pray.

Amen.

✚ All make the Sign of the Cross.

PRAYER FOR **MONDAY**
JUNE 23, 2014

OPENING

Today's Gospel is about those who condemn others' behavior because they feel superior. It's true that we progress more readily when we are supported and encouraged.

✛ All make the Sign of the Cross.

> **In the name of the Father, and of the Son, and of the Holy Spirit. Amen.**

PSALM

(For a longer psalm, see page xvi.) Psalm 85:8–9, 10–11, 12–13

The LORD speaks of peace to his people.

The LORD speaks of peace to his people.

Let me hear what God the LORD will speak,
for he will speak peace to his people,
to his faithful, to those who turn to him in
their hearts.
Surely his salvation is at hand for those who
fear him,
that his glory may dwell in our land.

The LORD speaks of peace to his people.

◆ All stand and sing **Alleluia.**

GOSPEL

Matthew 7:1–5

A reading from the holy Gospel according to Matthew

Jesus said to his disciples: "Do not judge, so that you may not be judged. For with the judgment you make you will be judged, and the measure you give will be the measure you get. Why do you see the speck in your neighbor's eye, but do not notice the log in your own eye? Or how can you say to your neighbor, 'Let me take the speck out of your eye,' while the log is in your own eye? You hypocrite, first take the log out of your own eye, and then you will see clearly to take the speck out of your neighbor's eye."

The Gospel of the Lord.

◆ All sit and observe silence.

FOR SILENT REFLECTION

What are some of the logs in my own eye? How does recognizing my shortcomings help me be more understanding of others?

CLOSING PRAYER

Let us stand and bring our hopes and needs to God as we pray, "Lord, hear our prayer."

◆ All may add their own prayers here.

Let us pray: **Our Father . . . Amen.**

Lord Jesus,
we need your guidance.
You know how human nature
likes to compete for
its own glory.
Help us to love with compassion
instead of harshness
when we see something
that needs correction.
In your name we pray.
Amen.

✛ All make the Sign of the Cross.

OPENING

Today, on this Solemnity of the Nativity of John the Baptist, we hear the Gospel about his birth and his naming. We learn how his parents allowed God to work through them to bring this mighty prophet to our world.

✛ All make the Sign of the Cross.

In the name of the Father, and of the Son, and of the Holy Spirit. Amen.

PSALM
(For a longer psalm, see page xvi.) Psalm 85:8–9, 10–11, 12–13

The LORD speaks of peace to his people.

The LORD speaks of peace to his people.

Let me hear what God the LORD will speak,
for he will speak peace to his people,
to his faithful, to those who turn to him in
their hearts.
Surely his salvation is at hand for those who
fear him,
that his glory may dwell in our land.

The LORD speaks of peace to his people.

◆ All stand and sing **Alleluia.**

GOSPEL
Luke 1:57–64

A reading from the holy Gospel according to Luke

Now the time came for Elizabeth to give birth, and she bore a son. Her neighbors and relatives heard that the Lord had shown his great mercy to her, and they rejoiced with her. On the eighth day they came to circumcise the child, and they were going to name him Zechariah [zek-uh-RĪ-uh] after his father. But his mother said, "No; he is to be called John." They said to her, "None of your relatives has this name." Then they began motioning to his father to find out what name he wanted to give him. He asked for a writing tablet and wrote, "His name is John." And all of them were amazed. Immediately his mouth was opened and his tongue freed, and he began to speak, praising God.

The Gospel of the Lord.

◆ All sit and observe silence.

FOR SILENT REFLECTION

Why was John the Baptist so important in the life of Christ and relevant for us today?

CLOSING PRAYER

Let us stand and bring our hopes and needs to God as we pray, "Lord, hear our prayer."

◆ All may add their own prayers here.

Let us pray: **Our Father . . . Amen.**

God almighty,
thank you for this great prophet,
who declared
the way of Jesus.
May we also prepare the way for you.
We ask this in the name of your Son Jesus.

Amen.

✛ All make the Sign of the Cross.

PRAYER FOR **WEDNESDAY** JUNE 25, 2014

OPENING

Today's Gospel is a simple message about the fruits of our faith. Listen to what Jesus proclaims about trees without fruit.

✝ All make the Sign of the Cross.

> **In the name of the Father, and of the Son, and of the Holy Spirit. Amen.**

PSALM

(For a longer psalm, see page xvi.) Psalm 85:8–9, 10–11, 12–13

The LORD speaks of peace to his people.

The LORD speaks of peace to his people.

Let me hear what God the LORD will speak,
   for he will speak peace to his people,
     to his faithful, to those who turn to him in
       their hearts.
Surely his salvation is at hand for those who
     fear him,
   that his glory may dwell in our land.

The LORD speaks of peace to his people.

◆ All stand and sing **Alleluia.**

GOSPEL

Matthew 7:15–20

A reading from the holy Gospel according to Matthew

Jesus said to his disciples: "Beware of false prophets, who come to you in sheep's clothing but inwardly are ravenous wolves. You will know them by their fruits. Are grapes gathered from thorns, or figs from thistles? In the same way, every good tree bears good fruit, but the bad tree bears bad fruit. A good tree cannot bear bad fruit, nor can a bad tree bear good fruit. Every tree that does not bear good fruit is cut down and thrown into the fire. Thus you will know them by their fruits."

The Gospel of the Lord.

◆ All sit and observe silence.

FOR SILENT REFLECTION

What does Jesus mean about the fruit that we produce? How do I care for my own spiritual tree?

CLOSING PRAYER

Let us stand and bring our hopes and needs to God as we pray, "Lord, hear our prayer."

◆ All may add their own prayers here.

Let us pray: **Our Father . . . Amen.**

Lord Jesus,
we can be assured
that our fruit
(or the works that we do)
will reflect who we are.
Our acts of kindness for others
are the delicious fruit
which we can all enjoy.
Help us Lord to produce gifts of
life-giving food for others
through an active faith life.
In your name we pray.

Amen.

✝ All make the Sign of the Cross.

OPENING

Today's Gospel provides a clear image of Jesus as the rock of our spiritual lives.

✠ All make the Sign of the Cross.

> **In the name of the Father, and of the Son, and of the Holy Spirit. Amen.**

PSALM

(For a longer psalm, see page xvi.) Psalm 85:8–9, 10–11, 12–13

The LORD speaks of peace to his people.

The LORD speaks of peace to his people.

Let me hear what God the LORD will speak,
 for he will speak peace to his people,
  to his faithful, to those who turn to him in
   their hearts.
Surely his salvation is at hand for those who
   fear him,
  that his glory may dwell in our land.

The LORD speaks of peace to his people.

◆ All stand and sing **Alleluia.**

GOSPEL

Matthew 7:24–29

A reading from the holy Gospel according to Matthew

Jesus said to his disciples: "Everyone then who hears these words of mine and acts on them will be like a wise man who built his house on rock. The rain fell, the floods came, and the winds blew and beat on that house, but it did not fall, because it had been founded on rock. And everyone who hears these words of mine and does not act on them will be like a foolish man who built his house on sand. The rain fell, and the floods came, and the winds blew and beat against that house, and it fell—and great was its fall!" Now when Jesus had finished saying these things, the crowds were astounded at his teaching, for he taught them as one having authority, and not as their scribes.

The Gospel of the Lord.

◆ All sit and observe silence.

FOR SILENT REFLECTION

What helps me to know where to build my trust? What does it mean to build our house on rock?

CLOSING PRAYER

Let us stand and bring our hopes and needs to God as we pray, "Lord, hear our prayer."

◆ All may add their own prayers here.

Let us pray: **Our Father . . . Amen.**

Lord Jesus,
you are our rock,
the solid foundation of
our hope and grace.
Guide us as we learn and play
this day, even as we face
challenges and strife.
We ask this in your name.

Amen.

✠ All make the Sign of the Cross.

PRAYER FOR **FRIDAY** JUNE 27, 2014

OPENING

Today we remember this Solemnity of the Most Sacred Heart of Jesus. The Gospel today makes us aware of our need to stay humble.

✚ All make the Sign of the Cross.

In the name of the Father, and of the Son, and of the Holy Spirit. Amen.

PSALM

(For a longer psalm, see page xvi.) Psalm 85:8–9, 10–11, 12–13

The LORD speaks of peace to his people.

The LORD speaks of peace to his people.

Let me hear what God the LORD will speak,
  for he will speak peace to his people,
    to his faithful, to those who turn to him in
      their hearts.
Surely his salvation is at hand for those who
    fear him,
  that his glory may dwell in our land.

The LORD speaks of peace to his people.

◆ All stand and sing **Alleluia.**

GOSPEL

Matthew 11:25–30

A reading from the holy Gospel according to Matthew

At that time Jesus said, "I thank you, Father, Lord of heaven and earth, because you have hidden these things from the wise and the intelligent and have revealed them to infants; yes, Father, for such was your gracious will. All things have been handed over to me by my Father; and no one knows the Son except the Father, and no one knows the Father except the Son and anyone to whom the Son chooses to reveal him. "Come to me, all you that are weary and are carrying heavy burdens, and I will give you rest. Take my yoke upon you, and learn from me; for I am gentle and humble in heart, and you will find rest for your souls. For my yoke is easy, and my burden is light."

The Gospel of the Lord.

◆ All sit and observe silence.

FOR SILENT REFLECTION

How does Jesus reveal his messages of hope for those who are burdened?

CLOSING PRAYER

Let us stand and bring our hopes and needs to God as we pray, "Lord, hear our prayer."

◆ All may add their own prayers here.

Let us pray: **Our Father . . . Amen.**

Lord Jesus,
you reach to take the yoke
of our burdens from our shoulders.
Guide us through
the difficulties of
this day, for we know that you
are our truest friend.
In your name we pray.

Amen.

✚ All make the Sign of the Cross.

PRAYER SERVICE
LAST DAY OF SCHOOL

Prepare eight leaders for this service. The fourth leader will need a Bible for the Scripture passage and may need help practicing the reading. You may wish to begin by singing "In the Lord I'll Be Ever Thankful" and end with "Send Forth Your Spirit, O Lord." If the group will sing, prepare a song leader.

FIRST LEADER:

Our school year is drawing to a close, and we can see in ourselves so much growth! With each passing day, God worked through each person to make a new creation. Together, let us thank our Creator for the many blessed memories we've shared in our time together.

SECOND LEADER:

◆ All make the sign of the Cross.

In the name of the Father, and of the Son, and of the Holy Spirit. Amen.

Let us pray:
God of all creation,
we are blessed to be with each other
in this time and place.
We are excited to start our break,
yet we may feel sad as we
think about friends
we may not see for a while.
In these times of change,
help us to stay
connected with you, Lord,
for you desire happiness and peace
for all your brothers and sisters.
We ask this through Jesus Christ our Lord.

Amen.

THIRD LEADER:　　　Psalm 119:1–3, 10–11, 41–42, 89–90, 105

Let us repeat the Psalm Response: Your word is a lamp to my feet and a light to my path.

ALL: Your word is a lamp to my feet and a light to my path.

Happy are those whose way is blameless,
　who walk in the law of the Lord.
Happy are those who keep his decrees,
　who seek him with their whole heart,
who also do no wrong,
　but walk in his ways.

ALL: Your word is a lamp to my feet and a light to my path.

With my whole heart I seek you;
　do not let me stray from your
　　commandments.
I treasure your word in my heart,
　so that I may not sin against you.

ALL: Your word is a lamp to my feet and a light to my path.

Let your steadfast love come to me, O Lord,
　your salvation according to your promise.
Then I shall have an answer for those who
　　taunt me,
　for I trust in your word.

ALL: Your word is a lamp to my feet and a light to my path.

The Lord exists forever;
　your word is firmly fixed in heaven.
Your faithfulness endures to all generations;
　you have established the earth, and it
　　stands fast.

ALL: Your word is a lamp to my feet and a light to my path.

PRAYER SERVICE
LAST DAY OF SCHOOL

FOURTH LEADER: Romans 12:9–18
A reading from the Letter of St. Paul to the Romans

    ◆ Read the Scripture passage from the Bible.

The Word of the Lord.

    ◆ All observe silence.

FIFTH LEADER:
Let us bring our hopes and needs to God as we pray, "Lord, hear our prayer."
For our teachers, administrators,
volunteers, coaches, and school staff
who worked hard to produce our
quality learning time together.

We pray to the Lord . . .

For our parents, grandparents,
and family members who helped us
with homework and other tasks
throughout the year.

We pray to the Lord . . .

For the friends we've made
and those on the horizon,
may they reflect the warmth and compassion
that Jesus feels for us.

We pray to the Lord . . .

For those who are dealing with sickness,
job loss, or other difficulties in life,
for those who have gone before us
to the other side of life,
may they experience the peace of Christ.

We pray to the Lord . . .

SIXTH LEADER:
Lord Jesus,
your gentle Spirit has
nudged and guided us
these past several months.
May we continue to seek your wisdom
as we daily pray to you,
ever mindful of
how much you care for us.
We ask this in your name.

Amen.

SEVENTH LEADER:
Let us offer to one another a sign of Christ's peace:

    ◆ All offer one another a sign of peace.

EIGHTH LEADER:
Let us pray:
Creator God,
you are Lord of all things,
and you are always with us.
May we embrace
all our new experiences
in our break from school.
Help us to listen to you,
source of all truth,
and go forth to
new adventures,
cherishing the love that
we've shared this year.

ALL: Amen.

    ✚ All make the Sign of the Cross.

CHILDREN'S DAILY PRAYER 2013–2014, © 2013 Archdiocese of Chicago: Liturgy Training Publications. All rights reserved. Orders: 1-800-933-1800 or www.LTP.org.

PSALM 23

This psalm is appropriate during all liturgical seasons. It may be prayed in times of difficulty or stress, when comfort is needed, or to meditate on Christ's presence in the sacraments.

The LORD is my shepherd, I shall not want.
   He makes me lie down in green pastures;
he leads me beside still waters;
   he restores my soul.
He leads me in right paths
   for his name's sake.

Even though I walk through the darkest valley,
   I fear no evil;
for you are with me;
   your rod and your staff—
   they comfort me.

You prepare a table before me
   in the presence of my enemies;
you anoint my head with oil;
   my cup overflows.
Surely goodness and mercy shall follow me
   all the days of my life,
and I shall dwell in the house of the LORD
   my whole life long.

PSALM 51

Psalm 51:1–2, 6, 10, 12, 15

This is a penitential psalm that is especially appropriate during a communal celebration of the Sacrament of Reconciliation. It can also be incorporated into any Lenten prayer service.

Have mercy on me, O God,
   according to your steadfast love;
according to your abundant mercy
   blot out my transgressions.
Wash me thoroughly from my iniquity,
   and cleanse me from my sin.

You desire truth in the inward being;
   therefore teach me wisdom in my secret heart.

Create in me a clean heart, O God,
   and put a new and right spirit within me.
Restore to me the joy of your salvation,
   and sustain in me a willing spirit.

O LORD, open my lips,
   and my mouth will declare your praise.

PSALM 139

Psalm 139:1–6, 13–16

This psalm expresses the wonder and awe of our mysterious relationship to the God who knows us intimately and loves us completely.

O LORD, you have searched me and known me.
You know when I sit down and when I rise up;
　you discern my thoughts from far away.
You search out my path and my lying down,
　and are acquainted with all my ways.
Even before a word is on my tongue,
　O LORD, you know it completely.
You hem me in, behind and before,
　and lay your hand upon me.
Such knowledge is too wonderful for me;
　it is so high that I cannot attain it.

For it was you who formed my inward parts;
　you knit me together in my mother's womb.
I praise you, for I am fearfully and wonderfully made.
　Wonderful are your works;
that I know very well.
　My frame was not hidden from you,
when I was being made in secret,
　intricately woven in the depths of the earth.
Your eyes beheld my unformed substance.
In your book were written
all the days that were formed for me,
　when none of them as yet existed.

343

CANTICLES

THE MAGNIFICAT OF MARY

Luke 1:46–55

Mary prayed with these words when she visited her relative, Elizabeth, after Elizabeth declared, "Blessed are you among women and blessed is the fruit of your womb!" For centuries, this beautiful song of praise and trust has been the Church's evening prayer.

And Mary said,
"My soul magnifies the Lord,
   and my spirit rejoices in God my savior,
for he has looked with favor on the lowliness of his servant.
   Surely, from now on all generations will call me blessed;
for the Mighty One has done great things for me,
   and holy is his name.
His mercy is for those who fear him
   from generation to generation.
He has shown strength with his arm;
   he has scattered the proud in the thoughts of their hearts.
He has brought down the powerful from their thrones,
   and lifted up the lowly;
he has filled the hungry with good things,
   and sent the rich away empty.
He has helped his servant Israel,
   in remembrance of his mercy,
according to the promise he made to our ancestors,
   to Abraham and to his descendants forever."

THE BENEDICTUS OF ZECHARIAH Luke 1:68–79

Zechariah had been struck mute during the pregnancy of his wife, Elizabeth. After their baby was born, on the day when they gave him his name, Zechariah's voice was restored and he spoke these prophetic words over his child, John the Baptist. His prophecy is part of the Church's traditional morning prayer.

"Blessed be the Lord God of Israel,
　for he has looked favorably on his people and redeemed them.
He has raised up a mighty savior for us
　in the house of his servant David,
as he spoke through the mouth of his holy prophets from of old,
　that we would be saved from our enemies and from the hand
　　of all who hate us.
Thus he has shown the mercy promised to our ancestors,
　and has remembered his holy covenant,
the oath that he swore to our ancestor Abraham,
　to grant us that we, being rescued from the hands
　　of our enemies,
might serve him without fear, in holiness and righteousness,
　before him all our days.
And you, child, will be called the prophet of the Most High;
　for you will go before the Lord to prepare his ways,
to give knowledge of salvation to his people
　by the forgiveness of their sins.
By the tender mercy of our God,
　the dawn from on high will break upon us,
to give light to those who sit in darkness and in the shadow
　　of death,
　to guide our feet into the way of peace."

345

BLESSING
FOR BIRTHDAYS

✛ All make the Sign of the Cross.

ALL: In the name of the Father, and of the Son, and of the Holy Spirit. Amen.

LEADER:
Loving God,
you created all the people of the world,
and you know each of us by name.
We thank you for N.,
who today celebrates his/her birthday.
Bless him/her with your love and friendship
that he/she may grow in wisdom, knowledge,
and grace.
May he/she love his/her family always
and be faithful to his/her friends.
Grant this through Christ our Lord.

ALL: Amen.

LEADER:
Let us bow our heads and pray for N.

◆ All observe silence.

LEADER:
May God, in whose presence our ancestors walked, bless you.

ALL: Amen.

LEADER:
May God, who has been your shepherd from birth until now, keep you.

ALL: Amen.

LEADER:
May God, who saves you from all harm, give you peace.

ALL: Amen.

✛ All make the Sign of the Cross.

In the name of the Father, and of the Son, and of the Holy Spirit. Amen.

CHILDREN'S DAILY PRAYER 2013–2014, © 2013 Archdiocese of Chicago: Liturgy Training Publications. All rights reserved. Orders: 1-800-933-1800 or www.LTP.org. Blessing prayer adapted from *Book of Blessings*, additional blessings for use in the dioceses of the united States of America. © 1998 USCCB, Washington, D.C. All rights reserved.